Before Spin

By

Keith McDowall

Published by

MELROSE BOOKS

An Imprint of Melrose Press Limited
St Thomas Place, Ely
Cambridgeshire
CB7 4GG, UK
www.melrosebooks.co.uk

FIRST EDITION

Copyright © Keith McDowall 2016

The Author asserts his moral right to
be identified as the author of this work

Cover designed by Melrose Books

ISBN pbk 978-1-910792-17-9
ISBN hbk 978-1-910792-20-9
epub 978-1-910792-18-6
mobi 978-1-910792-19-3

Printed and bound in Great Britain by:
Latimer Trend & Company Limited,
Estover Road, Plymouth PL6 7PY

MIX
Paper from
responsible sources
FSC® C013436

CONTENTS

ACKNOWLEDGEMENTS

To Brenda Dean, my wife, who not only urged me to keep writing my story, but was vital in getting it to print; to Tom Dodson, my grandson, who made time to read, assess and advise on the first draft; and Ron Atkin, my friend, who cut it with sympathy, encouragement—and like a former good *Daily Mail* features sub—with ruthless, timely efficiency.

FOREWORD
by Peter Hennessy

This is a book of multiple pleasures and fascinations. Keith McDowall has a gift for evocation—for summoning back an era, a mood or a moment. He has a gift, too, for finding himself at the epicentre of a crisis as a press officer who has to make sense of what is happening, advise his minister and senior officials while all the time handling as best he can the journalistic profession to which he belonged as an ace getter of stories. Like most journalists, he rather despised press officers until he became one in the late 1960s during the last days of the Department of Economic Affairs, Harold Wilson's attempt to inject a dash of growth mania into Whitehall. I got to know Keith when I was a young journalist and he was helping Michael Foot ease himself into the Department of Employment after the industrial crisis and the three-day week which had brought down the Heath Government. I thought then—and still do—that he gave press officers a good name. He was tough and direct, but he did not mislead. He was great fun, too.

In between the DEA and the Department of Employment, he had three tours in Northern Ireland helping Jim Callaghan, the Home Secretary when the Troubles … in 1969; ditto his successor Reggie Maudling who lacked grip. And finally the ministerial partnership of his lifetime with the great Willie Whitelaw in late 1973 when Heath called him back to tackle the mounting industrial crisis. When you reach the Callaghan section savour the dreadful, but unforgettable moment when Jim tried to soothe the Rev. Ian Paisley by pointing out that we are all children of God.

There are rich pickings in these pages for students of contemporary

British history and politics. Keith's heyday as a reporter was his time as the *Daily Mail*'s Industrial Editor in the late 50s and early 60s. He is fascinating, for example, on the maturing of Harold Wilson as Opposition Leader in the run-up to the 1964 election as a formidable public speaker and media operator. One of my favourite photos of that election is Harold Wilson on the steps at Transport House shortly before going to the Palace to 'kiss hands' with the Queen as her new Prime Minister. Next to him is an aged, smiling, Homburg-hatted Clem Attlee. Behind Harold Wilson is Keith and his friend and rival the great Ian Aitken.

Away from the high politics and policy, *Before Spin* offers us several bonuses, not least Keith's evocation of early post-war South London and the last of the docklands as Sherlock Holmes would have recognised them. Keith was one of the sharp-eyed young journos on the *South London Press* feeding the nationals with good stories which ensured, as he intended, that they would soon snap him up from his 'University of the Old Kent Road'.

Keith was one hell of an operator in Whitehall yet he does not care for the deeply spun sound-bitten world in which we live. But let him tell you about that.

Peter Hennessy is Attlee Professor of Contemporary British History at Queen Mary, University of London.

CHAPTER 1
Betrayal at Dawn

I groped for the phone by the side of my bed—a 'scrambled' line on the Government's exclusive FEDeral exchange, which in those days could protect calls from phone-tapping. The caller's voice was unmistakable, but the timing was very unusual. William Whitelaw, the first ever Secretary of State for Northern Ireland, was waking me at home abruptly.

"It's all over, Keith—I am going to have to resign," he said. "The IRA have blown the secret talks. I have let down my colleagues—I will have to go. There is no other option."

"Wait a moment," I interrupted as, quickly, the fog cleared. I'd never lost a minister yet, and I was not going to start now. My brain went into accelerated mode. "You've got to make a statement to Parliament. Come clean with them. That's your strength."

Whitelaw had been Chief Whip of the Tory Party in Opposition, and in the Heath Government had been Lord President and Leader of the House. If anyone knew the Commons it was him. The thought seemed to calm his panic.

Quickly we worked out a plan for the day. We were scheduled to be in Belfast that morning, Whitelaw flying from Cardiff in an RAF HS125, and me going from Gatwick Airport near my home in Woldingham, Surrey, to be in Stormont Castle by around 9.30 a.m. We decided to stick to it.

Our plan was to appear unfazed by this latest dirty tactic of the IRA and hold a 'business as usual' Monday morning security meeting with the Army GOC, the Chief Constable of the Royal Ulster Constabulary, a number of civil servants responsible for security, and those who had been involved in planning the secret talks with the terrorists.

Then we would fly back immediately to Westminster and Whitelaw would make a full statement to Members of Parliament. In effect, he would be throwing himself at their feet. Either they backed him—or they sacked him.

Until then, we would be saying nothing. I would be telling the media that there would be no statement or questions answered about the secret talks they now knew had been held with six Irish Republican Army representatives.

Of course, the media were desperate for more facts, more colour. Where, when, how was it done, who was present? The questions poured into my press teams based at Stormont and Whitehall.

But for once I too was keeping my mouth shut. I did not want one scintilla of information out until my Secretary of State had stood and faced Parliament—and answered the MPs' questions. Taking the Commons into our confidence was our only chance. If it failed, Whitelaw would be on the back benches and I would be either heading for what was known as 'gardening leave', or flung to the wolves by my masters in the Government Information Service, who I knew would be only too keen to see me off the premises.

In less than an hour we were on our way out into the garden by way of the steps from Whitelaw's Belfast office, straight aboard the RAF helicopter which had come down on to the lawn alongside Stormont Castle. Everyone working inside the building—including me—had at some time cursed these noisy beasts, because apart from drowning out all that was being said, they would also scatter our files and papers with the downdraught.

On this occasion, though, nerves taut even without the threat of a sniper, we were thankful to be on board. We would be at Aldergrove within ten minutes and aboard the waiting twin jet to carry us to Northolt in North London. We worked on Whitelaw's statement on the plane, and continued as we were whisked by his Government driver down the A40 to Westminster.

Once inside the Palace and into the ministerial offices behind the Speaker's Chair, we were all set to go. All of us—Whitelaw most of all—knew that either he won the sympathy of the House or the major effort he had made as Minister in charge of direct rule to wrest the initiative from the IRA and to return the province to some state of normality was over. Direct rule had been imposed by Parliament on the Province of Ulster, taking back powers it had delegated, imposing direct control of the police, judicial system, prisons, civil and local administration—putting one man in charge as 'supremo' of the six counties to try to end the murders, bomb attacks and shootings by terrorists.

Our small team had survived a lot since just before Easter 1970; we had gathered in Whitelaw's office, and were rapidly bonded under the leadership of this quite exceptional politician. In the room then were Lord David Windlesham, to be Whitelaw's number two; Sir William Nield, permanent secretary, something of a maverick who had once been head of Labour Party research; Neil Cairncross, a deputy secretary; Philip Woodfield, later to head up the appeals procedure for 'whistleblowers' in MI5; and several other able civil servants.

Whitelaw quickly put us all at ease. "This is going to be a difficult task," he told us. "We are going to have some tough moments to face. So we'd better to get to know each other and to learn to laugh together."

Over the next few months, as bombs killed people in appalling circumstances, Catholics and Protestants slaughtered each other in a wave of tit-for-tat murders night after night, and as troops were shot down by sniper fire out in the bogs of the Irish border, we often needed to remind ourselves of Whitelaw's enjoinder.

But now it looked as if the desperate drive to try to outwit terrorism, while winning the hearts and minds of both communities in the Six Counties, had run out of time.

Repeatedly, Whitelaw had been challenged on why he had made no attempt to parley with the terrorists. "At least find out what they want," argued MPs, supported by some commentators in the newspapers. Britain had done it with the Mau Mau in Kenya, with Makarios in

Cyprus, and in Malaysia. Go further back, and Britain had eventually judged the moment right to talk to Irgun in Palestine and Gandhi in India.

But all those places were a long way from London, and tentative contact could be made without the media getting in the way. In Northern Ireland, as the Americans had discovered in Vietnam, we had to learn how to operate under arc lights and doorstep coverage by journalists seeking to expose all in thirty seconds with a single quote. Not easy to try to unpick a highly explosive situation in that atmosphere.

Nonetheless, tentative contact had been made with the IRA, and gradually the prospect for some kind of probing discussion began to emerge. Six names were given to us, including Gerry Adams, Martin McGuinness, Sean MacStiofain and three others. Several of them, Whitelaw was well aware—and as intelligence confirmed—had plenty on their conscience as soldiers and civilians died in the seemingly endless clashes.

Even so, if it became known that negotiations of any kind were taking place with the IRA the initiative would be stillborn.

Plenty of right-wingers in Whitelaw's party—people like Enoch Powell, who hated him for his expulsion from Edward Heath's Shadow Cabinet, and Andrew Alexander, at the *Daily Telegraph* and once vetoed for a Parliamentary seat by Whitelaw—would seize the chance to settle scores.

We had the perfect cover for the talks. On the day they were planned, 7th July 1972, I had arranged for Whitelaw to be the guest of the Press Golfing Society at Walton Health, Surrey. I fixed it with Monty Court, the chairman, an old *Daily Mail* friend and colleague. But I had not told him why that date was so suitable for Whitelaw's diary.

Meanwhile, cars with darkened windows had collected the IRA at Northolt and whisked them to the Cheyne Walk home of Paul Channon MP, one of our ministerial team. It was the perfect location, though I doubt if any of the Irishmen had ever seen the inside of such a well-heeled place on the Thames Embankment, as Channon—heir, ironically, to a Guinness fortune—possessed in their country.

On the drive back to Westminster, Whitelaw and his private secretary, Terry Platt, went through the speech yet again. Then as soon as we reached Parliament I was off to the Press Gallery, where news of my arrival swept through the corridors. I was invited to address the Parliamentary lobby in their very private room in the tower of Big Ben.

That room has seen plenty of exciting moments, but I reckon this one rates a mention. I recounted the pressure for talks—written by some in that very room—and said it had been judged by Whitelaw that the time was ripe for such a meeting to try to find out what the terrorists really wanted. Ostensibly they wanted a united republic of Ireland and a British withdrawal. But what was their bottom line?

As a former Fleet Street journalist myself, I doled out what detail and colour I had gleaned about the meeting. But my difficulty was that I had not actually been present. It had been decided that since the British intention was to keep the negotiations secret a press officer in attendance would arouse IRA suspicions. I had agreed with that decision.

So then I threw in my best card. If the lobby would adjourn for ten minutes I would try to persuade my Secretary of State to come to meet them. That was what they wanted, I knew. I burst into Whitelaw's room. Would he agree?

It is at times like this that the relationship between a politician or a senior businessman and his public relations adviser are tested. If the relationship is right they will take advice. And that advice has to be right. Make a mess of it once and the bond is broken.

Whitelaw quickly agreed and we shot off to the room in the tower.

In my heart I knew if we got it right, Whitelaw was through the hoop. Wrong, and the media would make mincemeat of him.

As it happened, Whitelaw was brilliant. At the dawn of the day he had been on the point of resignation. But as it progressed, he had picked up confidence and momentum—an impressive reminder of a good politician's ability, indeed resilience, to take blows and yet keep going.

I could feel the Westminster journalists warming to him as he poured out what had happened, how he felt 'unclean' during the talks, and how he now felt betrayed by the IRA. As to their agenda, the talks had been well worth it, said Whitelaw, because he now knew the terrorists really did not have an agenda.

Whitelaw had been dominant on the floor of the House. There were plenty of right-wingers itching to pull him down, but most MPs were on his side, as were Harold Wilson and the Opposition.

Whitelaw apologised for being late to make a statement to the House—always a good start to throw yourself at your opponents' feet—but then told how, following a ceasefire by the IRA, they were threatening to restart killing and bombing.

Whitelaw said he had judged it was right to listen to the terrorists to outline their real demands. "Before I could even discuss these matters with my Cabinet colleagues, the fragile truce was broken. If the British Government cannot resolve this problem, I do not believe anyone else will."

As he sat down there was strong support welling up for him from most of the House, but it would depend on what the press made of it. And him.

After the tower session came interviews with television and radio— and especially, I made sure, with RTE in Dublin so that the Irish could hear for themselves how the mean bastards of the IRA had sought to represent them. And the same for US media so that those in Boston and the east coast would find out the kind of people to whom they were sending their dollars.

David Wood, the authoritative Political Editor of *The Times* with whom I was on good terms, wrote it up well on the front page. "One thing is sure: Mr Whitelaw carried widespread support in the Commons, with some reservations here and there about his wisdom in agreeing to meet the deputation," he wrote. "As on other recent occasions, Mr Whitelaw becomes a larger politician as his ordeal intensifies, and the Opposition particularly watches his growth as a portent. There are times when he has the air of a character in a Greek tragedy as he takes his stand, as he did yesterday, for reason and human decency in a setting of unreason and brutality."

It had been a very long day, but at the end of it we knew we had turned the tables on the terrorists. Triumph had come from the near wreckage of a political career. And once again the floor of the House of Commons had been unsurpassed as the place to stage a fightback.

For me, facing up to situations like that meant drawing on an immense amount of experience which had begun as a young journalist knocking around in South London. I had no idea at the time, but that training and background took me to a senior level in Fleet Street reporting politics, industrial relations and economics, and engaging with the major figures of the day—people like Hugh Gaitskell, Harold Wilson, George Brown, and union leaders like Frank Cousins, Sidney Greene and the TUC general secretary, George Woodcock.

And then my career took me into Whitehall to be the confidant and adviser of senior politicians as varied as William Whitelaw, James Callaghan, Peter Walker, Michael Foot and Reginald Maudling.

Later I was to be involved in the nationalisation of British shipbuilding, and then for eight years to be the press and public relations chief of the Confederation of British Industry, which were all rewarding experiences. I held quite a few top information jobs in Whitehall, graduating into public relations from twenty-one years in active journalism. For eight years I was in charge of information at the Department of Economic Affairs, the Board of Trade, Housing & Local Government, the Department of Environment, twice at the Home Office and finally at the Department of Employment.

But right in the middle of that experience was the Northern Ireland post, which was probably the toughest I ever held, as well as the most exhilarating. A loose word to a journalist, a failure to check a fact, meant not just a ticking-off—it could mean a death.

In the two-year period I was with Whitelaw in Northern Ireland there were nearly 800 deaths. Close shaves for us, personally, too. We tried to vary our routine, never to give in advance details of where a minister might be going to appear and moving fast when an air force helicopter was picking us up, say, at Warren Point alongside Carlingford Lough, where an IRA sniper with a telescopic sight could pick someone off while safe on the Republican shore.

I had had a taste of what to expect in 1969, accompanying James Callaghan, the Labour Home Secretary, to the province on what was expected to be a forty-eight-hour tour, but which lasted six days. And it produced the very first casualty: Royal Ulster Constabulary policeman James Arbuckle, killed near the Shankill, ironically by a Protestant bullet.

Those vital six days turned out to be training for a much closer involvement in those years ahead with Whitelaw. And the training I had absorbed whilst working in South London as a young reporter would eventually equip me for one of the toughest and most difficult jobs in press and public relations work of the era.

So let me take my readers back to the helter-skelter days of life on a busy local newspaper—an experience, sadly, that nowadays so few will ever be able to enjoy and learn as we did then.

But really my upbringing as a schoolboy during the war and losing my father when he was only forty-four years old was the starting point. Learning to cope with life and becoming extremely self-reliant was invaluable in a career where there were few guidelines and one backed a hunch or relied on instinct to guide me through exciting and challenging experiences.

CHAPTER 2
Wartime, Childhood—Growing up Fast!

The idea of no school for days on end sounds attractive and there was so much a boy could do around Addington in Surrey where I lived in 1939. There were the woods at Addington Palace, once a residence of the Archbishop of Canterbury, which I knew like the back of my hand, and behind the fairly newly-built houses in the area there were plenty of open fields and hedgerows.

But after a while, when there is no one to talk to or play with, the freedom starts to lose its magic. All the other children in the village had been evacuated away from areas likely to be bombed by the Germans. My sister and I were determined we were not going anywhere and our parents accepted that if we were going to die we might as well all be together.

But I was certainly getting a little bored. And then something magical—at least, to a small boy—happened. One spring morning in 1940, up the little hill called Crossways, the unmade road in which we lived, came some khaki-coloured army vehicles. With my parents and sister, Jean, I watched as the 2nd Field Regiment of the Royal Canadian Artillery motored into our village, Addington. And into my life.

They took over all the newly-built, but empty, houses in Featherbed Lane and Palace Green, they commandeered the Farm House Cafe and turned it into a soda bar and shop for toiletries. They even moved into Gravel Hill Service station and took over the workshops.

Virtually overnight, we had become a miniature army town and Addington was buzzing.

If the Canadians were here for a while, though, this was my chance, I told myself … without a mention to my family, of course.

As I sat on a low wall outside one of the empty houses in my own road, a Ford V8 light truck pulled up, two officers dismounted and walked up the front garden path. One of them was to have a profound impact on my life.

The major and a lieutenant tried the front door in vain and peered through the windows into the empty rooms.

"Do you want to get in?" I enquired.

"Sure do," said one, "but we have no key."

Having been in and out of the empty house several times, I said I could let them in if they wanted.

Seconds later, via the rear window I had carefully left unfastened the last time I had climbed into the kitchen, I opened the front door for Major Jack Ross and Lt Rolph of 7th Battery, RCA.

They had found their officers' mess courtesy of a ten-year-old schoolboy and were highly pleased. Swiftly, No. 7 Crossways was requisitioned.

Furthermore, Jack Ross invited me to climb into the passenger seat of his truck as he went on a whirlwind visit to see how his men were bedding in. I was his guide around the area, showing him how to get into the grounds of Addington Palace, where the 25-pounder guns were being uncoupled from the four-wheel-drive Quad vehicles that pulled them, to Palace Green where weary troops were sorting out their gear.

Off again to a special school along Featherbed Lane, selected as the mess for Major Ross's hungry troops. The ovens were already alight. Food smelt good, too.

Then it was off to find regimental headquarters which I guessed would have been set-up in an empty development a couple of miles up the road. I was right, too, because there Major Ross spotted the parked car of his regimental commander, Lt Colonel Tremayne.

By the time Ross dropped me off at my home, I had had a wonderful day, thinking that would be the end of it. But Ross told me I could ride with him next day if I wished and the next three months, I had one of the most exciting periods of my life. The regiment adopted me as an unofficial mascot and even gave me a proper steel helmet with the regimental flash to one side and called me Captain Keith. I could pop into the messes of other units, get a snack in the cookhouse … best of all, climb up into a Quad, learn about the angle of elevation required for a 25-pounder, see how a Lee Enfield .303 rifle needed to be cleaned and admire the occasional .45 revolver carried by officers and motorcycle despatch riders. One day I was allowed to fire one too. Oh yes—and they rode Harley-Davidson motorcycles, without the chrome plating, but not so different from the Hells Angels' machines we see gleaming on today's roads.

Within a few weeks I only had one ambition when I grew up. I wanted to be an officer in the Royal Canadian Artillery.

The summer of 1940 was to go down in weather records as one of the best for many years. Clear, cloudless skies, barely a shower. For several weeks, with my father and a next-door neighbour, a police sergeant, we stood in the front garden at dusk and watched German planes flying to and from London, silhouetted in the searchlights. Not a shot was fired at them—we did not know there were so few guns available at the time. So for the Germans, it was simple to pinpoint landmarks like Crystal Palace and check distances.

My father took it as a warning and very soon we took delivery of an Anderson air-raid shelter. This consisted of six or eight sheets of curved corrugated iron together with a bag of bolts and a spanner.

What my dad had to do was dig a hole in the back garden into which our Anderson was to be installed and then pile the displaced soil on top. There was a wood slatted floor with a bunk to either side, all of which seemed to make it rather cosy. But for now there did not seem to be much need to be down in the Anderson.

I soon discovered that all the Canadian gunners were territorial volunteers and had been called up as soon as war was declared in September 1939. After initial training, they boarded one of the Queen liners with their equipment and were soon in Britain—among the earliest troops sent by the Dominions to help the mother country. And were we pleased to see them because we knew, in terms of resisting the Germans, we were up against it.

Major Ross had been on secondment to the British Army and was not a 'terrier', unlike the rest of the Canadians. He was actually a regular soldier and took part in the BEF evacuation from Dunkirk. So he had seen plenty of action.

I sensed, however, that my hero was not too popular with his men. He was too much of a disciplinarian for them, insisting on clean equipment, smart appearance and full maintenance of everything. But, of course, he had been dive-bombed repeatedly in France only a couple of months previously and knew his men were totally under-prepared. They still clung to the idea that the war would be over in six months and they would soon be back picking up the threads of their civilian life.

Major Ross had other ideas. He showed me on an aerial photograph taken by one of our planes, which clearly identified where the regiment was based, the tyre tracks of their vehicles through the fields, men lined up outside the houses—it was all there in remarkable detail.

A day or so later, Major Ross told me there was to be a real dive-bombing demonstration at Hayes, Kent, about five miles from Addington. And yes—I could come if I wanted. Did I? I marched along with the men, spotting new friends I had made and chatting. How on earth a regiment on its way to war put up with me I will never know, but they did; and in a field I sat with the Canadian soldiers as three Blackburn Skua planes with Royal Canadian Air Force markings screamed down on three 25-pounder guns dug into the earth.

The planes dropped flour bags as bombs and came remarkably close to the artillery, but the real impression was the terrible noise of the planes as they tore down at us. I don't know if the troops were scared, but I have never forgotten that day.

Towards the end of the summer holidays, there was talk of the schools re-opening as children came back from evacuation and their parents and teachers decided nothing much was happening. Our village school was to re-open in September and I could see my happy solitude was coming to an end.

Then one day in August it suddenly all changed. I was with three or four other boys one tea-time when we noticed a number of twin-engined planes high above us. No one was shooting at them, and the presumption was that they were 'friendly'. Not for long.

Suddenly we saw them start to dive on what we later realised was Croydon Airport, four or five miles away. *Crump*, *crump* and *crump* we felt, as big black canisters were dropped from the planes.

We just about got out 'Wow' before one of the mothers hurled us all into an Anderson air-raid shelter and told us to keep quiet.

An 'All Clear' siren, after about an hour, said we could come out, though no one could recall ever hearing a warning. The attack had come all too suddenly and taken us by surprise. We did not know it, but that day, the 15th August 1940, was the opening day of the main phase of the Battle of Britain.

Croydon Airport had been attacked in the first major air raid on the London area. At around 6.20 p.m., twenty-two Messerschmitt 110 and 109 fighter-bombers mounted a final raid of the day, intended for RAF Kenley nearby, but they attacked Croydon (four miles further north) in error. Some error! The armoury was destroyed, the civilian airport terminal building badly hit, and a hangar was damaged by cannon fire and blast. Another hangar and about forty training aircraft in it went up in flames. Six airfield personnel died. Factories next to Croydon Airport took most of the bombing.

The worst was the nearby Rollason Aircraft factory, which received several bomb hits and accounted for many of the sixty-two civilians killed and 192 injured. We were concerned because both my father and my sister worked at Redwing, the aircraft factory next door, which was also badly damaged. But my father was away from the factory that day and my sister had turned down a request to work overtime—an instinct urged her to get away home, she told me.

Of the raiders, eight aircraft were downed by the Hurricane squadrons, but the huge tower of smoke reaching into the summer sky told us that the Germans had indeed hit their target. And we braced ourselves for more.

The pace of war was about to quicken and at Addington I was to have a ringside seat because the village lay equidistant between Croydon, Kenley and the most famous of all Battle of Britain aerodromes, RAF Biggin Hill.

From mid-August until late September the Battle of Britain raged overhead. We could identify the planes instantly and also knew the different engine sounds. Many of my age can still today tell the sound of a Rolls Royce Merlin engine compared to the different, harsher tone of the German planes like Heinkels, Dorniers and Junkers 88s, which we knew carried the bombs, and the Me 109 fighters which protected them.

My Canadian friends had anti-aircraft positions set-up all around, continually manned, so at Addington we felt quite fortunate to have some defence; but the real protection lay with the fighter planes, Spitfires and Hurricanes, which chased the Germans in the brilliant summer of 1940.

On one occasion, I watched a German fighter plane plunging to the ground as its pilot drifted down by parachute. The Canadians raced off by vehicle to find him and I watched Major McCormick, the regiment's second-in-command, bring the scared young blond German, blood streaming from a head wound, to the regiment's medical bay in Featherbed Lane.

A large crowd of civilians jeered and might well have lynched the Luftwaffe pilot had it not been for his army protection. After treatment, he was driven away and people dispersed, but not before I heard the major telling friends he had grabbed the German's parachute and fancied turning it into a pair of silk pyjamas.

Then, quite suddenly, it seemed my perfect world was coming to an abrupt end. My hero, Major Ross, told me he was being promoted to Lt Col. and leaving Addington to go to another regiment. I managed to hold back the tears, but the man who had changed my life so drastically in that summer of 1940 was to leave it so suddenly. I waved him off, wondering if I would ever see him again. In fact he did come to see us twice later and every now and again for several wartime years a wonderful food parcel would arrive, sent by Ross's fiancée, Donnie. Butter in a tin, ham and sweets—candies, they called them—for me.

But for a while I was quite upset. I had lost a wonderful friend and at the age of eleven that seemed very hard to accept, even though, as a parting gift, Jack Ross had given me a Westclox wristwatch, my first ever, as a memento.

And then I found a new hero. Captain Harley Jamieson, of the rival 8th Battery, 'adopted' me, and once again I was riding around to see the regiment's 25-pounders, as they were moved to Frylands Wood, which provided far better cover. I little realised then that years later I would camp in that very same wood as a scout.

Captain Jamieson took me into Croydon in his truck to visit the Davis Theatre, to see what he called 'a movie'—a film to me—and then to have tea with him on the theatre balcony.

Looking back, I suppose it all seemed rather strange that another fighting man would take a shine to me, but in these awful times when there is so much attention rightly devoted to the dangers of paedophilia, I can honestly say that nothing ever occurred of the slightest impropriety, and I don't think it ever crossed the mind of Jamieson or Ross. As Jack Ross put it to me many years later, "I just liked kids."

I had lots of other pals in the 2nd Field Regiment, most of whom signed my autograph book.

There was George who, every Thursday night, would come to my home and play me at table tennis on our little dining room table as my parents were off to the pub. In effect, George was baby-sitting, but I was learning more and more about the game I came to love and at which I was later quite proficient.

Then there was a great cook named Gill who gave me some of his food one day at Frylands Wood. Next time I found him, he was in charge of the Sergeants' Mess kitchen and thereafter I was always assured of some tasty snack when I dropped in—plus one or two items in my saddlebag for my mother ...

The Farm House Cafe, with little to sell and few local customers, was concentrating on supplying my Canadian friends, and whenever

I put my head in there I was assured of a Coke or a Pepsi—absolutely delicious. And free. I did not know until then that these American soft drinks existed. Nobody worried about the damage to children's teeth in those days.

It was at the Farm House Cafe where, for the first time I heard a new kind of music—'In The Mood', 'American Patrol', 'String Of Pearls', 'Juke Box Saturday Night' played by a wonderful band led by a guy called Glenn Miller. And there were other bands, like Benny Goodman's and Harry James's. So it was there and then that I started a journey into swing and jazz which has stayed with me all my life and given me immense enjoyment.

Two other Canadian friends, a young woman and an equally young man, both civilians, ran a vehicle serving tea, coffee and snacks. They staged amateur dramatics, films and other home-from-home events to entertain the artillerymen who were becoming increasingly bored.

They had, after all, come to Europe to take on the Germans and most had yet to see one.

But on the night of 7th September 1940 they certainly heard a lot more of them—as did we in the little van which my two welfare friends had driven to Oxted, and taken me along to see an amateur play in which the Canadians were involved.

We soon forgot all about the play as our van laboured up the hills of the North Downs and it seemed all hell had broken out. Planes were constantly overhead, bombs falling, and searchlights and anti-aircraft guns seeking out the attackers.

The Blitz on London had begun, and a light car on a darkened road with tiny pinpricks for headlights was not the best place to be sheltering. My two friends were remarkably calm, and eventually we got back to Addington and I was dropped off at my house. There seemed no one at home, but round the back I found my family in the Anderson shelter. Dad's handiwork had paid off.

For the next few months we were to spend most nights down there, long enough for my sister and I to learn to play whist, but it became damper and colder as winter approached. Often one of my Canadian friends would put his head into the shelter and ask if we were all right. Sometimes, too, a welcome bar of Hershey chocolate would be passed down to us. Later I realised just how lucky we had been because 40,000 civilians were killed in the Blitz—and half of those were in London.

Eventually my Canadian dream came to an end. One day, word went round that the 2nd Field Regiment's 25-pounder guns were wanted elsewhere, along with the rest of the 1st Division. Overnight, Addington went strangely silent. No more trucks or motorcycles zipping up our road, no soldiers milling around, no Cokes at the cafe, no high tea in the mess hall … just an impossible strange silence. My Canadian world of adventure had come to an end and it was time for my feet to get back on the ground. I knew in my heart that was right, too. But that did not help to hold back the tears.

School had re-opened, and there were friendships to renew and lessons to be learned. On the other hand I can see now that my months of freedom had turned me in to a cocky, stroppy, even insolent child, and there was a need for discipline. Not that I agreed just then.

What was known as a 'selection' test was to be held at New Addington, about four miles away, and Miss Forster did her best to prepare us. No one explained though that this test was crucial to our lives and everything we wanted to do with them was about to be decided in that grotty classroom.

Looking back, I do think that my parents could have discussed it and tried to help me better prepare. Not a bit of it. On the morning, my dad gave me two new sharpened pencils and wished me good luck. One has to make allowances. Dad was working up to sixteen hours a day, then walking five miles from Croydon to Addington, often through the bombing, spending the night in the air-raid shelter with us, and then setting off again next morning for work. His then job was production manager of a light engineering factory in Croydon, producing the compressors which operated the sliding hoods of Spitfires, Hurricanes and other warplanes.

Even so, just a bit of time with me on arithmetic would have been a godsend, I thought to myself, as I sat looking at the maths paper with all its unanswered questions plus my guesses for answers which I knew were wild shots in the dark. I had sailed through the English and the General Knowledge—both right up my street. Now here I was in trouble. If they had asked me about the angle of elevation for a 25-pounder gun I could have given the answer—but no such luck.

Two or three weeks later, as we sat in our columns in the tiny church school in Addington village, Miss Forster read out the results and gradually I learned where all my fellow pupils would move. She left me till last, and had me squirming.

"McDowall—Heath Clark Selective Central School," she told the school, who were probably as wise as me. None of us had heard of the place.

As the class packed up, Miss Forster called me over. "You had me concerned there for a while, Keith. I was wondering what was going to happen to you."

"So was I, Miss."

I was in fact lucky to get quite a good school place, but now I realise that I undershot considerably. With a little preparation, and explanation of the importance of the exam, I should—and could—have done a whole lot better. I ought to have made it to a grammar school like John Ruskin in Croydon. From there I could perhaps have taken what was known then as Higher Certificate and aimed for university.

Had that happened, my whole life would have been different, though not necessarily for the better. I did not know it then but my path to achievement was to be journalism, and leaving school at sixteen to fight for a place on a local paper was quite a good jumping-off place. I often joked that I had been at the University of the Old Kent Road. Certainly, all life was there, and it was a place to learn about it at close quarters.

Still, I would have liked the choice.

My mother took me into Croydon to get my first-ever school blazer in black with its rather smart embroidered badge offering the motto 'Laborare est Orare'—'To work is to pray'—and some other bits and pieces specified in the list sent by the school. The school had just returned from evacuation in Wales so it was almost getting off to a new start—and we were it.

On the next Monday I set off to my new school, but first I had to find it. Self-reliance was the norm those days. So I caught a 64 bus which terminated down by the Farm House Cafe and paid my fare to West Croydon station, about five miles away, and then walked to London Road where I got a tram towards London, which went to Thornton Heath. I learned quickly which tram went where, but on my first morning the tram was filled with lots of kids like myself in new uniforms so it seemed a safe bet. And the conductor told us to get off at Winterbourne Road where Heath Clark School was located.

I had not hung around, but I suppose the total journey took about an hour, and Mr Abba, the headmaster, was already on his feet as the last of us crept into the back of the assembly hall. Not a good start, as we could tell from his black look.

At the end of the quite exciting first day I had to make the return journey to Addington with a satchel containing my first-ever homework. Not too onerous—just checking, I suppose, whether we had absorbed anything. I quickly dropped into the routine, learned little ways of improving my journey time, and sometimes arrived at Heath Clark in time to meet my new friends in the playground. That, as any child knows, is where the real adjustments in relationships are made and how one finds new friends—and potential enemies.

But after a week or so I was surprised to get home one day to find my father in bed. He was away from work, I was told, because he had throat trouble and was unwell.

Each day when I got home I told him about my day's adventures, how I was enjoying learning about Henry VIII, the correct way to spell Katharine as distinct from Catherine and all about that cunning Cardinal Wolsey. My dad was good at history so we had interesting conversations. But his coughing, I could see, was getting worse, not better. And I have a very clear recollection of Dad showing me the *Sunday Express* which led on the story of the discovery by Alexander Fleming of what was to become known as penicillin, a wonder cure of the age. But not in time for him.

A few days later when I came home, Dad was not in bed. He had been taken to Mayday Hospital, Croydon—named after a road I passed each day in my tram. But there was no chance I could get to see him. In those days there was a strictly enforced rule that children under fourteen could not make hospital visits—and I was eleven. There was bombing on again, too. Not as bad as the Blitz, but almost nightly we would get attacks from a handful of bombers slipping out of the clouds to scatter their bombs and scuttle off again. It was before radar-equipped night fighters were developed to hunt them down, so we just got on with it.

However, the rising casualties were causing a bed shortage problem for Mayday and Croydon General Hospitals, so we were warned my father would have to be moved. Overnight, patients like him were driven to Horton Emergency, near Epsom, a former mental institution and, once, a World War I recovery unit composed of wooden sheds linked by covered walkways which were wet and cold. A nasty, unwelcoming place.

My mother seized her chance and took me to see my father in bed there, and I was told to act like a rather small fourteen-year-old and to keep my mouth shut. I had not seen my father for weeks and I could see he was weaker. Every few minutes it seemed he would have a coughing fit and need to spit into a container. He made a joke of it, but I have never forgotten that sound.

I did not realise it but that was the last time I would see him. It was shortly before his forty-fourth birthday, and I went with two school friends to Thornton Heath at lunchtime to buy him a birthday present. With my friends' help I chose a notepaper and envelope set so that he could write to us at home. He was never to use it.

One week later I was roused from my bed and told to dress. The Post Office had brought a message that my father was seriously ill— we knew that—and his next of kin should go at once to the hospital. This was eleven at night. There were no trains, no buses running, taxis did not exist, there was no petrol for private cars, and we did not have much money anyway as my father had not been working.

My mother decided she and Jean would get to the hospital somehow, and asked a young friendly couple who were new neighbours if they could take me in overnight. I joined them in their bed and soon dropped off, little realising that my whole life was about to be shattered.

Next morning, instead of getting me off to school, my overnight hosts told me they had received a message from my mother to give me some money, and that I was to make my way to New Eltham where my cousin and great pal Brian lived with his parents, my mother's sister Muriel and Uncle Harry.

To be told to take a day off school seemed too good a chance to miss, and I happily set off on the even longer journey right across South London by 54 bus, arriving mid-afternoon.

That was 27th November 1941—the day my father died—but the way I was told was pretty insensitive. The radio was playing 'Danny Boy' when my aunt asked me if I realised how ill my father really was. Did I know that he had died? I burst into tears—that hated 'Danny Boy' still bleating on, and my aunt consoling me even though, I learned later, she had been expressly asked not to tell me and to leave it to my mother to break the news.

That night, as I cried and cried, my cousin Brian, sharing the bed, tried hard to comfort me, but it was no use. A crossroads in my life had been reached and I had been utterly unprepared.

I stayed with my relatives for several days, one of which was to be the day of the funeral, but I was not allowed to go. My mother seemed desperately keen to shield me while my sister Jean, admittedly nearly five years older, was assumed to be sufficiently grown up to take it in her stride.

It was, apparently, a bitterly cold day for a funeral and there were not all that many at the interment, but even after all these years I would still have wished to be there. Many years later, when I could afford it, I had a tasteful headstone installed at Croydon Crematorium and added the name of my mother, since her ashes had been scattered in the little garden at a bungalow in Banstead where she ended her days.

But straight after the funeral when we gathered together again at Addington, it was a very purposeful and determined mother who took charge. She was virtually destitute; no savings, no job, not even a widow's pension, because to qualify there had to be a minimum contribution of two years (or 104 weeks) to the National Insurance scheme—and Dad had about ninety.

My mother could have put my sister and me into care and fended for herself, but she was determined to keep the family together. We would have to move, though. There was no way we could afford the rent of our detached house in Crossways.

My mother found a ground floor, self-contained unfurnished flat at 34 Elmwood Road just off London Road near West Croydon, usefully much nearer to my school, and she found a job in the office of an optical firm at nearby Addiscombe. Jean went to the Labour Exchange, as women then were being 'directed to jobs where there was a need'. After several jobs my sister was sent to the main office of the South Suburban Co-operative Society in London Road where, quite shortly afterwards, she objected to paying the political levy towards the Labour Party's funds and bravely 'opted out' as it was known. Not a good way to make friends with the activists … but that's Jean.

We needed her income too because we were so close to the breadline that I went on my mother's instruction to collect money from the Poor Law, as it was known, from a tiny window in a house in Mayday Road; again, right next to that hospital. It was to see us through until the first pay packet arrived. But when people ask me why I support the Left, I remember how uncomfortable I felt that day, and vowed then that I would not wish that on anybody else if it could be prevented.

In my case I could now ride a bike to school and save the tram fare. But even though I was much nearer I could not engage in the after-school activities like debating, which I would have loved. My mother chatted up Frank Wheeler, the manager of the UK Tea Co in London Road, and I soon started there as the delivery boy. For two hours each day after school, except Wednesday early closing day, I was at the grocery shop delivering orders, cleaning and polishing the brass below the shop windows and all the weighing scales—and helping Tiger the tomcat get the rats in the back yard. The shop assistants used to slip me chocolate digestive biscuits—rationed—when Mr Wheeler was not looking, and tell me saucy jokes. I learned a lot.

Riding the big delivery bike with three or four orders on the front took me all over Croydon to parts like Thornton Heath, Norbury and Waddon, and I got to know the borough well. I also had a newspaper round in the morning before school, and the combined income each week meant I bought most of my own clothes.

It was not long after moving that a school friend named Lionel Chapman casually asked if I was interested in joining the scouts, and invited me to a church hall off Mitcham Road the following Thursday evening. I turned up and found a hall of boisterous boys indulging in what was known as British Bulldog: a small group occupied the middle ground and the rest of us dashed from one end of the hall to the other, only joining the middle squad if intercepted and picked up off one's feet. Ten minutes of that and I was in the scouts all right—in fact, in it for eight years.

The movement became a major part of my life. Eventually I became a patrol leader, a King's Scout, and even, at 17, a scoutmaster in my own right when the 44th Croydon's leader was called up for the Army.

I lapped up Baden Powell's book *Scouting for Boys* once I had decided to join, and was proud to go with my mother to the Scout shop in Croydon to get my first uniform. I had explained to Frank Hepworth, the scoutmaster, that I wanted to join but could not afford it, so he arranged to lend me the money from scout funds, which I repaid monthly.

I still have vivid memories of my first-ever camp one weekend when our patrol leader announced we were to go to Orchard Farm in Woldingham. He might as well as told us we were going to the Moon. How was I to know that one day I would bring my daughters up in that Surrey village, and they would take their first lessons in horse riding at the same farm?

We staggered off the train at Woldingham station with our massive backpacks, and eventually found Orchard Farm and pitched our tiny tents. After seeing how a fire was lit we wolfed down some food and were ready for bed. I had no sleeping bag but a couple of blankets, so the patrol leader did his best to make me comfortable. Then sternly he told us if there was any 'larking about' we would 'feel his slipper'. We took one look at the size of it and shut up. Not that I slept much. I had no idea the ground could be so hard. Or so cold.

We set off home again on Sunday afternoon and the walk did not seem so bad. I had a spring in my step because I had been to my first camp and, miraculously it seemed, survived it all. Over the coming years I was to lead many patrols on such adventures, even running a major camp myself for thirty or so boys.

I was actually the only Boy Scout in Croydon to hold the Horseman badge, which came about in a strange way. For some time I spent weekends on a kind of farm a family friend had created out of the large gardens of bomb-damaged homes in Streatham. He convinced the local authority he could create a small farm and rear pigs, chickens, geese and help to feed a hungry nation. They even gave him a grant so he could acquire a horse, Sally. So I learned to wash, groom and brush the horse's coat and mane, to coax her into accepting a bridle—and eventually a saddle—and then to accept a thirteen-year-old on board who was convinced he was a Texas Ranger.

Years later I was to be proud of a granddaughter, Fiona, who was not only extremely successful as a three-day eventer, but was destined to become a talented veterinary surgeon. Anyway, I stepped forward one parade night at the 57th Croydon Troop to be declared 'Horseman'. It would be a long time before they saw another.

Another Scout occasion I recall was when I was much more senior and holder of a First Class—the King's Scout, and green and gold cords. I looked like a Christmas tree in uniform, and I was asked to telephone the District Commissioner. He told me that along with Charlie Burchill of the 8th, I was to go to the annual King's Scout Parade at Windsor Castle for a service attended by the King in St George's Chapel.

No instruction or advice on getting there—no bus fare either. Just be there. It's probably why the Boy Scout motto is 'Be Prepared' and we were. Charlie and I got on our bikes, worked out a route, and cycled from Croydon to Windsor and back. It was quite a long way, but we took our places representing Croydon's Western Division and reported to the DC 'job done'.

That was not long after every Boy Scout over a certain age in Croydon, then England's largest town, were assembled in a large hall in great secrecy. There we were told that a sudden emergency might hit our town in the near future, and if a certain password was distributed we were all to stop whatever we were doing and to go to a series of assembly points. In fact, the message never came, but the flying bombs certainly did. Hitler launched the V1, a jet-propelled missile, zooming over our heads at around 400 miles an hour, then suddenly cutting its engine and dropping to the ground causing a massive explosion. Of all the London boroughs, the most V1s fell on Croydon and thousands were killed and injured.

The message to summon the Scouts had been planned because the authorities thought all telephone lines would be cut and communication would break down. We were to act as messengers using our bikes and knowledge of our areas to get messages through. It was quite a neat idea but fortunately one that was never needed.

At first the 'doodlebugs', as Londoners nicknamed them, were terrifying and we cowered in shelters. But we had to come to terms with them. So long as the engine kept going we were safe. When it stopped, though, people learned to dive for cover very fast indeed because the blast effect was devastating.

As I found out when I got out of the Anderson shelter of a school friend, wondering where exactly a nearby V1 had fallen, so loud had been the explosion. As I cycled up the little hill towards London Road I had a sinking feeling I knew where it had come down … yes, right in Elmwood Road where I lived. It was a direct hit on Elmwood Hall, a multi-purpose/use dance hall which served the neighbourhood well. But not anymore. Several houses were flattened and every other house in the road was badly damaged, including ours.

I was home first. The front door was dangling on its hinges and most of the windows had been blown out. I do not think I had ever seen so much glass in my life, and by then I had seen plenty of bomb damage.

As I was just wondering where to start my mother arrived, followed shortly afterwards by Jean. We made a start, sweeping glass with that terrible, awesome screech into buckets and boxes. That sound was to come to haunt me again when I worked in Northern Ireland in 1972–4.

Would we be able to patch enough windows sufficient to keep us warm and dry overnight? Just then, as if by magic, a friendly face appeared at one of the open spaces and asked if we wanted it covered in with black pitch paper? It was an RAF serviceman on a ladder—one of a squad of service people quickly drafted in to shattered areas like Elmwood Road to patch us up and help get us sorted. It was an inspired idea by someone in Whitehall, and as dusk fell we were reasonably cleared up, our beds were glass-free, and we could safely put a kettle on the stove.

Because of doodlebug damage three Scout troops had been combined into one, which turned out to be a break for me because I came under the eye of an inspirational character named Ted Mayne, Group Scoutmaster of the 8th Croydon, founded in 1912 and one of the oldest in the country. Ted had been there then as a kid so he knew a lot about Scouting.

I learned that Ted, a relaxed pipe-smoking bachelor, spent every night at Mayday Hospital, where throughout the war Scouts were on duty as stretcher-bearers. On their breast pocket they wore a special ARP badge—quite an honour because the public could see a boy was doing important war work. They slept in their own quarters at Mayday so were always on call in an emergency. And there were plenty of those.

Trouble was I was not yet sixteen—the qualifying age. Even so I asked Ted if I could join this elite band of brothers. I never mentioned the age question but he obviously knew it. After a moment's reflection he told me to report to the hospital that evening. I was in. As the raids continued virtually non-stop I got used to the sight of blood, the sadness and worry of relatives as we carried their loved ones from the ambulances to the casualty station, the tears.

But there were happier aspects. If I got to Mayday fairly quickly after school, once my grocery shop work was done, I could sit there and do my homework—often assisted by some of the bright young nurses.

Across the English Channel the D-Day landings which began on 6th June were bearing fruit and the British, Canadian and American troops were starting to drive inland.

Though still under continuous attack by the V1s, we were following the progress of Canadian troops as they worked their way along the coast towards Belgium and Holland. Each day or so they overran a V1 launch site, one less place from which the Germans could aim a lethal weapon at us. These Canadian troops were not 'my' regiment, though—the 2nd Field Regiment I knew was in Italy, toiling up that mountainous country in the teeth of fierce German resistance. Even so, these other Canadians had our best wishes … "Keep at it lads," we thought.

There was a break for the Scouts of my troop (the 57th) when it was announced a fruit picking camp had been arranged in Cambridgeshire. We were all for it—a week in the country well north of London and away from the V1s sounded like paradise. And once in the orchards of Chivers, the famous fruit and jam company, we could see the potential. We split into pairs—a big boy and a smaller one. My little pal was Alf Spink, who had reached the top of the cubs and just come up to our Scout troop.

We quickly worked out that, rather than pick greengages one by one, if I got up the tree and shook it vigorously the fruit would fall, and Alf could nip round below and fill our basket. It worked a dream, and as we were being paid by the basket the omens looked good.

On Day Three, after our system had been adopted on a wide scale by other teams, worried production managers arrived from the jam factory to find why all the fruit was arriving bruised. They stood in the orchard, amazed at their trees swaying violently and fruit tumbling down as below, small boys went to work. Our speeded-up process was ended on the spot and we were instructed to pick by hand. Our credit for fruit already weighed would stand, though, and at the end of the week Alf and I had loaded 86 stone 4 pounds of greengages on to the scales and we were in the money. Soon enough, it was back to the daily air raids and a much more sinister turn of the wheel. Rumours of major incidents in London were circulating in which there was no sound of an engine, but just a sudden massive explosion with far more devastating damage than could be caused by a doodlebug.

At New Cross in South London, we heard on the grapevine that 164 people had been killed as they queued at Woolworth's because they had heard a supply of biscuits had arrived. At Smithfield meat market a similar mystery explosion had killed and injured many.

This in fact was Hitler's second secret weapon, the supersonic V2 rocket. It arrived literally out of space, killing and maiming. We were, quite frankly, scared.

The V2 weapon was so terrifying because there was no way we could prepare or take cover. I have never been sure how Londoners, or soon the rest of Britain, would have been able to cope with a prolonged V2 rocket attack. Fortunately, the Canadian soldiers and systematic low-level bombing by the RAF gradually knocked out or overran the launch sites by September and the attacks petered out.

It is only my view, but I believe on the home front in June 1944 war-weary London was on its knees and came very close to defeat because of Hitler's rockets.

Things slackened off at Mayday Hospital, but we continued to put in a nightly spell just in case there was some other dastardly device up Hitler's sleeve. Then one day, the 8th May 1945 was declared to be VE Day—Victory in Europe. At the hospital, led by the nurses and white-coated doctors, we paraded around the grounds, banging dustbins and blowing horns as patients came out on the balconies to wave. The noises might have seen off a few, but most seemed to enter the spirit of the magnificent day.

Now, although we were warned not to get carried away because we still had to win the war in the Far East, we did start to think about the future.

At school I was in my last six months, and passing the Oxford School Certificate was firmly on the radar screen. I had sat the Royal Society of Arts English exams in the air-raid shelter because of the V1s, but passed easily. A good omen, perhaps. And I puffed out my chest when Mr Edwards the English master suddenly told the class, "McDowall has the best vocabulary in the school … Why, why? Because he reads, he reads, he reads … " Well, he was right about reading. And I did seem to be making some status progress because I became a prefect.

Even so, I had no clear idea what I wanted to do when I left school. In the playground one day with my two particular friends, Ron Simmons and Brian Saker, the latter was quite clear. He was going to be a reporter, a journalist. Well, that was a thought. I reckoned I was better than him at English, and maths would not matter. If he was on that road, so was I. A decision that selected my route in life was chosen as easily as that.

No careers advice, no company teach-in, no parental input. That was it. My mother did admittedly raise her eyebrows and indicated doubt. "You want to get a good job with a pension," she urged. "Why don't you become a telegraph boy and work your way up in the Post Office. You'll never be out of work."

But try telling that to a sixteen-year-old with the world at his feet.

In my other world of Scouting there were big developments too. One day the doorbell rang and Ted Mayne stood there. "I've got a job for you," he said. "I want you to run a whole troop yourself. The fellow running the 44th has just got his calling-up papers and they have not got a Scoutmaster. I reckon you could do it." He knew how to play me. Cocky but capable, I think, was his definition of me. I took the bait—a chance to run my own show. Well, in theory anyway. What I had not grasped was that the troop leader and patrol leaders of the 44th were a tightly knit crowd and close friends away from the Scouts. So a newcomer, only a year or so older than them, was going to have to be on his toes to achieve any kind of discipline and leadership. I managed it over some months but was sorely tested. However we went camping, took joint cycle rides to places as far as Eastbourne, some sixty miles away.

Then came the really big test. I decided we had to have a Summer Camp. There had always been one, the leaders assured me, so … though I had done lots of camping and led a patrol, I had never organised a whole troop of thirty or forty boys for a week. Well, so what?

We located a camp site at a farm on the South Downs towards Forest Row, and I next had to organise transport with petrol still tightly rationed. I tried several well-known haulage companies but thought they were too expensive. Then I found a man-with-a-van advertising in the local paper who was very friendly when I rang him. "Yes," he could do it, "absolutely no problem at all."

Simple. After all, I was in charge, wasn't I? Out went notes to the boys' parents giving details of our plans, and asking for parental approval. Soon it was all tied up. I don't think I asked anyone about it or took advice. And the camp went well. We had splendid weather and my team of leaders pulled together. Their specialty was what they called corned beef hash, which consisted of throwing into a dixie any food to hand. Who said, for example, that you can hardly mix corned beef and condensed milk? "You can in the 44th," I was assured.

Then came the day to prepare for the return home, but our friendly van man was nowhere to be seen. He eventually arrived several hours late, full of apologies, but pulled me to one side. Though I had paid him up front, including for the return journey, he was not only short of money but short of petrol too.

Still, we loaded up the camping gear, got all the boys in the back and set off. I rode in front listening for the engine to peter out but it kept going until we neared Blindley Heath in Sussex when the engine spluttered to a halt. The boys were not at all worried, and climbed out seeking somewhere to put their sleeping bags and seemed to enjoy the adventure. It was about eleven o'clock at night and not a petrol pump in sight.

The driver did not appear to have a clue what to do and it was obviously up to me.

It was very dark because of the blackout, and there was nothing like a police station or even a phone box. Even so, the nearby houses looked pretty grand. But why should they help me?

There was no reply at the first three houses I tried, and as I moved further and further away from my charges I was getting pretty desperate. At the fourth house my knocking and ringing the bell resulted in a figure in a dressing gown appearing, looking suspiciously through the glass-panelled front door. Why he opened the door I will never know. Maybe it was the Scout uniform. Maybe he had been in the movement himself. I explained my desperation. Could he help? "There's a gallon of petrol in the garage—I'll get it for you." That kind gentleman would take no money and wanted no thanks. "Just leave the empty can in the front garden—good luck." And the front door closed firmly.

Scarcely able to believe such luck I walked back to the driver and told him to pour in the fuel carefully without wasting a drop. We still had a long way to go in the middle of the night. The boys all clambered back into the van, still remarkably upbeat.

Not so their parents. They were ringing my home and my sister Jean was coping with their calls but unable to answer their questions. I had not told her what was happening, and in any case, had not seen a telephone box. We tend to take phones for granted these days and forget just how rare they once were.

Though there was now petrol in the engine, that was not the end of our troubles. As the van crested the top of the hill and began to accelerate down the Caterham bypass there was a loud noise at the rear. We had a puncture. Furthermore, the spare the van carried was not inflated—it probably already had a puncture and we were riding on the spare.

By now I was exasperated and demanded to know what the driver intended. He had no answers, so at five in the morning we ran on the rim of the tyre down the hill and crept on through the centre of Croydon. It made a dreadful noise and at any moment I expected a red hot wheel to collapse under us.

But slowly, slowly, the Methodist church tower opposite the Croydon

General Hospital came into view, and then—almost, it seemed, in a cloud—we stopped and the tired kids clambered down into the arms of waiting parents. Few grumbled—they were just relieved to see their boys. Some fathers even helped us to unload.

I suppose they could see it had been a very long night indeed for all us.

Chapter 3
Learning to Chase the News in South London

The Mayor of Bermondsey was on his knees, tears streaming down his florid, flabby face.

"I am appealing to you—please forgive me," he begged.

Mayors were nothing new to me. As a young, but by then fairly switched-on, district reporter in South London, I had seen them come and go—in Battersea, Lewisham, Deptford and Camberwell. But never had one been pleading with me like this.

"I can't forgive you, Mr Mayor," I told Councillor Albert Culling, a stevedore from Rotherhithe. "That's up to the people of Bermondsey. But judging by their letters, they're in no mood to forgive you. You embarrassed them."

Well, maybe that was overstating it just a bit. But I had received several letters about Culling's astonishing performance when the comedian Norman Wisdom visited a Bermondsey Council housing estate in 1954. The mayor had ruined the show, seizing the mike repeatedly and completely upstaging Wisdom.

But what made me decide to confront the mayor in his parlour at the town hall was a phone call from a resident of Arnold Estate, barely a stone's throw from Tower Bridge. The woman was quite blunt. "What are you going to do about the silly old sod? He shouldn't be mayor—he made a bloody fool of us."

So here I was confronting Culling, who had been a disaster since his colleagues on the all-Labour council had chosen him under the 'Buggin's turn' rule to be the new mayor. It was Albert's turn. Never mind that he could scarcely read or write; he was elected, wasn't he?

Labour had held Bermondsey Council since before World War II. There was no opposition at all; no one on the other side of the chamber to put another view, or even a question. The Labour councillors had forgotten that completely. It meant the council meeting lasted a bare five minutes or so as they went through the formalities. By contrast, the party meeting two nights earlier could last two or three hours as the Labour councillors argued it out behind closed doors.

So for several years I had become the opposition. As the *South London Press* reporter for the borough, I set out to open those doors and shed a little light onto the one-party domination. I cracked the party meeting, getting some accurate leaks on housing, social policy and, indeed, who was to be the next mayor and how they were chosen.

You could say I already had Culling's number.

But when I confronted him I simply saw it as a good story for the coming Friday's issue. Having the mayor on his knees and begging the forgiveness of local residents was pretty good. It would read well, I told myself, as I climbed into my pre-war Singer two-seater and set off for the office at the Elephant and Castle.

What I did not know was that the moment I left, the Town Clerk and a colleague confronted the emotional Culling and told him he had to resign. I had set-up the situation which the officials who ran Bermondsey awaited. In his emotional state Culling agreed to go, and a letter of resignation—already prepared, it turned out—was placed in front of him.

The mayor signed with a cross.

Not only the officials breathed a sigh of relief, but also Culling's council colleagues accepted the decision as word quickly spread round the borough of the mayoral coup.

Everyone, it seemed, except Albert Culling.

Some hours later he discharged himself from the hospital, which the officials persuaded him was where he should rest, and tried to enter the mayor's parlour where a good stock was generally held in the wine cupboard. But the town hall officials were prepared, and Albert found his way bolted and barred. Nothing for it but to get in somehow. So

Albert went off and returned with a hammer and chisel. And started to break in.

High above, in his flat on the top floor of the town hall, that was all the Macebearer needed to hear. He dialled 999 and told police 'someone' was trying to break into the town hall.

Poor Albert resisted arrest, insisting he was the mayor, and was trying to gain access to his parlour. I never heard if one of the policemen replied that he was really Napoleon, but not long afterwards the ex-Mayor of Bermondsey found himself this time inside a secure mental ward at St Francis Hospital, Dulwich. Albert's brief reign as mayor was over.

I have gone into some detail on this incident to show that when dealing with stories about the successive Mayors of Bermondsey, you could not really make them up.

Over the years they provided me and my predecessors with good copy. There was the mayor who used his official limousine and driver to go thirty-three times to New Cross Speedway. Once was enough, decided the district auditor, and surcharged the mayor several thousand pounds for repayment.

And plumpish Miss Eileen Greenwood, mayor in 1950–51,was persuaded by the *South London Press* to object most strongly when a councillor in Bognor Regis declared that the town did not want 'fat ladies from Bermondsey in comic hats' arriving by charabanc to lower the tone. She demanded a public apology from Bognor to Bermondsey for this scurrilous slur on the good folk of her London borough. Bognor squirmed, but Miss Greenwood of Bermondsey put her foot down. Bognor Regis gave the public apology she sought, Bermondsey was delighted, and the *South London Press* revelled in it.

Joe Geoghegan took the mayoral chair for 1954–55 and was determined to leave a personal mark. He was a full-time official of the Transport and General Workers' Union which had an office in Tooley Street where Joe worked. Which was where the union served the needs—and tried to cope with the incessant unofficial strikes—of 10,000 dockers working the wharves and quays south of the Thames.

Into them every day came Britain's supplies of frozen lamb, mutton and butter from New Zealand and Australia.

On the paper we called Tooley Street 'London's larder'—and there was something in it.

Joe wanted to commemorate the name of Ernest Bevin, who had forged the union from a ragbag of smaller ones to create Britain's biggest union. As a tough negotiator Bevin was known as 'the Dockers' KC' and throughout World War II was Churchill's Minister of Labour, and then in the Labour landslide victory of 1945 he became Foreign Secretary.

No wonder he was Joe's hero. The mayor set-up an appeal fund to erect a permanent statue, and I gave it as much coverage as I could manage in the *South London Press* to keep the donations rolling in.

Today if you walk down Tooley Street, the wharves are silent, the warehouses gone—replaced by restaurants and office blocks housing financial white collar workers toiling, but not sweating as was once the case around there.

But still watching those changes is the late Ernest Bevin. A striking bust of him still stands on a pedestal at the junction with Queen Elizabeth Street where the citation declares 'A forceful and inspiring leader of democratic principles'. You could say that again.

It was unveiled there on 13th May 1955 in the presence of his wartime colleagues Clement Attlee, George Isaacs, and Bevin's widow Florence. And a young *South London Press* reporter who was pleased indeed with a very large 'thank-you' wink from Joe, Bermondsey's mayor, as he unveiled the memorial.

That was my background and it was great training. I never had the privilege of a university education, and with my mother widowed early in the war and left virtually penniless, I was extremely lucky to have been able to stay at school until I was sixteen.

My sister, Jean, from whom I learned of art, classical music, opera and, above all, good books, actually increased her contribution to the family weekly income so I could have my chance of a start in journalism. Maybe I was bright enough at school because I did well in subjects like English and History, but no one told me about university. In any case, not only was it out of the question, I wanted to get off on my own—maybe to my own 'University of the Old Kent Road'. It was quite a journey but, looking back, my 'university' served me well.

One of the best features of journalism is—or certainly was—that it puts you on a par with virtually everyone with whom you come into contact. Maybe it was also something of the attitude inside the *South London Press*, which by any standards was a remarkable local paper. Publishing twice weekly, it sold over 100,000 copies, carried over 3,000 classified advertisements, and did not bother with parish-pump items like weddings or obituaries. We bent at the knee for no one. Not for us, the reporters, the chore of getting down names and addresses at a funeral in the hope that they would buy the paper.

Instead we dug out the real news as we covered eight metropolitan boroughs south of the river; from Wandsworth and Battersea in the south-west to Lewisham and Deptford in the south-east, an area in which no fewer than twelve local papers operated. Our weekly sales were more than theirs combined and we wiped the floor with them.

Our editor was a Fabian, Eric Kinton, who set the tone but rarely interfered with reporters. His editorials generally came down on the side of Labour; unusual in a local paper, but as Kinton pointed out, they almost weighed the votes for Labour at election time when people like George Isaacs and Bob Mellish romped home with majorities of more than 30,000. So not a lot of point in trying to carry the standard for the Tories. In Southwark they gave two aldermanic seats to the Tories so that there was a token Opposition. But in Bermondsey they just did not bother, and a Tory had not sat in the Council chamber since 1937.

Each reporter had his own 'district'—a complete borough—and it was our job to find the real news there. When I had completed my National Service in the RAF I started off on my own in Battersea— where we were not so strong—and gradually progressed up to Deptford and finally Bermondsey. There was little guidance on what to cover from the News Editor, H.H. 'Max' Wall, but though he recognised everyone could have a poor week, an absence of copy from a reporter for more than a few days did not pass without comment.

But we needed little stimulus. The competition in the office as each of us vied for the front page lead story, the first item in the diary or an inside page lead, was intense. And we knew if we moved fast we could sell that copy to the Fleet Street evening papers, or better still, to the *Daily Mail*, the *Daily Express,* the *Mirror* or the *News Chronicle.*

Eventually we were doing so well on what was called 'linage'—the term descended from the days of a penny-a-line payment—that we would almost have paid the SLP to let us work free for them.

So a combination of competition from other journalists locally, the nearness of Fleet Street which meant a national daily man could be in your district within half an hour, and the intense rivalry among colleagues, kept us on our toes. And we loved it, but seldom admitted it.

What it also meant was that we were getting top quality training though no one ever mentioned that benefit. Seldom, after my very earliest days on a local, did I receive help with writing copy or handling an interview. You were on your own, to make your own mistakes; and maybe get an exclusive. Better still, and very occasionally, for a really well-written piece of copy, to see a 'byline': one's name in print. Which meant drinks all round.

The kind of story which really sold throughout Fleet Street concerned an ex-Guards officer, Major Richard Carr-Gomm, who I found on his knees scrubbing the floor of a tiny house in Eugenia Road, Bermondsey. My card had been marked by John Thomas, the local Labour agent, who was smart enough to keep me onside in the interests of his Member of Parliament, Bob Mellish, but also liked to see a good story in print.

John's tip-off about 'that Army bloke' took some believing. He held the Military Cross and the French Croix de Guerre, and obviously had a dazzling post-war military career ahead of him. Yet he had resigned his commission, used his gratuity to buy a worn-out house and invited in four old people. Each had his or her own room and was able to bring with them some items of furniture, personal possessions and a picture or two.

And Carr-Gomm cooked lunch for them, did the chores and chatted up his new 'guests'.

Why? "Well, I reckon my family has taken enough out of this area and I felt it was time to put a bit back." Just like that!

Certainly the family name rang a bell with me as extensive property owners locally, and in the 1931 landslide a Lady Carr-Gomm had won the seat for the Conservatives. The local Tory party offices were actually named after her.

"My mother," offered the major as he untied his apron and handed me a cup of tea. Wow!

Would he be willing to have his photograph taken … er … perhaps scrubbing a floor? I tentatively probed. No problem, it seemed, and when I reappeared next day with the SLP photographer, the major could not have been more helpful.

So within hours there were pictures of him on his knees in every daily newspaper looking the part—Guards moustache bristling, cavalry twill trousers, and a very big grin. And that apron.

It was the nearest I felt I had come to meeting a real Christian. And maybe there was an inner purpose of which I was just a part. For from that initial burst of publicity which Major Carr-Gomm had obviously wanted, came the Abbeyfield Society which he founded twelve months later. Within two years it had established six houses in Bermondsey and by the end of 1960 eight London boroughs had also gone with the major's idea.

Today Carr-Gomm's initiative of sheltered accommodation for older people, lonely but mostly fit and well, has spread throughout Britain. There are 300 local member societies, 700 houses catering for 7,500 residents involving over 5,000 volunteers.

Some story … some scrubber …

Oh, and my wife, Brenda, has become the President. I am proud of that.

In early December 1952, a thick, putrid smog engulfed London, reducing visibility to a few feet around the Elephant and Castle and most of South London. You could get about slowly during the 'daylight' hours, but as the darkness closed in around 4 p.m., thick, choking fumes grasped at one's throat. It was horrible. Buses and cars were abandoned in the streets, Heathrow Airport closed, Sadler's Wells theatre abandoned a performance of *La Traviata*, and cattle at Smithfield Market, there for the annual show, suffocated in their pens. London had never experienced anything like it.

And then my phone rang. "When are you coming down, Keith?" Fred Wingrove, the manager of the New Cross Empire, one of the last music hall theatres still open in London, was turning up the pressure.

I pleaded that there was no way I was going to be able to get from the Elephant and Castle to New Cross, but Fred would hear none of it. He was staging *Pick Up Girl*, in those days a 'near-the-knuckle' play about a risqué young woman, in response to local appeals that the theatre should stage some drama instead of strip shows and circus acts.

He had me over a barrel because I had certainly run those stories and Fred Wingrove had responded. "So where was the *South London Press*?" he demanded.

I agreed I would try to get there, and walked the two miles to London Bridge Station from where I hoped some surface trains would be running to New Cross. They were, but it took a long time for my train to limp the five miles; but eventually I did arrive. A further walk of about a mile and I staggered into the theatre.

Seated halfway down in the stalls I could just about make out the stage—and locate the other half dozen people in the audience. The play may have been risqué but no one in New Cross or Deptford seemed willing to go out in the worst smog to hit London for centuries. They were probably right, for in the next four days 4,000 people, mostly the elderly, died in their homes, quietly suffocated to death. It was only when undertakers reported that they were running out of coffins that we on the *South London Press* grasped that we were sitting on a very big story.

But here I was in the New Cross Empire wondering what I was going to do about the manager's complaint. He wanted something in the next edition of the *South London Press*—whether there was an audience or not.

In the interval I went backstage—mainly, I must admit, to have a closer look at the leggy young actress who had the leading role. I introduced myself and asked her name. It was Sybil Lishner and—great—she came from New Cross in the midst of my patch. "And how old are you?" I enquired.

"Fourteen—well, fourteen and a half," came the reply.

Sybil had a real Londoner's voice and I enquired where she went to school.

"Mary Datchelor," she replied.

This girl went to the best grammar school in South London, so clearly she was no fool, but I was really shaken. What was Sybil doing in this seedy play about gangster London?

I asked if her head teacher knew she was spending her evenings in this kind of drama, but it was clear the venerable lady had no idea. It seemed Sybil had not got round to mentioning her move across the footlights.

I took some more notes and told Sybil I would be in touch next day.

That was after I had stumbled home, handkerchief over my mouth to protect my nose, and once indoors stripped off to find my vest blackened with soot – the smog had passed straight through my clothes.

Next morning I arranged to meet up with Stanley Jaanus, our photographer, and to get Sybil to pose from some rather raunchy angles. No matter what awkward pose we suggested, Sybil was game. She wanted her picture and her name in print—that was very clear to us.

The following morning, just as we were closing to go to press, I rang Mary Datchelor School in Camberwell and asked to speak to the head. In those days, schools kept the local press at arm's length, but when I revealed to the school secretary that I had information about one of the school's pupils, the head was suddenly available to talk.

41

I explained that I had been surprised to find one of her pupils in a play at New Cross Empire and wondered if she had any comment. There was a long silence and then the head said she would get back to me. A couple of hours later I received a short statement to the effect that Sybil Lishner and another girl pupil, also in the play, had been suspended.

Bingo—the head had made my story. If she had said nothing and had quietly remonstrated with Sybil I would not have had such a good tale for the SLP front page. Nor one which sold to every newspaper in Fleet Street complete with Stanley's photos. We both cleaned up.

I always felt slightly guilty about Sybil though. Had I ruined her academic future?

I needn't have worried. Some months later, in a ballroom above the Co-operative Society's headquarters in Woolwich, I noticed a shapely knee which was vaguely familiar. It was Sybil. As we cruised round the ballroom floor she told me her acting career was taking off and the publicity had been just marvellous.

"Mary Datchelor school?" I enquired. "No idea—I never went back. I hated the place," she told me. "I'm really happy now—thanks a lot for your help."

There was a payoff to the smog too. It was so bad that even the House of Commons at Westminster had to be adjourned. Now that was serious. Four years later the Clean Air Act came into force and smokeless zones were introduced in London and other major cities in the UK. The chimneys of industry were controlled for the first time ever.

It was probably the first-ever piece of environmental legislation in Britain. It was not the 4,000 deaths—it was when the smog started to seep into the chamber and rooms at Westminster that the authorities conceded something needed to be done.

Covering stories like that gave us the training and confidence to ready ourselves for Fleet Street—the generic term used to mean going to work on one of the national dailies, which from a local paper seemed like joining a crack regiment. Nowadays it is television which has the glamour to attract and break the hearts of the young. But then it was the excitement of deadlines, scoops, intense competition, name on a story—the byline—big belted Crombie overcoats, oversized egos. Maybe even a car.

Nothing would have made my mother happier if I had accepted her advice and found a job—with a pension forty years hence—in the Post Office. Instead I made my way by way of office boy in an import business, working in a jeweller's shop, readers' boy on the *Croydon Times* and assistant in the *Daily Telegraph* library before getting a twenty five shillings a week job as a young trainee reporter.

I was soon working what was known then as 'a Saturday turn' on *The People*—a big-selling Sunday newspaper—and sometimes an illicit Friday afternoon too, and also taking in a couple of stories picked up in South London during the week. Money was good. We would go up each week to the accounts department in The Strand of Odhams Press, owner of the *Sunday* and the *Daily Herald*, to collect our pay in cash. I still have a distinct memory of walking away having pocketed about £28 for a weekend's work, big money in those days.

But Sunday exposés and foot-in-door journalism were not really to my taste. I wanted to be on a daily, and only one—the broadsheet *Daily Mail*. I never considered its politics. What I liked was the style of the paper, and the way its top writers were projected, and obviously better paid. The *Express* would have been an alternative but I always hankered after the *Mail*.

Competition was extremely keen. There was plenty of bright material around, and unless one had a contact on the inside somehow one had to attract attention in another way. That was with the big linage story which had Fleet Street running to your door.

One story which fitted that criterion was the tale of the man named in Parliament as 'the slippery emperor of the slums'. And we on the *South London Press* had unmasked him.

Each of us in our districts kept coming across cases where people living in war-damaged tenements or as families, crowded in with others into tiny houses meant to take a single family, just could not get basic faults fixed. The rain could be pouring through the ceiling, floorboards rotting, the toilet blocked or mould coming through the wallpaper, but the landlord never responded.

And when the local authority served what was known as a sanitary notice on him, still nothing happened.

Slowly the penny dropped that we were not dealing with different landlords or property owners all over the eight boroughs of South London but the same person or the same company.

In many cases where a sanitary notice was served it went to an address outside London. One used repeatedly was that of D. Brady, 17 High Street, Olney, Bucks, which turned out to be an accommodation address at a newsagent's. At another so-called landlord's address we forced the door—quite illegally—and found lying there hundreds of unopened notices from the town halls of Southwark, Lambeth, Camberwell or Bermondsey.

It was clear we were on to something big. But how big? And how did we firm it up?

Several SLP reporters were involved, but I worked closely with Laurie Manifold, who covered Southwark, and was a couple of years older than me. We were a formidable team. Laurie went on to be full-time on *The People* and eventually was in charge of all the paper's investigations. It was Laurie who brought down the head of Scotland Yard's Flying Squad for corruption and led many other of the paper's major enquiries. Alastair Campbell, Tony Blair's press supremo, worked for a while for Laurie, and paid him a public tribute in the columns of *The Times* for making him pay attention to detail and check facts.

Laurie and I had a breakthrough which helped us to identify the properties owned by the Slippery Emperor. He continually started up shell companies to own the run-down properties he was acquiring, and somehow could not resist using a local street name for the company. But he always reversed it. Thus Kranal Estates was a name at Companies House—but it was Lanark Road when reversed. The firm Arffe was from Effra Road. Acre Lane became Erca Co. And so it went on.

It was an interesting foible by whoever was responsible for setting up the Emperor's companies, but we found it an extremely useful pointer.

Each SLP reporter contacted his local Labour MP, who at our suggestion formed an action committee to pool information. That was the information we were digging out and we did not want it frittered away piecemeal by a headline-hunting Member of Parliament. But it meant the MP could explain to voters he was on the case.

And rapidly our 'dossier'—a favourite Sunday newspaper name for a file—expanded, and we knew a lot about the mystery landlord. So much, in fact, that we became convinced the whole dirty racket of exploiting hundreds, even thousands of poor tenants, who were existing in appalling conditions, was being run from Brixton by a property company called Water and Waters.

The boss was a man named Arthur Bertram Waters who lived in a splendid double-fronted house in Court Lane, Dulwich—well away from the riff-raff who paid for it.

The racket became clearer as we identified a former employee who had a grudge against his ex-boss; and, indeed, was living in one of the slum tenements just off New Kent Road where today one of the worst Sixties-type developments stands on the site. (We wanted to clear the slums but we never dreamed a huge modern slum block, like those, would replace them.)

Gradually we persuaded the man to talk, and the pieces began to fall into place. The racket was to buy up at auction blocks of war-damaged property, often whole roads, even small estates. Every property had damage, and surveying them all led to terrible delays in the long, politically sensitive housing problem. So surveyors had tended to look at a property or two with fallen ceilings and mark down replacements for all the properties, unseen. And if the two ceilings seen were replaced the tenants were lucky—even if the paper used did not match. But the others living in the road could whistle!

The sums involved ran into many thousands and the racket was not untypical of the 1950s with its shortages, power cuts, clothes rationing and queues. This was the age of the post-war 'spiv' and racketeer, and we seemed to be on to a very big one.

Unfortunately, the MP for Brixton could contain himself no longer. Lt Col. Marcus Lipton was notorious for headline-grabbing and prided himself on asking more questions than any other MP. His standing amongst his colleagues was nil but the thick-skinned Member for Brixton cared not a fig—his constituents knew he was at work because they found his name in the newspaper virtually every day.

As we cursed in our tiny reporter's room above the Elephant and Castle Tube station we had to admit grudgingly that his phrase 'Slippery Emperor' had something! But the Colonel had shot our fox. Instead of being able to sell a major exposé perhaps to a Sunday paper or put the story out everywhere, our phones were overwhelmed by Fleet Street reporters demanding facts and figures. With little intention of paying us.

Then came an interesting call. A detective inspector at Scotland Yard wanted to meet us to 'discuss the Waters case'.

The get-together was in a Lyons tea shop opposite Big Ben and just around a corner from Norman Shaw House on The Embankment, which in those days was known as Scotland Yard, the headquarters of the Metropolitan Police.

The policeman knew a little about Waters but not much. To us it seemed that much of his information was drawn from newspaper cuttings, most of which we had provided.

Laurie Manifold and I had a quick word together and agreed we could no longer hold back our dossier. It was going to be eroded rapidly anyway, but what we really wanted to see was those who were exploiting tenants getting their just desserts.

We handed over a thick file which represented over a year's work—much of it in our spare time. The policeman thanked us and gave us his direct telephone number. Not exactly a fair exchange, but he hinted we would get an exclusive if charges were to be brought.

Some hope. A few days later we picked up the *Evening Standard* to read that Arthur Bertram Waters, who ran a Brixton property agency, and some of his co-directors were to be charged with conspiracy to defraud the War Damage Commission.

We felt sick in the stomach that we had been scooped on our own story but set off for the Dulwich address we held for Waters. We could now confront him. There were lights on in the house but no reply as we beat on the door and rang the bell repeatedly. To try to provoke some reaction, I drove my car noisily into his drive and parked outside the front door.

But the man we had pursued over several years was not going to show himself. Instead, shortly after we had given up, he fled with his family to Dublin where he announced he had a full answer to the charges and would surrender himself—with dignity—to the authorities when the time came. He had fled, he said, because of harassment by the press. Us! Having seen the misery in which so many of his tenants were existing we had no regrets, and revelled in the day when he handed himself to the police to be charged with conspiracy to defraud the War Damage Commission.

Back in the *South London Press* office we marvelled at the coolness of Waters and wondered whether any of his tenants, perhaps behind with their rents for one of the slums he owned, would have had such kid glove treatment.

It left a bitter taste …

That was towards the end of 1953 when we were beginning to see that at last Britain was easing itself out of the exhaustion of being on the winning side of World War II. The Festival of Britain in 1951 had been a great success, and the feeling it generated of an exciting and better 'new world' was definitely percolating through. Mind you, petrol had gone up from one shilling and nine pence (about ten pennies in the decimal world) to two shillings and sixpence A GALLON. We were furious at this impost.

But it did not prevent me from shooting around the streets of South London, often skidding on the tar-covered wooden blocks laid between the tram tracks. At first I had an aged Austin 7 two-seater, but by 1950 I had traded up and owned a Singer Le Mans four-seater, nine horse power, open car which was decidedly good-looking. So much so that I went to Deptford public library to see if I could find more about Singers and why they laid claim to the name of the town where the famous 24-hour race was held. And there I found that the Singers had indeed acquitted themselves well in that endurance event, winning their class for under-1000cc engines in 1933. And performed well in subsequent years.

From there I dreamed up the idea of a gathering of Singer owners, and wrote a short piece to announce it in the motoring press. But imagine my surprise on turning into the car park alongside the Salisbury Arms Hotel in Hertford to find it thronging with Singer cars and their drivers. At twenty-one I had obviously started something.

Today, over sixty years later, the Singer Owners' Club is a thriving one-make club in the motor sport firmament in Britain—and has branches in USA, Canada, Australia, Germany, France, and a number of other countries. The club produces spare parts, advice and, above all, enthusiasm for a marque which ceased production when owned by Rootes in the mid-Sixties. That takeover by Rootes killed my enthusiasm for Singer, but I had no idea that the club I started would have such strong roots. Certainly not until I had a phone call in 1991 asking me if I would speak at the fortieth anniversary dinner. And again in 2001 for the golden jubilee!

But back to the Fifties. My four-seater was replaced by a two-seater, one and a half litre Singer, and it was a familiar sight around South London. It also helped me win three first class awards in the Lands End Trial and race in the Six Hour Relay at Silverstone. But maybe I should have eased the accelerator as I shot down the New Kent Road one Monday morning on my way to complete a round of the police stations just before the mid-week edition of the *South London Press* was about to lock its pages.

Suddenly, into my path came a uniformed policeman waving me down. Out of my eye to the left there had indeed been a sharp downward arm movement. I had driven into a speed trap—long before the days of our so-called 'safety' cameras which are really modern-day speed traps.

I said nothing as my details were laboriously noted down, but once released I shoved the car into first gear and accelerated away towards Tower Bridge police station. As the desk sergeant went through the Occurrence Book with me I left him in no doubt about my irritation. At Paradise Street station—magical name—in Rotherhithe, I reiterated my displeasure. And at Deptford where the station officer was Sergeant Mellish, brother of my friend Bob, the Member of Parliament, I went into more detail.

By the time I had driven back to the Elephant and Castle office I had cooled down, and was immersed in typing up my reports from the various police stations when an incoming call for the reporters' room was indicated.

The caller asked my name. Then—"I am the fellow who stopped you this morning in the New Kent Road. If you call off the dogs, I'll forget all about it. OK?" And the line went dead before I could blurt out my agreement.

Pity today's speed cameras cannot reach such sensible arrangements!

So the hectic pace of life in journalism roared along—local in fact, but almost cheek by jowl with Fleet Street, only a short Tube or bus ride away. And yet the size of the gap between one and the other, in career terms, yawned like a chasm. How could it be that our copy could often appear without a word changed in the three London evenings, in the *Daily Mail* or the *Telegraph*? Yet we never heard when there was a vacancy. We just noticed a new byline in the paper … someone else had made it.

There were others just as deeply frustrated. One day Laurie Manifold came back from Southwark inquests with the news that 'a cheeky bastard' had sat at the press table and announced himself as South Side News! His name, it seemed, was David English.

We already had plenty of competition south of the river from other local newspapers but more so with an outfit that called itself the South London News Agency. It offered its coverage service to all the nationals, but more importantly lifted any line it could find in our paper worth filing to Fleet Street. But not if we had anything to do with it—we had already sent it ourselves before it could be 'milked' by the agency.

English, however, was different. He had charm and a cheeky chappie approach to life. Even so we were not sufficiently sentimental to leave any morsel lying around for him. After a few sparse weeks he announced he was abandoning his quest on our side of the Thames. And to show there were no hard feelings we arranged a party to bid him farewell. David brought with him his fiancée, an extremely good-looking brunette West End chorus girl, and they stayed the night at Manifold's home.

It was a good party, but though we detected English's journalistic talent, none of us would have forecast that not only would he go on to save the *Daily Mail*, but become probably the most successful Fleet Street editor ever. Or that a knighthood would come, and he would be politically influential with Margaret Thatcher. Odd that, since when we rubbed shoulders with him David was well on the Left politically, a keen member of the National Union of Journalists, and when he left us went off to work on 'space' on *Reynolds News*, the Co-operative-owned paper right at the bottom of the Sunday market.

A couple of years later when I had made it to the *Daily Mail*, David was on *Weekend Mail*, a cheap, easy-read tabloid weekly knocked out by Associated Newspapers. With him was John Knight, who went on to be a highly successful columnist on the *Sunday Mirror*. But in those days the pair had little to do, and were constantly urging me to leave the reporters' desk at the *Daily Mail* to slip out for a drink—tempting but dangerous on a busy daily.

Later on it was clear English had talent as he demonstrated when the *Daily Express* placed him in the US and when he came back to edit the *Daily Sketch*. But he was much better than that, and demonstrated it by the way he turned around the *Daily Mail* and was a Fleet Street editor for over twenty-one years until his quite sudden and unexpected death in his own bathroom.

Another future editor who crossed our path was Robert Edwards and, again, we would have taken bets against the chances of his rise to the top. But Sam Campbell, the ruthlessly successful editor of *The*

People, came over to the Saturday news desk in 1954 and told us to expect a newcomer who was coming on board that morning. "Look after the f.....," he directed. "He's thick with Labour and you never know, they may win the next General Election."

Shortly afterwards, the beaming, anxious-to-please Bob Edwards turned up. It seemed he was doing some work on *Tribune*, and got on well with Michael Foot. He was even the Labour candidate for Horsham, fighting a much-decorated World War II army officer where he never stood a chance. He seemed to know precious little about the way newspapers worked down in the engine room, either.

We showed him how to put his carbon sheets amid the paper to go in his typewriter, to put his name and date top left, and be sure his machine was set to double-spacing. Things we had learned on local papers. But there was little we could do about his naiveté when it came to writing his copy or interviewing someone.

Bob was on the temporary staff, however, and we were part-time workers so we only saw him once or twice a week. But on Saturdays, when the early proofs came up, there would be his copy and like an anxious-to-please puppy, Bob would seek encouragement. Was his angle right, what about the heading? Above all, was his byline ok?

We chuckled as we gave our support to this likeable lightweight. But not one of us on the Saturday staff would have taken a bet on the chances of Bob Edwards twice becoming editor of the *Daily Express*, then editor of *The People* and eventually editor of the *Sunday Mirror*.

As the saying goes—you couldn't make it up.

Bob was never very popular as an editor, despite the ever-present smile. The *Express* staff felt he was only really interested in No. 1, and loathed him so deeply that eventually Lord Beaverbrook got the message and decided Edwards had to be moved to Glasgow.

The reaction was jubilant, so the story goes, and a call was made to Fleet Street's church, St Bride's.

"How much for a peal of bells?" Told the price, there was an immediate whip-round in the *Express* editorial and the fee went across to the church in cash.

Not many editors could claim to have been run out of Fleet Street. Mind you, Edwards had the last word. Within a year or so Beaverbrook sent him back for a second try. Bob had learned to improve his personal relationships but he was never popular.

There was another editor-to-be on *The People* at the time—a young messenger who prided himself on the alacrity with which he carried out our requests for cuttings or phone directories. But what really dazzled us was the speed he could produce hot buttered toast and tea from the slow *Daily Herald* canteen.

What did he want to do, we enquired—was he going to be a printer?

"I want to be a f...... journalist like you," shot back the kid with a marked Glaswegian accent. He was so keen we fixed him with an interview on the *South London Press*. But he went off for National Service and, not surprisingly, served in the Royal Marines. We were on to something, though, because Charles Wilson became deputy news editor and then sports editor at the *Daily Mail*, edited the *Glasgow Herald*, started up the new *Sunday Standard*, and then went on to become Editor of *The Times*, and introduced the new technology. Not bad for a kid who left school at sixteen and was quick at producing tea and toast.

Scouring around Docklands for news was good training for my future, but I did not realise it at the time. It was there I learned about trade unions, Labour politics, strikes and restrictive practices around the food importing wharves of Tooley Street where 10,000 men toiled, and at Surrey Commercial Docks where 7,000 unloaded timber imports. Looking around the area now, with its luxury apartments, boutique shops and expensive waterside restaurants, it is hard to grasp. Though, even at the time, I always felt the magic of the place had more to offer.

Contacts of course were paramount. One of my best was Dickie Golding, a crane driver at Mark Brown's wharf unloading butter or refrigerated lamb imported from New Zealand. From his high vantage point he could often spot an incident below. But, crucially, he also had a telephone up there which in those days was comparatively rare. It meant he could call me—and, more importantly, I could call him back.

One day Dickie called excitedly to recount how he was watching a scuffle aboard a Polish ship, the *Jaroslaw Dabrowski*, where crew members were grabbing at a man—while onshore dockers were urging him to jump to them. Eventually the man was overcome and hustled away below.

The man was Anthony Klimowitz, who had stowed away in one of the holds to escape from a police state and seek his freedom in London. So near and yet so far.

With only sketchy details, I phoned what I knew to the London evening papers and to the Press Association. And that set in train a remarkable series of events.

Early that evening a huge crowd gathered outside the Tower Bridge police station demanding that the stowaway be set free. But the police had no powers to board a ship flying a non-British flag. Their impotence inflamed the crowd which feared for the stowaway's life. Fleet Street's nationals demanded the Government 'did something'. But what?

All the next day crowds increased, but quietly, in the early evening, the *Jaroslaw Dabrowski* cast its mooring lines and headed off down the Thames on the top of the tide. Sadly, everyone felt for the man who so nearly had won his freedom, yet now seemed doomed.

But suddenly came news that all was not lost. As the merchant ship reached the end of the buoyed channel and was about to head for the open sea, a Royal Navy destroyer signalled it must instead slow down to take on a boarding party.

In the best of naval traditions, the officer in charge demanded the stowaway be handed over, and refused to accept the bland denials of the ship's captain. The Master was informed he was going nowhere until he complied. The Royal Navy had that on the orders of the Prime Minister, Winston Churchill. So the old war lord still had salt water in his veins …

That night, Anthony Klimowitz was brought ashore and granted asylum. I never heard any more of him, but I always hoped he had a happy life here, saved as he was by an alert crane driver and a local reporter who could smell a good story.

With stories like the Klimowitz tale we were not only getting noted and noticed in Fleet Street—we were getting richer. We no longer worried too much about eking out our wages for the week, nor fiddling our meagre expenses from the *South London Press* with quite the same intensity. Quite apart from our weekly earnings for our Saturday turn on *The People* every month, round about the tenth of the month, through our home letterboxes would drop familiar envelopes from Associated Newspapers, *Express Newspapers*, the *News Chronicle* and *The Star*, *Odhams Press*, the Press Association and several others. Our best payers were the three London evenings—the *Evening News*, *Evening Standard* and *The Star*—which daily produced up to ten editions and always needed 'overnight' copy for the first edition which was out on the street by 10 a.m., carrying all the day's horse racing events, prices and tips.

All the envelopes sent us contained cheques, often quite large amounts, so that I was able to forget the Post Office Savings Bank and instead walk in to see the manager at the Midland Bank, New Cross, and open my first account. Commonplace nowadays, but quite a moment for a young man who not all that long ago had a hole in his shoe and a threadbare overcoat.

When the cheques came in there was often a haggling session in the office as cash for a shared story was handed over or a debt settled. Then maybe a visit to our tailor—we had discovered the joy of a bespoke suit, and went to Kingston, where a smooth gentleman's tailor, who proudly boasted among his clients none other than Sir William Haley, then editor of The Times, would measure us.

Double-breasted, twin vents at the rear, hand stitched reveres—we were up with the fashion. Our tailor even made me a double-breasted dinner jacket in barathea. He said it would last for years and he was right.

Then, to make us look like proper Fleet Street reporters—even if we were not—we went to Mr Levy at the Elephant and Castle to buy Crombie overcoats, belted and bulky, but good and warm when hanging about on windy corners in South London or down by Thames-side wharves.

By 1954 I was doing so well I could afford to buy, brand new, a one-and-a-half litre Singer Hunter saloon—twin carburettors, two-tone finish, and even a glass-reinforced bonnet. By the standards of the time it was quite luxurious, and when eventually I did get to the *Daily Mail* I discovered I had a far better car than the Standard Vanguard owned by the news editor.

The call for a Fleet Street interview for a staff job came first not from a daily, but the *Evening News*, then a broadsheet owned by Lord Rothermere's Associated Newspapers and selling over a million a day.

Well, if I couldn't make it to a daily in one jump, a halfway stage via a London evening certainly was a breakthrough. It came about in a curious way.

Working again with Laurie Manifold, we had spotted at the back of the midweek edition of the *South London Press* a small space advertisement headed 'Apology'. The advertiser, grovelling, named a young woman and withdrew an allegation about her. It was intriguing.

We found out through our advertising girls—who should not have told us—that the advert had been placed by a Bermondsey solicitor named Freddy Baldwin, who I knew reasonably well. And when I rang he was quite happy to tell all since he had extracted the apology and some cash from a loudmouth who was accusing Baldwin's client of stealing money at a flat on a Bermondsey council estate. But it emerged that the accuser had only seen a young woman's legs going around a corner on a staircase—and on that had made his accusation. At that time, though, the young lady had an unbreakable alibi in North London, far away from the council estate.

Finding the young woman was difficult, but we agreed I would drive miles out of our area to track her down for interview while Laurie held the fort and made excuses to cover my disappearance. And he phoned the copy through to the evening papers as I was on my way back.

Laurie had given the *Evening News* the copy under my name, even though he had written it. To our amazement, while the other evenings used the story, a picture of a very attractive pair of silk-stockinged legs disappearing down a staircase was front page in the *Evening News* under the heading 'So Sorry', with a byline of '*Evening News* Reporter'. And the copy was exactly as sent.

Later that day I sat down and wrote to Frank Starr, news editor of the *Evening News*: 'So sorry,' I wrote, 'but that was no *Evening News* Reporter—it was me. How about making me a staff reporter?'

It worked. Back came a letter from the news editor apologising and inviting me for an interview. Bingo!

A few days later, wearing my best suit, I reported to Old Carmelite House, from which Northcliffe had started his empire. I was ushered into the latticed lift shaft and taken up to the editorial floor.

This was it. I was confident, and the interview with Frank Starr went well. We shook hands, and there was a broad hint I would be receiving a favourable letter in a couple of days.

Wrong again. When the letter arrived, Starr apologised and wrote, astonishingly, that due to 'conditions beyond my control' he was unable to make me an offer of a job. But he would retain my name on file, he promised.

It was bitterly disappointing and mysterious. What on earth had gone wrong?

Not long afterwards I noticed a new byline in the paper—Geoffrey Wareham, the same surname as Arthur Wareham, editor of the *Daily Mail*, also in the Associated Newspapers stable. He'd got the job.

It was soon forgotten, but just as well, as it happened. Within a week came a letter from the *Daily Mail*, the paper I really wanted to join—not for its politics but its journalism—inviting me to come for an interview with the news editor.

Back again, but across the road to Northcliffe House, a much smarter, modern venue, where I was taken to the second floor to meet Donald Todhunter. Immaculate in white shirt, tie, slicked-down hair, he looked—and was—on top of his job, and became renowned as the best news editor in Fleet Street. So much so that the *Daily Express* was to pull out all the stops to try to get Todhunter—and Associated vowed

Top left: Major Jack Ross. *Top right:* The eleven-year-old that Jack Ross befriended.
Bottom left: My sister, Jean, pictured at the end of the war when we obtained a precious
film – and peace had broken out! *Bottom right:* With my mother, Edna, and my new – and
first – suit from Burtons.

Top left: I enjoyed my national service in the RAF (1947–9). Most of my time, I edited a magazine. *Top right:* My father. *Bottom left:* Major Richard Carr-Gomm, MC, Croix de Guerre, where I found him in 1954 scrubbing the floor in a tiny house he had bought with his gratuity in Eugenia Road, Bermondsey to care for old people. It was the foundation of the nationwide care home charity, Abbeyfield. *Bottom right:* South London Press – shoulder's Bermondsey's new ceremonial mace.

Top: *Former Premier, Clement Atlee congratulates Harold Wilson on his 1964 general election victory at Transport House. Even though I felt ghastly with food poisoning, I was determined to be on the scene with Ian Aitken, then* Daily Express. *John Harris, Wilson's 'minder' watches proudly.* **Bottom:** *Is the national rail strike off? Sidney Greene, General Secretary National Union of Railwaymen, leaves No.10 Downing Street with deputy Sid Weighell, followed by industrial journalists Keith McDowall and Geoffrey Goodman. Sidney Greene kept press at arm's length, but we had a good relationship and visited and sent letters to him at his care home.*

Top: *Replying for the press at Trades Union Congress, Blackpool.*
Bottom: *Caught napping. Keith Harper,* Guardian *(right) and I doze off after my birthday champagne during Neil Kinnock's Bournemouth Labour Party (October 1989) speech.* The Sun *helpfully put us on the front page.*

it would spend anything to prevent it. And it did.

But that was some months later. My interview went well and Todhunter indicated he had followed my work. Would I be interested in £18 a week? I made it clear that as a successful linage man it was not attractive, but we shook hands and I left, confident I would be hearing more.

Next day came a letter offering me £20 a week—a thousand pounds a year before tax.

I worked out that I was earning, easily, £35 a week. But the crunch had arrived. At the age of 26, I was confident I knew my business, but I also knew I would never be able to prove it unless I threw my hat in the ring and took on the competition.

So it was really the end of an era. In November 1955 I set off for my first shift at the *Daily Mail*. But though I was eager for fresh fields, and I said goodbye to the *South London Press* after almost ten years, I did leave bustling, noisy Elephant and Castle with a tinge of regret.

In those cramped, crummy offices over the Tube station, we had staged our version of *Front Page Story* and seen a very large slice of life. But all of us from 'south of the water' were destined to see a lot more.

CHAPTER 4
Daily Mail—My Northcliffe Moments

I had always been an avid reader of the *Daily Mail,* and knew the names of the best writers and the most competitive reporters. Now suddenly I was one of them—or I hoped to be.

I reported for work to start on the 11 a.m. shift which I thought was rather congenial—little realising that after the first week in that slot on the roster, I would not see many more. The real shifts started as the London evening papers were winding down, so it could be 3 p.m. until 10 p.m., 5 p.m. to midnight—worse, 7 p.m. until 2 a.m. And the graveyard shift from midnight until dawn. Ugh.

A neat trick of the night news editor was to send a reporter out late on the 3–10 shift, knowing there was little chance he would be through by the end of it and would be expected to stay on without complaint. Reliefs on a story were unknown, and in this way the night news editor knew the 5–12 reporters were still to hand if a big story broke.

My first day was unproductive and I suppose the news room, not sure of the new recruit's abilities, were taking no chances. So I hardly got out of the office, but I began to get an idea how it all worked. Sitting nearby was Jeffrey Blyth, then called the shipping reporter, but eager to grab whatever looked like the best news story of the day. He went on to become the *Daily Mail*'s man in New York and stayed there for the rest of his career.

Late afternoon, after a good working lunch with a contact, Tommy (T.F.) Thompson, the air correspondent, arrived, tie awry, but with a pretty good idea he was working up a front-page piece. I was to learn quite a lot from Tommy.

Another late afternoon arrival was Arthur Tietjen, one of a famous journalistic family, who covered the Old Bailey for the paper, chatting up officials and detectives in the bars across from the Central Criminal Courts. It was Arthur's job to get the inside story of a court prosecution, and in exchange for an ample liquid lunch Scotland Yard men were usually only too willing to cough up. That was the way it worked in those days, long before a Crown Prosecution Service or the thought that a man in the dock might just be innocent.

On the reporters' desk were names that were as yet unknown—Walter Terry, to become political editor and, for a mad period, the partner of Marcia Falkender, Harold Wilson's political secretary; Patrick Sergeant, destined to become city editor, probably the best paid journalist in Fleet Street and to collect a knighthood; Barry Norman, film and show business reporter and film-world expert—the list of the talent that passed through the *Mail* ranks was unbelievable. My two close pals on the reporters' rota soon became Frank Duesbury and Paul Sargent.

One man who could not be overlooked was Vincent Mulchrone, to become chief reporter, and one of its best ever writers. Sadly, he died quite young from leukaemia. Vincent covered the Big Stories, a decent but perhaps an insecure person.

Vincent always had a sharp eye for colour, and it was that and the brilliant phrase that lifted his copy from the rest. Some years later he came to Scarborough when I was covering the Labour Party conference at which the late Hugh Gaitskell was to throw down the challenge to the Left and risk splitting the party over the nuclear bomb issue. Vincent's task was to write a backgrounder while I concentrated on the political power struggle, and he sought my help.

"Any chance," he asked, "of having a look inside Gaitskell's suite in the Royal Hotel?"

In today's high security world it is hard to contemplate, but in October 1959 not even a detective guarded the Leader of the Opposition, let alone his room. I was on friendly terms with Tom Laughton, brother of actor and film star Charles, who owned the Royal and was proud of his valuable collection of art. Every bedroom had its own oil or watercolour. Laughton's reception staff knew that, as a *Daily Mail* man, I was a big spender, so within a few minutes a spare key to Gaitskell's room was quietly produced, and Vincent and I went to have a quick look.

I must admit there seemed nothing out of the ordinary in what was a comfortable suite, and after a few notes by Vincent we were out again. But he had his angle. When the main feature page carried Vincent's piece next day, he used the title of the oil master on Gaitskell's bedroom wall entitled *The Hedger and His Mate*. It led neatly into the hole the leader seemed to be digging for Labour, followed along by his deputy, mud-besmirched Aneuran Bevan, seeking to calm the issue.

Sometime later, the Midland Bank unveiled its Personal Loan scheme and would lend its customers £500—a lot then—with remarkable little security. Vincent, as usual, was broke, but I urged him as a Midland customer to seek an appointment with the manager of the Fleet Street branch and explain he needed cash to buy a car. Half an hour later, Vincent tapped me on the shoulder. "Got time for a quick one?" he asked as he produced a rolled bundle of fivers. A few days later he was the proud owner of a neat, second-hand Austin A40.

But back to Day 2 for me at the *Daily Mail* in November 1955. I had not really had much of a chance to show what I could do, when a Press Association tape message was given me. A young boy who had climbed virtually to the top of the BBC transmitter at Crystal Palace had appeared in juvenile court in South London.

Someone on the news desk had seized on the fact that that was my part of the world and I had a car. Within minutes I was on my way to Penge, and quickly traced the boy's home address. My luck was in— his father wanted to talk even though, by law, I was not able to use his name nor identify the boy in any way.

But I made him 'The Loneliest Boy In London' when he looked down in darkness from the top of the transmitter pylon to see, below, police cars and flashing lights. All he had to do now was to get down! It took him two hours.

Next morning my story was centre column on the front page,

bylined '*Daily Mail* Reporter'. At last I felt I was one.

And my luck improved next day too. I had always wanted to see Winston Churchill, no longer prime minister, but to those who had survived wartime Britain, our leader and a hero. And I was sent to his London home at Hyde Park Gate to report the comings and goings on his 81st birthday, Wednesday, 30th November. Eventually the great man appeared on the arm of his wife Clementine. The effects of his stroke were not apparent, though it meant he had nothing to say. But he beamed and waved for photographers. Even so, it made a great colour piece, and I was soon back knocking out the copy at my desk. Later that afternoon, Donald Todhunter, the news editor, called me in and set me a much tougher task about Churchill. The *Express* had scooped us with a picture of the splendid birthday cake being prepared for the great man at a top Soho patisserie, resplendent with a croupier's words 'Faites Votre Choix' and a mysterious box.

"Find out what's in the box," I was told. It was implicit—don't come back without the answer!

In Brewer Street I soon found the confectioner, but I also soon found out that the owners were sworn to secrecy, and no way was I to be told the secret of Churchill's birthday cake.

South London training came to the fore. I found a rear entrance to the cake maker and hung around. After about half an hour a young woman ran out, clearly off on an errand. I caught up with her and said, "Ten quid if you tell me what's under that croupier's box on Winston Churchill's cake."

She did not hesitate. Ten pounds in 1955 was a lot of money to a teenager. "A pair of dice!" she said and swiftly pocketed the money. Pretty obvious when one thought about it. But good value, I felt, to save my job.

Surprisingly quickly, one settled down and the weeks flashed by. But for a long time I felt a thrill as I strode past the smartly uniformed commissionaire who commanded the *Daily Mail* front hall. No one got past him. Now, quite suddenly, I did, and even merited an occasional salute.

In the rat race all around me I grasped that the news editor really did not rate the specialists—the senior men who covered politics, the law courts, industry, finance and the city, defence. He wanted energetic younger journalists reporting to him on these beats—never mind experience. So he singled out a newsroom reporter to shadow each specialist. Cars, motor racing, engineering—that was my world. So I was given the hint to keep an eye on Courtenay Edwards, the motoring correspondent—who held the post I coveted.

One Friday, Courtenay himself threw me a bone which was well worth a chew. A public relations firm had sent out a teasing invitation saying it would reveal the name, the following week, of a mysterious inventor who had designed a completely new engine, with only a small number of moving parts, which would revolutionise the industry. In those days Britain was big in manufacturing, and boasted more than a score of car makers. Such an engine would indeed have an impact.

But Friday evening loomed, and Courtenay was drawn to his weekend retreat. Despite the urging of the news editor to find out the name of the inventor, Courtenay gave up and said he was off to a pressing engagement. "Put McDowall on it," he suggested, confident that he had done all the checking possible.

A distinctly irked Todhunter, immaculate in white shirt but eyes glinting, stood by my desk with the news release. "Find this inventor," he ordered. "We'll show that motoring correspondent how to get a story." Then he departed, leaving me to do just that!

I read and re-read the cryptic press release which gave little away. But I quickly got through to its author before he, too, left for the weekend. He would not give the name, but eventually conceded that if I cracked the code he would confirm a name, and gave me his weekend phone number.

My time spent in motor sport had not been entirely wasted, and I had several useful numbers in my contacts book—every good journalist had the names and addresses of people and their phone numbers stored away for use at night and weekends. They were gold dust.

I tracked down Laurence Pomeroy, technical editor of *The Motor* and an authority on motor engineering. From the top of his head he reeled off the names of half a dozen inventive engineers who might answer the description. It was up to me to find them, though.

I also tried Cyril Posthumus, who wrote regularly in the new *Autosport* which had carried quite a lot about my equally new Singer Owners' Club, so I had more of a bond with him. "Read it out again," he told me. "It might be Granville Bradshaw—try him. He's the kind of guy who comes up with something like that."

Within a very short time I had established that Bradshaw had won Government financial rewards in World War I for his aero-radial engine designs, had founded British Automatic, the slot machine company, made a fortune and lost it in the 1929 Wall Street Crash, and had designed the ABC and the Belsize-Bradshaw light cars.

This could be my man!

I rang the public relations man—still in his office. Scornfully he agreed to listen to three names and tell me if any of them fitted the bill. I knew the other two names were extremely doubtful, but I held Bradshaw's name till last.

"Granville Bradshaw!"

Silence … it was as good as confirmation. Then the voice on the phone: "How the hell did you get that?"

"Never mind how I did it," I replied. "We did a deal. Now I want to talk to your friend. Will you help or shall I track him down?"

The public relations man wisely decided I might just manage that as well.

"Leave it with me. I will call you back shortly," he vowed.

He did, with the news that the inventor would like to speak to me at a number in Hampshire.

"Granville Bradshaw," offered the voice at the other end of the line. He very much wanted to talk—it was his PR man who had been stopping him. Quickly I established that he had designed a lightweight rotary engine which would lie flat in the car's engine bay, front or rear; would take less space; but most importantly, only had nine working parts. To my mind that meant less friction, less wear and tear, and more power for less fuel. If that was what was on Bradshaw's drawing board, the British motor industry, then big in scale and importance in the country, ought to be beating a path to his door.

He even had a name for the new engine, "I call it Omega," he told me proudly.

Now the great danger with inventors that all journalists learn in their training is that they can be nutty. Cranks, as we called them. You needed to be careful not to be taken in because an inventor's enthusiasm for their creation is not unlike the zealous protection of a mother for her child. And it can be contagious.

Bradshaw had a good track record, as I had established in the library, and I was certain I was on to a good story. But could I convince the sceptics in the news room—and more importantly, higher up the chain, where decisions were being made rapidly about what should go into that night's paper.

The night news editor caught my interest and told me to 'knock it out fast' while he shot off to attract the night editor's interest. Half an hour later I saw the first page proofs. My story was the front page lead—another ambition achieved. But no name on it, just 'Daily Mail Reporter'. The back bench, the men on the sub-editor's top table, were not going to go overboard.

Later that night the editor, Arthur Wareham, saw the proofs at his home and panicked. Had a young impressionable reporter fallen for a crank? I stuck to my guns and argued strongly that the story stood up, that I had checked everything. But then, yes, I only had Bradshaw's word for it. Had he built an engine? Where was it being bench-tested?

The questions niggled. Had I fallen for a 'nutter'? If I had, my short-lived career in Fleet Street would be over.

But the story held for all editions and, not surprisingly, they wanted a follow-up. I was earmarked to go to see Mr Bradshaw at his home next morning—a Saturday, which was supposed to be a day off. But I was to be accompanied. A more senior reporter, none other than Paul Sargent, would be joining me to establish that I had not fallen for a tall story.

I bit my tongue. My pride was hurt. But they did not employ prima donnas as reporters in Fleet Street, not at my level anyway.

Next day we were made welcome at Granville Bradshaw's New Forest home, and he could certainly talk. Stories kept falling from his tongue of famous moments in the First World War, how he had pioneered the slot machine—the stories kept coming. But where was the engine?

Eventually I coaxed him to show me the drawing office where he had worked out his ideas. At his board he allowed me a quick look but not long enough to be sure—even if I had possessed the technical knowledge—that the Omega engine was revolutionary.

But as we slowly progressed, the doorbell started to ring as a stream of visitors following up the *Daily Mail* scoop arrived; first, the motoring correspondent of the *News Chronicle*. They all left reasonably convinced, and gradually my colleague and I felt confident enough to call the office and confirm the Omega story stood up.

I never heard what happened to Bradshaw's invention, but a year or so later Audi-NSU announced their new rotary-engined car. The engine lay flat in the front compartment, it revved fast and the car really motored. But it was heavy on petrol consumption and was never rated a commercial success. I often wondered if that was where Omega ended its days.

Christmas was looming and Paul had no money for a Christmas tree so I offered a solution. As we were heading down to the New Forest area in Hampshire, I told Paul to put a saw in the boot of my car. Then, as we drove back to London, there was news on the car radio that warden patrols were out guarding against Christmas tree thieves, but I still pulled off the road and turned down a darkened track.

Paul leapt out and started sawing at the base of a tree. Up went the boot lid, in went the tree and the saw, and I accelerated away towards London.

"Do you realise we have just risked our careers for that tree?" said Paul. "We must be mad. Can you see the *Express* story—'Two *Daily Mail* journalists arrested in New Forest tree theft'?" I knew he was right. We could have been fired for the escapade.

It was only when we got back to Kingston and opened the boot lid that we realized it was no neat little fir we were hauling. In the dark and in the panic, Paul had hacked down a gorse bush.

As my Fleet Street career developed I was to have many dealings with politicians, but not in those early days. Towards the end of my first week the news room told me to head off for Mansion House, the home of the Lord Mayor of the City of London. When I asked about my mission all I was told was, "Harold Macmillan is there."

Well, the Prime Minister would not be calling on the Lord Mayor to wish him a pleasant day so I set off with a photographer in tow. Security was non-existent in those days and confidently I strode up to the impressive front door and announced to the flunky that I was from the *Daily Mail*.

The *Mail* had a long tradition, of which I was aware, that its founder had decreed that *Daily Mail* men were to be well dressed. "A *Mail* man can then go anywhere," Lord Northcliffe pronounced. And there was I, smartly turned out in one of my handmade suits bought from freelance earnings, ushered through with the words, "The Prime Minister is waiting for you, sir."

Me? How the hell did he know I was coming? I wondered as I scaled the grand staircase and was ushered into a magnificently ceilinged chamber in which the Prime Minister stood immaculate in morning dress—black tails, striped trousers, white tie and a gold watch chain across his waistcoat.

"Ah, dear boy—so good of you to come. May I introduce Herr Von Brentano, Her Majesty's West German ambassador," who smiled and offered his hand.

The ambassador, it seemed, was shortly to be receiving the Freedom of the City of London. Remember, this was only ten years after the end of World War II when the Germans had tried their best to level the City of London—and had very nearly succeeded. I could hardly believe we were giving someone like that such an honour.

Not for me to grasp that this was all part of Macmillan's master plan to get Britain into Europe. But the penny was dropping that the Prime Minister had been expecting a very much larger contingent of reporters—and all that had turned up was a lowly generalist from the *Daily Mail*.

In my embarrassment I stumbled and tripped over Macmillan's feet. As I proffered my apologies I looked down at the Prime Minister's shoes which a moment ago had set off his outfit with a final gleam. Not any more—a large scuff from my rubber heels defaced the Macmillan toecaps, and for a moment the warm smile froze. I knew it was time to go.

Back at the news desk there was a similar reaction to mine—what were we doing giving some German the Freedom of London? Most of those in the office had fought in the war and held pretty strong views.

Next morning I pored through the *Daily Mail* but found not one line on the Mansion House. The story was all about Britain's new ambitions to join the European Community under the name of the diplomatic correspondent, properly briefed by the Foreign Office. He did not even mention Herr Von Brentano.

Fairly soon I was sent out more and more on bigger stories. One of the best things about a reporter's life was that every day could be, and usually was, different from the last. There was no such thing as a routine. But I did begin to notice that I was being put on so-called stories about gamblers and socialites hanging about in night clubs. The news editor, Donald Todhunter, seemed fascinated by their lifestyle. As for me, I wondered when they would get a life. I think it was that revulsion that turned my thoughts more and more towards industrial and political specialisation. But how did I get myself into one of those fields?

I had kept in touch, from my local paper days, with Bob Mellish, the MP for Bermondsey, and sought him out one evening for a drink. I met him in the Central Lobby and we went down to the Strangers' Bar, known in those days as The Kremlin, because it was the haunt of Labour back benchers and most Tory MPs gave it a miss.

At the time I was aware that a prisoner named Parsons was on the run, having escaped from Wormwood Scrubs jail and cheekily posted his prison clothes to the Governor saying he would no longer be needing them! So I sat up sharply when Mellish told me he had received a letter about Parsons from a man named Jason Dibley who was a voluntary prison visitor. Dibley hinted that he might be in touch with the runaway. Bob had no hesitation in letting me copy the letter and the writer's details in my notebook, such was the long established trust between us.

I soon tracked Dibley and asked him to meet me. Did I detect a slight tone of relief in his voice?

There must have been, because it was not long before the prison visitor agreed he knew about Parsons—and was in touch. Indeed, he was the one who had posted the clothes parcel to the Governor.

I guessed Dibley was hiding the runaway, probably at his home in Croydon, but if I knew where an escaped prisoner was hiding I was under a citizen's obligation to tell the police. Better not to know …

Gradually I teased the story out of the prison visitor. Parsons, who the rival *Daily Express* had nicknamed Scarface, believed he had been set-up by the detectives investigating a big bullion robbery at London's Heathrow Airport. Parsons admitted he had done lots of jobs, but insisted he had never used violence and had not been involved in this particular crime. But the jury at his trial had found him guilty and the judge sentenced him to twelve years.

That was why he had scaled the prison wall and gone on the run, said Dibley.

I reported my progress to the News Room and was told to press on. But no advice was offered other than to be exceedingly careful. I got the message—I was on my own.

When Dibley and I met again he admitted he was sheltering the escaped prisoner at his own home.

I came up with my proposition. If Parsons was willing to give himself up and go back to jail, the *Daily Mail* would investigate his innocence and his claim to have had a rough deal from the detectives.

The next day Dibley phoned. Parsons was ready to meet me and was prepared to be convinced.

The tension in the car as we waited for Parsons was tangible. I had with me Johnnie Twine, a staff photographer, and so bad was the tension that I, a lifelong non-smoker, asked Johnnie for a cigarette. I must admit that the fag helped me through the wait. Then suddenly there was a bang on the side of the car and Dibley was there with another man. It had to be Parsons.

They got in the car and we drove away, all the time expecting to hear the siren of a police car. But nothing happened and I explained to Parsons we had to go somewhere safe where I could interview him and where he could be photographed, so I was taking him to my home in Harlesden where, with my then wife, Shirley, I had a dairy and a grocery business—honest. I used to joke I was Britain's only journalist-milkman.

Shirley had rigged up the shop to look like a pub. She had a sheet hanging down behind the counter to hide the stacks of groceries, some bottles of beer on the shop counter and an ashtray or two. Our cash till was prominent. Parsons was keen on a beer and as he swallowed it gratefully the photographer snapped away.

In the better light it seemed to me Parsons' face was unmarked. Where was the scar?

"I never had one—my nickname has always been Jumbo," he replied. "The police gave me that nickname—makes me sound nasty, doesn't it?"

That explained why the *Daily Express*, our deadly rival, had gone so hard on the nickname. The police wanted it. From then on, I promised, the *Mail* would use the term Jumbo.

He poured out his story, which I had to admit to myself seemed quite plausible. Parsons said the police had decided to 'fit him up' for a bank robbery involving violence on the reasonably sure ground that if convicted, Parsons would be sent to jail for some time.

"But I didn't do that job," he insisted. "I have done others—I'm not denying it. But I have never used violence. So why would I start now?"

Then came the time when we had to get Parsons back to jail. So after we photographed 'The Last Drink' we took others of the returning prisoner as he made 'The Last Walk' to the gates of Wormwood Scrubbs prison. And then, as he was about to step through the small entrance which opened in the huge prison gates, Parsons turned, as I had instructed, and gave 'The Last Wave'.

I watched the prison gates close from across the road, and then went to a nearby phone box to pour out the story. There was no time to write—I just had to tell it 'off the cuff', as the saying went in Fleet Street. But that sometimes turned out to be the best way, and if one had an ability to dictate a story in sharp crisp paragraphs it often read surprisingly well. That was what happened. It was the lead story with the three 'last' pictures, and we had a major scoop. No other paper had a whiff—principally because I had kept well clear of the police. The only other possible source of a leak was from Parliament where Bob Mellish had astonished Rab Butler, the Home Secretary, with the news that a prisoner on the run was giving himself up. Mellish asked for an assurance there would be an inquiry into Parsons' allegation that the police had framed him.

Meanwhile, having phoned my copy I waited in my car from a vantage point across the road from the prison gates. A police car screamed up, soon followed by reporters from other Fleet Street papers. Then the Governor of the prison, Gilbert Hair, arrived from his nearby home. He seemed affable and stopped as we journalists gathered round. He asked each of us which paper we represented.

I knew if I named the *Daily Mail* I would be a marked man. I took a chance and said, "*News Chronicle*," in the hope that that paper's news desk was so dozy it would not yet have sent down to the prison. I was right.

"Well, I can tell you," said the Governor, "that the *Daily Mail* has scooped you all. They have found the prisoner who escaped from here—Parsons—and brought him back. He is banged up inside again. Goodnight to you."

As the Fleet Street reporters gathered to pool their thoughts I drifted away. Back in my car I watched the gates like a hawk, and about an hour later I was rewarded. Suddenly the small entrance opened and out stepped Jason Dibley.

I slammed my car into first gear and shot forward, wound down the window and shouted to Dibley to get in. Together we raced off towards the Western Avenue, convinced we would be followed by angry rivals, but to our astonishment, once again we had caught the rest of Fleet Street napping.

We badly needed a drink but in those days the pubs closed at 10.30 p.m. so we had to settle for a coffee at an open air refreshment bar used by taxi drivers, as Jason told me what happened once the gates clanged shut behind them.

Parsons had been spirited away quickly, and then Jason faced interrogation. As a prison visitor he knew he was extremely vulnerable. Choosing his words carefully, he insisted he had only that day been contacted by Parsons and had persuaded him to give himself up. Eventually the police let Dibley leave, but said they would want to talk to him again. I drove to the Underground and put him on the Tube to Victoria, and then went to a phone box to add the later information.

It had been a great beat on the rest of Fleet Street and everyone felt good about it—not just me. There is nothing like trouncing the opposition and that had certainly been done. And by a relative rookie—a fellow, name of Keith McDowall. They knew that, because my name was at the top of the story in bold black type under the splash and a story that took up the whole front page of the broadsheet newspaper.

Next morning, as I walked through the swing doors to the entrance of the *Daily Mail* editorial on the second floor of Northcliffe House people of all ranks started coming up to congratulate me.

Donald Todhunter could not have been warmer. "You've done yourself a hell of a lot of good—congratulations." And then he added, "Write your own expenses," which was a strong hint to put in whatever I liked and he would sign them.

Then I was called to see the Deputy Editor, William Hardcastle, probably one of the best news men in Fleet Street, who we all knew would one day—maybe quite soon—edit the *Daily Mail*. He had been news editor when I was sending in linage so he knew all about me.

"Keith, you're getting a £50 bonus in your pay this week—that's one of the best exclusives I have seen for years."

A few minutes later it was drinks all round in the back bar of The Harrow, the *Daily Mail* pub, as I started to spend my way through the bonus.

The words that stuck in my memory were Todhunter's, and I thought long and hard on how I was going to exploit my new-found status. There is an old Fleet Street adage that 'You're as good as your last byline' and it was worth remembering.

What I did know, though, was that my qualifications and experience were no longer open to challenge. I could take on anyone, and was well rated by those running the news desk.

So plenty of good stories came my way and I was often sent out of town on big ones, particularly if a car was needed. Possession of my blue and silver Singer Hunter definitely gave me an advantage.

A few days later I was called over by the news desk and asked if I could drive an automatic. I had not driven many but I knew what I was doing with such a vehicle. So they gave me the keys to Hardcastle's three-and-a-half-litre Rover parked outside the office and asked if I could move it. I must have arrived.

What was quite a break, although it did not seem so at the time, came when I was asked to report to the legal director, Donald Geddes, for a special mission. It all sounded rather mysterious, but instead of the daunting, stern figure I anticipated I met a charming, soft-spoken man who had something of the gentle Scots accent I recalled my father possessed. Within a short time I established that Geddes was indeed from Dumfries, like my father, and there were several links— such as schooling. From that day I was on very good terms indeed with the lawyer, who was on the board of Associated Newspapers and a very big shot indeed.

But my mission was a tough one. There had been a wild story on the front page of the *Mail* alleging expense fiddling, drunken sex parties and Communist manipulation within the Fire Brigades Union. The story had the byline of Walter Farr, not of the industrial staff, but the paper's diplomatic correspondent.

I told Geddes I recalled the story and had wondered about it at the time. From my knowledge of the unions, the FBU was indeed a left-wing outfit, but I hoped the *Daily Mail* could substantiate its charges.

"That's the problem—we can't," said Geddes. "That's where you come in. We need you to stand the story up. We have received two libel writs from the FBU, and at the moment there is not a shred of a case to enable us to resist them."

This, I told myself, is where they find you out. I warned Geddes it was a tall order, but I would dig around and see what I could find. He seemed relieved.

First I went to see Walter Farr. If he was worried, he did not show it. The story, he told me, came from 'a source' which was impeccable. But no, he could not tell me who that source was nor could he ask it to provide any facts to back it up.

I could see I was not going to get any help from Farr so I retired to think hard. In my days on the *South London Press* I had known quite a bit about the Fire Brigades Union and had a particularly good contact in Bill Keyse, the London member on the union executive. But that was several years ago … and a phone call, coldly received when once Bill and I had been the greatest of pals, told me I was not going to get any help there.

On the other hand. it did tend to confirm that all was not well within the union, otherwise my old friend would surely have been trying to disabuse me of such thoughts.

I waded through the *Daily Mail* library cuttings on the union and also looked at the work of other papers. Not a lot there, except it became very clear that on any political issue such as the campaign to ban the nuclear bomb or opposing the moderate leadership of the Labour Party, then the Fire Bridges Union was right up front—led by the general secretary John Horner and his deputy Jack Grahl, both Communist Party members.

Over the weeks I gradually built up a better picture of what was happening inside the union and how it was riven internally between the Reds and more moderate members. And I started to get some of their names, so I set off to visit a number of fire stations turning up unannounced—often shown the door, but in some cases invited in to hear a catalogue of complaints at Communist manipulation of the union.

My progress led to a circular being sent out from the FBU headquarters warning against a curly-headed reporter arriving from the *Daily Mail* who was bent on mischief—he was daring to enquire into the way the union worked internally! Too true.

But the circular proved counter-productive. The ratio of doors open to those closed improved markedly, and when I arrived I was often greeted warmly. "We've been waiting for you," I was told.

The real breakthrough came though when Jack Grahl, the deputy general secretary resigned—forced out, I learned later, by the Communist Party industrial organiser Peter Kerrigan.

From what I gathered Grahl's life was in turmoil and his wife, Helen, had committed suicide. News of a Communist union official's wife's suicide posed the question: what made her do it?

The police report into Helen's death gave an address in Harrow. My careful enquiries established that Grahl was indeed living there and on very friendly terms with his dead wife's sister, but a phone call to that address established that Grahl had gone off to Burntisland, across the Tay from Edinburgh.

Did they have an address there for him? Yes they did. I scribbled it down and put the phone down quickly before I was asked why I wanted it.

Back in the legal department Geddes and I went over the material I had collated. There was quite a lot—I even had a copy of the heavy expenditure on alcohol at the union's Blackpool conference. But nowhere could I find anything about a mystery flat which Walter Farr alleged had been funded by the communist officers at union expense where sex parties and drunken orgies took place. It was alleged that

Grahl, clearly quite a ladies' man, had an affair with a secretary at the union's Fulham offices and she would often accompany Grahl to the flat.

All I had to do was prove it.

Geddes agreed that I should travel up to Scotland and confront Grahl with all that "we knew." It might be enough to get him to drop his own case against the *Daily Mail*.

I checked into a good quality hotel in Burntisland and sent Grahl a telegram inviting him to come and talk—possibly to our mutual advantage. Would it come off or would he just go to ground?

But about 10 a.m., the deadline, I heard a loud voice in the garden and through the lounge doors—not through the front entrance, I noted—stepped Grahl. I was face to face with the man I had been tracking for weeks. My quarry was equally silent for a moment or two as he at last confronted the reporter who had been asking so many questions at fire stations all over Britain.

We shook hands in silence.

Then I asked if he fancied a drink and there was no hesitation. A large Scotch—"And never mind the watter."

Gradually, as we talked, the picture built up. I learned how Peter Kerrigan, the industrial organiser of the Communist Party, virtually ran the union, instructing John Horner, the general secretary, and officers like Grahl, on the line they should take. He even fixed the officials' wages. When Grahl, who was a powerful platform speaker, seconded the resolution at the TUC conference urging that Britain reject the nuclear deterrent, I learned it was at Kerrigan's behest.

So where was the secret luxury flat to which he had taken his mistress, I enquired of Grahl.

He roared with laughter. "There was no flat, laddie."

So where did he conduct his amorous relations?

"In the back of the car, of course." It was obvious when I thought about it, especially as it was a union car. No wonder I could not find the flat. It never existed.

After about two hours I had heard enough and phoned Geddes in the London office. I said I reckoned Grahl would come over to our side for money.

I was told to go ahead and negotiate up to £5,000. For £2,000, Grahl agreed he would drop his libel action against the *Daily Mail* and tell all he knew. Better still, such was his hatred of John Horner, I learned, he was willing to become a witness for our side if ever the case reached the High Court.

As the days went by, it became increasingly apparent that the Fire Brigades Union action would ultimately be withdrawn. The *Daily Mail* had almost certainly avoided a costly High Court case or a major payout, and the humiliation that would represent.

So after almost three months away from the news room I reported back, but with a good friend in Geddes who I would one day find very helpful indeed.

The 'halo' effect soon wore off—newspapers live for today—so I had to assess how I was doing and where I was going. Alex Kenworthy, the agricultural correspondent who had been recruited to the *Daily Express* and was shortly to leave, called me over to his desk. "Why don't you put in for this job?" he suggested.

"Don't be daft—what does a South Londoner know about farmers and cows and things? It's not my cup of tea."

Alex insisted any good journalist could cope with any subject if he put his mind to it.

"You could do it," he said. "But the most important thing is you would be drawing attention to yourself. It's not a bad idea to put in for a job you don't want—it tells them you're getting restless."

I took Alex's advice and applied to be the *Daily Mail* agricultural correspondent which, if I got the job, meant flogging my way round the county agricultural fairs, monitoring the price of grain and getting to know farmers. What a fate!

I was summoned a few days later to see the editor, Arthur Wareham. "What's this all about—you're not cut out for this job," he told me with a smile.

I insisted I could do the job, saying I was a competent journalist who could tackle a complex subject and it would not take me long to master it.

When Wareham pressed me I said I really wanted to be a specialist—motoring or industrial. But agricultural would do in the meantime, I argued, until a vacancy opened up.

"We already have a specialist writer lined up for the farming job but you go back and carry on. You are doing very well, and I assure you your time will come."

Much relieved at not getting the job, but insisting to the editor that I really did want it, I returned to my desk.

And then my luck changed, very much for the better.

My phone rang. It was Morley Richards, a name we all knew on the *Mail*. He was the news editor of our deadly rival, the *Daily Express*. "Come and have a drink, dear boy," he said. "I think we need a chat."

We agreed to meet in a Fleet Street bar not far away but slightly off the beaten track, where an assignation between staff of the two highly competitive newspapers would not be noted. Richards came quickly to the point. He wanted me to cross Fleet Street and become an *Express* staff reporter as their stories were bylined. "I've been watching you, old boy. You're good. That story about Parsons was a winner."

The *Express* money was good. A figure of £40 a week—compared to my current £22—plus a guarantee of £20-a-week expenses, straight into the pocket.

I told him I was interested, but I did not want to come as a reporter. I wanted to be a specialist, either industrial or motoring. I knew that both these posts were filled by highly experienced journalists like Trevor Evans—later Sir Trevor—and Basil Cardew, known in *Private Eye* as Basil Mildew, but highly rated in the world of motor sport.

To my surprise, that did not dent Morley's enthusiasm at all. As it happened, he explained, Ian Aitken, Trevor's deputy was leaving to join the *Daily Mirror* in the top industrial job. The vacancy was made for me, said the smooth Morley Richards.

It did sound that way and when, a day or so later, lunch was arranged so that I could meet Trevor—and he could sum me up—I agreed to join the *Express* and went back ready to submit my resignation from the *Daily Mail*.

But it was not so simple. Unknown to me, there had been a number of raids by the *Express* on the *Daily Mail* staff, the most notable of whom was Donald Todhunter, our highly regarded news editor. It seemed the *Express* had almost got him over the wall when the top brass produced a contract he had signed as night news editor in which he had agreed to give six months' notice. They intended to hold Toddie to that apparently. That meant I would almost certainly have to work out my full notice if I wanted to move. But the *Mail* people were determined nobody was going to be lured away. They would match any offer, it was being said. Even so, I could not see how they could match the *Express* offer of number two industrial man. But I was wrong.

It now appeared that Ian Aitken was no longer leaving the *Express*, but had been promoted to go to New York—a plum job. And all that meant was that the *Daily Mail*'s number two industrial man had been snapped up by *Daily Mirror*.

"The job's yours," I was told by Bill Hardcastle. "You wouldn't work on the *Express*, surely?" I was in a turmoil. I had accepted the job at the *Express* and working for the affable Trevor Evans would do my reputation no harm at all. By contrast, I was being offered deputy to Leslie Randall, a somewhat remote, gruff man that few seemed to know.

As I agonised I had an idea. I went to seek the advice of Donald Geddes, the office lawyer, with whom I had become friends. I told myself he would be objective, unlike my reporter pals who were all too close to the subject. And he certainly was.

"Put the money to one side, what matters is where you would feel more comfortable and would fit in. You know the people at the *Daily Mail* . Over the road you would be starting from scratch and it might not work out. Could you jump back? I doubt it."

Geddes' advice basically was to stick with the devil you know, and suddenly I realised that was my own gut feeling. I was, after all, a *Mail* man, through and through.

So I decided to join Leslie Randall. It was one of the best decisions of my life. That man became my father figure, my mentor and my lifelong friend. I had made the right choice.

CHAPTER 5
Making a Name in the Street of Ink

As I walked from the reporter's room to the one occupied by some of the specialists, however, I was anything but confident. Randall seemed a grumpy old man who did not have much of a sense of humour. Wrong, wrong, wrong. Leslie Randall stood up with a broad smile and held out his hand. "I have always believed in welcoming a new colleague one hundred percent," he said. And he added, "I have had all the bylines I need in this world; help yourself."

That was true. Randall had been in America as New York man for the *Daily Express*, and had covered the St Valentine Day's murders in Chicago, where he had mixed bootleg gin in his bathroom during prohibition. To be staff correspondent for a London daily paper in the United States in those days really meant something. During the war Leslie had been chief reporter for the *London Evening Standard*, covering food and rationing, a big issue to the starving British. And he had also been among the first British war correspondents into the Belsen concentration camp. So Leslie had certainly been about and knew his way around journalism, as I was to discover.

He did not set out to teach me about becoming an industrial correspondent. He just offered the occasional word of advice. After making an early trip to a coal mine in South Wales I told Leslie I had been knackered just by the effort involved in the long, stumbling descent to the coalface. "Well, remember that when you think of writing a knocking piece on coal miners," he counselled. "There's blood on the coal, you know."

My very first day out of the office as 'an industrial man' involved me with the seven-week-long London bus drivers' strike of 1958, led by a new figure on the national scene, Frank Cousins, who had made clear he was not going to fall in line with the 'don't rock the boat' approach of the trade union leadership of the day. If a boat needed rocking, he, Big Frank, made clear, he would not hesitate to rock it, even if the passengers fell out. Cousins held a daily news conference at Transport House in Smith Square, near Westminster, and on my first day I was shown the way by a lovely guy, Bob Garner, number two on the *Daily Telegraph* industrial team with whom, I was to learn, we on the *Mail* quietly co-operated, unknown to our bosses.

I was sitting with Bob when Cousins arrived and stalked to the mike. "Who's here from the *Daily Mail*?" he roared. Without a pause for thought I raised my hand. Wrong again! It brought forth a torrent of complaint from Cousins who, unknown to me, had been accosted by a team of *Daily Mail* reporters and photographers as he had left his home that morning at Tattenham Corner, near Epsom racecourse. As he climbed into his chauffeur-driven car, the *Mail* men had asked why he was not taking a bus. The *Mail* car pursued Cousins twice round a roundabout before letting the furious union man make off for his London office. Nothing had been achieved except to make Frank Cousins very annoyed. And I had walked into it. I squirmed.

It was hardly a good start in industrial journalism. And I would never have believed that years later, when Cousins quit as a Labour Government minister, he would give me his personal story exclusively. Or that I would organise a farewell lunch for him when he retired.

But that was the way it was between industrial correspondents and the people who led Britain's trades unions—the Fifth Estate as they became known. Increasingly in the post-war years, industrial relations became the great issue of the time, and I was to make my name in that sphere. We were seldom off the front page as strikes took place in the docks, on the railways, and in the motor car industry.

The top brass of the union world was the Trades Union Congress, which held an annual conference but met monthly in their headquarters at Great Russell Street in London. Most of the prominent union officials were elected to the General Council which ran the TUC and picked its top officials. Each month they met in secret, and it was our job to find out what had happened. All of us had contacts inside the meeting who, for a lunch or a drink or two, would spill the beans and even hand over the odd document marked 'Confidential'.

This was the interface between the Government of the day and the leadership of working Britain and while I worked in the field, the TUC claimed to have twelve million affiliated supporters—half the labour force in the country. So the movement at that time had real clout.

Another of our jobs was to watch the Labour Party closely. Although in Parliament this was the role of the political correspondents, because the unions had created the party originally we clung to our right to cover its headquarters at Transport House and to report its important activities. The unions coughed up most financial support and tended to call the shots within the Labour Party, and we industrial reporters argued we would find out more accurately what was happening inside the smoke-filled rooms at party headquarters. We also took precedence on the coverage of the Labour Party conference which was nearly always a front page story as the politicians squabbled in their pursuit of power.

In my early days on the beat we did not enjoy a very good relationship with the TUC General Secretary, Vincent Tewson, who clammed up when talking to journalists and never appeared to wish to help. But soon came his retirement, and in his place was elected George Woodcock, who had waited many years to fill the shoes. George was interested in change and knew that soon the movement would have to start to put its house in order or possibly perish. So he wanted to cultivate the press—'our lads', as he called us.

He was to lead the unions into discussion on the leapfrogging pay claims which only led to rising inflation which then eroded the hard-won negotiated wage increases. Eventually it would lead to an incomes policy and an attempt to share out the spoils. But that was yet to come.

I had just become secretary of the Industrial Correspondents Group when George took over, so I came up with a suggestion that we should challenge the TUC General Council to a cricket match. I put the idea to my friend Geoffrey Goodman who knew more about cricket than me, and together we went to see George.

Woodcock, who had twinkling eyes and large bushy eyebrows which made him a wonderful subject for the cartoonists of the day, smiled at the idea and pointed out the age gap. The TUC General Council members were no chickens but he thought they might accept the challenge. Next day George told us the match was on and he would expect us to organise the event.

That year, the TUC Conference was being held at Southsea for the first time so no one knew any of the local officials. But the public relations man of Portsmouth saw the publicity potential, and agreed to find a ground and lend us some cricketing gear.

Most of our colleagues agreed to join in and to contribute to a fund to buy some drinks. There was just one snag—who would be wicket-keeper? "It's your idea so you can do it," was the unanimous view.

I had not thought of that. I had an eye for a ball, but more the tennis variety, and had no experience of people deliberately aiming that nasty hard ball at you. Sir Trevor Evans and the boilermaker's leader, Ted Hill, kept score, recording the runs—and the numerous byes that hurtled past me.

Some of the trade union people turned out to be pretty good, too. George Woodcock had played at quite a high standard in the Lancashire League and Vic Feather, his number two, was also a veteran from the Yorkshire League and an excellent wicket-keeper—to put me to shame.

They won easily, but there was one delicious moment when Frank Cousins came to the crease, clearly intent on knocking us all over the field. Our bowler skied one, which dropped straight on the Transport leader's stumps. That was in 1960, the year he was leading the nationwide, headline-filling campaign to ban the nuclear bomb. It was the major political issue of the day. "That's what you call fallout," I said from behind the wicket. An angry but humiliated Cousins stalked off.

The event, however, achieved a lot in improving the relationship between the press and the union leadership, and its success was judged by the fact that the annual match continued for forty-five years, and was eagerly anticipated each year. It was only the fall in TUC membership, the declining numbers serving on the General Council, and the way newspapers cut industrial coverage that finally brought down the curtain in 2008.

As well as union leaders, we also hobnobbed with Labour politicians. My friendship with Bob Mellish, the Bermondsey MP—who went on ultimately to become the party's chief whip—had been excellent training, and over the years I got on good terms with Hugh Gaitskell, Harold Wilson, George Brown, Ray Gunter and scores more.

The *Daily Mail* had a bruising reputation with the Labour Party so as the *Mail* man I had to overcome plenty of suspicion, but gradually I convinced them that I could be trusted.

That was the reason I was furious over an article headed 'Our Man at the Docks' in a magazine called *Time and Tide*. The industrial correspondents debated the article, and the consensus was that Eric Wigham of *The Times* and I had been wronged. The piece said I would be prepared to sell my grandmother to get a good story, the inference being that one would deliberately ditch a contact to get a scoop. I felt that was pretty damaging, wasn't true, and would not do much to reassure my contacts.

Wigham was adamant that he would not go to law but, naively, I decided to chance my arm and seek legal advice. I went to a libel specialist firm in the Temple and, before I knew it, was authorising a writ to be served. I was cocky and really did not appreciate the deep waters into which I was heading. But I did stress to my solicitor that there was no way I could go into a witness box and face questioning on my contacts. At that point I would have to pull out and meet the costs.

A week or two went by in negotiation and then the *Time and Tide* side played what it felt was its leading card—they quoted an article under my name about a twelve-course meal in Soho's Gay Hussar, then the haunt of the left wing, held by the shop workers' union for just nine people at a cost of around £160. That worked out around £17 a head, nearly twice the average weekly wage the union had negotiated for its members. I had obtained the menu, and quoted the lines of poetry between each course and the quality of the wines served. It was quite devastating for the union but, as I was able to tell my lawyer, I had written it as a general news reporter sent out on an assignment, and it was long before I became an industrial reporter.

Suddenly, the pace quickened. The magazine's lawyers advised them to settle and, without clearing it, published a retraction. My lawyer pounced—we should have approved the text and we wanted a full apology. The magazine grovelled and offered to pay up.

And that was how I walked out with a cheque for £350, money which deserved to be spent on something I would not normally be buying. That was also how my first boat got its name ... *Time and Tide*.

I was involved with a rather larger vessel, the *QE2,* when the *Daily Mail* splashed under my byline that *Q4*, as it was then known, would be built on the Clyde. It was a story of enormous significance to the shipbuilding industry as the Tyne, Belfast and Glasgow tussled for such a major order.

I worked with Geoffrey Goodman, then on the *Daily Herald,* and Ron Stevens of the *Daily Telegraph* on the story, but in Scotland I had an advantage because the *Daily Mail* had a Scottish edition and was first on the streets. It was just before Christmas 1964, and as the news broke Glasgow's church bells were rung jubilantly. The only gloom was at the *Scottish Daily Express*, who could not bring themselves to follow up. It took five days before the *Express* admitted the Q4 story in the *Daily Mail* was true.

Goodman, Stevens and I had discovered the Wilson Labour Government was to put £17.4 million into the deal. The reason was the economic impact the order would have and the 'ripple-out' effect.

Some months later I travelled up to John Brown's yard on the Clyde where the new liner was having its keel laid. The yard manager proudly showed me round, assuring me that not only would the ship be delivered on time, but it would a testimony to all that was best in

Clydeside pride and skill.

On its proving trials there were some engine problems—anyone who knew anything about ships knew that was the point of having trials. Unknown to me, the then news editor, Jimmy Anderson, had pocketed the invitation to the 'shake-down cruise' and taken his wife aboard. His headline, which led the paper, was 'Ship of Shame', the story written no doubt as its author downed another glass of Cunard's champagne.

The *QE2*, as she was formally named by Queen Elizabeth on launching in 1969, cruised fifty million miles as Britain's best advertisement for forty years, earning billions in foreign exchange and amply repaying the Government investment. And that was not counting her role as a troopship in the Falklands conflict.

It was embarrassing hype like 'ship of shame' that had me wondering whether I wanted to spend my entire career trying to report serious affairs when cheap stories like that of Anderson's could lead the paper, and undo all that had been achieved by winning the story in the first place.

A constant theme underlying the trade union scene was the 'entryism' of the Communist Party and its attempts to manipulate events—particularly when Labour was in power—through the union movement. The Communists were strong among the miners, the engineers, the dockers, and even the print workers. They could not officially play a role in the Labour Party because they were banned, but by manipulating the unions they could pull strings on the political scene.

That, of course, was meat and drink to the *Daily Mail*. While I tried not to get too intense on the threat of the Reds, I could be pretty sure if I turned in a story on those lines it would get a good show. After all, I had had my experience with the Fire Brigades Union, and another story concerned the engineers—the Amalgamated Engineering Union, the second largest in the country. But I had a tip that the Communist cell in the AEU was to meet that weekend to plan its tactics for the impending policy-making conference of the union's National Committee, which was where real power lay in the AEU.

Better still, the meeting was to take place, amazingly, at the King Street headquarters of the Communist Party of Great Britain, a stone's throw from Covent Garden.

At that time I had a Morris Minor van which I used both in my journalistic work and also while I had a dairy business in Harlesden, North London—but that's another story. The van was ideal to park discreetly across the road from party headquarters and watch the comings and goings. I had a *Daily Mail* photographer with me, and we squeezed into the rear compartment, and waited.

Several hours went by and I was about to call off our monitoring when suddenly the doors to the King Street office swung open and people began to emerge. The photographer shot off reel after reel of his film, cursing that he could not use a flash, while I simply sat quietly taking notes in the hope that I would be able to link them to the film when it was exposed.

Next morning, on my desk was a pile of contact prints of the photographer's work. He had done a brilliant job. Now all I had to do was to put names to the faces and their roles in the union.

In later years I would have known some of the faces and been able to put names to them, but not in the early stages of my *Daily Mail* industrial career. But I did know a union official working in the North London office of the AEU who might be able to help, and when I found out he was attending a weekend conference in Shere, Surrey, I decided to drive there and try to get him out of the conference. My luck held. Tom Chapman came with me to a pub and was knocked sideways by the prints. He identified Claude Berridge, a CP member and a full-time member of the union executive. Another shot was of Reg Birch, then president of the North London area, but later to win a seat on the executive and ultimately to break allegiance to the Russians and identify with the Chinese.

I raced back to Fleet Street. I needed to confront some of those in the photos and ask what they were all doing at the Communist office. Was it true they were being given their tactical instructions by the

Party's 'industrial commissioner', hardliner Peter Kerrigan?

The union's National Committee was meeting on Monday morning at Clacton, Essex, and it seemed likely those attending would take trains from Liverpool Street Station. I gambled that the delegates would be passing through the station late afternoon to get to their hotels in time for dinner. My luck held, and I spotted several coming up the platform as I waited, pictures in hand.

"Excuse me, Mr Berridge—could I show you these pictures?" Berridge, known to his colleagues as 'Calamity Claude', was off guard, and stopped to look through his horn-rimmed spectacles. "These were taken outside the Communist Party headquarters yesterday," I said. "Were you discussing union affairs there?" A furious Berridge spun on his heel and climbed aboard the train. But we had snatched a picture of him looking at the *Daily Mail* photograph.

As the train pulled out I noticed another union member, face wreathed in smiles, obviously loving the event. He turned out to be John Boyd, a strong anti-communist on the executive, who battled non-stop with the Reds. That event and the front page pictures in the *Daily Mail* next morning were just what Boyd and his allies needed. Boyd, later AEU general secretary, a governor of the BBC, and eventually Lord Boyd, was to become quite a good contact in the years to come. And eventually I even became on reasonable terms with Calamity Claude, though I had certainly created one for him on that occasion.

Getting to know Labour politicians was an important part of the work of an industrial correspondent, and as I have explained, we were on better terms with them sometimes than the political correspondents. That was the era of Tory Governments, and for thirteen years the Labour Party was destined to be the Opposition, though gradually the voters were becoming sick of the Tories and seemed to be looking more favourably on the Opposition.

Hugh Gaitskell, a Labour Chancellor of the Exchequer, was Leader of the Opposition and not an easy person to get to know. But as secretary of the Industrial Correspondents Group, I did manage to penetrate the gatekeepers around him and arranged lunch. He specified the Stafford

Hotel, which was nicely off the beaten track, and clearly Gaitskell knew his way through the menu. Though the occasion was not over-relaxed, and I felt Gaitskell was summing up me and my colleagues, it broke the ice and meant that later he would acknowledge us.

Gradually my relationship with Gaitskell improved, but I never got as close to him as I did later to other senior politicians. I was once with my then wife, Shirley, at a Parliamentary Press Gallery dinner at which the Labour leader and his wife Dora were the guests. The leader was in his element on social occasions and came up to sweep Shirley on to the dance floor. "Careful," I warned him. "I don't think she's one of your supporters."

"Oh, we'll have to do something about that," he called back.

When she got back Shirley surprised me. "You realise he's a ladies man, don't you?"

Frankly I didn't, but it was an interesting observation from just one quick dance. And subsequently it turned out that Gaitskell was indeed something of a charmer, and had a number of conquests—notably, it was said, with Lady Pamela Berry—then the leading hostess in town.

The moment I recall most vividly about Gaitskell came in 1960 when he took on the Left at the Labour Party conference in Scarborough over the nuclear bomb issue. They wanted a commitment from the leadership that, if elected, a new Labour Government would abandon nuclear weapons and leave NATO.

Gaitskell had been supported by Nye Bevan, his deputy, who was well to the left but who also saw that such a commitment would doom Labour to permanent opposition. But Bevan had died suddenly, and Gaitskell had to fight alone. He knew, though, the US Government, extremely influential behind the scenes, would do all in its power to ensure his electoral defeat.

So it was an extremely unpleasant atmosphere at Scarborough with left-wing politicians and trade union leaders, notably Frank Cousins, clearly out to defeat the leadership. When Gaitskell stood up to speak, I felt strongly that I was about to witness an historic event as the leader took on the Left and most of the conference, underlining his determination to keep the nuclear deterrent.

As Gaitskell reached the key phrase—that he and party members like him would not accept a vote against the H-Bomb, but 'would fight, and fight again, to save the party we love'—it was so exciting I could hardly get it down in my notebook. But I knew, long before the term sound bite had been invented, that it was the quote that summed up the stupendous battle of wills.

The conference went wild with anger. Delegates were on their feet shaking fists and hurling insults. Never had I seen such hatred on the faces of prominent political figures like Ted Castle, husband of Barbara. If he could have reached Gaitskell I was sure he would have hit him. But coolly Gaitskell stood his ground, though he must have been shaking.

There was a similar party conference battle a couple of years later at Brighton when Gaitskell spoke for over an hour, and came down firmly against Britain giving up its sovereignty to join the European Common Market, as it was then known. After the bomb this was the other divisive issue in British politics, and a substantial number of the right wingers were strongly in favour. The left did not like it; Russia and the other communist countries in Middle Europe were opposed. But that was another good reason for joining Europe—who could foresee the crumbling of the Berlin Wall and the collapse of the Communist system?

Gaitskell's deputy, George Brown, who was due to wind up the debate later in the day, came to lunch with me and some colleagues. George was shattered and furious because Gaitskell had not told his deputy how his speech would end, and the line he would take against the Common Market.

To his credit, George, suitably wined and lunched on my *Daily Mail* expenses, went into the conference hall and put the opposite view. No way was he going to abandon a position he had adopted for years as the party's defence spokesman. "One in the eye for George," said the headline on my front page story next day, with George holding a hand up to his eye as if given a black one by his leader.

My new relationship with Hugh Gaitskell, alas, did not have long to develop. In 1963 he was admitted with a mystery illness to the Manor House Hospital in Hampstead. Known as the trade unionists' hospital, it did not enjoy a high reputation for its recovery rate, and people were relieved when Gaitskell was discharged. Shortly afterwards he was re-admitted to one of the main London teaching hospitals where he died from an immune deficiency, but there was speculation, never substantiated, that he had been murdered by the Russian KGB.

This was all low-key until Ray Gunter MP, a member of the party executive and president of the railway staff union, rang me as I was about to leave for Moscow as one of the industrial correspondents covering the visit of the Trades Union Congress leadership.

"What's wrong with Hugh, boy?"

Funny question. How the hell did I know? But Ray was not so much asking as marking my card. At a committee meeting of the Labour party executive earlier that day, the leader's health had been mentioned. There were several gloomy faces, I learned.

It was just a tip, a hint, but it came from a very shrewd political observer. Ray had an instinct that something was up. I replaced the phone, walked round to see the news editor, and told him I had decided to cancel my trip to Russia. He seemed surprised at my abandoning a nice jaunt to Russia. "No caviar and vodka, then?" he observed. But it was the right move. With all my rivals stuck in Moscow in the days when phones were non-existent and copy moved laboriously by old-fashioned telex, sadly I was in the right place at the right time. Within a few days Hugh Gaitskell was dead.

Almost certainly his successor would be his deputy, George Brown … or would it? The view was that he had a drink problem. He certainly had a temper and he could be mercurial. On the other hand, he was intensely loyal to his friends and so I had an open door to him.

When I had joined the Labour scene, Leslie Randall had suggested I should try to get close to Harold Wilson, then the number three, but quite disliked because he seemed such a schemer and was renowned as a fence-sitter. Easier said than done to cut through the wall his secretary, Marcia Falkender, had built around him. But gradually I did manage to strike up an acquaintance with Wilson and found that, if it suited him, he could be quite helpful.

So when Gaitskell died so suddenly, and an election was called in the Parliamentary Labour Party to choose a new leader, Wilson was nominated. There were other candidates, but it was soon apparent that the real contest would be between Brown and Wilson.

Promptly the word went round: "Would you want George Brown in a room with Khrushchev [the Russian leader] and a bottle of whisky?" It was a very successful smear. Wilson won, and Brown had to settle for number two, which set the field for a tumultuous relationship, especially in 1964 when Labour won power, but by a wafer-thin majority.

We in the Industrial Correspondents Group later had a special regard for Wilson because he saved our bacon one night at the newly-built Hilton Hotel. I had come up with the idea of a special celebration for the Group's twenty-fifth anniversary, and had the nerve to book the ballroom for a major black-tie dinner. Every member had invited his editor, and used the occasion to bring along to their tables the top industrialists, trade union leaders and senior civil servants as guests. It was destined, it seemed, to be a lavish affair.

All was looking good until the 35th President of the United States, John F Kennedy, was assassinated on Friday 22nd November 1963. Everybody of my age knows where they were at the time they heard of the tragedy—I was inside a wardrobe I was building.

As the news poured in it dawned on me that the world would be in mourning. Everybody who was anybody would go to Washington. And that would include quite a few of our guests. Worse—the speakers.

We certainly lost our government minister who was due to speak. But to his eternal credit Wilson flew to Washington, attended the funeral and the various events at the British Embassy and then flew straight back to London. That evening, shrugging off jet lag, he was our main speaker and saved the event for us.

In opposition, Wilson was on top of his job and set a cracking pace against the Government, especially as Harold Macmillan faltered and gave way to upper crust Alec Douglas Home. Wilson loved it and claimed that the new Tory leader had to count matches to work out economics. It wasn't true, but it was just one of the good lines from Wilson who was out to end 'thirteen years of Tory misrule'.

I was in the press party which followed Wilson during the 1964 General Election, and for three and a half weeks several of us hardly took our eyes off him. Gradually as we toured the country and Wilson faced huge public meetings—television had not yet come to dominate the hustings—we watched him mature into a good public speaker. He was known to be good in the House of Commons, but facing big public meetings at first Wilson was nervous.

Gradually, though, he worked up his speech, and each night would insert a newsy item which he knew would give us something to work with. And at the same time Wilson reached an arrangement with Harold Webb, then BBC northern industrial correspondent, to signal to him when the BBC News at nine o'clock was live and Wilson, with impeccable timing, would speak straight to camera and be beamed into Britain's homes. It may sound pretty easy stuff nowadays. but then it was state-of-the-art and it wrong-footed government ministers.

At Watford the election tours of Wilson and Alec Douglas Home criss crossed, and the *Daily Mail* newsroom came up with the idea that I should go to report the Tory leader while my colleague, Eric Sewell from the parliamentary team, would take in Wilson.

It was an eye-opener. I could not believe just how terribly the Tory leader performed. In the House, as an experienced diplomat, as a Cabinet team player, he surely had his qualities, but on the hustings as an aspiring candidate for leading Britain, he was awful.

Both Sewell and I were asked to write side-by-side pieces on the main feature page and I gave Wilson a very high mark for sheer professionalism. I had just witnessed chalk and cheese, side by side— and it showed, I reported.

Wilson came up next morning to thank me, surely a long time since a Labour leader thanked a *Daily Mail* man for the objectivity for his report. Only then I muffed it. I was recoiling at the danger of being thanked by a politician and did not want Wilson to think he had me in his pocket. I thanked him, but said I would be watching how he played things once elected … ah well, there went my gong!

Three of us, Geoffrey Goodman, (*Daily Herald*), Cyril Aynsley (*Daily Express*) and I, were determined never to let Wilson out of our sight. Just as well, because when we were in Huddersfield, where Wilson grew up, his car suddenly veered off the intended route and we gave chase. Through some narrow back streets we raced, and then the Labour leader's car came to a halt outside a small, neat terraced house. It was his home as a schoolboy, and there waiting was Harold's father, a former chemist with ICI. This was the father who had taken his son to London and photographed him wearing his school cap on the steps of Number 10 Downing Street. What a story! What a picture!

There were other moments before the 1964 campaign tour ended. In his Huyton constituency, at an old folks home, Wilson quietly asked me to pay for the tea and cakes the old age pensioners were scooping up during his visit. It was only a small sum and the *Daily Mail* would never notice, but Wilson explained a candidate was not allowed to pay for anything that might constitute a bribe. I never mentioned it in print. I doubt if such a relationship between politician and journalist could exist today without leaking.

Speaking of relationships, there was of course the one between Wilson and his personal assistant, Marcia Falkender. Most of Fleet Street suspected Wilson had had an affair with her, and there was no doubt she was a tremendous influence with him. But I was never convinced that a politician as shrewd and calculating as Wilson was going to run the risk of hopping into bed with his secretary.

Lord Hailsham, generally regarded as a loudmouth, certainly hinted at the secret relationship. But unlike today when there are few secrets, the story remained largely under wraps.

Wilson's wife, Mary, was on the tour but she clearly hated it and kept a low profile. Cyril Aynsley, the *Express* man with whom I had a non-aggression deal for the three weeks of the election campaign, told

Geoffrey and me that he had been in the same class as Mary at school in Workington. I urged Cyril to talk to her, which he did subsequently. He met her a few times but never let her down by spilling it in the *Express*. Hard to imagine nowadays.

After three and a half weeks on the road the end was in sight. The count on election night was in a school hall in Huyton, but suddenly I did not care where it was. I went down with what became known as Adelphi Berri—I had food poisoning, as did others. And we blamed it on the once famous Adelphi Hotel in Liverpool, where we had our doubts about the cleanliness of the kitchen.

Next morning, as the train carried Wilson, his aides and the press party southwards I was still under-performing but determined not to surrender my place, doorstepping history.

The BBC tried to bounce Wilson claiming victory, and arranged a camera in the dining car. Sweeping the cutlery and crockery to one side, Wilson stormed at Robin Day, "I am not a performing seal"—a sentiment we of the doomed writing press much approved of. But Wilson had done his sums, and knew the finish was going to be extremely close. Even as his car swept him to Transport House, the party headquarters, he refused to speculate.

It was not until mid-afternoon that the final results came in and showed Wilson had won by just four votes, which subsequently dropped to three.

Wilson struggled into his black morning suit which had been waiting for him at party headquarters, and the car took him off to Buckingham Palace to kiss hands with the Queen. That was the last we saw of him because from the Palace, Britain's new Labour Prime Minister went straight to Number 10 Downing Street.

We industrial correspondents looked round the coffee cups and cigarette ends in the hall at Transport House and closed our notebooks. Those cursed rivals, the political correspondents at Westminster, would now take him over.

A couple of weeks later, however, came a call from Number 10 Downing Street. All those who had been in the press party following

Harold Wilson's campaign were invited to have drinks with him there.

It was quite a night and my first visit to the seat of power. We had drinks in an upstairs reception room and were then offered a tour of the building. We went into the Cabinet Room where Wilson showed us where the Prime Minister sat. "This is where I work," he explained. There was a single telephone with a green-coloured handpiece in front of his seat. So we all leaned forward and started to note down the telephone number—they were 'currency' to us, the chance to get through to a key contact.

Wilson laughed. "You won't get through—and if you do, my private secretary will be listening in and writing it all down."

As a senior member of the *Daily Mail* staff there were many 'highs' including some exciting foreign trips. I got to Canada for the 1967 Expo in Montreal which, with sixty-two nations taking part, was one of the most successful ever World Fair events. The British stand rated well, I reported. And as it coincided with Canada's Centennial Year there were all kinds of other events to report. That got me to Toronto, where I wondered if I could trace my wartime pal Major Ross. Did he survive the war, I wondered.

I made contact with the Canadian Army records office in Ottawa, and told them of my boyhood link with a young Canadian officer. An official became interested and promised to try to help. He rang me back in under two hours. "Found him—he is certainly alive. Do you want his address? He lives in Kingston." I dialled the number and when Ross came on I said, "Voice from the past—do you remember a kid named Keith McDowall?" There was a pause. Then I heard, "Good God."

Kingston was only a short distance by train from Toronto, and Ross arranged to meet at the railway station there next morning. He had not changed a lot, but of course I had. That kid Ross last saw in short trousers was now a curly-haired family man stepping off the train.

I spent a splendid time rebuilding our friendship, met his wife Donnie, who used to send us those precious food parcels, and arranged for Ross's daughter to stay with us in Sanderstead when she came to

London some months later.

Ross won the DSO, ended the war an acting major general, and led the Canadian Army victory parade when Field Marshal Montgomery was on his worldwide tour after the end of the shooting. He came out of the service as a brigadier some years later, and lived first at Kingston—an army town akin to our Aldershot—but later moved out to the warmer temperatures of British Columbia. There, with many of his old comrades, he lived out his final years and I visited him again.

Another exciting overseas trip was to make it to Japan—then the most successful industrial nation in the world, knocking spots off the UK and other industrialised nations. One by one our industries were being knocked over by the Japanese—motor cycles, machine tools, radio, TV, electronics.

I travelled to Tokyo with about thirty company representatives of some of the best known trading firms in Britain. They were using an exhibition there as a chance to open doors and get face to face with the inscrutable Japanese. Ron Jones, for example, representing Castrol, had but one mission. He had to visit every Japanese motor manufacturer and persuade them to recommend Castrol. At the British exhibition stand we were showing the Triumph Herald and a Rolls Royce—both in their way, we thought, technically advanced. Ron told me, "The Japanese are light years behind us in motor cars, they'll never catch us." They did, of course. Triumph went bust, and Rolls-Royce cars are now owned by the Germans.

I was proud of a series of articles I sent back from Tokyo with the strap line 'Wake up, Britain'. I revealed the new VHS video about to be launched by Sony, described the world's largest tanker then being built in just five months at a modern shipyard on reclaimed land at Yokohama, and how the Japanese Camera Institute was forcing makers like Nikon, Canon, and Fuji to raise their competitive standards to compete better in exports. Which they did, of course. My reports made good reading, but though the *Daily Mail* readers seemed interested, British industry hardly blinked.

My old friend and colleague, Leslie Randall, my mentor, had a theory that in journalism you get three good editors—and then you get someone with whom you cannot hit it off.

That was to become my position. I had had a marvellous run at the *Daily Mail*, was well paid, had a Jaguar from them—which meant free petrol, free service and a weekly car wash—but I was getting distinctly restless. And looking back I can see I was getting distinctly cocky, too, and uncooperative. On the other hand, the paper did not seem to be using my copy as much as it had and other *Mail* men seemed to be infringing my 'patch'.

Quite suddenly came upon the scene Arthur Brittenden, who took over as editor from Mike Randall, stricken for months with a slipped disc. Under Randall the *Daily Mail* had become 'Newspaper of the Year' and we were all invited to the Dorchester Hotel to a celebration dinner. Now Mike was trying to edit the *Daily Mail* from his bed, but rumours were rife that Lord Rothermere had decided it was time to call a change. Enter Brittenden.

Arthur's own phrase 'the fastest smile in the West' tended to sum him up, I felt, and there was a distinct feeling that a lightweight had not only taken over but stabbed our favourite editor in the back. Unwisely, I made my opinions too clear. I should have relaxed and waited for the big industrial story to break, and then I would have been back in my element.

But there was a new ingredient in that thinking.

Before he had gone sick Mike Randall (no relation by the way) had called me into his office and said, "You need a proper deputy."

"Well, Mike," I said, "I know who it is."

"A fellow named Monty Meth. He's on the *Daily Worker*."

"For Christ's sake, they already think here I am a soft touch for the Left. How the hell can I hire somebody from the *Worker*?"

I pleaded that the least he could do would be to meet my nominee. Reluctantly, Mike Randall told me to fix a lunch date, but to be sure the venue was off the beaten track. I chose a dark cellar restaurant called Odins opposite the Connaught Rooms, near Drury Lane.

I had spotted Monty months ago when covering a trade union event in York, and liked the look of him. He was well turned out, but what attracted me was his sense of humour. Most communists I knew in the labour movement were surly characters. Deep down, I felt maybe Monty was not quite so dedicated.

I must have been on to something because the conversation quickly became very relaxed, and Monty had the *Daily Mail* editor roaring with laughter. Monty departed first, and as we mounted the stairs Mike said, "OK—how do we get him?" We hatched a plan that meant the *Mail* would not appear to have been coaxing Monty to cross over. It would take a little time.

But Monty had his own problems. He was trying to keep his wife and two young children on miserly wages, from which *Daily Worker* staff were then made to pay a regular slice to the party.

Though he wanted to join the *Mail*, immense pressure was placed on him. His wife, Betty, came from a dedicated Scots family who did not approve of anyone straying from the ranks. In addition, Bert Ramelson, a diehard communist who had first recruited him, came down from Yorkshire especially to try and dissuade him, and on several occasions Monty wavered.

What really bothered him was Ramelson's suggestion that the *Daily Mail* would gloat in print that it had been able to lure away a key specialist from the dedicated ranks of the *Daily Worker* staff.

Monty and I met in the Black Friar, a few yards away from the Printing House Square offices of the old *Times*.

He was wobbling. The Ramelson jibe about the *Mail* gloating had hit home. "You must be joking," I told him. "The last thing the *Daily Mail* is going to announce is that it is recruiting from the ranks of the Communist Party. Do you think we want to frighten all our readers away?" If the project went ahead it would be done quietly, I assured him.

Suddenly Monty got it. We worked out that he would simply resign from the paper, lie low for three months, and the *Daily Mail* would then, equally quietly, recruit him to its industrial staff. Monty and his family had to survive for that period and it was tough going. I managed to send him two or three credits for tip-offs on stories but it was not much.

It was interesting that he had other offers. The moment it became known Monty was a free agent, John Cole and Bernard Ingham, then a strong left-wing Labour supporter, offered Monty a job on the Guardian. First, he would have to make a public declaration he was renouncing the Communist Party, but Monty was not willing publicly to denounce his former colleagues. It was a grave miscalculation, particularly by Ingham—who went on to become Margaret Thatcher's press secretary at Number 10 and moved well to the right. I don't remember Ingham announcing that his membership and writings for the Labour left in Hebden Bridge had all been a ghastly mistake (even if they were).

So Monty came to the *Daily Mail* and my former editor was right. Having a highly dependable deputy with his own contacts and judgement was great relief to me. But I had, of course, also recruited my successor, which Brittenden and the others now running the *Daily Mail* had noted.

If McDowall quit there was no problem replacing him, they probably calculated. Rightly. Years later, Monty joined me when I set-up my own public affairs business, Keith McDowall Associates, and worked happily with me for over ten years. We have remained firm friends.

That day back in York when I liked the look of Monty Meth turned out to be a very good hunch. It was amusing, though, on his first day in the *Mail* office how all kinds of colleagues found an excuse to call into our room to see what one those communists looked like. "Look, no horns!"

I was thirty-eight, and another piece of advice Leslie Randall had offered was, "Get out before you are forty." It had seemed ludicrous when he said it, but now I was beginning to wonder. Was Leslie right? He was sixty, and the last few years had seemed to be very hard work. He had lost interest and the thrill of seeing one's name in print held no interest for him any longer. Was I getting like that?

I had begun to see that, despite a journalist's contempt for public relations people, maybe they were interesting jobs after all. As *Daily Mail* Industrial Editor I had come to know some of the big names at senior public relations level in industry—people like Geoff Kirk at the National Coal Board, Eric Merrill of the British Railways Board, and the redoubtable J.H. Brebner at British Transport Commission, one of the pioneers.

And now a new prospect opened up. Steel was to be nationalised, and the future British Steel would be a Very Big Beast indeed. Whoever had the job as the PR adviser would have a top role. In charge of the steering committee to create the new industrial monster would be Lord Melchett, whom I had come to know a little. And Ron Smith, the general secretary of the Union of Postal Workers and one of my best contacts, told me he was joining Melchett's team in charge of personnel. On top of that, steering the legislation through Parliament to take over the industry would be Richard 'Dick' Marsh, with whom I enjoyed good relations too.

It seemed to me I ought to get a good hearing if I threw my hat into the ring, so I went to see Lord Melchett, who was interested and told me to send in details of my career. But then I ran into Will Camp, the PR adviser of the Gas Council, who was regarded by many of us as a devious, wily fellow who was never too worried if a story he pedalled was true or 'slightly embellished'—as he might put it.

Camp asked me bluntly, "Are you in for this British Steel job?" I did not answer directly and shrugged it off. A mistake. A week or so later, a paragraph appeared in *Private Eye* saying I had got the job. Highly embarrassing—it looked as if I had been talking. I learned later it was a technique Camp used for dishing other people, and he had certainly wrong-footed me. I explained to Lord Melchett I was not responsible for the *Private Eye* piece. He dismissed it. But he told me Camp was to be the new public affairs director and asked if I would join the fledgling organisation as number two. I declined. "Send for me," I told him, "when Camp's vivid imagination drops you in the soup, as surely it will."

Maybe I was a bit hasty, but a couple of years later Melchett fired Camp when it became known that he had been lobbying against the new Conservative Trade and Industry Minister, John Davies. There was a major political row, and Camp was shown the door. However, all of this tended to add to my feeling of uncertainty and that it was time to move on.

Monty tried hard to persuade me I was wrong. We were a great team together, he argued. We had the labour and industrial scene sewn up. But I also sensed that I had perhaps overdone it at the *Daily Mail*, and I had outstayed my welcome.

In recent times I became friends with Arthur Brittenden, kept in touch, and visited him at his home in Woodstock, near Blenheim Palace; but in those days I felt, perhaps wrongly, that we did not click. I rather regret that now. He died in May 2015.

Then events moved suddenly very rapidly for me. A small PR company called, and I found myself being berated for failing to respond to an invitation to attend a press conference. My first inclination was to tell this upstart where to go but for some reason I listened as he explained he wanted me to see a wonderful new invention ... a plastic brick.

I thought I had misheard him. But that was what he said. The press conference was to show the brick, and a film of a demonstration bungalow under construction. I could easily have shoved this off to the news desk, but something intrigued me, and I decided to go next morning to the Waldorf Hotel in Aldwych to see these wonder bricks for myself. That decision changed my life.

I found the demonstration suite and, sure enough, two youngsters were busily building a wall using hollow components they called 'bricks'. But what was novel and unusual was the way they interlocked. They turned corners, built cubes, buttresses—or, turned on their sides, half a dozen made a super wine rack! The potential uses, it seemed, were legion. They could be infilled with any material like heat-retaining vermiculite, sand, rubble or timber framing.

I had a photographer with me, and we quickly lined up a picture of the young girl throwing a block of twelve interlocked bricks to the boy. That was a picture that was about to go around the world, exclusively, as I seemed to be the only journalist who had bothered to turn up. Maybe I was not the only one who failed to appreciate the invitation.

The inventor of the plastic brick, Geoffrey Hern, gave me his undivided attention and explained he had patented his new brick idea all around the world and was in talks to manufacture them in large quantity. Two major industrial groups, Guinness and Courtauld, were going to manufacture the bricks in millions.

I have previously mentioned that journalists have a built-in scepticism about inventors and wonder ideas, but try as I might, I could not seem to find a flaw.

Next morning, the *Daily Mail* went to town on page three. It turned over the whole broadsheet page to this splendid new British invention which, according to their industrial editor—me—was going to revolutionise the building industry. The splendid picture of the youngsters throwing the bricks took up half the page.

I was pleased with our exclusive, but even more impressive was the way the story took off. The Central Office of Information, the Government's own news agency, sent the story round the world, and took our photo for worldwide distribution. It meant all three phones in our office did not stop ringing for the next couple of days as caller after caller sought more information. I even had calls from Hong Kong and elsewhere in the Far East, which in those days was quite remarkable.

One caller was the inventor himself, Geoffrey Hern. He wanted to thank me and to invite me to dinner. Normally I would not have bothered but, strangely, on this occasion I was intrigued. I wanted to know more. In fact, if Hern was going to make his fortune, could I get a slice of it?

We met the next evening at Grosvenor House Hotel in Park Lane, where Hern had a suite. He clearly was not stinting and pushed the boat out well.

Hern cut to the quick. He was overwhelmed and needed help. Fast. He liked my style—would I join him? I tried not to be too eager and continued to ask questions. But Hern seemed to have the answers. His venture was backed by the Bank of Butterfield in Bermuda. Most of the investment had gone into pending patents all around the world.

His new company had been named Inca Construction since the Incas were the first people to build without using mortar. That was what we would do with the new plastic brick.

As we talked into the night I told him I had itchy feet and was actually looking around. But I had a good job—the *Daily Mail* even gave me a 2.4 Mark II Jaguar. I had a wife and two children to provide for, and the *Daily Mail* paid me well. Hern waved that aside and named a salary of £5,000 a year and a brand new 3.4 Jaguar S-Type. I must admit Jaguars—after Singers—have always been my soft spot.

Suppose the venture hit the big time—would those who had helped to get it there have a share of the action? Hern pledged that Cyril Smith, his partner I had yet to meet, and I would have a share in the bonanza.

Even so, I did not jump but said I would come out to Stokenchurch, near High Wycombe in Buckinghamshire, to see the bungalow which had been built.

Two days later I turned up at the small industrial plant of Cyril Smith, industrial toolmaker. It was his firm which had produced the steel tools which stamped out the PVC plastic material from which the bricks were made.

I found Cyril an extremely friendly, smartly dressed and sharp businessman. He explained Hern had not been able to make the appointment, but he was happy to show me around and answer all my questions.

We strolled to the back of the factory where stood a large single-storey building made of the new plastic bricks. I walked round tapping the walls and hearing a hollow sound, but the structure certainly seemed strong enough, capable of taking the weight of a heavy tile roof. It was remarkable.

Smith's enthusiasm came through, too. He said, as an engineer, he had never seen anything like it.

I was hooked.

What I did not know at the time was that my enthusiasm affected Smith, too. From where he stood, a cynical, hard-bitten reporter from Fleet Street thought it was a winner. Any doubts Cyril possessed were swept away too. Without realising it, we were convincing each other.

A few days later I resigned from the *Daily Mail*. Nothing actually happened. The editorial floor continued to operate as normal. Lesson number one in life—no one is irreplaceable! Including me.

Looking back, it was the height of irresponsibility. I had a wife, two young children, and a mortgage to pay each month. But my first wife, Shirley, raised no opposition though she would have been quite entitled to do so. Perhaps she had become aware of my itchy feet and did seem to have complete faith in me. After all, she had helped to run the dairy business and knew how we had gone on to sell it and acquire a big bungalow in Sanderstead. So maybe she decided to see where her husband was going to get to this time.

Among my colleagues at the *Daily Mail* there was speculation as to what 'big job' I was going to, or whether perhaps I was going to a rival. When, some days later, it emerged I was going to the plastic brick venture there was incredulity. Monty, Geoffrey Goodman, and some others still tried to talk me out of it, but my mind was made up and it all fitted with a philosophy I had held for some time—when a door opens, walk through. It had certainly worked well in recent years.

A few days later I drove up to Stokenchurch, from where I was to build up the team to run Inca Construction Co. UK. Geoffrey Hern intended to leave it to me. He was going to continue travelling the world, setting up patents to protect his invention and making new contacts. Meanwhile I had a clean sheet, it seemed.

Clearly I needed help. Letters were pouring in as a result of the publicity. The phone never stopped. A great character, Bert, who was a handyman and had had a lot to do with putting up the original structure behind the factory, came to see me. "How do I get a slice of this action," he wanted to know. "I'd like to get involved." I took him on and it was an inspired decision. Bert and I had to find all the things about Inca bricks that the inventor never mentioned, or maybe never noticed. How do you put in a door frame or windows into a plastic brick wall? How does it pass a fire test? What would stop rainwater creeping through the faces of the bricks? As fast as we found the answer to one poser, up came another.

But as we toiled there came a call from the BBC. Would we be interested in putting up a plastic brick bungalow in the studio of *Tomorrow's World,* the premier scientific/technology programme of the day? Would we? I consulted Geoffrey Hern and Cyril Smith. We all agreed it was too good a chance to miss, and would raise the profile of Inca bricks ahead of the planned launch.

These days I go hot and cold at the thought of a building in that studio with absolutely no foundations and supporting a heavy roof. But, quite unfazed, Bert and some of his pals built a magnificent bungalow to a sketch plan provided by an architect, a stylish project which featured a translucent version of the brick for a picture window, and made splendid images. So spectacular was the programme that the BBC switchboard was jammed for several hours. And more and more letters flowed into the sleepy village of Stokenchurch.

But then came a call from the *Daily Mail.* "Would I come back?" I waited to hear those words, but it was not a call from the editorial department. Instead it was the top man in the exhibition department, which ran the prestigious Ideal Home Exhibition at Olympia. "Would we build one of the houses in the show?" Of course we would, I almost blurted out. And again, after some discussion, it was decided to go ahead.

This was a far bigger venture than the BBC programme. For a month the public was to queue to visit our bungalow, bang the walls, slam the doors, and ogle our furnishings, fabrics and fittings. We were carrying an eight-ton tile roof again without so much as a foundation stone to our name.

Over three quarters of a million people passed through the bungalow, admiring its stylish design and asking when they could have one. One of the visitors was the Duchess of Kent, who stayed asking me questions for twenty minutes.

With a team of girls hired for the show, I ran the public side, answering the visitors' questions and demonstrating the versatility of the wonder British invention—the Inca Brick—for which an advertising man I had engaged wrote the slogan 'Inca Bricks slot together, stay forever'. A good slogan but, as it turned out, not exactly true.

Gradually my small team grew, and it was then that I learned how to manage people. Journalists are loners and have little experience in this respect. It is one reason, I believe, why editors so often fail. They have no training in man-management, and yet are suddenly flung in by their proprietors to lead a team of undisciplined people.

The promotion of the bricks went from strength to strength and the queue of callers at Stokenchurch was never ending—even the boss of Polycell products came for a demonstration and suggested they should be called Polybricks! No way, I told him, when actually I should have snatched his arm off.

Guinness and Courtaulds signed contracts with us, and agreed to mass produce Inca bricks and deliver them to main agents. Meanwhile we took £20,000 worth of advertising telling the DIY market that Inca Bricks that slotted together and stayed forever were coming their way.

But there were all kinds of problems. The tolerances of Cyril Smith's machines could be fine-tuned to turn out the product but in mass production that was not possible. And when the bricks were bundled together and strapped there were plenty of breakages.

Then the cost structure began to creak. Compared with a clay brick, our product was not in the same league. I came to realise just how clever those bricks which dated back to the days of Moses really were. If one clay brick did not fit, the brickie just lopped a piece off with his trowel while we needed a foundation laid to engineering tolerances and the bricks had to be perfectly in line to fit. And they cost one shilling and nine pence each compared to sixpence—maximum—for a clay brick.

Then, if an external wall was to be weatherproofed, it needed mastic between each joint—a messy and not necessarily successful method. Time consuming, too. So it went on. Problems piled up. As we solved one, another dropped on my desk. And there was little to be seen of the inventor of this wonder product. Airily, Hern would dismiss any of the problems I reported.

But worse, there were few repeat orders after the initial deliveries. And that was the key. If the product was going to take off, we should have been swamped with new orders. Courtaulds and Guinness switched their machines to other work, the phone went quiet, the post slackened to a trickle. Mostly bills.

Money also got tighter. The bank would give us no more cash. There were wages to pay and nothing to pay them with.

I had moved my wife and children up to Stokenchurch, which meant I no longer had to do a 108-mile round trip each day to and from the office. But fortunately we still had the bungalow at Sanderstead. I told Shirley to pack up and go back home.

Geoffrey Hern had become even more elusive. But then, suddenly, on my desk was a letter from him. I was fired. I was angry, yet relieved. But I felt guilty, too. My little team was on its own, and the future for them was equally bleak. Yet I knew I could do nothing for them as I cleared my desk, and I told the accountant to tell Hern I was keeping his car until he paid me redundancy money.

Had I fallen for an inventor's blandishments? Problems he dismissed with a wave of his hand? Yes, I had almost complete independence, but I had very little input from him. On reflection, maybe the marketing, for which I was responsible, was all wrong. Should the product ever have been a called a brick? It meant it was in direct competition with highly successful, established building materials. Maybe we should have called it internal partitioning.

I had been clever at publicity and getting the product talked about. That was my journalistic experience coming through. What I did not really understand was marketing—getting a product right, launching when it was really ready, at a price which made it profitable.

It was a bitter final lesson. Yes, I had learned a hell of a lot. But I had also found there was lots I did not know. And for a cocky blighter like me, that needed time to digest.

Gradually I realised there was going to be plenty of time to digest all this. The phone rarely rang and no one was rushing to make me an offer to go back to Fleet Street. Monty and Geoffrey Goodman tried to keep my spirits up but they had to get on with their work, too. Monty, in fact, got on with it so well that he won Journalist of the Year in the Press Awards with a series of industrial scoops.

Meanwhile, I had to keep my spirits up and keep my finances going. Fairly quickly, I started to run down my savings, though there was a fillip when Geoffrey Hern's accountant turned up with a cheque for £1,000 to take away the Jaguar. I had it in the bank so fast the ink hardly had time to dry. I started thinking about writing and, looking back, maybe I should have set myself up as an industrial commentator and columnist. But the months had slipped past, and I had to face the fact that I was not now as well known as perhaps had been the case.

Time was going, so were my savings, and I was nowhere near finding a job or deciding what I was going to do.

One irony was the discovery that articles I had written about unemployment pay and helping people change careers were rubbish. I signed on for the unemployment pay which I had written about, suggesting that people would get half their salary, but that was just pie in the sky. If I wanted to get the basic I had to travel five miles regularly from my home in Sanderstead to Croydon to prove I was really out of work. I gave up and actually never drew a penny from the State, even though eventually I was out of work for six months.

So later, when people used to talk to me about workshy people and how easy it was actually to get work, I had at the back of my mind my own experience. Being out of work can be a truly humbling, unpleasant experience, and ever since those days I have never joined the chorus of the ill-informed and uncaring. It is a lot harder than it looks out there.

Then, one day, I spotted a newspaper advertisement seeking a chief information officer for the Department of Economic Affairs. It was a two-year appointment but the pay wasn't too bad. The minister, I was aware, was Peter Shore, with whom I had been on friendly terms when he was head of economics at the Labour Party headquarters. Better still, the Permanent Secretary was Sir William Nield, someone I had got to know and taken to lunch several times. But I knew that after the departure of George Brown from the DEA, the department was in decline. Even so, I decided to chance my arm and give Nield a ring, though I was well aware there were rules in the Civil Service about the way jobs were filled.

Bill Nield took my call and was extremely friendly. He said there was to be an interviewing board which he would be chairing, and while he urged me to apply, he was careful to make no promises and stressed that everything would be done correctly.

I then put a call through to Peter Shore, the minister, and eventually he called me back from the House of Commons. Again, he was careful, but said he needed to replace the current incumbent who was going off to the Ministry of Defence and he hoped I would apply.

So I wrote a strong application and crossed my fingers. I reasoned that I might not be keen on a Civil Service post, but it was a job with some status and it would give me a chance to bounce back. Who knows—after a period in Whitehall, I might be a more attractive proposition for Fleet Street … perhaps leader writer, I daydreamed. Some hopes!

Though the contract was only for two years, at that moment two years seemed like a lifetime of certainty. So I was on for it. A couple of weeks later I heard that I had got the job. Neild told the minister, "You can have a saloon or a sports car. I recommend the sports car." I was in.

CHAPTER 6
Crossing the Bar … into the Civil Service

In the past when I had visited the Department of Economic Affairs, I was used to filling in a visitors' pass application and then being accompanied to meet the official with whom I had an appointment.

Today it was different. For a start, the staff at the entrance gave ME a pass, called me 'sir' and led me to my new office to meet my personal assistant/secretary. She showed me to my desk—totally clear apart from a couple of empty filing trays—and asked if I would like a cup of tea. When I assured her I loved tea, she replied that was excellent news because I was expected to contribute two shillings and sixpence to the weekly tea club. "Oh, and biscuits are extra—unless it's official business," she added without so much as a smile.

I opened a door which I assumed led somewhere and there was the Press Office team—James Currie, Dick Seaman and Henry Klokow.

And if I was pleased to see them, it soon became apparent that they were very pleased to see me.

Elsewhere, I learned, I had a speechwriting team and a unit working on producing a monthly economic newsletter and a punchy tabloid for use on factory noticeboards.

I had known the three press officers as a journalist and was on good terms, but now, of course, the relationship was to be different. They had not had a boss for some months since my predecessor had been promoted to head the information division at the Ministry of Defence, and there was a definite air of drift. Rumour had it that the department's throat was about to be cut—now that George Brown was no longer the First Secretary of State—and the Treasury could see off the upstart

DEA as it had always intended. The Treasury had been rudely shaken about by George Brown's team and disliked intensely the 'creative tension' between the two departments in the economic field. The Labour Government's policy was that the new DEA would concentrate on longer-term planning, try to stimulate industry and build a tripartite consensus between Government, industry and the trade unions, using the National Economic Development Council which had been set-up. The Treasury would concentrate, meanwhile, on keeping the books and looking after the nation's finances, but otherwise was to keep its nose out of wider departmental affairs. That was to be the role of the DEA.

Some of the best and brightest from all across the Civil Service had volunteered to leave their safer departments to staff up the new DEA—they were the brand of civil servants who wanted change and were fed up with drift. But they had taken a career risk, and now were in danger of being marooned if the DEA lacked clout or appeared ineffectual under a weak Secretary of State. That was, of course, Peter Shore to whom I had earlier spoken about the job.

But he was also carrying a nasty label round his neck. The trenchant Tory, Iain MacLeod, in Parliament had labelled Peter as 'Harold Wilson's pet poodle', and suggested he only had the job of Secretary of State for Economic Affairs because of his former close relationship with the Prime Minister. So was there really a job to do for Peter Shore? And for me?

All this was explained to me by James, Dick and Henry. It was gloomy stuff and I did not fail to notice that all the time they talked, the phones in the press office did not ring. Once one of the busiest press offices in Whitehall, the DEA had become akin to a graveyard.

Quite a challenge for someone brand new and unfamiliar with the inner workings of Whitehall. And someone keen to get back in harness and start to make some waves.

Back in my own office I noticed my in tray had started to pile up. Papers began appearing regularly, and at first I read them with interest. Then it dawned on me that if I continued reading this mass of material I would achieve absolutely nothing on my first day. So I let them pile up until Day Three when Dick Seaman asked why they were not getting anything coming through. I was supposed to read what mattered and write on the top sheet who else should see them, explained Dick. "Then put them in your out tray and the messenger will bring them to us. Simple." But why couldn't I just bring them through myself?

Dick gave me a pained look. Almost a wince. He had joined the Civil Service before World War II as a telegraph boy in the Post Office—the lowest rung in the Civil Service career structure. Just as my mother had urged me to do. In those days jobs were hard to come by so lots of people without higher education had started like Dick. He had gone on to pilot Stirling bombers in the war and had flown a number of operational missions. But now he was back flying a Civil Service desk there was no way he was going to let me put a messenger out of work. I took the hint.

I decided it was time to find out more about my new colleagues elsewhere in the corridors of the New Public Buildings, and climbed the two flights of stairs to the main ministerial floor, where Peter Shore was located as were several other ministers like Fred Lee from Newcastle, whom I knew, and Alan Williams from Cardiff, who was new to me. I also went in search of my mentor Sir William Nield to see what ideas he had for helping me raise the profile of the downwardly drifting DEA.

Everywhere I went it was clear they were pleased to see me. Even though most had never met me, they seemed to have heard of, or seen, my name from the *Daily Mail* days. To some it seemed I represented hope that the DEA could be pulled out of its steep dive, that a blaze of new publicity material would get the department back on course.

I listened and asked questions, but I began to suspect that even a much more experienced information man than me would be up against it. I needed the department to be creating policies and solving problems, sending material to Parliament and making waves. With activity like that, yes, I could raise the profile of the department. But I could not make bricks without straw. All I had so far was the clay. Not even plastic!

But one major project was under way. The DEA had spent months building up a National Plan, identifying key sectors of industry and what was holding them back. Businessmen had been put in charge of so-called Little Neddies—committees drawn from industries like engineering or construction—to try and pinpoint the problems preventing growth and the elusive, sought-after exports which would bring in vital overseas earnings to Britain's coffers.

But it had all gone sadly wrong when the Wilson Government had been forced to devalue the currency. Suddenly all that work had been shown to be futile as the pound plunged against the dollar.

Now, it seemed, the economists in the DEA had been toiling away trying to salvage something from the National Plan. We met in Peter Shore's large, beautiful room overlooking St James's Park, and I was surprised to find so many people working on the project. It was fairly well advanced, and the talk was of publication plans, the timetable and how it would all be handled.

And what, I asked, was this plan to be called?

Economic Assessment to 1972!

I did not exactly say 'You must be joking', but I made it fairly clear that was what I thought.

It needed a snappy title, something to catch the eye of a newspaperman. Or what we called 'an angle', I explained. The acid test was to see that title next morning in a headline or, better still, above a major comment piece in the leader column.

The civil servants appeared to be looking down their noses, but Peter Shore took the point. Before he became a minister he had been in charge of research for the Labour Party and knew the importance of catching the public eye.

What did I suggest?

It is at a time like that one needs either a piece of luck or to have thought up something in advance. Fresh to my new role, I had neither. But my survival instincts came to my rescue and I said, "How about 'The Way Ahead'?"

It was not exactly original, but it was sharp and to the point. Peter

Shore liked the idea, as did Bill Nield. We kicked phrases around the polished board room table. Then Shore made a decision. "The Task Ahead—that's it. Perfect."

A few weeks later when we published and had successfully briefed a number of senior journalists from the 'heavies', I was delighted to see the magic phrase 'The Task Ahead' over the main leader in *The Times*. We had made a bit of a splash, and the lift to departmental morale was almost tangible.

So that everyone knew what was going on, I had a noticeboard erected in the staff canteen, and pinned up all the cuttings, both national and regional, for the staff to read.

Having given an indication of what I could do, my next suggestion went down fairly well. While out of work I had got to know Michael Bunce the first producer of a new kind of television programme on BBC called *The Money Programme*. It was quite a trend-setter and had a punchy theme tune.

I contacted Michael, who became a friend and for many years was a colleague as he became the director of press and public relations at the BBC. My suggestion was that I might be able to get his cameras into the department and allow interviews with civil servants which would be a real breakthrough. It may not sound all that original today, but it had never been done before in Whitehall to the best of my knowledge.

Bill Nield, once again, was all for it in the attempt to present the DEA as a department busy with drive and new ideas. Some hopes. Bill interviewed well, as did Campbell Adamson, then an industrial adviser with the department, having joined temporarily from the steel industry. He went on to become Director General of the CBI, and the TV appearance probably did him no great harm.

All in all it was quite a coup for the DEA and led to other departments beginning to open up to the relatively new influence of television which, like it or not, was going to become more and more influential.

A short time later I was summoned to the equally large room of the Permanent Secretary, where I found Bill Nield with a number of officials. Bill explained a problem and asked me to comment.

In those days I was never short of views, ideas or confidence so I dived in, much to the obvious irritation of a dark-haired, thickset, and scowling official whose paperwork he felt I was clearly dismissing.

As we continued to lock horns, Nield looked at his watch and said he had another meeting. "You two go off and discuss this and tell me what you have decided," he ordered.

Out in the corridor I suggested my office. "No, mine—it's on this floor," snapped back my menacing colleague.

We walked in tense silence round the oval-shaped corridor, and he flung open a door on which the label read 'John Lippett, Assistant Secretary'—not a name I knew. Till then. In a bookcase stood two lonely cans of beer with the label 'Only to be opened in an emergency'. As I roared with laughter, Lippett opened the glass door and handed me one of the cans, snapping open the other for himself.

Quickly I reasoned that if this difficult customer had a sense of humour like that he could not be all that bad. So I softened my style. And so did he. John and I became the best of friends, and I learned a lot from a civil servant who believed in doing things—not shuffling paper. Over the years he made lots of enemies but had many good friends too, and an intensely loyal staff. They knew Lippett delivered and liked to be on his winning team.

We forgot the item we had been arguing about as Lippett probed me, and I asked him about the department. He named the people he thought were 'doers' and said they met Friday evenings in a pub appropriately called The Two Chairmen in Storey's Gate, near the department. "That's where we tell each other what's going on and pick up the gossip. Come along, and bring a few quid," he urged.

It was that chance meeting that led me to get on much better terms with some very bright civil servants and make some friends for life— one of whom, Michael Casey, would some years later recruit me to work at British Shipbuilders.

Lippett told me he was engaged on building up a case for new legislation, supported by some very senior British companies, which would smooth the way in which they could explore for minerals, aggregate, even oil in Britain and its surrounding waters. He got knocked back several times on this objective, but eventually persuaded the Government of the day to run with it.

It was in the Two Chairmen that with Lippett, Casey and several others we cooked up an idea to get some movement on the project for a bridge over the River Humber linking Hull to the opposite coast, opening up the east coast area around Grimsby southwards. I was keen because it meant I had a real news story for my minister to announce.

In a by-election in 1963, Barbara Castle had promised that if Labour won the impending General Election they would honour a commitment to build the bridge. Six years later nothing had been done. It was on the back-burner.

We put the thought to Peter Shore, who was enthusiastic, and departmental people went to work. On Humberside, they definitely wanted the bridge, but how did we prove it was really needed and would be an important stimulus to the local economy? Calculations on the cost/benefits were strained to meet the point while various departments like the Board of Trade, Transport, and the predecessors of Environment were stirred.

No one actually *liked* the idea of building a bridge, but on the other hand no one wanted to be seen to be opposed to what had been a party commitment. But where was the funding to come from?

Piece by piece, Lippett, Casey and co. made the case for Peter Shore to take to Cabinet and get his colleagues approval. We also found that Freeman Fox and Partners, the world famous bridge builders, had actually carried out design work—and, yes, they had a sketch. That, I knew, was what Fleet Street newspapers would be demanding if an announcement was to be made.

The fact that an election was due by late 1969 or early 1970 was obviously an important factor. Harold Wilson was shrewd enough to see that an announcement would do Labour no harm, and there would be no time actually to start to build the bridge, so arguments about funding could be deferred. And if the party said it was going ahead, that disarmed critics of Barbara Castle, who argued she had lied back in 1963. Oh, and there were two important Labour seats in Hull …

When the date was fixed for the announcement and we had Downing Street approval to go ahead, I came up with a way in which my minister could be in Hull to make the announcement and be back in London in time to address Parliament. I had discovered the Government had its own planes as part of the Civil Aviation Flying Unit which was part of the Board of Trade. A minister, could, I learned, charter a plane with departmental approval.

That was how it was I flew with Shore, Casey and Lippett and a private secretary to Hull to make some real news. My minister did well, too, back in Parliament. The Opposition did not like it but the Labour Party had their tails up over the Humber Bridge. Next morning the DEA had one of its best days for years in the morning newspapers.

Michael Casey worked on regional development. He had won a Leverhulme Scholarship at the London School of Economics, and if anyone carried a permanent secretary's quill pen in his knapsack it surely was Casey. I could not see then, his failings. One person who knew him said Casey was like a brilliant diamond which knocked your eye out until you held it up to the light and saw the flaw.

Casey was, however, highly rated, and when in 1969 the Catholics of Derry staged the Bogside riots, provoking the Protestant B Specials into running amok in full view of the world's television, James Callaghan, then Home Secretary, insisted something had to be done quickly to alleviate the Catholic pressure. That was how Casey led a team of civil servants to Belfast to cook up a package of measures to buy off the Catholics, particularly those in Derry and in the Falls Road area of Belfast.

I had no idea within a few months I would be following in Casey's footsteps to Northern Ireland.

There was one other memory of the DEA. I suggested to Bill Nield that a departmental tie might help morale. People felt isolated and under pressure, but maybe they could flaunt a tie like a regimental badge, I argued. Nield quite liked the idea so long as it was not going to cost any public money.

I went to my friend who had done the Inca Brick campaign for me, and as I watched he doodled with a pen on his drawing board. Suddenly he tucked a letter D inside the outstretched arms of a big letter E for Economic, and in the lower half of the letter he inserted an A. Then he put a royal crown over the top. It was very smart logo and, picked out in a golden/yellow thread on royal blue cloth, the tie looked the cat's whiskers. We soon ran out and had to order a second batch.

It was not long before DEA staff were seen sporting their ties at meetings around Whitehall. And, indeed, long after the department was wound up, people would wear their DEA ties as a defiant gesture. If one went into a meeting and spotted a tie it was a sign that an ally might be across the table.

We were swimming against the tide, however. Rumours thickened that there was to be a Cabinet reshuffle and the DEA was doomed. People like Lippett and Casey did not seem all that worried. They had seen it before. But whereas they were permanent civil servants and knew whatever happened their jobs were safe, that did not apply to me. I was on a two-year temporary contract which had about a year to run. And I had a wife and two children to feed.

The announcement of a Cabinet reshuffle was scheduled for a Sunday, and ministers were called to Number 10. Peter Shore arranged to keep in touch with me confidentially—this was long before mobile telephones or emails existed—and I arranged to ring him at his home in Putney late on the Sunday afternoon to be briefed. Just as well because all the chief information officers of the Government had been called to a meeting in the Cabinet Office so that we received the official news together. By the time it came through I already knew what was happening, but kept my mouth shut.

The Monday papers were full of the reshuffle, including the fact that the DEA was finished and Peter Shore would be Minister Without Portfolio. In the department there was the nearest I ever saw to a civil servants' rebellion. People felt betrayed by the Wilson Government which had lured them into a totally new, untried department where they had toiled hard. Now suddenly they were to be abandoned.

Across in the bar of the Two Chairmen, a packed meeting gave top officials a pretty frosty reception while former senior people who had gone off to other departments came to commiserate. It was a moment of mourning although, as usual, the beer flowed. And DEA ties were everywhere.

I suggested we should save the brass plate that graced the front door of the Department. When I went with John Lippett to look for it the nameplate had already vanished. But the resourceful team in the establishments department, as it was known, took us down to a scrap bin and pulled out the name plate. Not made of brass but plastic. "Two bob," they demanded—that was two shillings—and Lippett and I paid up.

That night we got it put in the Two Chairmen where it remained for a decade until some heathen took it down and no doubt shoved it in the waste bin again. But for many years it remained the flag under which we gathered on Friday evenings to pool information and remember the good old days of the DEA.

Next morning people were clearing their desks, shredding files and taking down pictures. The DEA was no more and it was rather sad. A third of our staff, like Lippett, were to join the new Ministry of Technology, the regional and planning people were to go to Housing and Local Government and would soon find themselves renamed again as the Department of the Environment. Others were shoved into Agriculture, to the Board of Trade, and indeed, a lot had to swallow their pride and become Treasury civil servants.

Bill Nield and I shook hands on farewell, but little did I know that within two years I would be working with him again—in much more strenuous times. And Peter Shore, with whom I had formed quite a strong bond, went off to be Minister Without Portfolio, a sinecure within the Cabinet Office where his job really was to draft the manifesto for the General Election due towards the end of 1969. Here again, Peter and I remained in contact and years later when I had a house in Falmouth, Peter and his wife Liz would come over from St Ives, where they had a shoreside cottage.

I went to see Harold Griffiths, in charge of information at the Treasury, an ex-*Guardian* man, with whom I had always got along. I told him the team producing the *Economic Bulletin* and other publications for the DEA should be retained. "Just rename it the *Treasury Economic Bulletin*," I suggested. And that was exactly what happened. The unit was saved. Other jobs were found for the rest of my team and I felt more at ease for them.

But in my case the phone did not ring, and I began to think I had burned my boats ... again.

CHAPTER 7
With Sunny Jim Callaghan at the Home Office and Ulster

The phone did eventually ring and it was Trevor Lloyd-Hughes from Downing Street. He had gone into the job as the first press secretary of Harold Wilson leaving his post as political editor of the *Liverpool Daily Post*, but had been elbowed out by Joe Haines. Even so, Trevor retained a role leading the departmental press officers and early attempts at better coordination of Whitehall announcements. It was a bit of a non-job, but it did not prevent Trevor doing me a good turn.

"Jim Callaghan has asked for you," he told me. "Give his private secretary a ring—a chap called Brian Cubbon." Trevor explained that Tom McCaffrey, the well-respected press officer at the Home Office, was going into hospital for a leg operation and would be out of action for about three months. Someone to deputise was needed quickly.

I had known Callaghan as a journalist, though not all that well. Indeed, I had clashed with him while at the *Daily Mail* over the issue of police pay because in Opposition he had been adviser to the Police Federation.

He had been one of the new Labour MPs swept into office in the 1945 landslide, and arrived at Westminster looking smart in his naval officer's uniform. He took a taxi from Paddington to Parliament where the taxi driver refused the fare. "Have it on me, mate, you've earned it."

Callaghan had climbed the greasy pole and held a number of junior ministerial posts before the party was swept into Opposition for what Wilson described, long before so-called 'sound bites' were invented, as 'Thirteen years of Tory misrule'. It was a phrase which stuck.

126

Then in 1967 Callaghan's reputation took a hammering when, as Wilson's first Chancellor of the Exchequer, Labour was forced to devalue sterling.

'Sunny Jim', as he liked to be known, carried the can for the devaluation, and was bundled off to the Home Office, so often a graveyard for ministerial careers, without much of a smile.

But events in Ulster changed all that. With his firm touch on law and order, drawing on his experience in handling police affairs, Callaghan appeared to be on top of events.

He took the initiative in August 1969 to order the Army onto the streets of Derry and Belfast when the Catholics rioted and provoked the vicious reactions of the reservist B-Specials, Protestants to a man. Civil rights had become an issue all over the world, and here it was on our doorstep. Soon the baton thumps on the streets of Northern Ireland were being seen and heard in Croydon, Coventry and Clydeside.

What had been swept under the carpet for years by successive UK governments could no longer be hidden or dismissed as a matter for the local administration of Northern Ireland. If British troops were on the streets armed with sticks and shields, the UK public had the right to know what was going on in their name. And what their Government was doing about it.

In the Province he had been hailed a hero by the Catholics. In the Bogside, the scene of much violence, Callaghan had climbed the stairs of one of the tiny houses and addressed the crowd from an upstairs window. He promised change—the corruption would be cleared up, the police would no longer be biased, justice would be fair, voting would no longer be rigged. It all sounded good that day in the Bogside.

Sunny Jim was cheered by the Catholics, but his message caused concern in other parts of the British Isles. Most UK residents had no idea such a state of affairs existed in their country. Callaghan sensed it, and was determined to seize the moment. He wanted to clean up the problem, but above all he wanted to clean up his own reputation. He did not want to be remembered in politics as the man who ruined the pound sterling. Here was his chance.

And what a time for his press man McCaffry to be carted off to hospital. As they say in politics and in life, when one door closes, another opens. It did for me that day and I was quickly on the phone to the private secretary.

"Ah, yes." Brian Cubbon had heard my name. The Home Secretary certainly did want to see me. Could I be in Whitehall in an hour, where the Home Secretary would pick me up in his car? I could, and I was. But I hardly expected the pace at events would then accelerate.

As I sat in the back with Callaghan, he reeled off all the major problems confronting him and why I was just the man to help him. Flattery often works and I was soon on board.

Jim said there was no time to lose in Northern Ireland before there was IRA violence. I laughed. Surely there was no question of that again. They no longer existed, did they? Callaghan gripped my arm. "You're wrong. I have to move fast before the IRA reacts."

It was then that I discovered the car in which I was riding was heading out towards the RAF station of Northolt, west of London, where an RAF Andover would fly us and several other officials to Aldergrove in Belfast.

I hadn't even had time to tell Shirley I would not be home that night or to pack a few overnight things.

Not to worry, Cubbon had said, all that sort of thing could be taken care of. And sure enough when we arrived at the Conway Hotel a few miles out of the centre of Belfast, in my room was a razor, toothbrush and even a pair of pyjamas.

After half an hour we convened in Callaghan's suite, where we were joined by the ebullient Oliver Wright, destined to rise right to the top of the Foreign Office and resplendent in his trademark red braces. From working in the private office at Number 10 he had been despatched to Ulster to live in a house outside the city where quiet meetings could take place and Wright could build up contacts and assess the situation. I found him impressive and very good fun.

Callaghan's briefing papers for confronting the Cabinet of the Northern Ireland Government had all been prepared, and it looked like being a very long day. Ostensibly, we were responding to the findings of the Hunt Report. Sir John, later Lord, had led the team that conquered Everest. He had inquired into RUC handling of the Bogside and Belfast riots which led to the Army being ordered onto the streets, a decision that was to take thirty years to rescind.

Callaghan would also report on the findings of an inquiry by Sir Robert Mark and Sir Douglas Osmond into the RUC structure and the B-Specials, an organisation of which they were extremely critical. There had been work done on a list of issues which would change the way Northern Ireland was run and would pave the way for ultimate power-sharing.

"I want all six of you civil servants to come with me into the Cabinet Room," said Callaghan. Someone warned that this was unlikely to be welcome to the Ulster politicians. After all, a British Cabinet would never accept it. "That doesn't worry me. I'll say I need to have you available for briefing. But really I want you all there as witnesses," declared Callaghan.

I was beginning to see why Sunny Jim was perhaps not the right description. Shrewd Jim, or maybe Calculating Jim. Certainly he was a good negotiator and he was thinking out the ground ahead.

"One more thing," he told Brian Cubbon. "I want to know the full extent of my legal powers. If this crowd won't play and decides to resign, how do I go about direct rule?"

This was dynamite. Fortunately, events did not force that issue, but though I did not know it at the time, two years later I would find myself very much involved in the imposition of direct rule.

After dinner we turned in, ready for an early start, and shortly after breakfast a fleet of government cars drove us to Stormont Castle, where the Northern Ireland Prime Minister had his office. Cameras flashed as we turned into the gate of Stormont and drove up towards the parliament building astride a hill, surely one of the most spectacularly sited legislative buildings in the world. Not that we had much time to enjoy the view, for in a few minutes we were at the Castle and being ushered into the Cabinet Room.

Nothing was said to indicate we civil servants were unwelcome, and Callaghan briefly introduced each of us, making it clear we were staying. James Chichester Clark, the Ulster Prime Minister, and Brian Faulkner looked closely at me as Jim announced, "This is Keith McDowall, my press adviser."

My surname is used by both Protestant and Catholic families in the Province, usually with a final letter 'a' by the Protestants who had come across to Ulster to take up the offer of free land from King James I. My forebears from Dumfries in Scotland, just sixteen miles across the water, and near the Portpatrick to Larne ferry link, no doubt had taken part in the land grab.

The two Ulster politicians probably decided, with my thick-set, bull-headed appearance, I was more likely to be a Prod than a Mick. In any case they knew they could quickly check me out with their own information staff.

Callaghan sat at the Cabinet table with those of us in his team to his left at a long table so that he could look at us, and we could catch any signal from him.

The negotiations lasted all day as, bit by bit, Callaghan ruthlessly stripped the Ulster Government of its powers, with a suave, charming approach—"This may hurt a bit but don't concern yourself."

The Ulstermen knew they were in a jam. There had been rioting on the streets, the police were exhausted, the world's media was against them—worst of all, this awful man in their Cabinet Room held the purse strings too.

How much more did he want? A hell of a lot.

Housing allocation had to change. The racket by which local authorities gerrymandered the voting locally by placing tenants according to religion rather than need had to go, declared Big Jim. Northern Ireland would have a new housing corporation which would assume control and supervision of all existing and new properties. New building, too.

A report condemned the Royal Ulster Constabulary's handling of the Belfast and Londonderry rioting, the deployment of the

B-Specials, the impression that the police were one-sided, the failure of intelligence—the list was endless. The RUC were to be disarmed, the B-Specials disbanded and a new Territorial Army support unit, the Ulster Defence regiment, to be created.

Callaghan wanted the head of the RUC, Anthony Peacocke, to go, and Big Jim had a replacement ready.

The Ulster politicians gulped. How was this going to go down in places like the Shankill Road area of the city?

Callaghan reminded the Ulstermen that the grant to fund the police came mainly from London and not much from the pockets of their voters.

So it went on until Callaghan reached what he regarded as the really tricky issue. He wanted a Civil Rights Act in Northern Ireland which would guarantee that every citizen, whatever their religion, was entitled to equal opportunity of employment and every aspect of the law.

In effect, no more second-class citizens.

There was silence. And then Brian Faulkner, clearly the most able of the Northern Ireland politicians in the room, broke that silence. As part of an overall package which would bring peace to the streets of the Province, he would accept it. The other politicians round the table nodded in agreement. It was a deal.

As the meeting broke up, Callaghan took me aside to discuss the press handling of the day. I told him we had to keep up the speed, and get out our side of the story as quickly as possible before Protestant extremists could start to unpick the deal. Callaghan, no slouch with the media, agreed. I had noticed a tall, thin, bespectacled man coming in to whisper in the ear of the Ulster Prime Minister and guessed he must be in the same business as me. That was David Gilliland, with whom, later, I would work closely.

Led by David, we all went along a corridor to a large room packed with newspapermen, many new to me, but some I recognised from London. Callaghan took the platform with me at his side.

There was no doubt that Callaghan could be a smoothie when he chose, and he recounted the highly successful day that Northern Ireland had indeed 'enjoyed'. He announced the resignation of Anthony Peacocke, the RUC Chief Constable—known locally as the Inspector General—which had been received with regret, the changes in housing allocation, and the new civil rights plans … the list went on and on, to gasps from the reporters as their notebooks filled.

When I asked for questions, one of the first wanted to know the name of the successor to the head of the RUC. "Ah, I'm glad you asked that because he is right here," revealed Callaghan, and I led in Sir Arthur Young, former head of the City of London police, who had headed the police reorganisation in the Malaysian uprising. I had arranged this flourish with Callaghan, who seized on it as a piece of theatre which would catch the eye of newsmen.

Young assured his questioners that he was in Belfast to take over immediately. He had a number of ideas for his new force, one of which was to replace the RUC's green uniforms with the blue of the typical British bobby. That, said Sir Arthur, would be a symbol of the changes he meant to introduce to the only armed police force in the United Kingdom. And they were to be disarmed immediately!

With the sense of a job well done—and no idea of the reaction that this list of sweeping changes was to provoke—we climbed into our cars and headed back for a wash and brush-up at the Conway Hotel.

An hour later there were drinks with the Northern Ireland Cabinet ministers, who, like most Ulstermen, became extremely friendly when the bottles opened.

One said to me, "Ah, you think you understand the Catholics, but you don't. They will take all these goodies from you, pocket them and then ask for more. Or just change the question—they've been doing that to the English for five hundred years."

An hour or so later I contacted an old friend, Roy Hodson, over from London to cover the story for the *Financial Times*. He was staying with several other London newsmen, and having filed their copy, they were about to go for dinner. I accepted an invitation to join him. We had just placed our orders when a waiter whispered in the ear of one journalist. There was shooting down at the Shankill, the epicentre of Protestant working class culture.

Within a few minutes we were on the scene. Suddenly bullets smacked into a wall behind us. Instinctively I threw myself into a gutter and tried to squeeze lower. It was the first time I had heard real automatic fire. And it was nasty.

Behind me came a chuckle from Hodson.

"Get your arse down, McDowall," he shouted.

"I'm trying—it won't go any lower."

There was a lull and we made a run for shelter where we found an RUC policeman willing to talk. He told us another RUC policeman had in fact been shot dead in the Shankill incident. There might be other casualties. Some policemen were, he knew, injured.

Suddenly, I remembered I was no longer a newsman myself. It was not my job to get the story. I was supposed to be at the side of the Home Secretary, not lying in gutters and getting too close to automatic rifle fire.

I bid farewell to Roy, who was to become a lifelong friend and best man at my second marriage, and I hailed a cab to the Conway hotel where I found a clearly irked Home Secretary surrounded by civil servants waiting for what they called 'a sit rep'—a situation report, I learned—but right then they had no idea what had been happening.

"Where have you been?" demanded Callaghan.

"In the Shankill Road," I replied.

The Home Secretary was obviously about to tear me off a strip publicly, but when I told him a policeman had been killed, he paled. It was his job to protect policemen, not to take actions that got them shot.

Callaghan quickly absorbed the significance and seriousness of the shooting. PC Arbuckle was to go down in history as the first of 300 RUC policeman who lost their lives in the thirty-year IRA campaign which began that night. Yet, ironically, the first shot had been fired by a Protestant at a green-uniformed policeman.

Callaghan quickly decided there would be no return to London next morning; he would have to face the music. And so would his advisers.

In fact, we stayed for four momentous days.

Next day, we visited some hovels in the Shankill—two up, two down, and an outside loo. Callaghan said, "Come with me, Keith," and we went around the back into the Falls Road, the Catholic stronghold, and into a similar house that stood virtually back to back to the one we had left in the Protestant enclave.

"These people actually have much more in common—they both have bad housing and should unite to put pressure on politicians rather than wasting their energies on arguing about the border or Unionism," he said.

Looking back, it was remarkable we could make those visits, for not long afterwards the Army commenced building the so-called Peace Wall which, in fact, created a major division between the Shankill and the Falls which was to stand for more than thirty years.

We also visited Bogside, where six weeks previously, on his first visit, Callaghan had been hailed as a saviour by the Catholics. Not this time. It was tense as we walked down the narrow streets. Above us the high wall surrounding the castle offered a magnificent vantage point for a would-be assassin.

The RUC security team kept scanning the heights and their fingers near the triggers as we moved along the road, led by Stormont MP John Hume, an articulate Catholic who was to pay a major role in the years ahead—and show great courage in trying to combat the extremism of the IRA. Eventually he won the Nobel Prize for his work.

Wearily, we returned to Belfast by helicopter.

Back at the Conway Hotel, Callaghan suddenly rounded on me in front of the rest of the civil servants. Well, he demanded, what was my advice? What did I propose should be done about the media?

It was probably a mark of my inexperience. I had assumed he and I would have a private discussion and evolve a plan. But here, quite clearly, I was on the spot.

There was no avoiding a full press conference plus television and radio, I told Callaghan. It was face the music time.

"Very well," he replied. "Fix it up."

After he left the room, Robin North, an assistant secretary who had for years been in charge of the once sleepy offshore islands like the Isle of Man, the Channel Islands and indeed Northern Ireland, sidled up to me.

"Keith, you have just tasted a bit of the Jim Callaghan method of running things, a lot of honey and a bit of stick," he said sympathetically. "You just got the bit of stick—across the knuckles."

It was a very apt summing up, and went some way to soothing my intense irritation at my humiliating treatment.

For the press conference I gave Callaghan what later became known a sound bite. We journalists were always looking out for one, long before TV came along—we called it an angle.

I scribbled on a piece of paper for the Home Secretary 'The No Go areas must become Will Go areas'—in other words, neither the RUC nor indeed the public were to be barred from certain areas just because the local tribal leader had decreed it.

Callaghan gave a brilliant, confident and authoritative news conference, and I was pleased to see the lead story of the *Belfast Telegraph* headed 'No-Go areas must be Will-Go areas'. Got that right, then, I thought to myself.

Before departing, Callaghan decided he should meet the Rev. Ian Paisley, a tub-thumper in a dog collar who had been whipping up the Protestants into an anti-Catholic frenzy. Some priest.

He arrived at the Conway Hotel, ushered in, I noticed, by a bevy of newspapermen obviously tipped off. Not by us!

As he flayed the Catholics, Callaghan tried to cool it. "Come, come, Dr Paisley, we're all children of God," said Sunny Jim.

"We are not. We are all children of wrath—Ephesians 2:3," snapped back Paisley.

Callaghan soon decided he would not get far trying to sweet talk 'the turbulent priest', as the *Daily Mail* had named Paisley, and swiftly brought the meeting to an end.

In recent times Paisley was said to have softened but I don't buy that. He had a lot to do with first stirring up the sectarian clash in the province and, in my view, had blood on his hands. At the same time he happily drew a salary as a Euro MP, as did his wife, and he was also a paid Westminster MP.

When one attended a service at Paisley's church, the collection was made by 'heavies' carrying plastic buckets, so anyone not dropping in a banknote was eyeballed. Where did all that money go?

As we flew back to London we were a lot less jaunty than when we had flown out. Brian Cubbon, the private secretary, was scribbling furiously—writing a statement the Home Secretary would give on the Belfast situation to Parliament later that day.

I was rapidly beginning to grasp that the mandarins in the Home Office operated at least a gear above, if not two, compared with the pace of my former department. "Any ideas?" demanded Cubbon. I came up with a couple of thoughts, one of which he incorporated in his brief. It was all finished by the time we touched down at RAF Northolt, where cars waited to whisk us to Whitehall.

Little was I to realise that not far in the future I would become very familiar with that airport and the journeys to and from Belfast.

Back in the office Dennis Trevelyan, then an undersecretary in the police department, with whom I was to become firm friends and later take sailing, put his head round my door. Each person in the team with the Home Secretary was being asked to write a report from their aspect of the Northern Ireland situation. Could I do one about the press handling?

I certainly could. I wrote that the press department in Stormont needed a major shake-up and the person in charge, a man named Montgomery, who had been on the civilian information staff of the army and seemed very thick with the Northern Irish Civil Service hierarchy, should give way to someone who knew the media and was a political animal. That man, I wrote, was Tom Roberts, then based in the Ulster Office in Mayfair, engaged on trade promotion, which hardly seemed relevant now with British troops on the streets dodging petrol bombs.

A few weeks later Tom called me to 'thank' me for assisting his rapid job and lifestyle change for him. But he knew I was right and told me so. So he went back to try to combat the rising efficiency of the IRA propaganda machine.

In Whitehall it became even clearer why Callaghan had asked for me in the absence of his own man in hospital. In the six weeks I worked for him we went from one crisis to another, and seldom had the luxury of only dealing with one at a time. But Callaghan seemed quite unperturbed.

Home Office officials learn to move quickly. The department has a slow-moving reputation—not true. Some of the most able civil servants I met were in that department and they were well aware of, and switched on to, events around them.

Over the rest of my time with Callaghan, we faced up to the implications of the largest prison riot in the country at Parkhurst on the Isle of Wight; the threat of a national strike by Britain's firemen and the introduction of the so-called Green Goddesses—worn-out vehicles left over from World War II which had been stored at an old airfield; exchanging a pair of top-level Russian spies for one of ours; and grappling with a report of the Boundary Commission which was going to torpedo up to twenty constituencies—the majority, Labour— on the eve of a general election. It was heady stuff.

Prison rioting has become more of a feature of our daily news schedule as the decrepit, worn-out Victorian buildings are forced to house double the number of inmates they were built to contain. In those days the issue was swept under the carpet. I took the view that no taxpayer was going to be persuaded to fund new prison building until he realised how dreadful it was behind the high prison walls. There were some new prisons being built, and on one occasion I accompanied Callaghan to open one called Coldingley, near Woking, Surrey. Prisoners were working in modern, factory-like conditions, making signs for motorways and trunk roads. Callaghan and I agreed that this kind of environment where prisoners could produce items really wanted by society and be paid for it, made more sense than having them sewing mailbags or wasting hours, in their cells.

It was while at Coldingley that I met Philip Woodfield, then in the prison department, and to play a key role in making contact with the IRA who was to be another close colleague of mine in the months ahead.

With the simmering prison situation I made it my business to get on good terms with the new Home Affairs man at *The Guardian*, Martin Adeney, with whom I formed a lifetime friendship. When Gus Macdonald of Granada's irreverent *World in Action* TV current affairs programme asked if he could visit a prison, I did not immediately give him the anticipated thumbs-down.

Instead I went upstairs to see Sir Philip Allen, the scholarly permanent secretary (who had a remarkable resemblance to Fernandel, the French comic film star). I put it to him that the time had come to encourage greater public awareness of the workings of the prison system. He took a few soundings and then gave me the go-ahead.

When I told Macdonald I could arrange for him to have an official visit to Wandsworth prison he was amazed, but quickly grabbed the offer lest it be withdrawn. Years later, Gus, after a meteoric career in television, went into the House of Lords and for a while was a minister in the Labour Government, where no doubt he discovered what it was like to be on the receiving end of the media rather than dishing it out.

The Parkhurst riot was in a secure block where some of the most evil men in Britain were imprisoned. But the restrictive 'lock down' was so oppressive that in the end the inevitable explosion occurred, and large parts of Parkhurst prison were extensively trashed.

William Pile, later to be the permanent secretary of the Education Department, was in charge of the subsequent inquiry, and I worked closely with him to get out the report and urge the changes Pile judged necessary, quickly, in Britain's prison system. They were, it seemed to me, a few steps in the right direction, but there was a long way to go. Almost half a century later not much progress has been made. In fact, in some respects, it has gone backwards.

One day my phone rang, and I was asked if I would 'step up' to see the Home Secretary. When such a call came one dropped everything and sped up the two floors to the ministerial offices. I was waved straight through the outer office and into the impressive lofty room of the Secretary of State. Callaghan was seated at the head of his long boardroom table, but I did not recognise many of the officials seated around him.

"Ah, Keith," said a breezy Callaghan. "We need your help."

And, to my amazement, he introduced Michael Hanley, then number two in MI5, the home security service answerable nominally to the Home Secretary, but allowed—or assuming—a large degree of autonomy. The rest of the team were introduced, but their names passed me by. I was still pinching myself that a former Fleet Street journalist like me was in the same room as the top brass of MI5. And being introduced!

They must want something pretty badly, I felt.

They did. They wanted to get the ringleaders of the Portland Spy Ring, Peter and Helen Kroger, out of the country in exchange for a British spy, Gerald Brooke. And they wanted to achieve it without a Fleet Street 'circus' which they believed would antagonise the Russians.

"What can you do, Keith?" asked Jim, rather as one addresses a magician.

I had to think quickly. I said it would depend how candid we were prepared to be with the press. If we were willing to give reporters plenty of facts and, above all, colour, it might just be possible to persuade journalists it was in their interest to go along with it. They would know it was going to be extremely difficult to get those kind of facts with a tight security cordon around the Krogers as they were virtually smuggled out of the country.

The Home Secretary told me to go off with Hanley and his colleagues and work out a plan.

I found him extremely good to work with, quite unstuffy and willing to listen. I wanted all the colour, I emphasised, from the moment the Krogers were reunited at a London prison and prepared for the flight home to Moscow. What they ate for breakfast, what they wore, what they said when they first met. What might seem trivial was important to me. I knew I needed to have enough facts to answer any question thrown at me. Hanley and his team ensured I had everything I needed, or could think I needed. Then I went to work.

Each newspaper was invited to send a senior crime man to the Home Office. The invitation was made extremely vague, but never before had such an intriguing call come from the department, so the bait worked.

I told the packed room that the spies who had been stealing secrets about Britain's first nuclear submarine HMS *Dreadnought* were being exchanged for a British spy. That was a big story and I had to hold them in the room; it was tempting to dash for a telephone outside in Whitehall.

I then explained that the Home Secretary was prepared to authorise me to give the press every fact and figure they wanted in response to a deal: no attempt was made to chase the car taking the spies to the airport, and there were to be no airport scenes. In other words, the newsmen were being asked to show some restraint.

I pledged that everyone would be treated fairly, and no journalist would be shown any individual preference or put at a disadvantage.

It took some time, but gradually there was an understanding that they would agree.

On the morning the exchange went ahead and by 8.30 a.m. I had plenty of colour. I knew how each of the Krogers had been awoken, allowed to dress in their own clothes. They had each had a decent breakfast too—probably the best they had ever enjoyed as inmates of HM prisons.

The flow of information was fed to the journalists, and the pact seemed to be holding. We gave updates steadily through the morning as the Krogers' car sped to Heathrow. There was no great skirmish outside the two prisons, and no scramble at the airport as the passengers filtered through to board their plane.

So far so good. I watched BBC television as the plane took off, and felt at last I could uncross my fingers. It seemed to have worked.

Michael Hanley phoned to express his thanks for what he reckoned had been a good operation.

But next morning it did not look so good. Everyone had kept their word, except the *Daily Express*. They had booked a seat on the plane to Moscow, and described how the Krogers enjoyed the food and chatted on their journey to Moscow. No other journalist was on board, although some Moscow correspondents of the Western press tried to get a word with the spies on their arrival.

Overall, the experiment of seeking cooperation with the press had succeeded. I blamed myself for not alerting the airline and asking them to watch for newspaper attempts to get on board.

But in the main MI5 seemed content, and my dealings with them were to stand me in a good position when our paths crossed again quite soon. Oh, and Jim Callaghan never mentioned the matter again. I contented myself with the thought that I would have heard all about it if my gamble had failed.

Another in the list of urgent problems facing Callaghan in the run-up to the 1969 General Election was the threatened national strike by firemen. Why on earth was the Home Secretary involved with firemen? It so happens that among the ragbag of responsibilities of the Home Office like the police, prison officers, drugs, mad dogs and fireworks, the department was also the place where Her Majesty's Fire Service Inspectorate was located and where firemen's pay and conditions nationally were overseen.

So in theory even this issue could end up on the desk of the Home Secretary. Of course it could never happen, until it did in 1969. Even so, the wise old birds in the Home Office had kept a card or two up their sleeves. On a disused airfield - Moreton-in-Marsh in Gloucestershire - they had stored a fleet of wartime emergency fire engines. They were to become known as Green Goddesses. In reality, these unroadworthy rust buckets were Bedford fire pumps which went out of service in 1956. But the Home Office mandarins were great believers in the theory of 'just in case'. And this time they were right.

I got a 'can you come up' call from Callaghan's private secretary, and was shown into the Home Secretary's room where he sat surrounded by civil servants. At the other end of the table was a familiar face—there sat Terry Parry, general secretary of the Fire Brigades Union, and some of his colleagues. He gave me a welcoming smile. I knew Parry from my reporting days to be a decent cove and not the usual left winger the FBU generally elected. But though he was big in stature I was not sure he would stand tall if his members were shouting the odds.

I soon picked up that Callaghan was in negotiating mode of sweet reasonableness as he manoeuvred Parry into a corner. There was a very final offer on the table and, as every union chief knew, the Government was itself in a corner. There was no more money available, and a general election loomed.

"You know what that means, Terry," soothed Big Jim. "I don't have to tell you." Parry knew exactly. A Labour Government going to the country with runaway inflation was doomed. And that was no use to the unions in general.

But the union leader had to have something to take to his executive. He could not go back empty-handed, he wailed. Callaghan produced a small rabbit from his conjuror's hat. He pledged to use his good offices to put the firemen's point of view, and would do his level best if they would lift the threat of a strike and resume normal working.

Not much there, I thought. But then I heard Callaghan say, "Now, Terry, you go off and take Keith here with you. He will give you all the help you need to get this across. You can count on him."

I looked at Sir Philip Allen, the permanent secretary, and whispered, "Is this alright?"

"No, it is not!" he told me. But he said nothing to the Home Secretary nor gave me a straight order. As a civil servant, albeit a temporary, what was I to do?

Within minutes the meeting broke up and we went our separate ways, but Parry hung on to me as we went down to the street and got into his car. Within minutes we arrived at a delegates' meeting, and Parry gave a detailed report culminating in 'the pledge' Callaghan had given.

"This gentleman here, Mr Keith McDowall, who some of you may know, can vouch that I am telling you, first-hand, what I was told. That's right, isn't it, Keith?" I nodded my head vigorously in confirmation. No doubt at all in my mind, I assured the firemen, and then I left the meeting before some industrial reporter woke up to the fact that a temporary civil servant was about a million miles out of his territory. And depth.

But it worked. After a couple of hours the Press Association reported the strike was off.

In theory the Civil Service is non-political, and pays no attention to the political climate in which it operates. In practice, those at the top of the pile are highly sensitive to the political environment in which they work. In 1969 we knew the general election could not be far away. Having scraped into power in 1964, Harold Wilson had managed to cling on with a majority of three, but as soon as he saw his chance he went to the country in 1966 and was returned with a 96 majority. Soon he had to face the electorate again.

The economic battle had been tough after devaluation of the pound, but Wilson's Government had shown itself reasonably competent, and there seemed a good chance Labour would win again if Wilson got his timing right. But no nasty surprises. If there were any lurking, ministers knew they had to resolve them—or bury them.

Jim Callaghan had a big one right on his desk. There had been some speculation in the newspapers that it was in fact a time bomb ticking away.

It was the report of the Boundaries Commission, which keeps all parliamentary constituencies under review and ensures that they are roughly comparable in terms of registered voters. But as manufacturing changed, pits ran out of coal, or perhaps farming declined, there was always the chance that one constituency needed to be topped up by moving in some voters from a neighbouring seat. Or perhaps merging one parliamentary seat into another.

In this case, the Commission report recommended changes which would hit the Labour Party hard. About twelve of its safe seats could become marginal. And twelve seats, Callaghan knew, could decide the outcome of the next election.

He called a meeting round his big table, and all the senior Home Office officials, including the Permanent Secretary, were there. I took the seat at the other end of the table, furthest from him, but in direct line of sight of the Home Secretary. Since I had worked in Whitehall I had decided it was always a good idea to sit in the same place so that the minister could see my face: if I did not like, or believe, what I was hearing, a frown, a grin or a nod often told the politician what I was thinking.

Callaghan went round the table taking views on whether to place the Commission report before Parliament or whether it could be allowed to collect some dust.

The officials made it quite clear the report should be published as soon as possible to give Parliament time to digest it, and then to debate the findings before an election. The projected loss of a dozen seats was not their concern.

"But suppose," asked Callaghan, "the Home Secretary was to take the view that he needed more time to study it?" 'No way' indicated the Men from Whitehall. The Home Secretary was simply the point of reception for the Commission's report. It was his duty to pass it to Parliament at the earliest opportunity.

"But suppose I don't. What can happen?" asked Callaghan, with just a trace of a smile. "Can they put me in the Tower?"

There was no actual sanction that could be applied to the Home Secretary. He could not be forced to publish. And he could not be sent to the Tower of London.

Callaghan looked at me. "Now put your hands over your ears, you civil servants. Keith, can I get away with it?"

It was so blatant that I almost gasped. It perfectly illustrated the difficult role the information man in Whitehall has to play, treading a careful path between the administrators and the politicians. In for a pound, I thought, and spoke up.

"I reckon you can, Home Secretary. There will be a row in Parliament and you will be accused of all kinds of chicanery. But your standing is good in the country after your achievements in Northern Ireland, and I think the public will give you the benefit of the doubt."

That was what Jim Callaghan wanted to hear. He instructed the department to sit on the report, and explain away the delay with the need to examine all the options and implications of the Commission's findings ... blah, blah.

The report stayed under wraps, but it made little difference. A few months later, in June 1970, Wilson called a general election, the result of which he seemed to have in the bag. It was a magnificent summer and he fought a low-key election. 'Let's just carry on as we are doing' was the line.

It did not work. The voters decided to give the new Tory leader, Edward Heath, a chance, and chucked out the Labour Party. And several of the seats for which Jim Callaghan had risked his reputation were lost, too.

But by then I had departed the Home Office. Tom McCaffry came back from sick leave and I started to pack my bag. Callaghan had another idea. Why not stay in his private office as his political adviser? he suggested.

I don't think it had ever crossed his mind that I was a temporary civil servant and that I was not a member of any political party, let alone Labour. But it wouldn't work, I told him. There wasn't room for two cooks in the kitchen, and if I was, McCaffry would be pretty brassed off.

I was lucky. If I had taken up Callaghan's suggestion, I would have been out on my ear when Edward Heath arrived. As it happened, a whole new series of adventures was to open up for me when the Tories came in.

Some months later, when I was walking out of Westminster, I saw Callaghan sitting in a parked car and he called me over. "What was the name of that policeman who was shot in Belfast when we were there?" I had never forgotten the name of Arbuckle, and Jim wrote it down.

Some months later his very readable book on Northern Ireland,

A House Divided, was published. Arbuckle's name was there. But though numerous officials were mentioned, my name was not among them. Which reminded me what I knew instinctively as a journalist: that one can get close to politicians, but not too close.

Tom McCaffry did stick with Callaghan, and later, when Labour won back power, joined him first at the Foreign Office and then at Number 10 when Big Jim became Prime Minister. Tom was awarded a knighthood. But when the Tories swept in under Mrs Thatcher, McCaffry's Whitehall career was over.

On the other hand, in 1969 after that period in the Home Office I knew I was a much more experienced and competent operator. I had learned a lot which was going to be extremely valuable in the years immediately ahead—and further on. Even so, once again, in my short Whitehall career, I was without a job, a title and, indeed, without a department. I was being paid, but hanging about on leave can soon become very boring, I discovered.

CHAPTER 8
Disney, Woad, Trade and Trips with Roy Mason

For a week or so I was indeed kicking my heels. Nowadays it is known as 'gardening leave' but that term had not then been invented. In any case the British public would have been shocked to find a public servant being paid for not actually working flat out. But the phone did eventually ring. It was Trevor Lloyd-Hughes again from Downing Street.

Roy Mason, the president of the Board of Trade, was not happy with the public relations support he was getting. There was a big team of press and publicity people at the department, but to Roy's chagrin his name rarely appeared. In opposition, when Roy had handled his own publicity, he was seldom out of the newspapers, but now he was missing the intoxication of daily publicity.

As the industrial man at the *Daily Mail* I had enjoyed good relations with Mason, particularly when he was Shadow postmaster general. I was not keen on generating his kind of personal publicity, but anything was preferable to a repeat of the silence of the closed-down DEA.

I was told to contact Roy Croft, the minister's private secretary, and was flattered to learn from him that my call was anticipated. When could I come? Straight away—but first it appeared I had to make contact with the office of the BoT permanent secretary, Sir Anthony Part, known to be a bit of a nitpicker. But a high flyer.

Part seemed pleased to see me, but pointed out there was already a Head of Information—a self-important type named Neville Shepherd. I had assumed he would be going and I would be taking his place but Part ruled it out. Though he admitted no one was enamoured with

Shepherd's performance, no complaints or adverse comments had in fact been placed on his file. So Shepherd could not be moved, let alone sacked.

Part suggested I should become Joint Chief Information Officer with Shepherd, which sounded like a recipe for disaster, but reluctantly I accepted. After all, I had the access and goodwill of the minister and his private office. I would soon demonstrate the difference between new and old, I told myself.

The information team worked on the ninth floor at Victoria Street offices, one floor below the ministerial team, where Roy Mason had a magnificent suite of offices overlooking Westminster Abbey and the Palace of Westminster. The last time I had seen that view was when, as a reporter, I had interviewed Douglas Jay, then President of the Board of Trade under Harold Wilson. I did not realise that the view would become quite familiar to me.

It did not take long to establish some rapport with the press officers, who were keen to have a professional lead after the cautious approach of Shepherd. But Ray Tuite, the deputy, who had once worked on the *Daily Mirror*, grumbled that it was difficult to be deputy to two men. He had a point. Gradually, though, Ray came round and became one of my best and most loyal friends in Whitehall. And a good deputy.

In those days the Board of Trade was absolutely huge. It oversaw everything from trade negotiation to insurance, financial regulation, HM Coastguard, civil aviation, air traffic control, shipping, energy— and just about every important industrial statistic like the crucially important monthly export trade figures, a political hot potato of that era.

Once my name was circulated, an avalanche of papers flowed into my in tray, most of them very interesting indeed. But deciding which to prioritise was overwhelming. There was a huge staff at the department, and no fewer than ninety undersecretaries—major general level in the army—each with a 'division' of civil servants reporting to them. I decided I needed to find a get-up-and-go type like John Lippett at the DEA. I noticed that the name Fell appeared on the circulation list of a number of the juicier documents, so I walked around the building one lunchtime until I found his office.

"May I come in?" I asked. "I'm the new chief information officer."

"I've been waiting for you for twelve years!" said Bob Fell. What had brought me to see him? I explained I kept noticing his name on the circulation lists of important memos.

Fell, who went on to become chief executive of the London Stock Exchange, and then set one up in Hong Kong, smiled. "That's very smart of you," he said.

He explained that there were several other names that would appear frequently at the head of departmental memos even if the subject had nothing to do with them. "That's because there are about twelve people who make real decisions in this department, and we keep in touch."

Bob Fell's theory is something I have ever since applied in all kinds of spheres. Basically, there are some people who want to make things happen, while the rest are content to let others take the tough decisions and keep their heads down. They get paid just as much as the 'worker bees' with no hassle.

As Sir Ken Stowe, another permanent secretary once put it to me, "There are two types of civil servant: the four fifths who say 'We can't' and the one fifth who say 'Why can't we?' I belong there."

Bob Fell explained that he brought this team together every Friday lunchtime in his office to kick ideas around and report on developments. I was invited to join them. Suddenly I had cracked the code. I was on the inside and, apart from having access to the material coming up to the minister's office, I would be involved in the targeting and timing of material down in the engine room.

One early project was the plan to build the National Exhibition Centre in Birmingham. The company which ran Earls Court and Olympia thought it had the Government-supported project in the bag, so naturally the new exhibition halls would be in London.

Not if Bob had his way. Apart from the fact that he himself hailed from Cumberland, he felt strongly the proposed NEC should be at the centre of the country, at a junction on the new motorway network and have its own station on the new electric train line linking London and the North West, but it was going to need strong backing from the departmental ministers. That was where I came in.

I marked the cards of the private secretary, Roy Croft, who agreed we should put Roy Mason in the picture. Officially, he knew nothing of it until the papers had wound their way up to the tenth floor via Anthony Part's office, as they did eventually.

But by then Mason was fully on board. As a former miner from Barnsley in Yorkshire, Mason knew the importance of getting major projects out of London and to the regions, so we were pushing at an open door.

When subsequently an announcement of the go-ahead for the Birmingham location was agreed by the Cabinet, and Roy Mason was to make a statement to Parliament, I came up with a quote for him to use: "This House must get away from the idea that everyone north of Watford wears woad," he told MPs. There was a roar of approval—the NEC was to be built in the Midlands. That quote still nestles in the Hansard reports of Parliament from 1969.

I was in close touch throughout the construction of the NEC with the Birmingham Chamber of Commerce, which had organised the project. They were proud that it was completed on time and to budget. It was such a good news story but I could never get anyone in Fleet Street interested. It was a long way from London!

As I have mentioned, the Board of Trade was quite remarkable for the range of its responsibilities.

The Queens Award for Industry and Technology came under the department, and studying the lists of awards I worked out that Imperial Chemical Industries (ICI) and Rolls-Royce had each won five in succession. No other British companies could match that success, so I put up the idea that we should use the front hall of the department's headquarters in Victoria Street to show off these products, and hold an official reception to publicise them—and our department.

Roy Mason was all for it, but the permanent secretary, Anthony Part, noted on my minute, "I have always felt the front hall has remained pleasantly uncluttered." Somehow, though, we got round him, and the front hall became a showcase for the best of British, seen by the thousands of home and overseas business visitors.

At the reception, I have never forgotten how when I mentioned carbon fibre to two Rolls-Royce executives, both seemed to be thrown. My journalistic antennae told me I was on to something—but, hey, I was a gamekeeper now, no longer a poacher.

It gradually emerged that the jet engine maker was in big trouble with the carbon fibre turbine blades, which kept disintegrating. So much so that the company was forced to revert to titanium, which meant a delay for overseas customers. Titanium was tough and durable but not as light, and therefore unable to give Rolls-Royce engines the power they sought. Eventually of course, they overcame the problem in the customary Rolls-Royce manner of no fuss and no publicity. But it led to major financial problems and the amazing decision by the Heath Tory Government to nationalise the company. But that was later.

Mason had been told by Harold Wilson to get out and promote British trade around the world. Roy loved overseas travel and needed little urging. While I was with him we travelled to California, Hong Kong, Singapore, Malaysia, Bangkok, Burma, the Philippines, and across Europe—to places like Bucharest, Vienna and Oslo. Twice a month we would lead the British delegation to EFTA, the Free Trade Area of those outside the six-nation group which had formed the European Common Market.

We usually met in Switzerland and had a good time building stronger ties with the Spanish, and the Scandinavian countries like Sweden, Norway and Finland. Most of them had stayed on the sidelines waiting for Britain to bite the bullet and join the EU. Then they would be in behind us like a shot before the door slammed shut.

Although it meant I was often away from home, I certainly had some wonderful travel with Roy Mason. Memories come back of swimming with the two Roys—the minister and his secretary—in the magnificent rectangular pool at the British High Commissioner's residence in Kuala Lumpur, Malaysia. A former Tory politician made high commissioner in the post-war years, probably around the time of the terrorist uprising, insisted on the construction of the pool as a condition for taking the job, such was the humidity. It's all gone now, but it really was a last taste of the way the British Raj once operated.

On another occasion, in Manila, Mason and the team paid a visit to the rice proving and testing station where the new RU8 wonder rice, forerunner of today's genetically modified variety, was under development. It was going to boost rice production throughout the world, was an exciting prospect, and might work wonders for the poor rice farmers, up to their waist in water almost daily in the paddy fields.

Mason went off with the ambassador to meet Ferdinand Marcos, the dictator, but it was felt the press man had better remain on the sidelines. Pity, as I might have caught a glimpse of all those shoes it later emerged his wife, Imelda, had stashed away.

In California I persuaded Mason to join me in a lift at the side of the skyscraper hotel which soared upwards to the Top of the Mark bar on the roof of the Mark Hopkins Hotel in San Francisco. "Got any more bright ideas?" demanded a queasy Mason as he looked nervously down at the sidewalk. As it happened, I had. I told him I wanted to visit Disney World when we got to Los Angeles.

"Be your age, McDowall—Battersea bloody Fun Fair!"

I assured Mason that what was then the first new Disney operation was worth seeing, a view fully supported by the British Consul, who was a dynamic salesman for Britain. He even laid on a chauffeur-driven Rolls-Royce to take us there on the Saturday.

We found Disney spotlessly clean with everything built a little smaller so that children were not overawed by the buildings. I little realised that one day I would go there fairly frequently with my own grandchildren, Tom, Fiona and Lucy, who were brought up in Los Angeles.

I got the minister to take a ride through the Pirate's Grotto, but terrified him when I shouted, "Put your head down—*Daily Mail* photographer!" Mason went white when he realised the possible headline: "British Trade Minister in Pirates' Lair—at taxpayers' expense." He was not too enamoured with my sense of humour but the private secretary could hardly contain himself.

As we travelled around the world, I took with me with my Olympia portable typewriter. I knocked out speech lines for Roy Mason, who picked them up quickly and put them across at meetings with British businessmen or with the press. We worked well together. But suddenly it all came to an end. Harold Wilson called a general election in June 1970 and it appeared he had it in the bag.

Roy Croft and I bid farewell to Mason at the Victoria Street entrance of the Board of Trade and said we would see him when he got back. It never crossed our mind that Labour was about to lose.

For me, it was the first general election when I had nothing really to do. Normally in newspapers it was a time for maximum effort, but as a civil servant closely involved in policy I was supposed to be stay above the fray. Frustrating. So another spot of gardening leave.

There was one crucial moment in the campaign when I was compelled to take a role. In those days the monthly trade figures were of maximum political importance—Britain's future seemed to hang on how well it was doing in visible exports and how little it imported. Unfortunately, in the middle of the election, in came the figures for importing three Boeing 707s and one of the new Jumbo 747s. Britain was in the red!

This needed a non-political explanation, and I was ordered by Downing Street on the instruction of Harold Wilson to write and sign a letter to *The Times*. Very unusual, but I did as I was told and the letter duly appeared. Come to think of it, no other civil servants—Sir Anthony Part, the permanent secretary, for example—were pushing themselves to sign it.

In hindsight it was not very smart. I should have refused. But I knew Wilson, I knew Mason, and they were all going to resume office after the votes were in … weren't they? Wrong. Wilson was out, and Edward Heath stood on the steps of Downing Street proclaiming victory for the Tories. I could be in for a bumpy ride.

At first the departmental structure carried on as before, and we welcomed to the department a charming Scottish MP, Michael Noble, who became President of the Board of Trade. He seemed as surprised as we were that he got the job. When he sat down to be briefed he made it clear he had not expected to be in office at all and he did not feel it would last for long. It turned out later that the new prime minister had discovered he had no Scot in his first cabinet and told his secretary to, "get Noble." But apparently there were two of that name representing Scottish constituencies and they got the wrong one. Encouraging.

For a while, though, the Board of Trade continued to operate, and I got on well with the new Trade minister. He had a number of investments, one of which was in sea fishing. While touring a Scottish port one day he noticed the fishermen cast aside small round prawn-like catches—"They're queenies, we call 'em—not worth bothering about," he was told. But Noble scooped up a bucketful and took them home. "Not easy to cook but once we found out how to do it, they were delicious," he told me. So Scotland's equivalent of Dublin Bay prawns were launched, and today queenies supply a lucrative and rewarding market.

Down the corridor on the ministerial floor was a new Minister for Aviation, the redoubtable Fred Corfield, who knew his field well, having specialised in aeroplane matters in opposition. Fred had an ambitious policy. He wanted to adopt an inquiry report which had recommended what he defined as 'The Second Force'—a merger of private enterprise airlines capable of providing competition to the state-owned monopolies, British Overseas Airways Corporation (BOAC) and British European Airways (BEA).

No one else seemed too enthusiastic, but when Fred brought the ailing British United Airlines and Caledonian Airways together in his room, it looked as if a deal might come off.

It was always my aim to get on good terms with the private secretary, and in this instance it was a likeable, lanky fellow with rather big ears and teeth. But, clearly, a pretty big brain too. He was Richard Wilson, who lent me his copy of *M.A.S.H.*, and for many years it has been a standing joke between us that I still have to return it. But in 1969 how was I to know that my friend was to climb the greasy pole to the top of the Civil Service, be knighted and become Cabinet Secretary. And even invite me to his retirement party more than thirty years later, before he became a peer. That was a long way in the future. Meanwhile, Richard Wilson made sure I got all the papers and was included in Corfield's meetings where it became clear this was a pretty big story.

As it developed and was about to be clinched, Corfield gave me the nod that he would quite like to see a hint or two of the deal in the newspapers and his key role in brokering it. Strictly speaking, he was supposed to tell Parliament about it first, but these were the early days of the pre-emptive strike, and seizing the headlines before the knockers, like the state-owned airlines, could get to work.

As an ex-*Daily Mail* man I knew I could not drop the story there. The finger would point straight at me. On the other hand, a splash in the *Daily Express*, then selling four million copies a day, would set the hares running. And one name would certainly carry impact—Harry Chapman Pincher was renowned for his Whitehall scoops.

We hardly knew each other but he recognised my name and started to probe around. Normal practice would be to play a very straight bat, but on this occasion, while I did not give a direct leak, I certainly pointed him in the right direction. That was all a good newsman like Pincher needed and next morning the *Express* led on the news of the impending creation of 'The Second Force'.

The story was out and Fleet Street was in full chase. The boss of British Caledonian, Adam Thomson, was delighted. He knew he could not buy publicity like that. The minister was also quietly chuffed, while officially concerned at this clear breach. I admitted nothing, and braced myself for the inevitable Whitehall inquiry into leaks. As usual it got nowhere, though I was quizzed quite intensely by the official in charge.

I got on quite well with two junior ministers, who were to become bigger names in the Conservative Party—Sir John Eden and a real character, Nicholas Ridley. He was very right-wing, but had a terrific sense of humour. Both liked my style of operating, and I remained on good personal terms with Nick for many years. Twenty years later he paid me a public compliment on my abilities as a totally unbiased chief information officer in Whitehall.

Sadly, that did not mean much at the time when the Board of Trade learned the new Government intended to merge it with the fledgling Ministry of Technology, one of Harold Wilson's creations which, surprisingly, had survived the cull of the incoming Heath Government. But not for much longer. The two departments would be combined and known as the Department of Trade and Industry, which seemed to me to be the right course.

But I was not to serve it. The incoming Secretary of State was John Davies, whom I had known pretty well when on the *Daily Mail*, and he became the first director general of the new Confederation of British Industry. Sir Anthony Part told me he was off to meet Davies at lunch. and hinted that with two departments being merged, there would be casualties.

At Technology, my opposite number was Derek Moon, formerly in the Lobby at the House of Commons for the Bristol evening paper. On experience I reckoned I had him licked, but Part sent for me on his return from lunch. "I'm afraid the tide is running against you," was the way he summed it up.

Part's position was secure. He would become the permanent secretary of the new monster department, but not for the first time the public relations man was going nowhere.

Davies had decided he did not like my 'abrasive style' and I suspect he thought I was on the left politically. Certainly, when I was an industrial writer on the *Mail*, I had not pulled my punches so I suppose it was payback time.

I put it to Part that since both Moon and I were journalists on short term-contracts, couldn't there be a board? "That's no good—that way we could lose both of you," he said.

I vowed to myself to remember that as I cleared my desk, but then I had a call to go back up to see Sir Anthony.

He had mock-ups on his desk of the new notepaper for the Department of Trade and Industry. The historic crest of the Board of Trade, which

Top: *Looking for peace among the bomb damage in Belfast. Second from right, Terry Platt, Whitelaw's private secretary © Century Newspapers Ltd.* **Bottom:** *The end of the miners' strike? Whitelaw surrounded by press as he builds relationships with miners' leaders when bomb scare forces talk outside No.8 St James' Square. Joe Gormley (left), Whitelaw, Mick McGahey and Lawrence Daly of the union try to talk as media jostles around. Far left, I try to hear what is being said.*

Top: *Michael Foot's first press conference as a minister. Had he swallowed Harold Wilson's bait?* ***Bottom:*** *Roy Mason, MP, former President of Board of Trade with whom I travelled the world 'selling' Britain.*

Top: Anthony Grant, Conservative Junior Trade Minister, enjoys a joke with trade promotion civil servant and me. **Bottom:** Survivors from the ill-fated Department of Economic Affairs – left to right: John Lippett, Michael Casey and Peter Shore, our minister before its demise – toasting my farewell from the civil service 1978.

Top: *James Callaghan (photo by Fred Jarvis).*
Bottom: *Keith McDowall and William Whitelaw.*

dated right back to the first plantations in the United States, had an embossed sailing ship with wording around it. It mentioned trade and the BoT. Part wanted to keep it but how could it survive? What did I advise? "Simple," I told him. "Just keep the ship but remove the words." Bingo—Sir Anthony's problem solved. It was to remain on the department's stationery for years.

"Good luck," said Part as he showed me to the door.

CHAPTER 9
Going Green with Peter Walker and Environment

As is so often the case, the unexpected happened and a new opportunity presented itself. If a door opens I am a firm believer in going through to see what is on offer on the other side. Yes, there may be a chance of coming unstuck, but if you have confidence in yourself it usually pays off. It certainly has in my life.

Mind you, I had never seen myself as the spokesman for the Ministry of Housing and Local Government—not as old as the Home Office, but pretty embedded in its ways. It was supposed to tell local authorities what to do, but it often appeared that the boot was on the other foot.

What happened was that Henry James, the smoothie who was chief information officer, was called in to Number 10 to take over as deputy to Donald Maitland, the diplomat chosen by Edward Heath as his new public relations man—Head of Information, as it was known, though it kidded no one.

Maitland was a Foreign Office man, expert in Arabian affairs, with very little experience of Fleet Street journalists. His idea was to tell them to open their notebooks and take down dutifully what they were told. He was totally devoid of humour, though he often thought he was very funny. In fact, years later his obituary in *The Times* commented on his brilliance in this area. I can only say it passed me by completely. A little man in stature, Maitland seemed acutely aware of his own importance.

Henry James was a natural to underpin him, so he lost no time in clearing his desk and moving round the corner to the Prime Minister's residence. He had worked there before in a previous period of Conservative rule so he probably felt comfortable—and hoped that before not too long Maitland would be called back to his first love— diplomacy. Maybe the Arabs would appreciate his jokes more!

I took over Henry's office on the ground floor of the New Public Office where the Treasury is located, and had a ground floor window overlooking Whitehall. My deputy was Shelagh Jeffries, who had no journalistic background but had climbed up doggedly from the Central Office of Information. Devoid of much imagination, she did things strictly by the book, so she was in for a shock as I got into my stride.

In the press office, though, were a fine bunch, itching to be given the green light instead of flashing reds. Jack Gee, a former newspaperman, was on my wavelength, I remember. He rose eventually to become head of information at the Ministry of Defence but died quite suddenly.

Up on the ministerial floor there was plenty of movement. The new Secretary of State was a very young Cabinet minister, Peter Walker, very knowledgeable on housing matters. And keen on publicity. Very.

He was to play a major role in the big miners' strike in the 80s under Margaret Thatcher, but when I first met him he had yet to show his mettle. I found him approachable and accessible. He had a good news sense, and when I went to him with an idea he was quick to pick it up. Walker was all for a bit of publicity – preferably every day!

He was not a toff, not a dyed-in-the-wool Tory. He had been to Latimer Grammar School in Battersea and started work in an insurance office where, he loved to tell, he took charge of the weekly collections to pay for tea, and by buying it at the Co-op made regular profits on the dividend stamps. That was his first ever profit. But soon he got into business.

He made money in the Slater-Walker partnership in the City with Jim Slater, but with his usual good timing had got out before his partner ran into financial trouble. Walker liked to flaunt his money. He had the Government pictures on his office wall replaced with valuable original paintings from his own collection just to let us know he could afford it.

Though he professed to like journalists I suspected that deep down there was a touch of disdain, though he tried not to show it. His public policy was that his door was always open and journalists were welcome.

I believed in first working out what exactly I was dealing with, knowing the answers to the nasty questions that could arise and not putting out so many stories each day that we were competing with ourselves for space. But so keen was Walker that sometimes it was a struggle. He had supreme self-confidence that he could talk his way out of any problem presented by a mere newspaperman.

There was a standing joke in the Press Office. The intro, the first eye-catching paragraph of a press release, was usually the hardest to write. In this case every press notice from Housing & Local Government had to begin 'The Rt Hon Peter Walker, Secretary of State for Housing and Local Government ...' Embarrassing. We would send up releases with bright, crisp intros but they always came back with the usual introductory words.

On one occasion, however, Walker told me he wanted a news release to go out with an intro and heading which listed *ten* points. "Minister," I pleaded, "when I was in Fleet Street, the most we would dare to submit was three points. That's as far as the subs can count. And they think that's as far as the public can count." Walker would have none of it, and insisted we put it out as he wished. Next morning, I groaned at the daily papers. Several had fallen for it. "You see, Keith, it works every time," chuckled Walker as I gritted my teeth.

The number one private secretary was John Rowcliffe, but I got on particularly well with his deputy, a good-natured girl called Mavis. Women had to be bright to get into the private office which is a chance in Civil Service terms to earn your spurs. I found Mavis to be on the ball and, what's more, on my wavelength.

I must have spotted something because Mavis climbed to the top, became Dame Mavis Macdonald and was permanent secretary at the head of John Prescott's department when, in 1997, he became Deputy Prime Minister under Tony Blair.

The Housing Department dealt with planning issues; the Rate Support Grant, which was how the local authorities were allocated funds from central government and much other worthy stuff. A bit boring, though.

But it quickly livened up as the department became another of Prime Minister Heath's Super Departments. Headed by Walker, it was the first ever Department of the Environment. With us came the Ministry of Transport and the Ministry of Works—it really was big. Now in his ministerial team were Tory veterans like Julian Amery, son-in-law of former premier Harold Macmillan, and the man who, as Minister of Aviation in 1962 had signed the Anglo-French deal to build supersonic Concorde; and John Peyton, former Tory whip, one of the old school, who did not take kindly to chasing headlines. He, too, was very experienced and made it clear he was none too keen on a pushy whippersnapper like Peter Walker upstaging him.

There was also the up-and-coming Paul Channon, Guinness heir and son of Chips Channon MP, who published his remarkable diaries of the internal strains within the Tory party as World War II approached. I got on well with Paul and was to work with him again later in Northern Ireland.

Another junior minister was a tall, handsome blonde man named Heseltine, with whom I hit it off. But at our first meeting, Michael— one day to be Deputy Prime Minister—was a little despondent. Coming from the Transport wing, it did not look good that he had just been off to open a new stretch of motorway and been clocked in his personal Jaguar at 104 miles an hour!

The merging of three ministries into one obviously had its repercussions on the information job. The combined staff totalled well over a hundred. Nominally, the three Chief Information Officers were all equal, but as I reported to the Secretary of State I was clearly in charge, and started trying to weld them all into one efficient outfit. But it was uphill work.

Nobody knew which one of the three of us would emerge as Director of Information, virtually an undersecretary grade, and all of us were keeping our powder dry.

But I had the sexy end of it. 'Environment' was a fashionable buzz word. You could work it into anything, and it was practically guaranteed to walk into a prominent position in the morning papers. Nowadays they do the same thing with 'sustainable'—the Greens purr as it is tacked on to everything and anything. Totally meaningless in most cases, but they all feel better. And the media fall for it.

I got a considerable brownie point from the weekly meeting of ministers when I found out that the number of species of birds located in St James's Park was over seventy and that was because Central London now had some of the cleanest air of any capital city in the world. A big improvement on the killer smog of 1954.

The ministers' meeting was interesting in that Walker brought all the political team together and barred entry to all civil servants, who naturally hated it. It lasted about an hour. At the time, Walker was the only senior minister in Whitehall to do so, but it went down well with his colleagues who no longer felt isolated and out of the loop, often the fate of junior ministers.

One of his achievements was identifying that the grants for upgrading substandard property were woefully underused. Walker called a meeting into how the old Ministry of Housing people were getting out the message that citizens could get cash towards a new kitchen, a modern bathroom, or installing hot and cold running water.

The civil servants explained there were leaflets, and occasionally a piece in local papers. "No wonder so few apply for grants," declared Walker. "They don't know a thing about it."

Within weeks we had four caravans touring the country displaying promotions for the 'new' grants.

The take-up rocketed. Walker was right that once Joe Public knew he could have a new loo and the Man from Whitehall would pay, the citizen with outstretched palm would not be able to get to the plumbers' merchant quickly enough.

As the figures went through the roof the Treasury started to grumble. Yes, the scheme was in the Budget, but no one expected it to catch on like this!

There is no doubt in my mind that with the kind of drive Walker brought to housing, Britain's post-war slum clearance would have been completely different. And better, faster.

Instead of tearing down old properties to replace them with concrete slabs which virtually imprisoned people, Walker would have given the public the materials to do up their own homes. Many of the houses I knew from South London could have been saved if we had encouraged the do-it-yourself boom 20–30 years earlier. And I am sure that would have applied to many of the mining villages and industrial areas, which could have then retained their identity and community sense. Instead they were destroyed by the soulless towers in which we dumped families.

Walker was a great believer in going out to meet a lobbying group on their own territory. The civil servants were secretly horrified that their minister not only knew about Shelter, but would encourage its loudmouthed founder, Des Wilson, to drop in to see him. That took the wind out of Wilson's sails.

Right-wing lobbyists with axes to grind would get appointments, convinced they were going to convert Walker to their tune. They would leave happy in the knowledge that the minister had listened enthusiastically and would pick up their ideas. Wrong. Walker had his own ideas—or would pinch them if necessary—but he was never an easy touch.

Mavis and I accompanied Peter Walker to the 'Conference of the Cities' in Indianapolis, which was one of the first to identify the crisis of confidence coming to so many cities as employment slumped, factories and warehouses closed, drug pushers moved in and crime soared. One place we heard about which seemed to have a better idea than most about tackling its problems was Baltimore, on the US east coast.

Not long afterwards, Walker called me to his office at the top of the new Marsham Street tower block to which we had decamped. Michael Heseltine was with him. He had an important story he wanted me to handle.

Walker unfolded his plans for taking over the whole of London's

Docklands, using the legislation which had been passed by the post-war Labour Government to create new towns like Crawley, Stevenage, Harlow, and Peterlee.

I gulped. From my reporter's knowledge of the London waterside, there would be entrenched opposition from the powerful Port of London Authority, which owned the Thames-side warehouses, and also from Labour-dominated local authorities like Southwark, Bermondsey, Tower Hamlets and Newham, They would fight like hell, I warned.

"That's the point," Walker assured me, with Heseltine's nod of approval. "If we move fast with this New Town legislation they can't stop us. If we wait for them, years and years will drag by, and East London will just spiral downwards. Like Baltimore!"

And when I see the towers of Canary Wharf, the waterside piazzas, the O2 Arena, and the smart apartment blocks down by the clean Thames, I have to admit they were right.

True, there is not much of the old London community spirit, but there are jobs, though not much for the 50–60,000 dockworkers who once got their living from the wharves, the barges and the lighters. But they were going anyway. The writing was on the wall for the docks, just as in Baltimore, and Walker and Heseltine seized their chance.

Some years later, when Heseltine was in the driving seat and setting up the London Docks Development Corporation, he rang my old friend Bob Mellish, Bermondsey MP, and asked him to be deputy chairman. Bob was worried, and asked me what I thought. I urged him to take it on and see if he could get some social housing into the new LDDC's plans. Bob got some stick for taking the job—but he did get some homes for ordinary folk, too.

Heseltine was to do it again a decade later when he breezed into Liverpool, grabbed the decaying city by the scruff of the neck, and started a rebirth of the port.

One day I was called up to Walker's office in Marsham Court by Rowcliffe. "Something big," he told me mysteriously over the phone. Three tower blocks made up the new super department, and Walker toyed with the idea of calling them Fire, Earth and Water with the argument that these were the key ingredients which made up the environment. Fortunately, the civil servants managed to kick that particular brainwave into the long grass—just as well, as the three blocks were eventually found to be stuffed with life-threatening asbestos.

Around Walker's big conference table were gathered an army of people from the Transport wing I had never seen—engineers, technical men and boffins, as well as the bureaucrats. There were also private company people present with tubular rolls of drawings. Normally they would have answered to John Peyton, who was in the room, but Walker was clearly in charge. He looked grim.

It transpired that in Australia a major British construction project known as the West Gate box girder bridge across the Yarra River had collapsed. There had not been much publicity in the UK—but there would be soon. Because what the Transport engineers were having screwed out of them by Walker, almost line by line, was that well over 100 box girder bridges of the same design were located through the British Isles.

An urgent survey was needed on every bridge. Calculations were required, traffic densities, crack-testing, load-bearing … we were hearing it all.

And how long would it all take? Well, it could probably all be completed in a couple of weeks, and then a full report would be presented to the minister so that decisions could be made. Of course, the bridges would have to be closed in the meantime. I didn't need to say much but I did scribble a note to Walker: *Secretary of State— you are about to go down in history as the man responsible for the biggest traffic jam in British history.* I often found that if I conjured up what the newspapers would be saying in the morning, it concentrated a politician's mind remarkably well!

Walker got the point and knew he was in a jam. He had to tell Parliament soon, that was clear, and press and television would be clamouring.

He tried various ideas. Could just one or two lanes on a bridge be closed to lighten the load while tests were carried out? What about really going to town on one bridge, totally closing it down, and subjecting it to stress-testing? And so on. No good, said the engineers. Every bridge is different.

They were not committing themselves. They said nothing, but their expressions told us, "This is why we have political masters—this is your problem, not ours."

Eventually Walker decided he would close one lane each way on every box girder bridge in the British Isles. We would announce it in Parliament and go big with the media, but it was impossible to say how vast the chaos would turn out to be. That night, the traffic cones were out, lights were flashing, and drivers waited. But there were no sensational traffic jams or accidents reported.

"Once again," said Mavis, "Peter Walker's luck has held." It's true that if you are going to be in politics you want to be lucky. But Peter Walker generally made his own luck. And it was usually good.

There was another big meeting in his room with all the bigwigs of the water industry present. The country was littered with all kinds of water authorities—some owned by county councils, some by smaller local authorities, and some by private companies. All falling over each other's feet and often working to different criteria.

A report now lay on Walker's desk calling for rationalisation—and shotgun marriages if necessary. The minister nagged away. It was uphill work, but Parliament was expecting him to deliver.

At one point I passed him another of my notes. *Secretary of State— you are in danger of going down as the Man who Nationalised WATER*, I wrote. For a Tory to be associated with the socialist concept of State ownership was too awful to be contemplated.

Walker settled for regionalisation as preferable, though he knew there would have to be a further round of mergers. Someone else could have that one, he decided.

He also had a gift for making eye-catching appointments, like the one he told me to prepare, to announce that Richard Marsh, Labour

MP for Greenwich—once tipped as a future Labour leader—was to be the new chairman of British Railways. I suggested it might not go down well with the Conservative backbenchers, but Walker waved it away. "The Labour Party will like it even less," he chortled. "And there's not much between Marsh and me."

Where I did disagree with Peter Walker was on his handling of the reorganisation of local government. A report was put on his desk from Lord Redcliffe-Maude, the conclusion of a three-year-long Royal Commission advocating a major shake-up of 1,200 local authorities and dividing the country into about sixty-three unitary bodies.

It was a thorough piece of work by one of the brightest former permanent secretaries in Whitehall, but Walker was not buying it, even though one of the last acts of Harold Wilson's Government was a pledge to accept it.

It was the purest piece of pork barrel politicking I think I ever witnessed in Whitehall. "Labour want it because their strength is in the county boroughs—they would come out running most of these new unitary authorities," Walker told me. "Our strength is in the county councils—the shires. That's where our votes are." It went through my mind to enquire what was best for the country, but decided to keep my mouth shut. Coolly, Walker announced he would be talking to the county councils on taking forward the proposals by Redcliffe-Maude. The man who proposed the biggest ever shake-up of local government kept his head down and settled for a life in academia nursing his life peerage. But it must have been bitter to find he had wasted three years of his time simply to see it tossed in the wastepaper bin in Whitehall.

The legislation was already in draft form within the department, and the officials had little to do but substitute county councils for unitary authorities. And so it soon started its passage through the House of Commons. To my amazement it included paying councillors' salaries, even in inner London.

Though I got on well with Peter Walker, and had shown him I was clearly on his wavelength, there were soon deeper waters to navigate. A new permanent secretary had emerged, and not from the three departments being merged. Step forward, Sir David Serpell—not a nice man. He sent for me for a chat, and when I went in had his feet up on his desk. And as we talked they stayed there.

He was obviously sizing me up, and it soon got through to me that stories in print were of little consequence to him. He would prefer they were kept out!

Pleasing ministers was not his business, either. I often wonder if he was the prototype for Sir Humphrey in *Yes Minister*.

I asked if he thought the proposal to build London's third airport at Foulness in the Thames Estuary would ever survive. A small area of shingle had been uncovered there and its existence was being monitored.

"Funny place to put all those resources—in the middle of the sea," he replied.

With opposition for major construction works entrenched like that in Whitehall, the project never stood a chance. Indeed, if Serpell had been a Dutchman they would never have started dredging, let alone build New York.

One way and another I sensed I was never likely to hit it off with Serpell. Ironically, after he retired he was called on by his old Transport department pals to produce a report for Government on the future of railways and another on the motorway network. Both ended up in ministerial wastepaper baskets. Those who live by the sword …

But by then I had departed Environment. Though I got on well with Walker and the ministerial team, I never felt I was on all fours with the senior civil servants who were engaged on bringing the three departments into one, admittedly a major task.

There was a board convened to interview the candidates for the top job as Director of Information. The three of us from the three smaller departments were all contenders for the super role, but suddenly a fourth runner appeared on the rails. Up came Henry James, who had left Housing for the attractions of Number 10, but if the pay and status of the new DoE information job was being raised, he was after it. And a Welshman from the Housing department was chairing the interview panel.

It came as no great surprise to me to find I had not been successful and Henry would take over. It was a bitter pill, though not all that difficult to swallow. But what did surprise me was the clear disapproval of the combined information staff. They had liked having a decisive ex-journalist in charge and made it clear they were sorry to see me go.

I had cleared my desk and was preparing to make my way out of the building when I got another of those life-changing calls—not this time from Trevor Lloyd-Hughes, who with the departure from power of his boss Harold Wilson, had also cleared his desk (though he did get a knighthood as compensation). My call was from Ian Bancroft, later to be head of the Civil Service, who was masterminding the DoE merger. He told me to make contact with the Home Office. It seemed I was wanted there.

I soon found out that Henry James' departure had meant Tom McCaffrey was moving to Number 10 as deputy to Heath's man, Donald Maitland. I was not surprised because he was extremely experienced in Whitehall ways and desperately wanted the Number 10 job himself.

I made contact with a man called Bunker, whose job it was to manage the manpower of the Home Office—no mean task at that time because, apart from the main departmental people, it included all the prison staff, immigration, and those who run the myriad of Home Office responsibilities such as police, fire, drugs, and young offenders. You name it, the Home Office was in there somewhere.

This time, the prospect of the Home Office was not so daunting. It had been less than a year since I was last there, and the uniformed messengers still regularly made up the little coal-burning fire in my ground floor office. Upstairs, Sir Philip Allen was still Permanent Secretary and there had been few other changes.

But the ministers had certainly changed. My new Home Secretary was Reginald Maudling who, in the Macmillan era, had been Chancellor of the Exchequer. And he had fought, and lost, to Edward Heath in the first-ever secret ballot for the Tory leadership. It looked interesting.

CHAPTER 10
The Maudling Era and Moving to the Northern Ireland Office

Reginald Maudling's private secretary was Graham Angel, new to me but a Londoner with whom I quickly established a harmonious relationship. Ushered back into the same office in which Jim Callaghan had presided, I found Maudling to be an amiable person and not at all demanding. He gave me the impression he was not at all fussed about personal publicity, or indeed any kind of it. He'd sooner have a good lunch! Another impression was that he was not over-stretching himself unduly. Second or third gear, but rarely in top, I felt.

He was a bit scruffy, too. I was expecting to meet a Tory Cabinet minister who might not necessarily be a toff, but who was reasonably turned out. Maudling often looked as if he had dressed rather hurriedly at home in Barnet without time to iron his shirt or sponge a stain off his lapel. It was common gossip in the Home Office that Beryl, his wife, formerly an actress, liked the high life and was inclined to spend anything that her husband earned.

But intellectually there was no doubt that, when he stretched himself, Maudling was a high flyer. He had been President of the Board of Trade, Colonial Secretary, Chancellor of the Exchequer, and had lost narrowly to Edward Heath in the Tory Party leadership ballot. When I came into contact with him he was Deputy Leader of the Conservatives, and holding the number two or three position in the pecking order as Home Secretary.

He clearly still hankered after an economic job, and Graham Angel showed me a paper his master had personally drafted on the current wages trend, warning that trouble loomed. He was right—that was what sooner, rather than later, was to bring Edward Heath's Government crashing down. But at that time Maudling's suggestion of an incomes policy was not a runner.

His interest in the daily turmoil in Northern Ireland was virtually non-existent. Again and again I would go to him with details of the latest outrage, but Maudling just waved it away. His policy was to steer well clear of Ulster—the six counties might well have been located in the Caribbean for all the interest he showed.

Almost daily, Tom Roberts, now in post as number two in Information with the Ulster Government, would phone me from Belfast as police stations were blasted, dustmen in the centre of the City were torn to pieces by a bomb in a refuse bin, soldiers were shot in the back. Roberts, quite rightly, kept pressing to know what the UK Government was going to do, and I was forced to tell him to expect very little.

But it was obvious to me, and indeed to several of my colleagues like Heath's spokesman in Number 10, Donald Maitland, and John Groves at Defence and others elsewhere in Whitehall, that we were losing the propaganda battle against the IRA. As we had so little ammunition, it was hardly surprising.

I bumped into Sir James Dunnett—Ned, as he was widely known— with whom I had been on extremely good terms as an industrial journalist when he had been permanent secretary at the Ministry of Labour. I took a chance and told him how unsatisfactory I was finding the media situation in the absence of much interest by ministers, notably mine.

Dunnett asked if it would help if he called a meeting in his office and invited all the public relations people to give their views. The upshot was that we started to meet in Sir James' office each day at 9 a.m. At last we started to pool our efforts and our information effort began to have some impact. I was not authorised, but I kept Tom Roberts in the picture and he continued to tip me off about developments at Stormont Castle.

Because of my earlier involvement with James Callaghan I had plenty of background in the subject and knew the officials. Robin North confessed frustration at not being able to get the minister to visit the province.

"After all, it is being blown up day after day and no senior politician reacts. Any other major provincial city would have a visit on the same day," he chuntered. I agreed and said I would try to bend Maudling's ear on my morning visit.

I chose a day when there had been a particularly nasty bombing incident and several deaths. Maudling agreed that perhaps he should make a foray to Belfast. Graham Angel rapidly made a note and, giving me a wink, made for the door before his Secretary of State could have second thoughts.

The visit was quickly set-up, maybe because I had tipped off Tom Roberts who had fed it in to his officials, and there was no hesitancy. But there was to be no advance publicity as there had been prior to Callaghan's journey. It was now recognised that a Cabinet minister was a target, and the growing audacity of the IRA made an attack on him a possibility.

The Home Secretary had meetings with Stormont ministers and a briefing with the Army and the Royal Ulster Constabulary. But he brought no 'goodies' to announce, and we were rather on the back foot when the obligatory press conference was staged at Stormont Castle. The decency of the man and his reassuring calmness cut little ice with the Belfast newshounds, who were looking for a chance to put the boot in.

It came when the Home Secretary suggested the British Government objective was to reduce IRA violence to 'an acceptable level'. My heart sank—it was the quote of the day, and there was no hope of undoing the damage. I knew instinctively any attempt to do so would make it worse. And within half an hour there it was, leading the BBC Northern Ireland radio news.

I warned Maudling, but he brushed it aside. Unlike most ministers, who would be looking for someone to blame – probably me – he shook hands with his hosts and got in the car.

On board the RAF plane at Aldergrove he called for a drink. "For God's sake bring me a large Scotch—what a bloody awful country," he declared, in what should have been confidential company.

There were no more than half a dozen of us in that tiny jet, excluding the steward, but someone leaked that quote. It certainly was not me. And whoever did I consider very disloyal and treacherous. Maudling did not deserve that breach of trust.

But Northern Ireland matters could only get worse. Within a few weeks Maudling had to persuade the Cabinet that, reluctantly, he felt he had to allow the Northern Ireland Government to introduce internment.

It was a tactic that had been used in the troubles in the twenties, and elsewhere in the world where the British colonial boot could be slammed in without a television camera recording the event. But not any more.

There were strong rumours that potential IRA supporters could be rounded up, so the very ones that were wanted had slipped away by the time soldiers or the RUC banged on doors or kicked them open. Before the night was out, something like 350 Catholics were rounded up. Not one Protestant, though.

It was a propaganda gift to the IRA and the Catholic community. There were all kinds of stories of cock-ups and mistakes, and the Irish can always tell a good story. Like the one about the Army knocking on a door and asking by name for one young man.

"He's not here, gone away," said his defiant mother. The soldiers asked the identity of another young man they could see indoors. It was the missing man's brother.

"Okay, you'll do," said the soldiers, and frogmarched him away, ensuring another anti-British story would to go round the world—particularly to places like Boston, on the east coast of America, where the exiled and Irish sympathisers were waking up fast to this new era of, as they saw it, colonialism.

In the years ahead this part of America would be the source of much of the IRA's funding; its senator, Edward Kennedy, would become a thorn in our side; and considerable British effort would be expended trying to get across an alternative view: the truth as we saw it.

And, of course, the level of violence soared. The IRA now had a more legitimate cause. Until internment a large part of the Catholic community did not support the terrorist agenda. Yes, they loathed the Protestants and hated being treated as second-class citizens, but internment changed everything. Just as Maudling had predicted.

As if matters could not get much worse we began getting hints at one of the morning conferences in Sir James Dunnett's office that there would be some kind of discipline meted out that coming weekend in Londonderry.

No. 1 Para, the leading regiment in the Airborne Division, was on a tour of duty patrolling the walls and battlements of the old city. Repeatedly, bricks and stones were flung at them by teenage boys keen to be seen on television—and not averse to tossing bigger stuff like bits of paving stone if the bribes from overseas cameramen were big enough. As soon as the arc lights went up so did the level of street violence, and round the world went pictures of 'war-torn UK', though in fact the incidents all took place in one area while the rest of the city was quiet.

We knew there was to be a Northern Ireland Civil Rights march in the city that weekend, and at our morning meeting on the preceding Friday there were hints that there could be trouble. Number 10 seemed to have heard something, and the Army spokesman appeared to us evasive. But nobody levelled with the meeting, although at one point Ned Dunnett raised an eyebrow to me.

We knew the Army was increasingly frustrated at seeing themselves on television, passive, as rocks and stones were flung at them by increasingly daring youths. Occasionally the soldiers would give chase but only for a few yards, and soon the teenage yobs would be back for another baiting session.

This was not supposed to happen to the toughest regiment in the British Army. It was not good for recruitment. Friends and relatives were asking the young soldiers what was stopping them, "sorting out those kids."

"Orders," came the reply through gritted teeth.

But the coming weekend, it sounded to us, would be different. Those Irish lads were going to be taught a lesson. I thought in terms of pickaxe handles and fit young paras chasing and thrashing a few Bogside youths so the message would get around—"Don't mess with the Paras."

We exchanged weekend telephone numbers, and discussed a common line to take if called at home by our contacts in journalism, TV and radio. But nothing had prepared us for the full impact of Bloody Sunday on 30th January 1972.

News did not travel then as fast as it does today, and it was several hours before the full picture—or what we thought was a full version—came through. Shots had been fired by the Army, but in response to those fired at them. Yes, there were casualties and some deaths. But no, no one in the Army had been shot. Odd that, I remember thinking. All those bullets flying about, and not a scratch on a para.

Eventually it emerged that in fact twenty-six people had been shot; thirteen had died instantly, and several more were to die in the next few hours.

A Catholic priest, Father Daly, no apologist for the IRA, had led a small number through the Army lines waving a white handkerchief, as a mortally wounded man was carried to safety. The priest was later to rise to the post of cardinal in the city, and his objective eye-witness account seemed to give lie to the Army claim they had been fired upon.

It was a propaganda disaster—and a gift to the IRA, who seized on its importance. They sent the picture of Father Daly round the world. And we had no answer. It was the final response to the Army insistence that if its arm was no longer tied behind its back it could, we were told, sort out Northern Ireland.

Maudling did not accept it as he made clear in Parliament, giving the first account to MPs of what had happened in Derry. He was on the back foot, but had some help when Bernadette Devlin, a recently elected Catholic MP from the Bogside, ran across the floor of the Commons and slapped his face.

Poor old Reggie wiped his glasses as attendants dragged away the shrieking Northern Ireland MP, but by her action she had demonstrated the near impossibility of talking to or negotiating with the minority in the Province.

The Prime Minister had got the message too. Almost immediately, but in total secrecy, Heath asked for the files to be dusted down on direct rule. They were not so dusty, it seemed. I remembered James Callaghan had asked the same question before we flew out to Belfast in 1969.

It went quiet as the issues were thrashed out, but not in Northern Ireland where the IRA considered they had been given the green light to unleash a campaign of terror. They really sought a united Ireland, but if that was a long way off they were certainly on the road to getting the undivided attention of the British Government.

There were plenty of other matters at the Home Office to occupy me—indeed, with a break from Ulster concerns it meant I could give some attention to other departmental matters. There was also an amusing moment when I had a call from the establishment department—what today is called human resources—asking if I had been positively vetted for security. By this time I had been working in the Civil Service, albeit on a temporary contract, for nearly two years, and in that period I had dealt with the top-secret trade figures, helped MI5 to bundle two spies out of the country, been involved with the police and army over Northern Ireland, and seen many hundreds of secret documents.

Now, it seemed, those in authority were concerned I might be a security risk! A detailed questionnaire was sent to me in a heavily-sealed double envelope for my eyes only. Wow! Most of the questions were pretty straightforward, but I hesitated when I came to one which asked blandly, "Do you know any Communists?"

I could have ducked it, but as a former journalist specialising in employment and trade union matters I knew a lot of party activists. I would not have been doing my job if I didn't. So in the blank space I simply wrote 'Lots' … and waited.

It took about a week before I thought I heard the sound of a train smashing into the buffers, and I received a peremptory call to present myself to a department across Whitehall at the Ministry of Defence. I was directed to an office in the eaves of the MoD, and had difficulty in suppressing a smile as I entered and found one of those office green lampshades shining in my face so that it was difficult to see who was sitting behind the desk.

The person did give a name, but made little effort to welcome me and indicated this was a formal interview. "You say on this form that you know lots of communists and ex-communists. Could you name them?" I could see where this was going so I looked straight forward where I hoped my inquisitor's eyes were located and said, "Well, how about Denis Healey? He was once a communist." At that moment Healey was currently the Minister of Defence and presumably my man's boss.

"Who else?"

"Well, how about Hugh Scanlon?" The engineering union leader had been in the CP when I first met him, but as he scaled the union heights he dropped out and moved to the right, and at that time was being courted by Heath to try to get an agreement on wages policy. A fairly frequent visitor to Downing Street and even Chequers, the Prime Minister's country residence, I had heard.

My interrogator seemed to realise he was not going to get far on this tack. "How do you know these kind of people?" he demanded. I pointed out that for more than a decade I had covered the labour scene, and it had indeed been my job to know those on the left just as much as those more to the right. How could I have covered major industrial disputes without meeting communists? I asked.

The session came to a fairly quick ending. I went back across Whitehall to my office, where there was the usual pile of papers in my in tray with several marked 'Secret'. I heard no more.

My other concern at the time was for the reputation of Maudling. *Private Eye* had got its teeth into him and was dropping brick-sized hints that the Home Secretary's relationship with the architect and developer John Paulson was, to say the least, unsavoury. It was right because in the years ahead Paulson would go to jail. And *Private Eye* seemed to have found a new bucket of mud to throw at the Home Secretary over his earlier relationship with the Real Estate Fund of America, whose CEO had been imprisoned for fraud.

Strictly speaking, it was none of my business, but I decided to tell Maudling it was doing him great damage. "Don't worry yourself, Keith. That *Private Eye* stuff does not cut much ice with the Fleet Street editors and I know them."

"You may well do," I replied, "but I know the journalists and they are itching to get at this story and bring it into the Fleet Street domain."

I urged him to take it seriously, but Reggie seemed unperturbed. I accepted his view, but I knew the issue would not go away. Bit by bit, it was chipping at his reputation, and if he did not defend himself the press—and the public—would draw their own conclusions.

As it happened, I was not to be there when Reggie's downfall came. Inside Downing Street a decision had been taken—a major one, as it emerged. There were rumours, but not until the Prime Minister announced the Government was taking powers away from the Northern Ireland Government, and transferring them to Whitehall, did we believe it. He announced the first Secretary of State for Northern Ireland would be his Leader of the House, William Whitelaw, who accepted the poisoned chalice in the Commons chamber with tears streaming down his face. He, at least, seemed to have an idea what he was taking on, I thought.

As for me, it was with a great sense of relief that at last I was getting rid of the issue. No more early morning meetings in Whitehall—I could go back to my later train. And no more midnight phone calls. Wonderful news.

But when I got back to my office, a lovely lady name Dreda Gorgas, who had become my PA, told me Sir William Nield had been on the phone and wanted me to call him back. Bill had been named in the House of Commons to be the new department's first permanent secretary.

"Listen," I told Dreda, "don't call him—I don't want to speak to him."

My assistant took note, but I knew she wasn't buying it. A couple of hours later, she told me Bill Nield was on the phone again.

"Listen, Bill," I told him. "I don't want to know any more about Northern Ireland. I have had my fill and it is time someone else had a go."

Bill chuckled. "There is no harm in coming and talking to us about it, Keith. Whitelaw says he knows you and wants you to come over for a drink." It was difficult to decline without appearing very rude. I was cornered. I agreed to go to the Lord President's office the following morning at 11 a.m.

CHAPTER 11
Back to Belfast, Bullets and Bombs with William Whitelaw

The Lord President's office at 70 Whitehall is an impressive historic building, and some pretty good political operators have had it as their base over the years. It even has a back door entrance to 10 Downing Street—very useful in delicate political situations.

Here was Willie Whitehall about to give it up to take on the crisis in Ulster, a part of the United Kingdom that has been the graveyard of too many politicians. So I could see he needed help—but why me?

Bill Nield was his smooth self as I was shown into the grand room where the Government's business of the day and the weeks ahead was sorted out.

I had just started to tell Bill Nield he was not on this time when the door opened, and in swept the Lord President, leader of the House and designate first-ever Secretary of State for Northern Ireland. Big, genial, affable, shrewd, Willie Whitelaw was to get more out of me than a dozen or so Cabinet ministers I served in my years in Whitehall. A tall man, big smile, hand outstretched—anything but standing on ceremony.

"Keith," he beamed. "I'm so glad you're going to join us … absolutely delighted."

"But I'm not," I insisted. "I am at the Home Office, which is very busy and has a hell of a lot on its plate. I don't think I can be spared."

Whitelaw looked at Nield, who seemed quite unimpressed. "I am sure we can arrange things," declared Bill Nield, to whom any problem was a small challenge which could be smoothly sorted.

"I am not even a civil servant. I only have a temporary two-year

184

contract. What about my wife and children?"

"What can we do about that?" demanded Whitelaw. Again, nothing that Bill Nield could not fix with a phone call which, considering the hurdles and interviews normally deemed necessary for a permanent post under Civil Service Commission rules, was quite an eye-opener to me.

"Well, Keith, we'll soon sort out that kind of thing, but now we are going to have a meeting of the team, and I'd like you to stay."

Short of being very rude and leaving there was nothing for it but take my seat round the big table as the team to take on direct rule filed in. Pretty high-powered, too.

Just before we went in, Whitelaw suddenly turned and said he had to raise one question—my political affiliations. There had been a nasty story by Robert Carvel in the *Evening Standard* naming me and Bernard Ingham, both journalists recruited to the Government Information Service, alleging us to be Labour Party supporters. The story obviously emanated from Tory Central Office, and Carvel kept stirring it.

Ingham was undoubtedly an avid Labour supporter, but changed when he was swept into Margaret Thatcher's entourage and became her press secretary. But I had no qualms. I told Whitelaw that, yes, I was a Labour supporter, but that I belonged to no political party as I firmly believed a journalist should remain detached and objective. I had been recruited as a temporary civil servant and accepted the civil servants' code.

"That's all I want to hear!" said Whitelaw and my impression was he had enough to brush the Tory Central Office knives aside. Whitelaw never raised it again with me but in discussion later when I repeated I supposed I was a Gaitskellite—the late leader of the Labour Party—Whitelaw confided that he too had been attracted to the man. "Our politics were not all that far apart," he told me.

Then he swept me in to 'meet the team' indicating that I was to be a member, too. It was quite an impressive assembly. Lord Windlesham—a Catholic, I was to discover, and later much involved in the launching of commercial television in the UK—to be Willie's deputy; Paul

Channon, Minister of State, who I had worked with at housing; Neil Cairncross, deputy secretary Home Office; Philip Woodfield—assistant secretary—one day to be the man appointed to hear problems of MI5 officers in the field; Dennis Trevelyan of the police branch, who had been with us on the Callaghan team in Belfast.

Others were to join within a few days—Joe Pilling, for example, just a principal then, but one day to be number two at the DHSS and then Permanent Secretary of the NIO. A number of younger high flyers also came from the Home Office, like Bob Whalley, Rob Stevens and Stephen Boys Smith (destined one day to be the Chief Immigration Officer), all willing to hurl themselves into the Northern Ireland issue. Quite remarkable. Was it only me who knew the issue was a quagmire and probably a political graveyard for our new master?

And more ministers: David Howell MP, then a backbencher, but to have a good career in politics as Transport and Energy portfolios, and one day to lead on foreign affairs in the Lords; and Peter Mills, a decent, down-to-earth backbencher from the southwest, who became Parliamentary Secretary and was to look after agriculture, an important industry in Ulster.

As soon as he sat down Whitelaw took command of the meeting. "The first thing we must all remember," he boomed, "is that we must all laugh together. We are going to be flung into some very difficult circumstances, and unless we can manage to laugh we are not going to get anywhere."

His second point was extremely important. This was the time, he said, for obtaining the maximum out of Whitehall, so everything the fledgling NIO wanted should be demanded now. The first thing to get agreed was the clear right to have use of an HS-125 executive business jet from the RAF, and plenty of cars. This was music to the ears of a former Fleet Street man who had often been irked at Whitehall penny-pinching.

We arranged that there would always be one minister 'on duty' in Northern Ireland, and another at his desk in Whitehall so that as the frequency of bombings, shootings and other terrorism soared, the department could never be accused of not being on the case.

Whitelaw brought the meeting swiftly to an end, and told us to be ready to fly out to RAF Aldergrove, the secure aerodrome at Belfast, next morning. That happened to be Maundy Thursday, the start of Easter. "Not this year, McDowall," I told myself, and prepared to tell my wife and children not to save me an Easter egg.

But within a couple of hours I was back that evening beside my new boss on our way to Lime Grove, the BBC studios, where Whitelaw had already committed to taking part in a major programme about the gathering Ulster crisis.

Next morning, a driver picked me up at my home in Woldingham, Surrey, and took me to Battersea heliport, where, with Whitelaw and the then private secretary Leonard Davies, we were whisked to RAF Northolt. As I read my newspapers, I thought about the previous evening at Lime Grove. Though a senior minister and an experienced politician, Willie was pretty green in terms of the media. Everything in the House was on lobby terms, but he was going to be quoted directly now. So I stressed the need to concentrate on a few simple points and not to sermonise. I told him he looked like a desperately keen man who had just taken Holy Orders and was too anxious to please.

And I resolved to toughen him up.

On the plane to Belfast I sat with Bill Nield, and we assessed our new masters and colleagues. Bill and I were used to working together and knew each other's methods, and we agreed that Willie had great potential. We just had to keep him on track.

Meanwhile, the minister himself had been doing some thinking. Somehow he had decided he had to break out of the internment spiral. Something like 600 men were now behind bars in Long Kesh without trial or even a charge. There could be no start to seeking a solution until they were out, Whitelaw resolved.

Secondly, he wanted to put an end to the ban on marches in the Province. The first challenge to that would come that very weekend when the Catholics traditionally paraded through the streets, thumbing their noses at the majority Protestants.

As it was Easter, it was agreed on the flight that it would be unwise to order the Northern Ireland civil servants to be at their desks. We could have swept into Stormont Castle like some whizz kid management team, but that was not Whitelaw's style, we found. He was much more adept at winning people round and bringing them into the fold. So it was resolved to let the civil servants have a day or two at home and time to think things over.

So on arrival, instead of heading for the Castle, we drove straight to Lisburn, the Army headquarters, where the redoubtable General Sir Harry Tuzo held court.

The army were keen to show us they were on top of everything, and that if we civilians would be good boys, not meddle or interfere, then they would soon have this little Irish problem sorted.

It was not the time (though I certainly said it later) to tell them the main reason we were there was because this time the British army boot going in was definitely NOT the answer. Nor was internment, where a place like Long Kesh was doing similar damage to Britain's reputation as General Kitchener's original concentration camps in South Africa during the Boer War.

Certainly not in the new television age. Just as the US military had come to grief in Vietnam when the US public could see their misdeeds on CBS, so the media could put an end to many of the myths the British Army liked to proffer.

And as a very large part of the world map showed Catholic majorities in countries like Spain, Portugal, Latin America and—most important— on the East Coast of United States, British exports were suffering.

But we knew we were on trial, too. The Army had been taking casualties and needed better political leadership. Were we the ones to supply it?

First things first—lifting the marching ban. The object of the exercise, the Army grasped, was to end it, and have the gesture interpreted not as weakness but magnanimity by the Incoming Man.

An initial draft of the announcement was produced, with every word chewed over, with one eye on the clock. I knew Willie had to have it on radio and TV by noon. In a break for coffee as the draft began to take shape, I went to the portable typewriter I had brought from London, and drafted twelve of the toughest questions I could think of putting to the new Secretary of State. Later, we worked through them with everyone round the table contributing, and in this way Willie prepared himself for his first real session with the media.

He had had an earlier session the previous weekend when, prior to direct rule being passed by the Commons, he had flown to Belfast with Bill Nield to meet the RUC and some senior Ulster civil servants. There had been a disastrous press conference at the airport. Although not as bad as Maudling's disaster when he used the phrase 'an acceptable level of violence', Whitelaw was bounced on questions about his own religion. I resolved that there would be no more airport press conferences. After all, if we had arrived by ferry or train, no one would presume it was a peg for a press conference, so what was so special about flying into a regional airport? The press never forgave me, but they never bounced us again when getting off a plane.

At Lisburn, however, I called up BBC and ITV, and Billy Flackes and Gordon Burns came out to interview the new Secretary of State. It was a great improvement, and I decided Whitelaw was a quick learner. So now we had to wait to see how the two sides of the Northern Irish public digested the announcement and how they reacted.

Whitelaw and his wife Cecilia stayed at Hillsborough, the official residence of the Governor, Lord Grey of Naunton, as, having taken the seals of office, he was now in charge. It says much for the patience and remarkable tolerance of Willie that he put up with Grey nagging at his elbow until 1973 when we could end the office of Governor under the Constitution Act. When Grey was not presuming to advise on policy he seldom missed a chance to drop hints at the difficulty he found in making ends meet on the Queen's payroll.

If de Gaulle was the heaviest cross Churchill had to bear during World War II, then Grey was the equivalent for Whitelaw. They formed a relationship of sorts, but it was very one-sided. Outwardly affable, yet very conscious of Royal 'status', Grey intrigued even to the point of invoking Royalty on his behalf. He frequently got at the small set that considered itself 'society' in the province to try to lobby Whitelaw.

The actual Hillsborough household was dominated by the butler. Everyone, including Whitelaw, seemed frightened of him. Yet the food was appalling and a constant cause of ministerial complaint. But to be a few minutes late for one of those meals, frugal as it was, led to stony rebuke. And a lukewarm meal.

Whitelaw's original plan was to get rid of the Governor as soon as he could. He discussed it with us at Whitehall and at Stormont Castle, promising us he would soon have Grey on his way. Then the magnificent rooms would be turned open to all the NIO staff. The tennis courts would give us some relaxation, and the gardens would be ideal for a stroll, to ponder the problems of Ulster. It sounded good. But it was not to be until the late Mo Mowlem moved in under the new Blair Government in 1997.

Throughout the whole period, however, Whitelaw never let the tension get out of hand, occasionally taking up a suggestion from the Governor and ensuring that, for the first time, he was allowed sight of Cabinet papers affecting the Province.

The decision to permit marching that Easter (1972) seemed to go down reasonably well, and there was no expected backlash from the Protestants. So Whitelaw went off to Hillsborough while the rest of us set off for the Culloden Hotel, about ten minutes from Stormont, and unpacked—but for how long? For almost two years, in fact, and for the whole of that time the hotel, despite coining it in from the British Government with a regular full house, never once allowed its dining room to produce a single fresh vegetable.

Out came the similar food, night after night, straight out of the freezer, served in the elegant dining room. The wealthier set of Belfast dined there and seemed satisfied, but of course there was little choice in a beleaguered city where most restaurants were closed. On one occasion I challenged the Culloden's head waiter to produce a fresh vegetable. There was a long pause then the chap's face lit up. "How about a tomato?" he suggested.

On the Easter Sunday morning Whitelaw planned to attend the Hillsborough church service with the Governor, so I went over in my new official car with young Johnnie Walker at the wheel. Though he made no secret of his strong Protestant feelings, Johnnie stayed with me throughout my Ulster tour of duty and became invaluable as a sounding board. And he never forgot to change his route constantly— too many had died in this kind of terrorist situation because they fell into a routine. Johnnie was determined we were not going to be ambushed in that way and it was a comfort.

I asked Whitelaw if he was a regular churchgoer, for he did not strike me as particularly religious. But he told me went to his local church in Penrith near his country home, Ennim, fairly frequently.

It was obviously trickier stuff in Northern Ireland, though. The venue was to be Hillsborough Parish Church, part of the Presbyterian Church of Ireland, where it was customary for Lord Grey to read the lesson, and he had his own reserved pew.

The security aspect needed watching and Superintendent Jack Morris of Special Branch, who was with us at the time, carefully vetted the congregation with the help of an RUC sergeant responsible for the Governor's security.

Lord Grey read one lesson and Whitelaw took the second—and it suddenly clicked that I had not checked to see if there was a hidden implication which might provide tomorrow's headline. The clergyman skated fairly near topical issues, but as there were no journalists present it all passed off safely.

After church, Whitelaw again followed Grey's tradition of walking back to Hillsborough through the lanes in the warm sunshine. There was little security around. But few people then knew Whitelaw by sight. Within a few weeks, something like that would become quite impossible.

Next morning I was up early, raring to go to work, but I could see there was not a lot of point in arriving and having to persuade RUC security guards that I was entitled to entry. As yet, I had no pass other than the usual Whitehall identification.

But at 8.30 a.m. I went outside and there was Johnnie Walker, his Austin gleaming and a big grin on his face.

At the entrance to Stormont Castle stood Tom Roberts, hand outstretched in welcome. "Come on in and see what you can do," he smiled.

I was clear in my own mind about my initial steps. I told Tom I wanted to meet the entire staff of the information section. Everyone, I insisted, not just the chiefs. Tom raised his eyebrows, but suggested that the meeting had better be in the conference room and that the switchboard should be told to hold calls.

It took about fifteen minutes for everyone to gather. I knew several of the NIO staff from my period there with Callaghan, but now it was to be quite a different relationship.

"Good morning," I began. "I'm told you are the people who have been losing the propaganda war to the IRA ... " and paused. "Well, now you are going to show me how to win it."

There was an audible buzz; people straightened their backs and began to look interested. *Maybe this cocky Londoner might be what we have been needing.*

I asked several people to describe their roles, and it gradually became apparent that many of them were working in isolation. I did not detect much of a concerted drive towards any particular objective. When I asked where people were located, it became clear they were in nooks and crannies all over the place in Stormont Castle and that there was no actual centre of activity.

I told Tom and David Gilliland I was going to ask for immediate office changes so that all the staff would be located together. Following the Whitelaw dictum of grabbing what was needed immediately, I sent for an accommodation man and told him what I wanted. He was delighted. It meant he could quickly find rooms for the newly arriving ministers if he could shunt out all those awkward information people. And now he could do it without a fight!

In return, he gave me a block of prefabricated offices set-up at the back of the Castle and connected by a short corridor. I knew I would have to do a lot more walking to get to ministerial offices and meetings, but now I had Tom next door on one side of my room and David and Fred Corbet, his number two, on the other side. Indeed, if I shouted loud enough, I did not need to phone them, so thin were the walls.

I always thought in newspaper terms, so in effect I was editor and Tom was deputy. On the other side David was the news editor dealing with the fast traffic. In another room was Cliff Hill, the Foreign Office liaison man—really, MI6—in effect my foreign editor. Round the corner worked the wonderful Freddie Gamble, who had been chief sub on the *Daily Mirror* in Manchester, and before that the top dog at the *Belfast Telegraph*.

Freddie wrote like a dream and could quickly translate my thoughts into tabloid terms. We hit it off extremely well, and Freddie produced some great counter propaganda material. 'Death of a Village', for example, was a tabloid inset produced within the local newspapers condemning a dastardly bombing of the tiny hamlet of Claudy. Another was the deadly chronology of Bloody Friday when the IRA let off a series of timed bombs within the centre of Belfast to induce panic as the crowds found there was no safe place to run for shelter. The pen was certainly mightier than the sword when Gamble produced our powerful *Daily Mirror* polemic scorning such callous cowardice.

In 1972 there were no photocopiers or computers. Every time we wanted copy it had to be typed—and retyped. If we wanted a change, it meant more carbon copies and our typing pool, headed by a girl called Rosemary, was our equivalent to the Downing Street Garden Girls. They were nearby too, and part of the team.

So suddenly the Northern Ireland office had an integrated information section, and it had taken only a few hours to achieve it.

I set about building my London office up too. I recruited Dick Seaman, who had marked my card on my first day at the Department of Economic Affairs, as my London deputy. I brought in Tom Roberts' London man, who was idling away his time at the virtually defunct Ulster office. There was not much scope for trade promotion at the time! But that was important because Dick, like me, was a Londoner, and a knowledge of the Northern Ireland towns and villages was extremely valuable, as was an understanding now and again of the Ulster psyche.

It was vital that both offices spoke with the same voice, otherwise journalists would quickly latch on to ringing one and then using what had been gathered to lever more facts from the other. After a short while I had a breakthrough in that respect. I spotted an advertisement by Rank for a new gadget which would enable me to have press cuttings sent from one office to the other in a few minutes. A Rank salesman brought one into my office in Whitehall and demonstrated what, at the time, was breathtaking technology.

I ordered immediate installation, and within a few days we had what were the first fax machines for general media use in Whitehall. The invoice went through without touching the sides—it was a joy to behold.

To get back to my first day in Stormont, Whitelaw arrived and, as we learned was his style, had been thinking overnight. He had resolved to visit Londonderry. He argued that though the violence had to be defeated in Belfast and the real battle against the IRA had to be won there, the psychological battle really had to be won in Derry, as the Catholics called their town. If you heard the London prefix it was usually from the lips of a Protestant.

The IRA campaign had started in Derry, said Whitelaw, and that would be where it would have to end. It was important therefore, he reasoned, to try to stamp his personality on Derry and to try to win over its people. Since at the time the Catholic areas, or Free Derry as it was known to the world, were a complete no go area, that was a fairly optimistic order.

We were helicoptered to Ebbrington Barracks outside Derry, mindful, as we hovered, that we were a good target for a sniper. The pilot told us nonchalantly that it was fairly common for the IRA to take a pot shot, but they were usually so much off target there was no real danger. That may have been the case in 1969, but only a few months later, better armed and equipped, the IRA were to become deadly in this aspect.

In Derry we made a tour conducted by the Army and by Chief Superintendent Frank Lagan, in charge locally of the Royal Ulster Constabulary. Lagan was to become one of Whitelaw's touchstones. Much maligned by the Protestants because he was a Catholic, and because the police dared not step inside the Bogside or the Creggan estate, Lagan nonetheless had a high reputation among the local Catholics, who made up eighty percent of the population.

It was no exaggeration to say that Lagan could go anywhere in the city in complete safety. Frequently he wore mufti, but in a town as small as Derry he could never hope to keep his identity a secret. Still, whenever in the months ahead Whitelaw flew in, Lagan was there to meet and brief on how well—or badly—the battle for political and public relations was going. Lagan was undoubtedly one of the heroes of the Ulster story. We could have used a dozen like him.

General Robert Ford also came to the barracks to meet us—'Old Charge of the Light Brigade' as Whitelaw later nicknamed him. It was Ford who had suffered the brunt of the IRA's political attack over Bloody Sunday. He was the man who committed the 1st Para on that fateful day—but did he then keep a tight grip on what happened? Subsequent enquiries revealed he did not.

Ford was not politically astute, unlike Harry Tuzo who knew instinctively when to bend and sway in tune with political thinking. But, as Whitelaw put it, Ford was the man to follow over the top, the man who would gallantly lead with dash and élan. Maybe get his head blown off, though.

Brigadier Pat McClelland was there, too. He was the top soldier at Derry, based at the barracks. He regarded Lagan as a Republican—which he probably was, agreed Whitelaw—and relations were frequently strained. But it was Lagan who picked up the vital intelligence in the city that was needed.

Having taken the plunge to visit Derry, we were agreed that the Northern Ireland Secretary had to be seen in town. So we went to the top of a nearby cinema, and from the sandbagged observation post—slap in the middle of a so-called British city—peered through binoculars at the terraced houses down by the city wall and up to the concreted Creggan estate.

The army officers pointed out positions from which shots were frequently fired at the post, before shepherding us into the back of a Saracen or a Pig troop carrier—later found to be very vulnerable to armour-piercing bullets—to visit Rosemount police station.

At first it appeared encouraging that somehow the RUC were managing to maintain a presence only a few yards from what had become known worldwide as a no go area. But the Secretary of State was to be rudely awakened.

Once there and shunted pretty smartly by the soldiers into a dingy house, there was only one policeman to be found, a rather frightened young man guarded by half a dozen British soldiers. If ever there was a symbol, here he was, nervous as hell and no idea what was happening. After Whitelaw had chatted and moved on the young policeman asked a soldier the identity of his visitor!

Whitelaw resolved to try his personal charm and approached some people standing in the street at the end of the Creggan. Beaming, holding out his hand, came the soon-to-become familiar line, "Nice to meet you—I'm Willie Whitelaw." The locals just continued chatting. Then one Ulsterman told Whitelaw, "You're a nice enough lookin' fellow, but we've yet to find out if you've anything in yer head."

The biggest laugh of all was Whitelaw's. And the laugh continued the rest of the day as Whitelaw recounted the story.

I left that story out as I phoned over details of the first official visit of the Northern Ireland Secretary to my new enthusiastic team. But we had made a start …

At Stormont Castle we started to develop a routine that would be roughly the way we would operate for the next two years.

I quickly established that I saw Whitelaw first thing after the private secretary, and over the months we built a close rapport. I discussed everything with Whitelaw in complete candour, other than security matters. I told him that I did not want to know these kind of issues unless they were likely to go public. Otherwise, I felt, when there were the inevitable leaks I would be an obvious suspect.

We would then have a major morning meeting attended by the RUC chief constable, Graham Shillington, the army's GOC Sir Harry Tuzo, Bill Nield, the security chief Alan Rowley, Northern Ireland Cabinet Secretary Sir Harold Black and his deputy, Ken Bloomfield. I would attend and take Tommy Roberts, which sometimes raised Northern Irish Civil Service eyebrows but established the status press and PR work held with the Secretary of State. His junior ministers, whichever were in Belfast at the time, would also attend.

Whitelaw concentrated on his strategy, which was to try to win over the Catholic minority, to separate them from their 'protectors'— particularly the IRA—and at the same time push the Protestants as far as he dare. Only in this way, Whitelaw felt, could he find out how the 'Protestant backlash', might be tested.

Willie called it his 'balancing act'. Often, if he was too far exposed on the Catholic side, he would make some gesture to the Protestant view to bring the scales back nearer to central. It was high-wire stuff but for several months it paid off.

Meanwhile the security forces, notably the Army, continued to look in only one direction. To them the IRA—and therefore the Catholics—were the 'enemy' and for many months it was extremely difficult to persuade them that Protestant elements were potentially just as dangerous.

Willie wanted to get a batch of the people interned in Long Kesh released as soon as he could. We knew many of those listed for internment had been scandalously treated anyway, which played beautifully into the hands of the IRA.

Those selected for round-up had had their names chosen by a Stormont Castle civil servant named Stout. This man had an appalling reputation among the Home Office civil servants, and in the very first weekend of direct rule Bill Nield persuaded Sir David Holden, his opposite number in the NICS that Stout had to go—fast. News of Stout's premature retirement on a good pension soon became known on the grapevine, but it was not to leak into the Republic's newspapers for several months.

I was told that the actual round-up of suspects had been based on names supplied by the RUC, and Stout had been content to authorise the arrest of over 380 Catholic men without query or demand for substantial evidence. This was a factor in the minority anger when Whitelaw and his team arrived.

There was precious little to go on for the special team set-up to sort it out. The bright young principal, Joe Pilling, came over from the Home Office in London to work on the files, assisted by a younger executive officer, appropriately named Dilling. These two worked through the files, such as they were, trying to produce a list of the lesser evils held at Crumlin Road and in cells aboard HMS *Maidstone*, berthed in Belfast Lough.

The IRA was making good propaganda out of the 'prison hulk' and the claimed poor conditions even though British soldiers were in identical accommodation in other parts of the ship.

Whitelaw asked me what I considered would be the right number of releases to make an impact without appearing to be taking a security risk. I visualised the likely headlines and suggested something over 50—nearer 70 if possible. And preferably an odd number so that it would not look contrived. In the event Pilling produced 74. We were halfway through the second week of our direct rule drive, having worked straight through Easter, and some of us were beginning to flag. Whitelaw was to fly back to London to attend Cabinet and then the new special sub-committee set-up to monitor direct rule. Since Edward Heath had pledged in the announcement of direct rule that internment would be phased out, this was the first real test. It also had to take into account the Army's sensitivity if they were to go with the decision.

The Secretary of State flew back to Aldergrove after his brief few hours in London. As soon as he touched down he signed every one of the seventy-four releases. As he dashed off his remarkably illegible signature—virtually impossible to read, but incredibly difficult to forge—he told us that while in London he had telephoned each of our wives personally. We were all taken aback. Such was the pace from

Maundy Thursday onwards that we had practically forgotten our home life.

But Willie hadn't, it seemed. We were to learn that this was typical of Whitelaw. Later, I learned, one of the London-based private secretaries, Rob Stevens, contacted each wife and alerted them to expect a call from the Secretary of State. It was just as well as my wife, Shirley, was not unaccustomed to leg-pull phone calls from journalists and told Stevens to 'pull the other one'. But my new minister came through shortly afterwards booming, "Willie Whitelaw here." He proceeded to thank Shirley, to tell her I was safe and well, and to apologise profusely for ruining planned Easter holidays. From then on Shirley, and all the other wives, I imagine, had been recruited at a stroke to the Willie Whitelaw fan club.

It was a completely genuine and thoughtful act on Whitelaw's part, but as a textbook way of getting total loyalty from one's staff it was a lesson some of today's ministers might well take on board.

We agreed that Whitelaw would announce the internment releases at a press conference in Stormont Castle that very next morning. The last thing we needed was a leak. I had resolved from the first that we would only hold a formal press conference when we had a genuine copper-bottomed news story to announce, and this was certainly in that category.

The dash to the door of the agency men running to the telephone (mobile phones had not been invented) confirmed that for me.

Needless to say, Whitelaw was accused of using the men in Long Kesh as political hostages, but we were prepared for that line of attack. "Not at all," boomed Whitelaw. "This is only the first lot—there will be more to come." From now on there would be a steady trickle as the internment camps were run down, so there would be no regular announcements from the Northern Ireland Office.

Whitelaw also declared, with an eye on the likely impact—that HMS *Maidstone* would no longer be used as a prison—another IRA propaganda weapon neutralized.

Calling on the Catholic minority to reciprocate and renounce the men of violence, Whitelaw made very good mileage in the newspapers, on TV and on radio, particularly on RTE, the Dublin state radio. His first bid to woo over the minority went well.

None of us could foresee that in the months ahead Whitelaw would have to reverse the decision to release many of these men, and pilot a bill through Parliament scrapping juries and holding judge-only trials to begin a new legal detention process. Soon, over a thousand men, some women, and even teenagers as young as fifteen, would be behind bars before the IRA would be on its knees. But at least the prisoners knew the charge they faced.

Still, that evening we flew back to the mainland on the HS-125 with our newly battle-hardened Secretary of State, content in the view that at the end of an intense fortnight we had regained the propaganda initiative and started out on a road to end the desperate Ulster situation.

We ached, it seemed, in every bone, and our brains were totally fagged. But we felt good. We believed we had done a reasonable job, and if not appreciated in Northern Ireland, certainly the rest of the country seemed to acknowledge it.

Pretty soon the morning discussions in the Stormont Cabinet Room, to which all the key personalities in the Northern Ireland scene were brought in, became unmanageable, and a stopper was applied, quite rightly, by Bill Nield. One had to have a very good reason to attend the meeting, or receive a summons because of a specific issue. This meant we were not stuck in the big room for several hours at a time.

Nield would be there, of course, until he was replaced by ex-Battle of Britain Spitfire pilot Frank Cooper, as would Jack Howard-Drake, an undersecretary at the Home Office, who was once in charge of an anti-aircraft battery there when Belfast was heavily bombed.

General Harry Tuzo, and later General Frank King, came to the meetings primed with the army view while Graham Shillington, the Chief Constable, arrived with the RUC version of events until he too was replaced by Jamie Flanagan, the first-ever Catholic to get the top police job in Ulster. He had a lot of guts.

We would also be joined by three senior Northern Ireland civil servants: Sir David Holden, Sir Harold Black and Ken Bloomfield—the three musketeers as Whitelaw called them.

Often the assembly would change with the issue of the day, but the regulars, as listed, were generally there as were the key private secretaries—notably Terry Platt, who had suddenly replaced Leonard Davies. Terry and I worked extremely closely together for two years—he always kept me in the picture with innermost confidential material, and I never let him down. Later Terry became the Home Office Chief Immigration Officer—and in this highly politically exposed task he survived! And then he became head of the Home Office Police Department before retiring as a deputy secretary.

Whichever junior ministers happened to be where Whitelaw had touched down were always invited. He was a great believer in keeping them in the picture and encouraging them to contribute. He strongly disagreed with the old-established Whitehall practice that junior ministers were to be seen but not heard.

At the London end Whitelaw would duplicate his morning conference with the outcome transmitted to Belfast and vice-versa. Wherever the conference was held, the permanent secretary and I would be there, but otherwise the cast changed. Communication between the two offices was at first primitive, and in the early stages there was a tendency to forget to tell the other end—where the Secretary of State wasn't!

Bill Nield made great efforts here and his administrative abilities shone. His initial appointment was a good Whitehall choice because he excelled in cutting through time-consuming procedures, but Nield increasingly came to irritate Whitelaw with his dogmatic views. So the offer of deputy chairmanship of the newly nationalised Rolls-Royce was not only timely for Nield, but a welcome relief to Whitelaw.

A fly on the wall at one of our early morning conferences might well have been shocked at the sight sometimes of Nield, hand in the air as ostensibly he scratched under the armpit. That was Bill's summing up of the latest Ulster outrage.

'Monkey business' would be identified as Nield raised his arm. That was the usual verdict on the latest gyration by the Rev. Ian Paisley, the so-called Ulster Defence Association, or by the prisoners in Crumlin Road jail. Nield argued that these tricks were not unlike the antics of monkeys in a zoo, and Whitelaw seized on it. The more he became familiar with the Province and its daily crises the more he became convinced that the theory held water. As fast as he grabbed one by the tail, another issue would be on the table clamouring for attention while another climbed the wall to distract attention or, more likely, to attract it.

I doubt if the Ulster population would have appreciated the theory, but the sight of Nield raising his arm was often a signal to those of us in the room not to be sucked into the latest clamour but to step back and make a cooler assessment.

Another of Nield's acute observations was that as each weekend approached, an issue would suddenly flare up and occupy all weekend attention only to subside the moment work started on Monday. "If we're not careful," said Bill, "they are going to run us ragged just as they did with their own politicians."

He likened it to a game of rugby; if we had the ball the other side could not do much. So from about midday Wednesday we had to work up an issue that would keep the agitators busy while we nipped home to the mainland on Thursday to return refreshed on Monday.

Basically, in my language, we had to keep the publicity initiative and not leave space for Ulster troublemakers to exploit.

But there were grim moments, too, in that Cabinet room, some of the tensest of my life. Fairly regularly, it seemed, the Army would arrive determined to shake us up or give us a fright.

One day General Frank King arrived with a letter bomb, defused fortunately, and showed us the fiendishly simple detonation plan which worked as the envelope was opened, dislodging a paper clip which fired the explosive—straight into the opener's face. Nice people.

Only a week or so later in my London office my secretary Dreda took a packet into Dick Seaman addressed oddly to the Deputy Director of Information. Dreda said she did not like the look of the envelope which had something greasy on it.

Ludicrously, Dick slit the end open with a stationery knife and saw it contained a book about classical music. He had been a RAF pilot in the war and was fairly calm. "Nobody sends me a book like that—I don't like classical music," he told Dreda, and put a paperweight on it. She called the department's security staff and they took the packet away gingerly.

That was about the time a similar packet blew up in the post room at Downing Street, seriously injuring a woman clerk; and there were other incidents elsewhere. Our packet, though, was very useful for the follow-up detective work, and some months later a terrorist in Londonderry was arrested and charged for sending six letter bombs. His finger prints on 'our envelope' clinched it. He went to jail for several years.

About that time the Army and RUC seized 250 mortars being prepared at a Protestant arms factory in so-called peaceful Co. Down.

The ingenuity was terrifying. The barrel was plastic drainpipe— easy to fabricate from material bought in a DIY store or at a builders' merchant. The tripod was in wood adjusted by wingnuts bought in a cycle shop. And the bomb was not unlike an aerosol can, but packed with explosive. Their accuracy may have been questionable, but there was little doubt that the concept of using mortars was under consideration by both Catholic and Protestant terrorists in a 'doomsday' environment on the streets of Belfast or Derry. It was awful to contemplate.

We hoped that by publishing stories and pictures of the weapons, and suggesting that they were blowing up and injuring their operatives, it would deter both sides sufficiently. But the mortars worried us for the entire two-year period of direct rule under Whitelaw, which was the most concentrated period of violence in what turned out to be a period of unrest spanning thirty years. Fortunately, the mortar threat never culminated in their direct use, but the potential was clear to us all in 1971. Crumlin Road jail, for example, was wide open. So was every military establishment in the Province, which now housed little short of 20,000 servicemen and women. The well-protected but isolated house of the GOC called 'Cloonah' was a sitting duck.

And above all, as we sat around the conference table before the large expanse of window opening onto the rising ground above Stormont Castle, we were quite vulnerable. The table was pretty hefty and I reckoned we would all need to dive under it, but I doubt if it would have protected us from a well-aimed mortar shell lobbed straight into the Cabinet Room.

When work was done for the day, and there were no evening engagements, those in town would gather for dinner with Willie and whoever of his ministerial team were around. The drinks would flow, which was how the joke got around that there were eight parties in Northern Ireland—the seven political parties and the one that was always on at Stormont Castle!

On one occasion I commented that Whitelaw seemed able to take terrorism in his stride. Had he previous experience, perhaps? It was a shot in the dark but he revealed that he had been with the Army in Palestine in 1946. That was when Britain tried to hold the Protectorate of Palestine together as the Jewish Stern Gang and Irgun pioneered the very terrorism which subsequently they so abhorred when employed against them by the Palestinians. Whitelaw had been through that daunting period so maybe he was more battle-hardened than we had imagined.

Remarkably quickly we settled into a routine—we would fly out on Monday morning to Belfast, work extremely hard for three days, and depart on Wednesday evening for London. On Thursday morning Whitelaw would attend Cabinet, and in the afternoon there would be a meeting of the Cabinet sub-committee which presided over Ulster affairs.

I went on several occasions as an adviser. More likely, though, I would be in the London office of the NIO sorting out my London in tray, seeing my staff there, liaising with the others in Stormont Castle, or planning for an upcoming event.

It was also a chance to go across to Parliament and get upstairs in the Press Gallery to meet up with lobby correspondents and take the temperature. At that time many of them were my former contemporaries from Fleet Street and I was usually given a good welcome. Often I would have lunch with capable journalists like Gordon Greig, *Daily Mail*, John Dickinson, *London Evening News* and Cyril Arthur of Press Association.

A regular beer was taken with Chris Moncrieff of the Press Association who loved me to give him a reason to argue with his News Desk why he should be sent over to Belfast for a few days. At the time he was fairly low on the ladder at PA but he was to develop into a journalist of major political influence in Westminster. Long after retirement he still had a regular column in *The House* magazine.

Thursday and Friday were also days to give a briefing to foreign journalists visiting London, and also to meet up with my opposite numbers in the Whitehall machine, like John Groves, chief information officer at Defence, or some of the Foreign Office people. That was important because they could update me on how our efforts were being reported in vital places like the eastern seaboard cities of the United States, from where substantial funding for the IRA was sourced.

Later, with casualties and then terrorism striking home in US cities, attitudes did change. But it was a long time before Americans began to grasp the true nature of the viciousness of terrorism in Northern Ireland, even when we had most of Washington on board. It was the same with much of Europe and Latin America, where often British policy was seen as anti-Catholic when we had been striving since the first attempts by James Callaghan to give them a fairer deal.

Continuing with our routine, if all was relatively quiet we would get home for weekends, but for Willie Whitelaw it was not always so simple. Friday was, if possible, his constituency day in Penrith, and then he would try to take a break at his beautiful Cumberland home, Ennim.

But quite often—and totally unreasonably, some of us felt—Heath would call a few of his ministers to lunch on Sunday at Chequers, the Prime Minister's country residence near Aylesbury. There was a view that, as a bachelor, Heath had little real social life, and if nothing was arranged for the weekend he would summon a few of his team for company and to make them jump through hoops. OK for some, but very unreasonable on the Northern Ireland minister, who seldom had time to enjoy much home life.

Our team had personal knowledge of Chequers for we all gathered there one weekend shortly after we had settled into a routine to discuss our strategy. We were installed in splendid bedrooms, and looked after by RAF men and women from the nearby Halton base. We met in the magnificent Long Gallery upstairs where we could all contribute as Whitelaw presided.

On Monday morning our arduous week would begin all over again. I had a breakthrough, however, when I discovered I could fly direct with British Caledonian from Gatwick to the civil airport at Belfast, adjoining the RAF base at Aldergrove, arriving around 9 a.m. It meant I did not have to trek across London to Northolt, could get breakfast on the plane (not always a speciality of the RAF on its HS-125s) and also read the newspapers. Vital research time for me …

That worked well for a while, but on one occasion the Gatwick plane was cancelled, so I was in a real jam. The RAF plane was held for a while for me at Northolt but then took off. I was in luck, though, because I was told another RAF plane would be flying a VIP out later that morning and I could get on board. It turned out to be the Defence Secretary, Lord Carrington, on an unannounced visit, and I had a very interesting session with him as he pumped me on progress in Belfast.

But at Stormont Castle two hours later I was sent for by Bill Nield. "Just make your bloody mind up what plane you are on, will you," he told me bluntly. With the help of my team I soon regained my spurs. We met briefly each morning but once a week there would be a big session and I made it clear that anyone's thoughts or ideas were welcome, an idea I used for the rest of my professional career. I brought in the press people from the RUC, the Army headquarters at Lisburn, and several of the Northern Ireland departments like Home Affairs.

On one occasion we discussed that overnight there had been a considerable amount of rifle and machine-gun fire in some flashpoint areas, yet there seemed nothing to report next morning.

That was not the point, argued Tom Roberts. "My poor old mother was worried sick all night," he told us. "Why can't she pick up the phone and ask someone what's going on?"

As we kicked this around we realised we were talking about a public information source, but Bill McGookin, in charge of the RUC press office, made it clear that his outfit was too busy to start answering the public clamour. In any case, it took time for facts to get through to his team.

But as we talked it became clear that maybe we were not exploiting the telephone facility at all in the Province. "So people are cut off and isolated even if they want to help us," said someone.

From this discussion slowly emerged the concept of the confidential telephone line on which people could ring in to a tape recorder and leave a message for the police; anonymously if they wished. They could have confidence that they were not speaking directly to a policeman and that there was no way their identity could be checked, nor that their call could be traced back to them.

With this concept Tom and I went to the next morning conference and strongly argued our case with occasional references to Tom's 'wee mother'. It did not exactly hit the meeting between the eyes. The RUC made noises about the difficulty, the manpower involved, the legalities—all kinds of problems. The army remained silent, so we knew we did not have their vote.

But, perhaps to let us down lightly, Whitelaw asked for the proposal to be examined and for a report. That meant our idea had to be looked at. But we were not optimistic as we filed out of the Cabinet Room.

However, two days later, Bill McGookin was on the phone. At the top of the RUC they liked it and wanted a meeting, so Tom and I went down to the RUC headquarters at Knock. It turned out that the police did not think the tape recordings would yield much at all, but Special Branch loved it. Now they could use the confidential phone as a cover to explain where secret information had been acquired. It took the pressure off possible secret informants and the use of illegal interrogation techniques.

Within a day or two we were ready to announce the service which turned out to be the first if its kind, copied all over the world, and vital in many counter-terrorist operations. The biggest compliment was the way it was picked up by Crime Stoppers in London despite some initial sniffiness by Scotland Yard, not keen to be seen copying a 'provincial' police force idea.

In Belfast, from our initial publicity launch, the phone was red-hot. Information flowed in. Everything had to be carefully checked and evaluated in case it was a come-on to trap security forces. But it soon became clear that many tip-offs were from mothers and wives who would rather turn their men folk in and have them alive behind bars than shot dead by a British Army patrol. Or, worse, blown up carrying one of their own home-made bombs.

I set out to publicise the confidential phone number with a big campaign, and again money was not a problem. So I bought space on the sides of buses which went through 'no go' areas like Anderstown and The Creggan, put the number on the back of bus tickets, and gave away free shopping lists in grocery shops, which—just by coincidence—happened to have the phone number on the back page.

And when the unemployment or social security monthly cheque arrived in the post from the much maligned British Government, there was the confidential phone number franked prominently on the envelope.

My biggest coup was with a private businessman who for twenty years had advertised through the earpiece alongside the *Belfast Telegraph* masthead. I persuaded him to surrender it to me. So from then on every night the magic confidential phone number was printed in red on the front page of the biggest-selling evening paper and delivered throughout the city.

Another successful counter-terrorist ploy to emerge from my morning meetings came through discussing why there was no equivalent, locally, to the highly successful programmes on the mainland enlisting public help for the police in solving crimes. Each commercial TV region had such a programme, but none existed in Northern Ireland.

"Ulster TV will never touch it," I was told. "They're scared of being blown up." I asked for an appointment at Ulster TV and went down to meet the programme controller, Sydney Perry. Was I mad? Didn't I realise how vulnerable the television studios were? Did I really want the station put out of action for days, weeks?

I argued back strongly. The programme I had in mind would not dwell on terrorism. There was plenty of 'ordinary' crime being committed. People were drinking and driving, speeding, knocking down pedestrians in unlit streets. Illegal booze was being sold in secret drinking dens. It was getting like Chicago in the Prohibition. Restoring respect for law and order was part of the process of getting Northern Ireland back to normal.

TV producers were also citizens, I argued. They had to stand up sometimes, and accept a share of responsibility for what was going on. Yes, even if there was a personal risk. Like the rest of us.

It must have gone on for two hours, but finally Perry agreed to put the proposal to his bosses. I was not optimistic, but I offered to script the programme and give it full backup.

Next morning the call came through that Ulster TV would give it a try, though they were distinctly uneasy. The programme would be called *Police Six* (because there were six counties in Northern Ireland). We had a week to prepare, and this was Bill McGookin's finest hour. He had been at Ulster TV himself before joining the Government service and could write and visualise a TV script without difficulty. And we had some luck—though a tragedy for the family concerned. A little boy was missing from a Protestant area and there was no terrorist connection. So we could go big on the manhunt to search for the child and enlist public support. The Ulster public, despite their noisy and vicious streak, are also softies at heart and love children. We were on a winner.

Our second story concerned the heist of a lorry load of whisky just before Christmas. It had gone, we suspected, into one of the dozens of 'shibeens', illegal drinking clubs, which had sprung up round the city, and were quite possibly ways in which the Ulster Defence Volunteers could launder stolen money. That Chicago thing again.

Police Six went out on a Monday evening, and within a few weeks was one of Ulster TV's most successful programmes, regularly topping its charts, and it continued in production for many years.

I used the success of *Police Six* in another way as well. I had wanted to promote McGookin, but I was up against Northern Irish Civil Service rigidity and even some opposition from Tom Roberts. I felt McGookin played a key role and really worked closely with us at Stormont Castle. With his extra responsibility as scriptwriter and part producer of *Police Six* I got Bill upgraded to chief information officer. Money well spent, I argued.

Fairly frequently, Whitelaw himself and the rest of us were challenged on why we were not trying to talk to the IRA. It was quite a useful stick with which to beat us, but we knew that the moment we did, the Protestant extremists and many more moderates would berate us for supping with the devil. And so would Whitelaw's critics on the right wing like Enoch Powell.

The policy line was that we did not talk to those who indulged in violence. The door was always open, of course, to those willing to lay down their arms and get round the negotiating table.

Whitelaw was quite clear that eventually he had to talk to the IRA. Indeed, it was in recognition of his innate negotiating skills that he had been picked out for the worst job in British politics.

So while persisting that there was no question of mediating with men of violence, he quietly agreed that Frank Steele, on our team, should put out some tentative feelers. An MI6 man who had carried out the secret negotiations with Jomo Kenyatta in Kenya, Frank was an extremely affable character, quite unlike the mysterious souls who inhabit dark alleyways in John le Carré novels.

He operated out at Laneside, the comfortable but isolated house from where Oliver Wright had based himself in the Callaghan days. A perfect location for a little skulduggery.

Soon after the declaration of direct rule and Whitelaw's appointment, the Official IRA, as they were known, announced a ceasefire. This was welcome, but it did not really address the violence question because the 'Officials' were really older men who had campaigned against the British in the 1950s.

Our concern was over the breakaway group of younger hotheads, who came to be called the Provisional IRA, many of whom were interned, and whose brothers—and some of their sisters—were itching to kill a British soldier. And to bring down the dominance of the Ulster Protestants.

On 2nd June 1972 they announced the fight would go on, but secretly, tentative contact by Frank Steele was making slight progress.

He set-up talks in a remote country house owned by a Colonel Sir Michael McCorkill, just over the border from County Donegal, which meant the Provisionals from the South could take part.

With Steele went Philip Woodfield, himself an experienced negotiator, and from my own team David Gilliland, who was from Derry and had the right accent and instincts for that part of the Province. It culminated with the announcement on 22nd June of a ceasefire by the Provisionals to take effect four days later.

I can still remember the atmosphere. It seemed a huge black volcanic cloud had lifted, the sun had come out, and an immense joyous feeling of relief flooded through the city. Drinks all round!

That could not last, surely?

Four days later, masked 'members' of the Ulster Defence Association emerged in military fatigues from their homes in places like the Shankill and Short Strand to barricade their streets in protest at what they called the 'no go' areas of the Province run by the IRA. "Where the Queen's Writ does not run," to coin a phrase from the claptrap of the day.

The UDA stopped and searched vehicles, marched up and down the streets in military formation, and demonstrated to us up at Stormont Castle that if we were thinking of talking to 'peaceful' IRA spokesmen, we had better think again.

The trouble was we knew, and maybe the Protestants suspected, that a meeting with Whitelaw was on the cards.

In strictest secrecy we had agreed to fly six of the Provisional

IRA, led by Sean MacStiofain of Dublin—real name John Stevens, of Acton, London—and their Chief of Staff. Among the others were Gerry Adams, Martin McGuinness, both of whom we knew played very dirty with the British Army.

Whitelaw had the perfect cover because that day, he had agreed to play in a golf tournament at Walton Heath with the Press Golfing Society. After a few holes he excused himself and was whisked by official car to the secret talks.

I made no effort to get anywhere near those talks because the presence of a press officer would simply encourage the IRA to go public, the last thing we wanted. So I was going about my duties in the London office, giving no hint, not even to my colleagues, that sensational developments were at hand.

Two days before, up at Stormont, we had held a meeting with the UDA led by their spokesman, Tommy Herron. I had argued strongly that we had to get the masks off their faces to strip away their mystery. So it was made a condition that before such a meeting could take place we had to know the identity of those attending (which meant the RUC could make a quick check of their files) and there was no question of a minister of the Crown sitting down and parleying with masked men. If they were Loyalists, now was the time to prove it, we argued. It worked—and now we knew the identity of Tommy Herron, a former petrol pump attendant, we learned!

So how come we could spirit into London six leaders of the Provisional IRA, grant their immunity from arrest—and not reveal this information? Were we being completely even-handed?

We could see the line of attack, but we were also being criticised for NOT meeting the IRA. And if we missed a chance to turn the temporary ceasefire into a permanent halt to violence, shouldn't we seize it?

For a few days there was no leak and all seemed well. The ceasefire held, even though Whitelaw and the negotiating team were not optimistic. He had asked for time to reflect on their position—total intransigence—and time to consult his Cabinet colleagues, which would have been a total waste of time.

But back in Belfast a new round of 'monkey business' was afoot to exploit the situation.

The British Army was involved in a dangerous standoff with Catholics attempting to rehouse families in the Lenadoon area of Belfast. For hours more than a thousand Catholics, led in reality by IRA activists, tried to move into the housing. A solid phalanx of Protestants were determined it was not going to happen. The soldiers were the meat in the middle.

Whitelaw and Bill Nield were down there and so were several civil servants, led by the redoubtable Deputy Secretary, Neil Cairncross.

It was so tense that the commander of the British troops asked Whitelaw, quite calmly and coolly, if he could give the order to fire if the order to disperse was disregarded and the crowd charged the small military unit.

"I have to have your answer. Is it 'yes' or 'no'?"

That was a hell of a question to ask a civilian minister in a democratic country, even if he had served in World War II and held the Military Cross for gallantry in D-Day tanks.

In normal circumstances I think Whitelaw would have looked round to me for input. Not this time—I wasn't there! Tom Roberts was deputising. Whitelaw had reluctantly agreed to me having the weekend off to take part with my friend, Roy Hodson, in the Round the Island yacht race from Cowes. Not that I could have done much about the confrontation, but I probably could have given my minister support and solace in one of his darkest moments of the two-year Ulster crisis.

"You have my permission to fire," said the Secretary of State for Northern Ireland. But the crowds got the message. Both sides hesitated, and there was a gradual dispersal. The soldiers re-engaged their safety locks.

In Dublin, though, a sheet of paper was slipped into a typewriter, and drafting began of an announcement that the ceasefire by the Provisional IRA was over. Early next morning, as I have described, the phone by my bed woke me—on 10th July 1972—for a momentous day in which it looked as if the Provisional IRA held all the cards. By the end of it the tables were turned, and Whitelaw was back in the saddle, but it was a close-run thing.

Now a completely new phase, bloodier and uglier, in what the Army described as the insurgency phase of the Ulster campaign, was about to commence. It was opened up on a Friday— 21st July— which meant that I was in London. Dick Seaman, my London deputy, had been itching to get over to Belfast, and was there when, about mid-morning, he had the fright of his life as the first of twenty-six explosions was touched off in the centre of the city. As the crowds reacted, more explosions occurred, timed to ignite as the crowds were running towards them. In the space of half an hour the bombs killed eleven, injured 130, and tore the heart out of Belfast. There had been little warning of the callous onslaught.

Dick's call through to me to say what was happening was far above the usual bomb incident with which the City had been coping.

Then Dreda, my secretary, alerted me to an urgent caller on the line. It was Maurice Tugwell, the colonel I had met at the army headquarters at Lisburn the day Whitelaw arrived in the province.

"Keith," he suggested, "what about calling it Bloody Friday."

I told him it was brilliant and to leave it to me. Immediately I instructed both press offices to put out the one sentence: 'It looks like Bloody Friday'.

In the next edition of the evening papers that was the headline. So it was in most of the morning papers and the comment all round the world.

It was small consolation to the people who had lost their lives or suffered horrendous injuries, physically and psychologically, but we had scored quite a propaganda coup over the IRA. We had avenged Bloody Sunday, a phrase they had hung round our necks. This meant we could point to plenty of blood on their hands, too.

But the day was not to end there. With Belfast still reeling from shock at the outrage, Whitelaw decided we should go to Ulster immediately, and very quickly a plane was organised at Northolt.

In the VIP waiting room we linked up with Lord Carrington and his retinue, and made our way out to the jet that could catapult us across the Irish Sea to Aldergrove in little over an hour.

At Stormont Castle a big group was awaiting us, and Whitelaw immediately went into conference. General Tuzo was there, as was Shillington, the RUC chief, and there was a collection of Northern Ireland civil servants ready to report on the dislocation to the city caused by twenty-six bombs.

Once we had heard the latest 'sitrep', the horrible jargon with which we had become so familiar, Whitelaw and Carrington turned to how we could respond. Their feeling was that the IRA had overplayed its hand and had provided the British Government with every justification for ending the no go areas.

These enclaves had sprung up in Catholic areas, initially designated with white paint on the road and guarded by shadowy, armed young men, in balaclavas and dark glasses, restricting entry. The cameramen loved it.

As the weeks went by, the fortifications had been strengthened, and to enter so-called Free Derry to get to the Bogside required guts and determination. The complete chassis of a truck had been sunk in concrete in the middle of the road to prevent access by British army vehicles. The locals claimed that the barriers and the armed guards gave them protection from marauding Protestant youths (true to some extent) but the areas also presented a defiant challenge to British rule.

The cost of this kind of public defiance was rising rapidly, as was the temper of the Protestants who kept demanding to know why the 'no go' areas had been allowed to remain—and the Queen's Writ, whatever that might be, did not run.

General Tuzo had been waiting for the order to do something about the enclaves, and now he got the 'go' from the Secretary of State for Northern Ireland and the Secretary of State for Defence. In person, no less.

Quite a bit of planning had been going on at Lisburn, and the

Army was itching to make a start. But not without considerable reinforcement. Tuzo first wanted several thousand more troops. The figure in the Province eventually reached nearly 20,000.

He also needed lots of equipment. My ears pricked up when he talked of flail tanks being shipped over. "These road blocks could well be mined," he warned.

Casualties? Inevitably, if the IRA put up a fight there would be quite a lot of blood spilt, and there was no way he could give any assurance on the number of likely civilian casualties. There would need to be the element of surprise and that meant there could well be a human cost. Maybe as many as 500! As I listened with Tom Roberts I was getting distinctly queasy. In exploiting the backlash on Bloody Friday could this turn out to be another Bloody Sunday?

There were working groups set-up, and I got the PR people together to kick it around. One issue which did alarm us was the use of British Army tanks on British streets. This had all the makings of a propaganda photo coup for the Russians—they could avenge Hungary.

My team came up with the idea that our Army would not be using tanks but 'armoured bulldozers', and it was agreed these words should be painted on the sides of the vehicles. Secondly, as soon as they had done their job, we urged they should be pulled out of the mission and returned to their base.

Maurice Tugwell arrived in my office from Army headquarters looking worried. The plan now was officially to be known as Operation Motorman. But more important was what went down the line to the troops. We agreed that no corporal or his squaddies had the time or inclination to work through the reams of paperwork being churned out.

Tugwell wanted a simple Q and A for them, but nothing existed. So I pulled over my typewriter and together we drafted in what I called *Daily Mirror* language crisp one-liners on what was happening. Why the British troops were involved. But we never used the term Queen's Writ!

When the time came the simple Q and A worked. Briefing the men right down to platoon level is now standard practice, but it was fairly new in 1972. The success was also the genesis of the TV training set-up to ensure that soldiers at ground level could speak up quickly and so counter the IRA propaganda. This has been copied by police forces all over the UK and subsequently around the world.

Tugwell and I also agreed that, despite the Army insistence on total secrecy to ensure surprise, there should be broad hints leaked out that Operation Motorman was on the way even if we did not indicate when.

Ten days after Bloody Friday, at dawn on 31st July, Operation Motorman began. The troops had orders to clear the no go areas in the Catholic districts and, at the same time, to remove any barricades in the Protestant areas, too. It meant we could not be accused of being one-sided.

The evening before, I met with Whitelaw and we agreed he should give a warning to the Catholic areas. But the problem was that few of them listened to BBC Radio or watched BBC television.

So I telephoned John Sullivan, the Belfast staff man of Radio Teilifis in Eire, and asked him to come up to the Castle. We could not be completely open with him and tell him what would happen next morning, but Whitelaw dropped some pretty deep hints and John got the drift.

In his response to John's questions, Whitelaw mentioned the friendly talk he held recently with 'the Ladies of the Bogside'. They had marched up to the Castle and demanded to meet the Big Fellah, as they called Whitelaw. To their amazement, we ushered them into the chintz-furnished anteroom by Whitelaw's office, and he offered them afternoon tea as he listened to their grievances. It resulted in a very good-natured atmosphere which I was able to disclose to the waiting reporters.

"What did he say to the women of the Bogside?" they clamoured.

I looked shocked. "You mean the Ladies of the Bogside," I admonished.

The incredulous Protestant-dominated media—and, indeed, many of the Castle staff—could not quite get over it. But Whitelaw had treated his visitors with courtesy and respect, and we hoped it might have gone down well.

The Motorman evening interview went out widely on RTE, and though we suspected Tuzo at Lisburn would be irked, if there were 500 casualties Whitelaw would be able to say he had given a strong warning.

It was pretty late by then, and Whitelaw said he was going to sleep in his office. The private secretary had already erected a camp bed for him, and we tiptoed away to the comforts of the Culloden Hotel. But we were back by 5 a.m. next morning in time to be there when one of our minister's police bodyguards took him in a cup of tea and shook his shoulder. "All going well, sir, no casualties," reported Special Branch man Cole.

The sigh of relief seemed to echo round the walls. "Thank God."

For a few hours alone in that little bed he had faced the prospect he was likely to go down in British history as the Cabinet Minister who authorised the deaths of many, maybe hundreds, on British soil. It would be a hell of a political epitaph.

A few minutes later and Whitelaw was in the outer room with us and seemed his normal self. We picked our way in darkness through the French windows and out to where a helicopter waited.

As we skimmed across the darkened city streets it all seemed remarkably peaceful—no sign of fires, or shooting—and we were soon hovering over the lawn of the GOC's home near Lisburn.

Tuzo had breakfast laid on, and we tucked in to bacon, sausage and eggs as he took Whitelaw through the events of the last couple of hours.

Apart from a single shooting incident in Bogside—not serious—there had been no resistance and no sign at all of armed response. It seemed a miracle. But maybe not. Only fools would take on the Army when it was organised, equipped, and armed to break through the barriers. But maybe, just maybe, the way in which Whitelaw had been coming across had had an impact. He had released men from internment, had striven to listen to all sides, appeared even-handed, and even listened to the Ladies of the Bogside.

Maybe those mothers and wives had gone back and argued that with the Big Fellah up at Stormont Castle things might at last be changing. Give him a chance.

The success and efficiency of Operation Motorman gave a fillip to morale, and the Army enjoyed a brief period of one-upmanship. With the resources of 4,000 extra troops brought from the mainland and good planning, they had demonstrated what could be done. Those 'armoured bulldozers' were not a lot of use, though. They were soon loaded back on the HMS *Fearless* and sailed away. So deeply were the trucks embedded in concrete that the only way for the army engineers to shift them was with pneumatic drills. It took them several days to reopen the roads.

With the 'No Go' areas cleared and some sense of normality around, there was time for policy and objectives to be reassessed. Initially we had to get the level of violence reduced. There was no chance of getting talks between the two factions or persuading local politicians to start to deploy some leadership when bombs, bullets, death and destruction was the daily diet of the people of Northern Ireland.

But Whitelaw was determined to keep his eye on the long-term objectives of getting power-sharing accepted, and the Protestants and Catholics co-operating rather than watching their extreme wings killing each other. It was important to keep reminding ourselves that the large mass of the community on both sides of the divide wanted nothing more than to see the violence stop, and normal life resume, so that kids could go to school in safety, so that people could set out to go to work and have a reasonable chance of returning home again.

Whitelaw devoted much of his time to meeting the local politicians, though he got on much better with the Catholics than with the majority of Protestants. People like Gerry Fitt, garrulous but witty; shrewd John Hume, more strategic with lines open to IRA in Derry; Paddy Devlin, blunt, crude, but gutsy. These were the leaders of the SLDP we cultivated. They had never been inside Stormont Castle before. They all carried a gun, licensed by the RUC for self-protection, and several had been attacked in their own communities by masked thugs. It took a lot of guts to talk to the British Government and to try to argue for peace in such circumstances.

On the Protestant side of the divide it was more difficult. There were the Unionists who had held sway and controlled the Province ever since it had been created after World War I. The key figure was Brian Faulkner, who had been the Prime Minister and was still smarting from the imposition of direct rule which had removed him from office, virtually overnight.

He kept attacking us in speeches and articles. On one occasion he overstepped the mark, and I whooped when I found an old news cutting in which he had said completely the opposite. I took it to Whitelaw. "I've got him—look at this." But Whitelaw shook his head and would not let me shoot Faulkner out of the water. "I'm going to need him— leave it," he told me.

He was right. Whitelaw was peering ahead much further than me. Eventually Faulkner did come on board and showed great courage. It was very sad when he fell from his horse and was killed; ironically, not from an assassin's bullet, but in a riding accident.

While Faulkner represented what might be thought of as the old school, there were the more hard-line, so-called Loyalists, who walked the streets waving Union Jacks and protesting allegiance to the British Crown—yet rejected the tolerance which it represented.

One of its worst advocates was the turbulent priest I had met with Callaghan—the Rev. Ian Paisley.

Frequently he was up at the Castle, and Whitelaw endured many bruising encounters. On one occasion, as he railed against the British Government with half a dozen hard-faced zealots on either side of him, Whitelaw solemnly folded a note and passed it along to me. Everyone, Paisley included, watched closely as I opened the scribbled note. 'All balls' it said. I marvel how I managed to keep a straight face. I still have a memory of the twinkle in the eyes of my minister. And I still have his scribbled note among my career souvenirs.

On another occasion, as Paisley drove up the hill to the Castle for a meeting on rents with Whitelaw, the zealot passed the famous statue of Carson, the Irish Protestant political leader who led the revolt against British plans to quit Ireland totally after WWI. He coined the famous 'no surrender' line.

As Paisley drove past, he saw there was scaffolding around the statue for repair and maintenance. And when he swept in to Whitelaw's office, he brushed aside the proffered handshake and declared, "You are not going to remove Carson's statue."

Puzzled, Whitelaw said, "Of course not, Ian." But Paisley persisted. "The Loyalist people will not stand for it," he thundered. Then he sat down and talked about rents quite sensibly and constructively for about half an hour. He knew by then reporters and cameramen would be awaiting him outside.

"What did you tell Mr Whitelaw?" he was asked. "I told him he was not going to knock down and remove Carson's statue," thundered Paisley. "I told him the Loyalist people would not stand for it." The reporters made a dash for the door to find a telephone.

So there we had it—a classic example of how to build a phoney story and create further bad blood among the hardliners when there was not a word of truth in it, as Paisley knew. For once, though, he did not have it all his own way. It so happened that thirty minutes later I was due to meet the press for the regular weekly briefings Whitelaw had authorised me to hold. I saw how to deal with Paisley—with humour. I was laughing as I gave the journalists a blow-by-blow account of what had happened in Whitelaw's office.

The reporters by now were grinning too. They could see a good story going down the drain, but I was offering them a funnier one in replacement and they took the bait. It was to be useful in the months ahead, too. Whenever one of Paisley's shockers came bouncing along I just waved it away.

"Oh, it's another Carson's statue," I would say. I found the regular dismissal of Paisley's machinations worked a treat that way.

But as we worked away on the political side, trying to get a gradual recognition that politics were really the only way forward, the terrorists seemed hell-bent on preventing that and making our efforts appear feeble and futile by perpetrating some dastardly incidents.

I remember being particularly saddened at the way a young girl, newly married, was gunned down in cold blood through a frosted glass panel in her back door. Her crime? As a Catholic she had dared to marry a Protestant.

Two soldiers were given the come-on by a couple of girls in a bar, and foolishly agreed to go with them to another bar. Outside, the 'come-on' girls stood back as masked IRA gunmen, armed with sub-machine guns, shoved the soldiers into the back of a car to drive them off to be murdered. Yes, they wore khaki uniforms—but they were in the dental corps!

Almost every day there was another outrage, as violence was jacked up, notch after notch, to shock and enrage the people of Ulster and catapult the story around the world's media.

Sometimes mere words seemed woefully inadequate, as they did at about 5.30 a.m. one morning when Tom Roberts rang me in my room at the Culloden.

Apparently, Senator Wilson, a Catholic who had been in the Stormont Upper House before Direct Rule, had been drinking with his secretary Irene Andrews, a Protestant, in a public house across the road from the Europa Hotel in the centre of the city.

They were seized at gunpoint and driven away, never to be seen alive again. When their bodies were found near a quarry on the Belfast outskirts, Wilson had his throat cut and had been stabbed 32 times. Irene Andrews had been stabbed 19 times.

The viciousness of the attack took my breath away, as it did so many when the city began to wake. Wilson had been a popular political figure and no physical threat to anyone. He was murdered just because he happened to be in a pub in the town centre with a Protestant.

They were targeted by an Ulster Freedom Force hit squad, led, it later became known, by a former butcher, John White, one of the founders of the vicious UFF—Ulster Freedom Fighters. He was sentenced to life imprisonment in 1978 but some years later was out in the Belfast Shankill again, and ultimately—thirty years later—would play a key role in peace talks. He even got a degree in social science!

One of the lessons from my Northern Ireland days was that in a democracy, undermining the police force is a dangerous route. Insist on a straight, honest regime, and throw the book at police who break the rules. But fail to support them and out from under the stone comes corruption, bribery, drugs, murder, you name it, and crooks who devalue everything in the society in which they can now flourish without hindrance.

That was what we were confronting in Northern Ireland at times. It was proven statistically that Belfast was a more dangerous place than Chicago had been at the height of the Al Capone era. At one point our police were so scared they would not come out of their barracks at night.

We started to suffer a series of random but incredibly vicious murders, and quickly a pattern began to set in. Perhaps a Protestant would set off to go home from work and fail to arrive. His body would be found in an alleyway, shot through the head. Word of the crime would spread quickly and a couple of hours later a Catholic would be similarly gunned down elsewhere in the city.

So it went on each morning, and we would dread to turn on the BBC Belfast radio news to learn of the latest grim developments.

Tom Roberts and I went to see Whitelaw. "You've got to do something," we told him.

"Yes, I know—but what?" demanded the Secretary of State.

"Well, how about a Task Force?"

"What with? The police won't come out of their barracks. They're scared."

Then I had an idea. In the Air Force I had been in the RAF Police. "What about getting some military police to go out with the RUC?" I ventured.

Whitelaw picked up the thought and asked Terry Platt, the private secretary, to make contact with the Ministry of Defence. Did we have any?

Back came Terry with a grin. Yes we did have some, a whole

regiment in fact, from the Corps of Military Police—the Redcaps—who were just packing up their kit in Germany and were returning to the UK to go on leave. No they were not!

The Redcaps were diverted to Aldergrove, and as soon as the advance guard landed that same afternoon they were shipped out to various police stations around Belfast.

Meanwhile, we announced with a fanfare that the Secretary of State for Northern Ireland had set-up a Task Force of joint RUC and Military Police, fully armed, to patrol the city streets from that night onwards.

I also tipped off the journalists that Whitelaw would be out himself that night—and I was with him—to see how the new patrols were settling down. In today's jargon it was 'a photo opportunity', but it was also intended as reassurance to increasingly jumpy Belfast residents.

We needed a bit of luck now, and we got it. One of the random Stop and Search joint patrols flagged down a small private saloon and went through it very thoroughly. Under a seat they found a homemade machine gun—known as a 'zip gun' locally because of the way it could be fabricated in a local engineering workshop. That made the lead for us in the next morning's news rather than the 'Tit for Tat Murders', as the campaign of indiscriminate slaughter had become known.

Slowly the wave of murders waned, but not before more than a hundred people had been killed—few of them connected in any way with the IRA or Protestant gangs. Just, as the saying went, people who were in the wrong place at the wrong time.

It had certainly given us a fright up at Stormont Castle. Our problem was that we would make a little progress, a step forward or two, and then some issue would blow up unexpectedly and back we would go for what would seem ten steps. Then we would start again.

A few months after our arrival a thick volume of paper landed on my desk. Just what I needed—a major report to read and on which to advise the ministers. This was Lord Justice Scarman's inquiry into what had led to communal rioting in August 1969 throughout the province. The RUC had been stretched well past breaking point, and calling in the reservist B-Specials, totally untrained in riot control, had poured petrol on the flames. The Catholics regarded the B-Specials as a bunch of Protestant bully boys, and the sight of them on their streets was sufficient to provoke a backlash.

Out of all this chaos Lord Scarman produced a report of great clarity with recommendations for the future. By the time he had got it out, however, Jim Callaghan had sacked the chief constable, scrapped the B-Specials, disarmed the RUC, and carried out a number of changes of his own. And then, on the decision to shut down the Northern Ireland Parliament, Whitelaw had taken over and promptly given the machine guns and pistols back to the police.

It was tragic. As I read the Scarman report, the first of several inquiries carried out into riot situations in the UK by a very wise judge, it seemed such a shame that his work appeared to have been a waste of time.

By the time Scarman reported, we were in the midst of a terrorist uprising.

I talked the report over with David Gilliland, who had been in contact with the inquiry, and he agreed that it was time for a personal chat with the judge. I was somewhat apprehensive, but need not have worried. Scarman appreciated the Government's dilemma and quickly set me at ease. Far from being removed or above the situation he had read it perfectly. But he courteously thanked me for taking the trouble to go to see him.

I showed him a comment drafted for Whitelaw welcoming the report, promising full and careful consideration. He smiled, thanked me, and handed it back. Months of his painstaking work had just slipped away down the drain.

While progress may have appeared slow to the onlooker, and certainly the media, piece by piece the machine which ran the Province was being taken apart, overhauled, and reinstated as fit for purpose.

The security set-up was a good example. Whitelaw recruited a new supremo to coordinate the various units engaged in this work. Alan Rowley came into our team from SIS, the Secret Intelligence Service. He held the Military Cross for wartime bravery in the jungles of Burma, and had had vast experience in the Far East in the post-colonial era. So Alan knew his way around. His experience was so acknowledged that none of the rival groupings could really challenge him. Gradually, he welded the intelligence effort together and turned it into a formidable resource behind the Whitelaw team. Affable, gregarious, a golfer, and friendly, he needed all these attributes to break down the suspicion between the special branch of the RUC, the intelligence section at the Lisburn army headquarters, MI5, the mainland security which is part of the Home Office, and MI6, the secret service looking outwards from the Foreign Office.

Alan succeeded in gently knocking heads together and, most importantly, getting the Army and RUC intelligence to work with each other. On the top floor of Stormont Castle the beginnings of an electronic surveillance system was created which was to become vitally effective.

Eventually an Army patrol could call in that it had noticed the curtains had been pulled in a house in which it was possible a man on the run had been hiding. Why were the curtains not opened during the day? Was it worth a sudden raid on the place?

This kind of sophistication was to take time to develop and settle down. The army at Lisburn was keen to involve itself in what the military called 'PsyOps'—psychological warfare—or lying, as we would call it in Information. In the early stages the completely amateur nature of the Army operation was almost laughable. A new laundry service appeared on the streets of Anderstown and offered to give free dry-cleaning to demonstrate the quality of its work.

But the name of the new firm was a dead giveaway—the Army called its new service Four Square Laundry. They could have put a Union Jack on the van! The soldier driving the van paid with his life. The plucky young woman soldier with him calling door to door was lucky to escape with wounds. Apparently some army officer had the idea that the locals would hand in for cleaning clothes that had been used in terrorist incidents, and so they could be examined forensically for traces of cordite or bomb-making material. The Army were to learn the hard way—that by the early seventies the IRA were much more sophisticated and would quickly have burnt every item of clothing involved in an incident.

Another arm of Government to be given this kind of reorganisation was in public prosecution. The Catholics had long felt the dice were loaded against them, and the Protestants, who regarded themselves as totally law-abiding, that the legal services worked for them.

The Director of Public Prosecution was Thomas Hetherington. I had become familiar with the name through reading it in newspapers, but I never thought I would get on friendly terms, and later commute, with him on Southern Region trains to East Surrey. He travelled to the Province regularly as he rebuilt the local service and overhauled their systems, so I saw quite a lot of him.

When it was complete the Attorney General, Sir Peter Rawlinson, came over to launch the new service, and I persuaded him to meet the press for what was a positive news story.

In those days the Government's chief law officers did not brief the media, but Sir Peter agreed to talk to the press so long as it was not attributed to him directly. It went well, no reporter let him down, and it was also the first ever press conference of its kind in Northern Ireland. Quite a little coup.

CHAPTER 12
NIO Inching Towards Peace

Step by step, and often with one or two backwards, we made what seemed to us to represent gradual progress. The public in Ulster generally, but not the terrorists on either side, seemed to come round to accepting the new way they were governed, how we operated, and that it was reasonably impartial. Of course, there was nowhere quicker in the United Kingdom to spot an injustice, alleged or more often totally unfounded, but generally direct rule was becoming the accepted way of life in the Province.

Both the Army and the police also seemed to prefer clearer, decisive orders from Stormont Castle rather than having everything cross-checked back in Whitehall. And there was a growing team effort, a spirit of cooperation and pooling of information.

Through it all Whitelaw remained remarkably upbeat, and although I am sure he had his own personal low moments, to all around him he came across as decisive, authoritative and extremely good-humoured. He could lose his temper, but not often. When it came, Whitelaw's face screwed up, brow furrowed, and it would seem at any moment he would stamp his foot like a small child unable to get his or her own way. Then, just as quickly, the mood was gone, an apology was tendered and everything was swiftly forgotten. If that was a minister in a bad temper, I knew I had seen considerably worse.

One morning I did deserve a ticking off. I had agreed Whitelaw would give an interview on newly arrived colour television to a major US television company, based in the Boston area. As I have explained, that was where much of the financial support for the Provisional IRA derived from, and it was important to get our counter-propaganda over. My problem was that I had committed to the interview, but forgotten to tell my boss about it.

At a reception at the Castle when the whisky was flowing I suddenly remembered, and sidled up to Whitelaw to break it to him gently.

"8 a.m., Secretary of State."

He gave me a very black look. He knew it was too late to get out of the interview. To call it off now would mean an unnecessary critic in Massachusetts.

So it was next morning I knocked gingerly on his door at the Culloden Hotel, where he had now moved, and heard the order to enter. As Whitelaw struggled into his trousers I saw the colour of his eyes, a glorious technicolour after the late-night session.

"Don't you ever do this to me again."

I would never have dared. But I ought also to record that Whitelaw never once mentioned my clanger again.

Another incident I recall was a much happier event. Willie's daughter Carol—the second of his four girls—was to be married in the crypt at the Palace of Westminster. Whitelaw and his wife Celia invited every member of the staff of the Northern Ireland Office in London to the reception—including the office cleaners, telephone switchboard staff, doorman, drivers and the messengers. A representative group was also brought over from the Belfast team.

It was a splendid occasion, though whether Carol and her new husband needed us all there to see the cake cut was doubtful, but everyone in the NIO knew we had a once-in-a-lifetime boss and one who deserved to have the very best of our efforts. We raised our glasses to that.

Back at base, Whitelaw inched his way towards compromise. He felt strongly that the projection of him by the media as a kind of Regent or Governor-General was not the acceptable image in a Parliamentary democracy. Nor did it send the right message. But if none of the local politicians would sit at the same table as others from across the divide, how could he take soundings?

Whitelaw decided to appoint an advisory group of citizens, drawn from across the board, to give him their input and also to warn if they saw trouble ahead. From his journeys around the Province he became familiar with the great and the good of Ulster, and took a view on who might have something original to offer rather than just bellyache. Not being local politicians they could keep their mouths shut surprisingly well, and little leaked from the meetings. Which meant Whitelaw could be much more open than would normally have been the case.

He was able to take soundings on the thinking behind the Green Paper published on 30th October 1972 which contained a potential flash point in a reference to 'The Irish Dimension' in which the British Government—for the first time ever—conceded that the Catholic community had strong links with the Republic of Ireland which needed to be taken into account.

While the British Government pledged it would do nothing without the support of the majority, it was saying they could not put their heads in the sand and ignore the minority view. My press team worked hard on all shades of media to stress that as a Green Paper it meant it was a consultative document seeking ideas and opinion.

Was it hell! It may sound innocuous now, but right then it was dynamite.

Whitelaw had a foreword which said 'The British Government has a clear objective in Northern Ireland to deliver its people from the violence and fear in which they live and to set them free to realise their great potential.

'We want to help them to draw together; to find a system of government which will enjoy the ideas and the convictions of the Northern Ireland people themselves. That is why there has to be a lengthy process of consultation, which I started on my arrival, and have been continuing ever since.'

Ken Bloomfield from Belfast, who wrote like a dream, was the main author, but all of the inner team signed a copy for Whitelaw and he was quite touched as we presented it to him. Next day he sent all of us a personal letter.

'Dear Keith' he wrote, 'I was touched by all your kindness in giving me a signed copy of the paper that my thanks yesterday was totally inadequate. You have all been so marvellous with me. We may not succeed but no one will ever say we did not try or did not enjoy ourselves trying together.' Willie Whitelaw.

So even though there was little slackening in the violence, we were inching towards some kind of a deal ... possibly. We had to get the local politicians more engaged, but one of the major problems was the way each side played to the gallery via the media, and the relentless pressure of the journalists on the politicians to produce a new story each day. If they didn't, they would encourage the opposition to come up with something which would start a new hare running.

Billy Flackes, the BBC political correspondent, was a past master. If things were quiet he would have 'a wee chat' with, say, Ian Paisley who would be coaxed into something inflammatory. Then a quick call would be made to, say, Gerry Fitt of the Catholic SDLP, or to the main Unionists. Someone would come up with a retaliatory quote and the 'story' would have legs and possibly lead the midday news on the BBC. We would then spend the afternoon insisting there was no truth in the story, and if something better came up the hare would be allowed to drop. But if more good comments came in to give the story further support, so it would go on and give the people returning home from work something to chew on.

When Billy was on leave his place was taken by Eric Waugh, who usually covered industrial relations and trade unions and was more inclined to a quieter life. Fewer hares ran and we were quite happy about that.

How did we break out of this cycle of comment, counter-comment, denial and abuse? At one of Whitelaw's round-table discussions I explained this was one of the reasons why Northern Ireland was seldom out of the news. Each side felt it had to get across, via the media, to its supporters that it was out there defending their interests. But were they?

So we hit upon the idea of a conference of the politicians away from their usual haunts, cut off from the phone, and removed from the need to shout the odds.

Darlington was chosen as a suitable venue, and in September the British Government took over a major hotel to which all the political parties were invited and their expenses paid. Brian Faulkner's Unionists agreed to come, as did the SDLP Catholic party, the middle-ground Alliance, and Paisley's Democratic Unionists—everyone except the Provisional IRA. We knew that if we invited them no one else would come!

All parties were told there would be no contact permitted with the media. Each day a press briefing would be given by me, impartially, and factual, with a bulletin on the day's progress, if any.

To our amazement, the politicians accepted. There was a sense of relief all round; maybe we were going to get some serious talking done at last.

Needless to say, the journalists did not like it at all. They had booked into the few hotels in Darlington, had established which were the best bars and then located the few decent restaurants, and were all set to go. Trouble was—no real story. Where were the bust-ups, the insults, the threatened walkouts?

I did my best each day to provide an angle, but it was thin fare and I knew it. I also understood that if I slipped off the careful straight line and gave a hint that one side was gaining an advantage over the other, it would be all over. Someone could stomp out and the collapse of the talks would be the story.

At one point, Whitelaw demanded to know why the press were complaining. I explained that they had seen no one, had no copy and not even a picture. We had Ulster's politicians virtually imprisoned.

"Right, we'll see about that," said Whitelaw as he summoned his security man, Detective Chief Inspector Brian Hayes, and told him to prepare for a walkabout outside the compound.

I still have a photograph of our Darlington sortie—I am walking at the front, talking to Whitelaw. Brian Hayes and his colleague, Geoffrey Bourne Taylor, are just behind the minister. Brian looks very smart and some people thought he was the PR man and that thick-set, thuggish-looking character next to the minister (me) was the copper. Brian went on to become Chief Constable of Surrey, then number two at Scotland Yard and, on retirement, head of security for the Football Association.

Some years later Brian was to give the address at the memorial service for Whitelaw in the Guards' Chapel—an occasion, sadly, I missed as I was abroad.

As we inched towards some kind of a compromise we were under increasing pressure from Downing Street, and Edward Heath in particular. Things were not going well on the economic side for him, as he introduced a statutory pay and prices policy, a walk out by the trade unions, militants in the miners itching for a fight–it was all looking very sinister for the Heath Government. The only bright spot being the apparent progress on Northern Ireland and the undoubted popularity of the politician in charge.

Heath had been over to the Province on several occasions, and I had always found him relatively easy to work with. Donald Maitland, the Press Secretary at Number 10, was content to leave it to me in terms of the media handling in Northern Ireland, which was, I suppose, a compliment.

I particularly recall the tenseness of the funeral of Lord Brookborough, the long-serving prime minister of the Province, who clearly had to be sent off in style. The funeral was to be held at Belfast's Cathedral, and Heath, Whitelaw, other ministers, and all the top brass of the Province would be among the congregation. We could be sitting ducks for a sniper from one of the tall buildings overlooking the cathedral entrance or, maybe a car bomb.

It was just like that moment in Freddy Forsyth's *Day of the Jackal*—any second I expected to hear the crack of a rifle. With Terry Platt, the private secretary, and several other civil servants we walked just behind the Prime Minister and our man into the cathedral. And then had to do it all over again as we walked out to the waiting cars. Neither Heath nor Whitelaw appeared to turn a hair, maybe due to their wartime experience. I know I did, and so did several of my colleagues.

As I have said, I found Edward Heath much more approachable than the public were led to believe. In my view, Maitland over-promoted the Prime Minister's rigidity and stiffness—all undoubtedly true—but we were told little of his sense of humour, compassion, culture and talent.

We had a dinner at Hillsborough with all the politicians. Even to get them all into the same room was an achievement. But there was no way they would mix. They all sat in their own groups. So the plan was that the ministers would move round the individual tables to keep the show on the road. William Van Straubenzee had become our number two minister, and he would give Willie the nod when it was time for each minister to move on. The trouble was that Heath got to table number twelve where we, the senior civil servants, were all seated, poured himself a largish glass of red wine and started to ask us questions.

"Prime Minister, you've got to move on," we told him. "You're not supposed to waste your time with us."

"No, I'm staying with you lot, you're much more fun."

And he stayed on our table for the rest of the evening much to the dismay of the local politicians and most of his ministerial colleagues.

However, there was another side to Heath which became apparent when he decided to tone down some of Whitelaw's shine. Stories were appearing hinting at a reshuffle in which the Northern Ireland supremo was going to be on the move. The shambles at the Department of Employment where Maurice Macmillan was the minister was becoming more and more apparent. The TUC and the unions were running rings round him and, to top it off, it was rumoured strongly that he was hitting the bottle. Even being the son of Harold Macmillan was not going to protect him for long.

Over lunch with Whitelaw in the Stormont Castle dining room, we urged him not to accept such a move. He was on the threshold of pulling off a ceasefire and persuading Ulster politicians to start to work with each other, ending four years of bloodshed. It was within his grasp, we argued. Surely not the time to make a change at the top?

Whitelaw shook his head. His whole life, indeed his philosophy, he said, was based on loyalty—to his constituents, to his party, to his leader. "If I am wanted somewhere else by my party, it is my duty to go," he insisted.

We left the lunch a bit saddened and feeling Whitelaw was making a very big mistake.

Whitelaw was soon called to see the Prime Minister, and then came the announcement of a reshuffle.

Whitelaw was to become Secretary of State for Employment, and his place at Northern Ireland would be taken by Francis Pym. That meant Pym, instead of Whitelaw, would attend the imminent conference at Sunningdale at which the Northern Ireland agreement was to be finally hammered out. But, more importantly, Edward Heath would take the chair.

At my desk in Stormont Castle I had a bitter taste in the mouth. Nearly two years of extremely hard work with final success so close, I was thinking ... and then the phone rang. I guessed it would be Willie. "I want you to come over here as soon as possible and join me at the Employment Department," he said.

"That will cause a hell of a row," I cautioned. I sensed that Bernard Ingham, in charge of Employment's information division, was not going to take kindly to the sudden change since we had clashed many times in the past. Our mutual dislike went back to our days as industrial correspondents in Fleet Street.

Whitelaw dismissed my objections. He had already cleared my appointment.

"I have told the Prime Minister that I insist you come back. I told him I want you in what is going to be a very difficult job. And if you don't get out now you never will," he warned.

I knew he was right and it probably was time to go. I had been neglecting my family and my home, and after almost two years flat out I was feeling the strain when I stopped to think about it.

I told Willie about my misgivings on Ingham, but he dismissed them. "I have spoken to him and explained our relationship, and that I have nothing against him, but I want my own man at my side and the Prime Minister had agreed. He took it very well."

Interestingly, Ingham's name had been on the original list of candidates for the Ulster role when I first deputised for Tom McCaffrey on Callaghan's tour of Ulster in 1969. So why could not Ingham just change places with me now and do a two year stint? But Ingham saw a much deeper plot by me, and stored it in his barrel of bitterness. Some years later, when I thought we had buried the hatchet, I proposed him for membership of the Reform Club, which he accepted. Yet when he left Number 10 after almost a decade of success with Margaret Thatcher he wrote a book in which he attacked me and alleged I had schemed to take his job at Employment. Quite untrue.

But back to my phone conversation with Willie across the Irish Sea.

"By the way," said Whitelaw, "I have got one of those political advisers here at Employment. I don't know what to do with him."

"I thought the idea was you brought in the politics," I replied.

"That's what I have always believed," boomed back Willie.

The young man's name was Robert Jackson, apparently, who turned out to be very bright, if politically naive. He went on subsequently to become a minister in charge of higher education policy for which, as a Fellow of All Souls, he turned out to be ideally cast.

I gave little thought to that though. It was all happening very fast. I sensed there was going to be a trouble ahead.

Before leaving Ulster I had to see the new NIO Permanent Secretary, Frank Cooper, and put him in the picture. He raised no objection to my departure; indeed, I thought I detected a willingness to help me to the door! He was probably right. I had become too powerful, and Cooper had his own ideas. Indeed, he embarked on making personal contact with Sinn Fein quite soon after the ministerial changes.

I also had to see my own team to break the news. That was tough. Tommy Roberts, David Gilliland, Fred Corbet, Bill McGookin and I had been through a hell of a lot together over the past twenty-three months and they seemed genuinely sorry to see me go.

Roberts, who sadly was to die within the next year, bought me a beautiful pair of dress cufflinks, which to this day I wear with my dinner jacket.

Johnnie Walker, my driver for almost two years, was similarly saddened. I thanked him for keeping me safe, and bought him a good quality water jug and set of glasses as a farewell present.

In the back of the Austin Maxi I took my last drive through the tatty, bomb-scarred streets of Belfast to Aldergrove airport, and within a few hours I headed for the Press Gallery at Westminster and got into the corner seat from which Government public relations men are just able to see the faces of their minister.

Whitelaw looked up and gave a big nod and a smile. Business as usual, he seemed to indicate.

He was right in one respect. The next few weeks turned out to be just as hectic as those we had left behind in Belfast.

We were heading into one of the biggest industrial confrontations seen in Britain since the General Strike of 1926. It would culminate in a General Election in which the issue was 'Who rules?'—the elected government of the day, or the trade unions.

And we would be bystanders as the Sunningdale Conference agreed on the formation of a Northern Ireland Assembly and accepted a system of power-sharing between the Protestants and the Catholics—a landmark in the history of that troubled province where we had seen so much blood spilt, most of it quite pointlessly.

CHAPTER 13
The Three-Day Week

It was quite like old times getting down to Woldingham Station in time to catch the 8.05 into Victoria rather than swishing through the darkened streets to Gatwick and later in still dark Belfast.

No car now, no driver and no expenses. Back sharply to the basics as a civil servant. Still, I could walk through St James's Park to my office on the corner of the Square, at Number 8. At the time that was probably one of the best known addresses in London, rivalling 10 Downing Street and Buckingham Palace for public recognition. The British knew that was where the beer and sandwiches meetings took place between the unions, employers and Government to try to head off yet another strike threat by the railway men, pilots, engineers ... one day soon, even by the Indian ladies who processed the public's holiday snapshots.

This time it was the miners hovering near the famous doorstep and the whole country dreaded the likely impact of a nationwide coal strike.

As I walked through the front door I received a welcoming smile from the attendant, who recalled my face and showed me into the ground-floor suite of offices used by the Information division. I was also familiar with the street corner office of the director vacated by Ingham, having been inside it plenty of times as a journalist, especially when I was chairman of the Industrial Correspondents Group.

My secretary was Kathy O'Brien, equally new to the Information division, so we were starting with a clean sheet. Kathy and I got on famously, and later she accompanied me when I departed to work at

British Shipbuilders. Then she married and went to Australia, but we kept in touch and at beginning of 2013 I asked for her early memories.

"I always found you energised, full of ideas, and always wanting to maintain contact by lunching every day and talking to people on the phone. Writing those speeches for the Ministers on your little manual typewriter, or dictating parts of them to me, rewriting, bashing out draft after draft. You were always in a hurry. There was always a long list of people trying to contact you when you were out of the office."

Amazing the memories you leave of yourself with someone else. Sadly, Kathy succumbed to cancer in the summer of 2015.

Within a few minutes of my arrival I was on my way upstairs to the second floor ministerial suites where Roger Dawe, the private secretary, greeted me warmly. Among his support team was another smart-looking young man with a twinkle in the eye—Richard Dykes. Our paths were to cross repeatedly because we both went to British Shipbuilders and then he became private secretary to James Prior when the Conservatives were re-elected in 1979. Later, Richard went on to the Post Office, which became one of my early clients when I launched my own public relations company.

Roger briefed me on the latest developments in the miners' dispute and then showed me into Whitelaw's second-floor office overlooking the lawn and trees in the square.

The Heath Government had defied all the usual caveats and introduced a legally binding statutory pay policy limiting pay rises to three and a half percent, with restrictions on any devices to get around it such as longer holidays, increased sick pay or whatever ingenious bypassing was dreamed up. There was a Pay Board, and also a separate one for prices with orders to monitor every development, hardly the coinage of a free society.

As their wages were pinned down ruthlessly, the British public were watching inflation soaring, and had become almost addicted to eyeballing the rate at which the monthly retail prices index rose. Each time the RPI went up half a point, so did everyone's wages and at the Employment department we had to put in special staff each month to handle the flood of phone calls.

It all had about it the whiff of failure, of a collapse of the system—rather, I imagine, as the Germans felt after WWI. As inflation there went through the roof they needed a wheelbarrow to carry worthless currency which would hardly buy a loaf of bread. We had not reached that stage, but there was a feeling it was just around the corner.

Through it all my press office, Number 10, and colleagues at the Treasury were supposed to keep repeating the mantra that the pay offer to the miners was 'fair and reasonable', that everyone else had reluctantly accepted this pay freeze, the struggle would be worth it, and so the miners really had to fall into line too. Trouble was, they had no intention of doing that, and would come out on strike if there was no more money. Clearly they meant it.

There was little mood for compromise because earlier the Heath Government had introduced the Industrial Relations Act, which required unions to register, to accept restrictions and ballot before a strike was called. There were many other ramifications, and the entire Act was anathema to the trade unions led by the TUC.

To a point the public had gone along with the Heath reforms, especially as under Labour at one time the streets were piled high with uncollected rubbish due to a strike by municipal workers. But now the inflexibility which seemed to be personified by Edward Heath was affecting the voters themselves and hitting their pockets. That was different. Support was draining away day by day.

This was the situation confronting Whitelaw. Could the emollient, conciliatory, listening, freer-thinking Willie Whitelaw pour on his magic balm, get the miners around the table, and persuade them to call off the confrontation? A Very Big Ask.

In his office we sat round the conference table to analyse the dilemma. There was Sir Conrad Heron, the permanent secretary, a very decent man, but one of the architects of the Industrial Relations Act. With him was Douglas Smith, in charge of industrial relations, who had made his name as private secretary to Barbara Castle when she headed the department. Her attempt to deal with the unions was in a White Paper entitled 'In Place of Strife' but the unions saw it off.

Also at the meeting was the formidable, and totally humourless, Donald Derx, architect of the prices and incomes legislation that was now tying us in knots. He was fiendishly clever, but maybe did not comprehend how ordinary people would react when they found their lives, pay and conditions suddenly controlled by law rather than through free collective bargaining.

Whitelaw heard them all through patiently, listening intently, rather like a bomb disposal engineer straining his ears for a clicking sound from inside an unexploded bomb. Eventually the meeting came inconclusively to an end and the officials were ushered out, but I got the well-known nod from Willie to stick around.

Once the door was shut he wanted my view. Willie and I had first met at one of those ministerial receptions when he was newly appointed as a parliamentary secretary, and I had been with the *Daily Mail* as industrial editor. He wanted my instinctive feel about where it was all leading.

I said I felt Willie had to meet the miners' leaders as soon as possible, but somewhere off the beaten track, with no publicity. I said I knew Joe Gormley, the miners' president, as a decent trade unionist with no strong political beliefs, certainly no screaming leftwinger. It was true Mick McGahey was a hard line communist, I knew, but Lawrence Daly, though also on the left, was no wrecker.

My instinct was that it would be possible to negotiate with them, but not if the Government kept going on about 'a fair and reasonable offer' which could not be increased. "Tell it to the birds," I told Whitelaw, who agreed that somehow he had to steer past that rock if he was to make any progress.

Though he wanted to get around a table with the miners' leaders, there was a clear need for a 'get-to-know-you' session at which the new minister introduced himself and listened, without any commitment, to the points the various parties wanted to make or reiterate.

There was little doubt both sides would be keen to get inside Number 8 St James's Square to put their point of view yet again. But, particularly in the case of the union side, there was a hunch that this new man over from Northern Ireland might just be able to break the logjam.

Whitelaw was briefed, and judged that he could not be seen to be giving any ground and so undermine the Government position. But he was confident in his own abilities to break the ice and get on good terms with them.

As it happened there was not much time. Someone put the skids under the meeting by alerting the police to a bomb allegedly planted in or around the building, and we all found ourselves out on the pavement by the Red Lion pub surrounded by press and television.

It would have been hilarious if it had not been so serious. Here was the nation facing a coal strike possibly shutting down most of its factories, schools and hospitals, and we were laughing and chatting with the people who could stop it all. But they could hardly negotiate in these circumstances.

I still have a photograph in my collection of this most unlikely gathering. Whitelaw towers above the miners, well-known journalists are straining to hear what is going on, and I am standing just behind Willie listening carefully to ensure he is not misquoted.

Across from the Ministry building where we were all gathered, a restaurant in Duke of York Street was setting out its tables for lunch, and the idea emerged to make it a meeting place.

My team shooed away the much aggrieved media as Willie sat at a table covered in a red-chequered cloth trying to break the ice. The miners' president, Joe Gormley, was affable enough—he had given me a big wink as he entered the room. But Mick McGahey was a hardliner and did not want us to shoot his fox. On the other hand he was a shrewd negotiator, and was not going to miss the chance to rub a Tory Government's nose in the dirt.

After an hour, the all-clear was given, the bomb incident declared a hoax. and it was time for the unlikely gathering to break up.

Though the talks were inconclusive, they did encourage Whitelaw to think that if he could get closer to the miners, it might be possible to find a formula to get the strike called off.

What was needed was a completely off-the-record session with the union to explore the options, the conciliation experts at the DE told him. It only took one call and the get-together was fixed for the coming Sunday evening at dinner at Brown's Hotel in Albemarle Street, near Piccadilly. The hotel was not the swish haunt which Rocco Forte and his sister have now made it. In those days it was brown paint and faded chintz, worn-out armchairs and self-effacing staff. Little danger of being spotted by anyone of importance staying there for the weekend!

It was Whitelaw who detected at that get-together a possible compromise. The miners' leaders explained that, somehow, they had to go back to their members and say they had broken through the three-and-a-half percent pay barrier, but they recognised it had to be done without embarrassing the Government overmuch.

So they had looked at pay and conditions and productivity, and argued that mining was one of the few jobs where, when a shift was over, a man could not get in his car or catch a bus and go home. He was in need of a shower or a bath, and that was going to take at least fifteen minutes. From this came the germ of an idea to get round the Tory pay policy—so-called Bathing and Waiting Time. It was an allowance, not a pay rise! Willie thought it a runner and promised to present it to his Cabinet colleagues. Joe Gormley was happy and convinced his negotiating colleagues they could sell it to a delegate conference.

Everyone left Brown's Hotel sworn to total secrecy, but it did not last for more than a few hours. By Monday morning there were strong rumours in the newspapers of a fudged deal on the cards. That meant Whitelaw went in to bat with his colleagues without the element of surprise. It turned out Gormley had marked Harold Wilson's card and who helpfully leaked it.

At the Cabinet sub-committee—attended by Heath, the Chancellor Tony Barber, Jim Prior and Lord Carrington—the group who had become known as 'The Hawks' would have none of it. Whitelaw—a 'Dove', it would seem—just did not understand, they said. There was a line in the sand which could not be crossed. In which case we had to ask, what was the point of bringing Whitelaw back from Northern Ireland?

As stalemate continued, we all became very busy indeed coping with the implications of the mounting crisis as the miners worked to rule and coal supplies began to dwindle. The maximum speed on the main roads was slashed to fifty miles an hour, and there were all kinds of other restrictions, such as limiting industry to three consecutive days of power and preventing them from using electricity or gas for the other two. Because companies could not work for two days, in most cases the pay of their employees had to be cut. They then had to sit at home shivering as electricity was turned off.

To make it all utterly miserable, Heath decided to order the television companies to shut down transmission at 10.30 p.m. each evening, just when the electricity was switched on again.

In vain, the heads of the information departments in Whitehall argued that this was counter-productive—you not only needed to tell the public what was going on, but had to use the opportunity to get the Government case across. Heath's head of information at Number 10 had come from the Foreign Office, and was part of the 'teach 'em a lesson' school, so he supported the view that the public backlash would come down on the miners. On the contrary, we argued, the man in the street would get the impression that Edward Heath was out to make everyone suffer for his punch-up with the miners. Disaster!

Quickly, a pattern of electricity shutdown and restoration times was implemented, and there were even charts in the local press setting out the schedule. I spotted that if I took my wife and children a few miles away where supplies were on, it meant the cinemas were open, and warm too. By the time we got back home the electricity was on again, and so was our heating, although the TV screen remained in darkness.

It was all pretty miserable. If I felt like that, knowing what was going on, how did the British public feel? It couldn't last, and I well remember the day Whitelaw came back from Number 10. His reaction told it all as he faced me, Roger Dawe, and the others in the private office. "It's all up—there is going to be a general election."

He disclosed that 'the Hawks' thought this was the chance to beat

Labour by bashing the unions, but that he had disagreed. Whitelaw told Heath and his colleagues, "If you go to the country and say 'We need more power', they will say 'We have given you that, and you have wasted it'." The Tory theme was 'Who Governs Britain?' In February the nation gave their answer—'Not you'.

It was a close-run campaign, though, and for several days Heath clung on in Number 10 while he tried to set-up a coalition with the Liberals and Ulster Unionists. Meanwhile, our ministers were clearing their desks quietly, and the civil servants were checking what kind of policies an incoming Labour Government would be wanting.

Very suddenly an era, and a very important experience in my life, had ended and it was all change. Thinking about it, I felt that Whitelaw got more out of me than a whole string of ministers. He had that extra something, and I would have gone to extraordinary lengths to please him or achieve a target he set me. The initial Northern Ireland team were flung together, but I know that most felt, like me, that it had been a demanding, exhilarating and sometimes very sad period in which we had very nearly pulled off a settlement in the Province in December 1973.

None of us realised that it would cost 3,000 deaths, including 319 RUC policemen before the Good Friday Agreement would be signed on 10th April 1988—*TWENTY-FIVE YEARS LATER* by Tony Blair, the Labour Prime Minister. But as one of the most distinguished SDLP members, Seamus Mallon, summed up: "The Good Friday Agreement? Ah, that's Sunningdale 1973 for slow learners."

CHAPTER 14
A Different Kind of Cabinet Minister

General elections take about three and a half weeks, and for most civil servants in those days provided a welcome interlude, even time off. For me it meant few calls from the private office, no demand for instant speeches or the need to gallop up four flights to the second floor ministerial suites.

For some civil servants, however, a likely change of the political party in charge meant writing briefs on current policy and anticipating the demand for it to change. It also involved reading carefully the party manifestos, though very often there was no mention of the thorniest issues.

Heath's three-day week and the standoff with the miners continued during the General Election of 1974, and we had to work on the basis that the Tories would get back into power. Privately, most of us doubted it. The interlude did not stop us, nor the press, from speculating on who might come in to head the department, which had been dubbed 'The Bed of Nails' by one former minister.

No one, though, came up with the name that caught us all on the wrong foot when it was announced by the new Prime Minister, Harold Wilson, that the Secretary of State for Employment would be Michael Foot. Wow!

One of the nation's finest orators, finest journalists, and most highly-principled politicians in Britain who had always refused to take office, preferring the independence of the back benches? Yes, the same man. More maverick than minister, surely.

Because of the continuing three-day week, all so-called gas guzzlers such as the ministerial limos were off the road. So on Michael Foot's first day as Employment Minister he was collected by Roger Dawe, his new principal private secretary, in a chauffeur-driven Mini.

If you sought proof of civil servants' even-handedness, there it was. Roger had gone from private secretary to shell-shocked Maurice Macmillan, hit it off brilliantly with William Whitelaw, and was now to run in a completely new secretary of state, Michael Foot, who had never held public office.

Unfazed, but perhaps a bit dazed, Foot arrived at St James's Square asking for me, the Director of Information, rather than the Permanent Secretary. He had enquired in the car who was the director of information and, when told my name, replied, "He's alright."

I had known the new minister as a journalist, but was somewhat embarrassed by this upsetting of the pecking order. I went into the office newly vacated by Whitelaw to find Foot sitting at the big desk.

"What are these fellows like?" he asked of his new civil servants. I assured them they were a good bunch, but he had to make his instructions precise and firm.

"Tell them clearly what you want and they will do it. They're alright," I assured him.

I explained that I was a little embarrassed that he had sent for me rather than Sir Conrad Heron, the permanent secretary. "You've got to see him straightaway," I urged. "Then get him to call a meeting of the top team with you, but make sure I am involved." Mandarins are quite prone to overlook the needs of journalists and PR men, I knew.

So he sent for Conrad, who promptly offered his resignation. The top official in the department was acutely conscious that he had been the principal architect of Heath's Industrial Relations Act which had ushered in the miners' strike, the three-day week, and had meant the British public giving the Tories the boot.

Foot waved that away. He might be new to office, but he respected the integrity of men like Conrad Heron and he was not looking for easy scalps. What the new Employment Secretary wanted was the miners' dispute settled at once, and the statutory counter-inflation and wages policy scrapped and replaced as soon as possible.

Donald Derx, the deputy secretary, who had constructed the legally underwritten policy and built-in elaborate penalties, then set to work undoing all his own work. It was like being asked to retrace your steps and dig up all the landmines you had just so cunningly set in place. Yet Derx seemed quite unperturbed when he was given the task by his new minister.

Then Foot asked, "What will the retail price index be?"

"Nineteen point six," said Geoffrey Brand, an undersecretary.

Foot went white and seemed about to leave the room. In fact the RPI went to twenty-six percent before Derx was able to get the amended legislation through Parliament which stopped wages going up automatically each month as the index rose.

Through it all Michael Foot kept his nerve and his humour, becoming very popular in the department. We held regular parties in those days, which we paid for ourselves, and Michael Foot and his wife, Jill, loved to join in. And they paid their way.

Working with Michael Foot was quite unlike being with any other minister I had known, Tory or Labour. He was quite unconventional. Indeed, he was the only minister for whom I never tried writing speeches. I used to joke that Foot, as a very skilled wordsmith, knew more words than I had ever read. The truth was that he never used written speeches, but got a theme and from there conjured up a flow of invective, sarcasm or passion to stir up a crowd.

On one occasion, when we went to Harrogate to address the personnel managers, he produced one of our press releases and proceeded to read it out line by line—"Because he down there," pointing at me, "wants it."

Then he tossed it aside and went off into overdrive. He had asked me earlier, though, if I could get the television floodlights turned down or directed away because he liked to see the faces of his audience to assess how his words were going down. I could tell him they were laughing quite merrily at the humiliation of a Government press officer.

While he was preparing for the first occasion when he was to speak as Secretary of State for Employment in the House of Commons, briefing material and paragraphs on policy poured into his private office. But Foot ignored the lot. Instead, he insisted in going off alone to walk around St James' Park as he composed in his mind his first-ever speech to Parliament, no longer as a rebel but as a Cabinet minister.

That was when he conjured up a brilliant phrase about the dangers of letting the lawyers get into labour relations, resulting in a 'trigger-happy judicial finger' in the courts: a memorable phrase I would wish to have authored. It was a brilliant performance, and we in the department were all proud of him.

On one occasion he was so annoyed about a critical report in *The Times* that, rather than instruct me to sort it out, he simply wrote and signed a letter himself. He told me about it at our morning meeting. I explained—journalist to journalist—that it just wasn't done. In any case it was quite contrary to the 'Guidance to Cabinet Ministers' issued by the Cabinet Secretary, which was the way Number 10 sought to impose its iron grip. Not on Michael Foot, it didn't. Like me, the first they knew of it was when they read their morning copy of *The Times*.

Nowadays it is not unusual to see a denial in the letters column signed by a minister, and they can thank Foot for achieving that breakthrough—though I doubt if they send them to the newspaper without first getting clearance from Number 10.

First, though, in line with his number one objective, in came the miners' leaders, Joe Gormley, Lawrence Daly and Mick McGahey. They were not exactly salivating. but the grins and the obvious relish with which, metaphorically, they rubbed their hands was obvious to us all.

There was already an offer of £4.50 a week rise on the table, which was inflationary. That was the 'bathing and waiting time' sop that Whitelaw had worked up with the miners. But by the end of the day, under Foot, the figure had risen to £11.50, which would certainly take wages in Britain through the roof. And with it Britain's inflation.

The miners scooped it up without having to give a concession worth a damn. If he was worried about inflation, Foot wasn't doing much to restrain it.

Dealing with the TUC and other trade unionists, it was sad to see he was even more of a pushover. When Len Murray, the TUC General Secretary, swept in accompanied by David Lea, Foot appeared to hold them in awe. While Murray listed his demands for the brothers, Lea thought nothing of picking up a phone in the outer office to make a call without the nominal courtesy of requesting permission.

That was how Murray got his nickname of 'the Deputy Prime Minister', and I got a laugh when I ventured the thought he had taken everything else so why not have the pictures from the walls?

Part of their demands was full restoration of the union rights taken away by the Heath Government as part of its Industrial Relations Act, which Foot was determined to repeal.

Whitelaw had been under no illusions; he viewed the Heath changes as disastrous, and he too would have scrapped them if there had been time. But I doubt it would have been such a costly exercise.

The repealing law became known as the Employment Protection Bill and Foot was very proud of it. So were the unions, who had ploughed the field deep and left hardly a blade uncut.

Around that time there was public concern at a succession of tribunal findings which imposed the closed shop on workers; if they were not in a union they could not work. This was against human rights, it was argued. Several groups of workers, mostly Left-led like the printers and the draughtsmen, forced it through—no union card, no job.

We tried to persuade Foot that as Employment Minister he ought to have the final say in such matters, possibly appointing a special committee or tribunal to hear a case.

Before we went into meeting the TUC, we urged him to make the unions leaders sweat a little for their concession. "They're bargainers, make them work for it," I emphasised. Foot assured me he knew that, and promised to keep the thought in mind.

But as soon as the concept of an appeals mechanism was aired, Jack Jones, the transport union leader, denounced it as just like Heath's

Industrial Relations Act. "We're not having it," he declared. And that was that—Foot just caved in when, had he indicated it was his bottom line, the unions would probably have bought it.

Having said this, Foot was a very pleasant, kindly and humorous person with whom to work, and we got on well.

There was a particularly difficult spat involving Lord (Arnold) Goodman, a lawyer on the Left, who had open access to Number 10 and just about everywhere else. One of his characteristics was his poor punctuality, and Foot always opened up with, "Ah, the late Lord Goodman." But it had no effect.

Goodman took exception to a situation where editors were claiming to be forced to join the journalists' union. Since they had the right to hire and fire they should be allowed, but not forced, to join.

It was a dilemma for Foot because in effect he was being asked to balance two essential freedoms—the right to combine, and the freedom of the press. Which freedom carried more weight? As a journalist, Foot was once the youngest editor of the *London Evening Standard* and a fearless columnist in the national dailies. But Foot, proud of his NUJ membership, was also an uncritical supporter of trade unionism.

It ended with a virtual surrender to Goodman, who had strong support in the House of Lords. A compromise was hammered out in the small hours at St James's Square. It was not pleasant for Foot, but he dismissed it when I mentioned it at our morning meeting. "When I took this role on I knew it meant compromise—all government involves compromise," he lectured me.

Another hairy moment involved a massive fine on the engineers' union resulting from Heath's Industrial Relations Act, which the unions refused to recognise.

If the deadline expired it meant the leader of the AEU, Hugh Scanlon, the second most powerful union leader in the country, faced jail. What would that do for productivity when engineering workers downed tools in protest all over Britain?

Foot and I were in the Reform Club when I got a call asking me to get my Secretary of State to a phone. Not easy in the Pall Mall gentlemens' clubs where phones are anathema. In the cramped telephone box in the club's front hall, the message was that an unknown donor had put up the considerable sum of money to meet the cost of the AEU fine and get them off the hook. The trouble was that Scanlon and his AEU colleagues were not sure they wanted that and, in any case, who was paying? It might be some right-wing outfit seeking to embarrass the unions.

Gradually we managed to get the deal done without turning the club over, but it was awkward and delicate. And to this day I have no idea who paid or why?

Was it Robert Maxwell, the print and newspaper owner, seeking to curry favour with the new Labour Government? But he could not keep a secret like that for long. Or maybe one of the firms of Labour lawyers had devised a way round the AEU's stubborn decision—and in fact, by subterfuge, the union was really paying up without admitting it. Or was the union really paying itself by a roundabout way?

One of Foot's weakness' was clothes. To put it mildly, he was pretty scruffy at the best of times and usually went to Parliament in a sports jacket—its collar thick with dandruff because of his constant battle with eczema—and slacks. Matching, if it was a good day.

His wife, Jill Craigie, a formidable lady in her own right, had been a film-maker when she met Michael contesting the Plymouth seat in 1945 when the war ended. She was strong on equal rights and an outspoken supporter of the Fawcett Society which campaigns for female equality.

As a young woman, Jill Craigie had been a very good looker and still dressed well. So she despaired of Michael's apparent lack of interest in clothes. She rang to tell me she had been trying to get him to wear a dinner jacket when he was going to lead his colleagues of the Privy Council to meet the Queen.

Foot had a thing about evening wear probably because his hero Aneurin Bevan, Health Minister in the 1945 Labour Government, had adamantly refused to dress up like the Tories—or waiters. "Not me," snapped Bevan. As Bevan's biographer that suited Michael Foot, too.

Jill told me she had laid out a dowdy dinner suit Foot had worn at university, green with mould. Alongside she placed a new black suit she had bought for him off the peg. It was not evening wear, but it would do.

Her husband said nothing, but took the dark suit and put it on for his first meeting of the Privy Council. A real breakthrough, I agreed with her.

Ironically, it was his lack of taste in clothes that later was possibly to cost him leadership of the country. He was bitterly, and unfairly, criticised for wearing what was said to be 'a donkey jacket' while laying a wreath of poppies at the Cenotaph at the November ceremony to remember the nation's war dead.

As he told me, it was a rather smart, new, half-length topcoat Jill had bought him at Harrods. But the Tory papers had found a stick to beat him with, and the coat certainly went into history as a donkey jacket of the type workmen wear on a cold building site.

Yet Foot got on extremely well with the Queen at their regular meetings. She seemed to enjoy gently teasing Foot, and he played along with good humour. And those black trousers had a very natty flare to them ... rather fashionable.

The Privy Council was one of the few places where Foot was not accompanied by his dog Dizzy—short for the Tory politician Disraeli. The Queen's corgis would probably have objected. Foot was often to be seen in the mornings striding across Hampstead Heath with Dizzy. One day as I climbed into the front of the ministerial Rover and saw Dizzy cuddled up against Foot, I enquired, "What breed is your dog, Secretary of State?"

Seemed an innocuous question, but there was a long silence. Foot looked at his dog, obviously a mongrel when I thought about it. "Shall we report him to the Race Relations Board, Dizzy?"

Winnie, our lady driver, exploded with laughter as we slid away from St James's Square.

It was not long afterwards that Foot asked me to stay behind after a meeting with officials. "I have a problem, I have to go into hospital," he told me.

That came quite out of the blue. "Nothing serious, I hope."

"Not breakfast time reading," was how Foot put it, a phrase I accepted without wishing to probe. Big mistake. As I learned later, I should have pressed for more precise details of an illness that was to take my minister into hospital.

Instead I was looking ahead. I said, "No private hospital for you—not even a private room. No special privileges of any kind."

Foot looked a bit crestfallen, but I explained the *Daily Mail* would be ready to pounce if a great socialist was to end up in a private hospital or receiving privilege of any kind.

He saw my point, and told his wife to get on to the National Health Service Royal Free Hospital, Hampstead, to insist that her husband sought no privileges.

Later, I went to see Foot myself at the Royal Free, and found him in a small room with three other patients. The nurses had brought a phone to him on a trolley—no more than any other National Health Service patient might receive.

My instinct that the *Daily Mail* would not let another socialist lie in hospital without its tender concern was soon proved correct. Into my office came Adrian Moorey, now my Chief Press Officer, to report that Lynda Lee Potter, of that paper, doyen, of Fleet Street bitchy women writers, had just given him an earful.

"She wants to know what 'not breakfast time reading' means, and she'll decide if her readers can brave it. She also wants to know what special privileges he is receiving in hospital. She does not accept that he is in an NHS hospital, and is not being looked after specially."

I knew that Potter's husband was the secretary of the British Medical Association and, as such, received private medical cover for himself and probably other members of his family. I also suspected that the *Daily Mail* still had a private medical plan for its staff. Certainly I had received that benefit while working there.

And here was this woman hammering down because Foot was in a small ward of four at an NHS hospital and had the use of a phone!

The injustice made the blood boil, but I had to keep calm as I called

Lynda Lee Potter back. She was not impressed that the Director of Information was calling her, nor seemingly aware that we had once been colleagues. Rather, she continued to sustain the treatment she had dished out to Adrian.

I insisted we did not know the minister's actual health condition and considered it a private matter. It was up to Mr Foot whether or not he disclosed the nature of his illness.

Oh, no, it wasn't, she claimed. The *Daily Mail* readers wanted to know.

The phones were not exactly slammed down, but they were replaced with firmness though I knew we had not heard the last of this, as I reported to the private office. We agreed that if we were to give details of Foot's illness it would make our concern for his privacy look shallow. But in any case, why on earth should a paper be able to demand to know the intimate details of a person's health.

The *Mail* ran a predictably snide article, but once his lump on a testicle proved to be benign, Foot was soon back at his desk. He told me he had been advised to sue the paper and he wanted me and Moorey to be witnesses.

This was delicate. It is one thing being annoyed with a Fleet Street newspaper, but quite another being a witness against your old paper. In any case, as I explained to my minister, as civil servants we really could not volunteer statements. "You will have to subpoena us. Then we cannot avoid giving you a statement," I suggested. He did just that and, some months later, Foot told us the *Daily Mail* had paid him a substantial sum in damages and paid his costs in full. He did not offer to buy us a drink, though.

Not long after this incident, a West Country visit was arranged for the Secretary of State which included Plymouth with which the name of the Foot family was always associated. Michael's father Isaac, a solicitor, had his practice there, and held the constituency as a Liberal until beaten by the Conservative, Hore Belisha, who gave his name as Transport Minister to the yellow-topped crossing signs which became known as Belisha beacons. He held the seat until 1945 when Michael trounced his father's old rival.

Foot's father must have been a hell of a man. Michael told us about him as Winnie drove us down to Devon. Apparently, the family home was about ten miles out of Plymouth, and each day Isaac would walk along the railway track to and from town reading Shakespeare, poetry, and the latest literature.

An argument developed between us when Foot talked of the original Plymouth settlers who had gone from the city to found America. I told him he had got that wrong—those people had set off first from Bermondsey, where the *Mayflower* had been provisioned, and had put into Plymouth prior to making the Atlantic crossing. So really they were South Londoners!

Foot would not have it. Rubbish! But I stuck to my guns because, as a local reporter in that area, I knew the exact location in Bermondsey from where the famous voyage began. When we got to his Devon city, Foot insisted we drove immediately to the famous quay steps at The Barbican, and examined the historic plaque. "No mention of Bermondsey there," he exulted, which I conceded.

"But it doesn't mean that it didn't happen, and I can prove it did. There is even a Mayflower settlement in Bermondsey. That can't be an accident."

I never did convince Michael, but it was a source of banter between us for many months.

In conversation the issue of diaries came up. At the time, Foot had the Cabinet Office highly alarmed as executor for the late Dick Crossman, insisting that the famous diaries could not be edited. He wanted everything published. In those days, politicians keeping diaries and having them published shortly after leaving office was quite unknown. A decent interval, perhaps several years later when all participants were dead, was the norm.

"Are you keeping a diary?" I asked him. At the back of my mind was the fear that if I was too candid I might end up being serialised in a Sunday newspaper. "No, I'm not—are you?" he snapped.

"No, neither am I," I assured him. "I do not agree with civil servants

Top: *Advising CBI President, Sir James Cleminson, MC, who fought at Arnhem.*
Bottom: *Tony Blair, then leader of the opposition, discusses education – not Iraq.*

Top: *Urging my Singer Le Mans up Beggar's Roost in the 1954 Land's End Trial—the same car I used on the streets of South London as a local reporter.*
Bottom: *Time and Tide—my first boat bought from a libel action.*

Top: *Rt Hon Michael Foot and his wife, filmmaker Jill Craigie, open employment exhibition stand in park at St James' Square.* ***Bottom:*** *Finding an angle!*

Top: Decorations will be worn ... dinner on board Nelson's flagship, HMS Victory, accompanying my wife, Baroness Dean of Thornton-le-Fylde, in her role as first woman chairman of the Armed Forces Pay Review body.
Bottom left: Cruising off to Scotland to retirement (photo by Sue Jones).
Bottom right: My new role as great grandfather with Margot, my first great grandchild, daughter of Edwina, eldest grandchild.

keeping a diary. I believe that is the right of the minister. I could have kept a diary in Northern Ireland, but I never did. I thought if anyone was keeping a diary, it should be Willie."

You get the best of relationships with politicians when you travel with them, I found over my career in Whitehall. I went with Foot to Ebbw Vale, the constituency he took over after his hero, Bevan, died, and though he was not Welsh, Foot clearly identified with the area. He pointed out the landmarks, even showing me the tiny miner's cottage he had bought for a song in the constituency.

As the car negotiated a tight bend he had us all laughing. "You know, Nye used to say 'The valleys are so narrow in South Wales— even the rivers run sideways!'"

While departments like mine were carrying on with their everyday duties, which in effect added up to running the country, quite a different struggle was taking place down at the Palace of Westminster. There, the Government whips under my old pal, Bob Mellish, the Chief Whip, were struggling to keep the Government from being defeated. They kept that going for three years, a remarkable achievement.

It meant many late-night votes, and often all-night sittings, which made it very difficult for ministers who were trying to run their departments.

Then, in the spring of 1976, came the bombshell that Harold Wilson was to stand down two years after winning the election. It was quite unexpected, and very few people, even among those in Downing Street, were in the picture. Foot, and the left wing MPs with whom he generally kept company like Tony Benn, Barbara Castle and others, were in non-stop contact. How to stop James Callaghan from taking over?

I was with Foot at Rothesay awaiting a ferry. He had just addressed the Scottish TUC when the news came through that there was to be a party contest, and Peter Shore, one of Foot's protégés, was the likely candidate on the left.

The whole timetable had been thrown out of gear by the sudden decision of the white-collar union leader, Clive Jenkins, to put Peter's name forward. You could see the argument. Foot was a much older man, still an outspoken supporter of the Campaign for Nuclear Disarmament and a dedicated pacifist. On the other hand he had great integrity, was held in high regard by a large section of the British public, and he was seen as a success as a government minister.

When I asked if he intended to throw his hat in the ring, he gave one of his quizzical smiles, but no reply. I reckoned he was going to have a go. And that was how it went in the first round with Callaghan, Shore, Healey, Roy Jenkins and Foot slugging it out. Not surprisingly, Big Jim came out on top, but Foot was in front of the others so a run-off between the two was declared.

Callaghan won by 176 to 137 for Michael.

Foot came back to tell us his days were over as Secretary of State for Employment. Jim, as the new Prime Minister, had asked him to be his deputy and to become Leader of the House. It was going to be Foot's job to keep the coalition with the Liberals going—somehow— if the Government was to cling to office.

We had a farewell party at the department that evening to see him off, but before he cleared his desk Michael Foot took me to one side. Would I go with him to be his press adviser at the Cabinet Office?

I knew there was no machine and no PR staff at Number 70 Whitehall, probably not even a desk. I would be hemmed in by the Number 10 press office where Tom McCaffrey, as thick as thieves with Callaghan, would not take kindly to having me around.

Reluctantly, I told him that though I had enjoyed working with and for him, I could probably do a lot more for Government by staying where I was. Michael quickly agreed; putting pressure on a person was not in his nature.

"But I would like to give you a gift. Is there anything you want?" he asked. I knew exactly. I told him I would love to have a personal copy of his biography of Aneurin Bevan. Next morning he brought me completely new copies of volumes I and II of the biography which, of all the books Foot had written, I knew he personally felt was his best ever work.

He wrote in the first volume: 'To Keith McDowall with best wishes and much gratitude for two years hard labour. Michael Foot, May 1976'.

And in volume II he added 'to make a belated conversion'.

In 1980 Michael published a collection of his work and called it *Debts of Honour*. I bought a copy and asked him to sign it. Inside, he wrote: 'He's a big creditor too. Michael Foot, December 1980'.

Then, almost as if in a puff of smoke—rather as he had suddenly arrived—Michael Foot was off to 70 Whitehall to take the historic office of Lord President of the Council. So Sunny Jim had neatly embraced his opponent and leader of the Left, and at the same time removed him from his nominal power base at 8 St James's Square, where the trade union leaders were increasingly prone to drop in. Not any more, thought Jim. "If they want to do that, they can come here to see me at Number 10."

The other consideration was that the Callaghan majority in Parliament was on a knife edge until he went to the country and sought a new mandate—and hopefully, increased support. It was going to be a close-run thing. Michael was anything but disloyal and Callaghan increasingly came to work with him. They were a good team.

Back at the Employment Department the awful truth of the changes was sinking in. Foot had urged the Prime Minister that his replacement must be Albert Booth, our Minister of State, and Callaghan was only too happy to oblige. He knew there would be no problem from Albert.

He was a very nice guy, Albert Booth, but if that was Cabinet material then I should have been in the Coldstream Guards. He was boring—no getting away from it—and the relative lack of newspaper interest in his promotion summed it all up.

Desperate to find some colour, I asked Booth about his career before coming into politics, and he told me he had been in the drawing office at a North East shipyard.

Booth represented Barrow, which was famous as the home of Vickers, and where the latest submarines were designed and built to take the Polaris nuclear missile to sea. Yet he had recently led a Campaign for Nuclear Disarmament rally in his own constituency and actually lay down in the street with others to protest against the bomb.

As shipyard workers went about their shopping on that Saturday afternoon with their wives and families, I could imagine quite a few decided their constituency needed an MP who supported their work rather than trying to cut its throat.

One good scheme worked up in the Albert Booth era was what became known as the Temporary Employment Subsidy. If a small or medium-sized firm was in financial trouble—usually cash flow problems—it could get a short term loan from the Government to tide it over. If the banks would not help, HMG would.

A large number of companies survived in this difficult time because of TES, dreamed up, I believe, by Donald Derx and his team and taken to Cabinet by Booth. All the companies eventually paid back their loans.

I met a printing employer in the Little Ship Club who told me gloomily his family business was doomed. When I mentioned TES he asked why his bank manager had never mentioned it when he was so desperate to pay the wages.

I rang the DE London region and asked them to investigate. Two weeks later my printing friend rang and asked if I was free for lunch? He had received a cheque for £36,000 and his firm was free to trade again. It had been saved.

Sadly, though his company was to survive, he was to lose his life a few weeks later in the Fastnet Sailing tragedy. His body was never found. And the TES sunk too by the EU in Brussels which had been alerted. Any mention of that taboo word 'subsidy' was banned ... even, as in this case, it worked.

The other presentational problem was that the Department of Employment was a shell of itself. The real power bases had been hived off. The beer and sandwiches phase and the all-night sessions trying to find the solution to a major dispute were virtually over. The new Arbitration and Conciliation Service (ACAS) had upped sticks and moved away to Cleland House in Westminster, presided over by Douglas Smith. So why should industrial correspondents come round our way anymore?

Health and Safety was in its infancy, having been set-up under Foot's aegis but really driven through by Harold Walker, another of his junior ministers. The aim was to improve worker safety and at the same time take the issue out of politics. That was a joke because in years to come it was to be a constant source of public irritation and scorn, though it certainly did improve worker safety. But probably at a huge cost to efficiency.

Another mandarin grabbed that empire—John Locke, a headstrong personality, who moved the whole section out to Baynards House at Paddington and set-up his own fiefdom, complete with its own press and PR team.

The biggest plum of all was that part of the DE that dealt with training, re-training, employment services and job finding up and down the country. That hiving-off had already begun, but now it accelerated under a former permanent secretary, the manipulative Denis Barnes, who had found himself the perfect number for his retirement years. Full pay, expenses, grand offices, and a committee of business people and trade unionists, putty in the hands of the calculating Mr Barnes.

At base, the DE still had some minor roles like looking after labour attachés and keeping an eye on economic trends—when the Treasury allowed it—but it was a busted flush. I was Director of Information and head of profession, but the various parts of the hived-off press departments only came seeking me when they had a problem.

It was so quiet I used to wander round the department looking for anything that might be of interest. A deputy secretary looked up a little sheepishly as I popped my head round the door. Well he might—he was looking at his stamp collection!

Then, suddenly, there was some action. In August 1976, from nowhere came a dispute that catapulted the name Grunwick around the world. That was the film processing factory in Willesden, North London, owned by a George Ward of Indian origin. Quite clearly, he exploited Asian women, paid very poor wages, and refused to allow them to join a trade union.

By the time it was all over, we had seen massed police units acting like paramilitaries in violent clashes with picketing unions there to support the strikers, 550 arrests, a blacking of all post in and out of the processing plant, High Court injunctions—the lot.

At first, though, it just seemed a regional news item. But on television news I caught sight of an interesting figure slipping in at a side door of Mr Ward's factory—none other than John Gorst, Tory MP for Hendon, and a very partisan rightwinger. I smelt trouble, and warned Albert Booth.

Within days, matters had escalated as Labour MPs, moderates like Shirley Williams, Denis Howell and Fred Mulley, went to the picket lines only to be attacked by Sir Keith Joseph in an intolerant outburst for which he was ticked off by his own party.

Behind it all was the issue of the rights of trade unionists, the closed shop and individual freedom which the Tories had pinpointed as worth escalating in the looming General Election.

But the impotence of the Employment Minister was on show, too. Hiving off industrial relations to ACAS looked fine on paper, but when the issue was big enough and occupied the front pages of most newspapers, and was top item on the TV news, MPs wanted a statement in the House of Commons. They wanted to know what the Employment Minister was doing to resolve the issue. Not a lot, as it happened, because George Ward refused all our ministerial invitations, and then tougher-worded summonses, to come to St James's Square.

Egged on by John Gorst and, later, we learned, the so-called Freedom Association, Ward seemed hell-bent on forcing a major confrontation. Not what Jim Callaghan wanted at all. It was playing havoc with his election prospects and Labour's place in the polls.

Eventually, with plenty of pre-conditions, Ward was coaxed into Number 8 St James's Square where he proved, as expected, to be a very obdurate and stubborn man. We did not know then that he was also playing for time as the Freedom Association was lining up an army of supporters to come into the factory in the small hours, and spirit away hundreds of mailbags containing customers' processed film. The postmen were blacking the factory and no post, on the face of it, could leave the building. Not so. The Freedom riders drove all night through the Home Counties, stuffing every postbox for miles. So George Ward's photos got through to customers, ensuring his cash flow. Once that was done, Ward eased up, and was talked into agreeing to a Court of Inquiry headed by the redoubtable Lord Scarman, my old acquaintance from Northern Ireland.

But the damage was done. Labour again looked to be the party of the unions, the closed shop, and against individual freedom.

There was no avoiding the conclusion that the right wing and the Conservative party had secured a major political and ideological victory which prepared the ground for Margaret Thatcher's sweep to power in the 1979 General Election.

There was another major dispute which flared up, it seemed from nowhere, and had serious potential. The helicopters supplying the North Sea oil rigs, ferrying in and out the men to operate them, were suddenly grounded when the pilots were refused the right to join a union. Alan Bristow, who owned and ran Bristow Helicopters, had built the company up from nothing and had a formidable reputation. He won the Croix de Guerre flying a Sikorsky under fire to rescue French troops surrounded by the Vietnamese, and had many similar escapades in his career. He was not taking kindly to being told that he had to negotiate with BALPA, the pilots' union.

But the nation needed the North Sea oil to keep flowing. Eventually, Bristow was coaxed into coming to St James Square, but demanded a minimum of two High Court judges to hear the case—nothing less. The meeting took place after lunch, and it was clear Bristow had had an excellent meal, but he was agitated and several times on the point of walking out. Booth dare not let Bristow out of the room.

I guessed Bristow was in pain with indigestion. I tiptoed out, went to my room where I mixed a mug of white powder and returned without a word to put it in front of Bristow. "Thank God," said Bristow, gulped it down, and then let out an enormous belch.

We now had his full attention, and Bristow finally settled for one judge, Lord McDonald, who swiftly produced a report to get both sides off the hook and allow Bristow to save face.

Not exactly beer and sandwiches, but useful stuff, Bisodol.

But these were highlights in a fairly boring phase in my working day and I started looking around for an escape. One had turned up in the shape of Harry Pollock, the US Labour Attaché with whom I got on extremely well and who was clearly a senior man within the Embassy. To my amazement, he offered me a one-month trip to the US under their Foreign Visitor Programme, all expenses paid by the US Government.

It was a great opportunity, but how would I get a month away from the department even though I felt there was so little happening I wouldn't be missed. Well, no harm in asking.

I went to see Tony Sutherland, the top man in the establishments department which ran the pay, rations and staffing of the DE, and I showed him the letter of invitation.

At first he was doubtful, but when I pointed out I had spent two years in Northern Ireland and lost a great deal of spare time, he seized on it. "And this would clear it?" he asked.

"Most certainly," I replied, quite pleased that the suggestion had not been thrown out on the spot.

"Off you go, then," said the Head of Establishments. I swear there was a twinkle in his eye.

A week or so later I arrived in Washington. For the first time I was there not as a working journalist but as an invited guest, with airfare, hotel and daily living allowance courtesy of the US Government.

By great fortune I had arrived in the midst of the Bicentennial celebrations, the 200th anniversary of the break with Britain in 1776. Apart from the fact that I was British, I could not have chosen a more fortuitous time to tour the United States of America. Lucky me!

I had to go to the office of the Visitor Program Service to work out with them where to go, and to arrange all the details of the tour, including a $30-dollar-a-day allowance. It may not sound much now, but if one was prudent it was quite adequate.

The first thing you learned was that America is a very big place and you cannot see it all in a month; maybe not even years. For example, I was keen to get to the middle of the country, and elected for Chicago and Detroit, but time did not allow me to visit both. I had to choose. So I went for Detroit because it was the home of the US auto industry and I thought it would be extremely interesting. As it turned out to be. To this day, I have always regretted giving the Windy City a miss, and not having the chance to get to some of the famous jazz venues like The London House and see where the great Count Basie first played when he made it to Chicago from Kansas City.

I was told to work out where I wanted to be each weekend because while in most cities there were marvellous people prepared to give up their time and to take you into their homes, they were, quite naturally, usually tied up at weekends.

That was how I had a fabulous time in places as diverse as New Orleans, Vermont and San Francisco. I even persuaded the Visitor Program to allow me to pop over the border into Canada and visit my old friend Major Ross, who had retired to the wonderful island of Victoria, a short boat trip across Puget Sound from Seattle.

I went to the United Automobile Workers to meet the great union chief, Walter Reuther, in Detroit, had three exhilarating days as a guest of Boeing in Seattle, heard the new 'bluegrass' music in the hills overlooking Burlington—and recoiled at seeing 'pot' being smoked under the magnificent foliage of the Vermont trees.

I found Seattle to be quite a city, and was very impressed with the great Boeing company. They had produced the first 747 Jumbo a few months previously so I was able to see the enormous hangar in which four of the planes were being worked on simultaneously. My guide gave me a magnificent pen and pencil as a gift from Boeing, and on the way to the airport showed me the hoarding on which two Brits, made redundant in the past with other aeroplane workers, had bought space for a week. 'Last one out please switch off the lights' it said—a piece of British humour that had apparently gone down well in one of the city's darker moments.

A highlight of my tour was undoubtedly Boston, where the Boston

Tea Party was staged in 1776—the spark for the spirit of independence that ended British rule. In that Irish city right then it was a good idea to keep one's British accent subdued, but I visited Faneuil Hall, and the dockyard where imported British tea was dumped overboard into the harbour. I climbed Telegraph Hill and I rode the subway—in fact, I quite fell in love with Boston and to this day it remains my favourite US city.

Back in Washington I asked to go to the Department of Labour and hopefully meet my opposite number. Waiting in his outer office I got a faint whiff of, "Another bloody visitor," but eventually I was shown in for fifteen minutes or so with the director, John Leslie. We went through the pleasantries and then suddenly we clicked. We discovered mutual friends, interests and problems. "What you doin' for dinner tonight?" he asked. I was doing nothing so an invitation was very welcome, especially when it turned out we would be eating at the Officers' Mess of the US Navy in Washington.

It turned out that John, who became a lifelong friend that day, had served in the US Navy and was allowed to use their Mess. He had even sailed in wartime into Falmouth, where one day I would own a waterside home—and he and his wife, Joan, would come to stay.

That evening he drove me round the sights of the city, and one of the most impressive was to stand by the grave of John F Kennedy and see its flickering eternal flame. A very moving moment.

On again to New York, which was to be the conclusion of my fabulous trip. I had been to the city a number of times so I had done most of the usual tourist visits, but I still had a great time. I went into Saks on Fifth Avenue and bought dresses for Clare and Alison—and suddenly I was homesick. I tried to work out with the sales assistant how big Clare might be and ended up with two nice dresses with smashing labels but it was about two years before either could be worn.

A day or so later my magic journey came to an end. I climbed the steps into the plane which would take a long time to get to London, but I had a lot to think about. And I had certainly absorbed the point that New York and Washington are not America—why, I now had new friends in Los Angeles, Detroit, New England and New Orleans.

Back at my desk at the Department of Employment it still seemed pretty quiet. Sifting through the mountain of paper on my desk I found little of interest. And the phone was pretty quiet. As was the press office and the rest of my department.

Though trips with the minister to places like Norway and Canada broke up the time, I realised the department was quite happy for him to go foreign. It saved them trying to think up enough to keep him busy at home.

Then a call came through which might change everything. It was Michael Casey, one of my old friends from the Department of Economic Affairs, who had ended up in the shipbuilding section at Trade and Industry. Mike was now running the nationalised British Shipbuilders and suggested dinner in Chelsea. I had no difficulty in clearing my diary to fit him in.

I had a hunch there was change in the air.

CHAPTER 15
British Shipbuilders—Trying to Save Dying Jobs

Yes, it was certainly the kind of restaurant I knew Mike liked. A bit Spanish, spicy, good menu—and expensive. If we had to go Dutch I was braced, but I need not have worried. Late as usual, he ordered a good bottle of wine as he arrived and we were soon into animated conversation as if we had been working in the office together all day.

He told me he was chief executive of the newly nationalised British Shipbuilders and there was an exciting period ahead as people in shipbuilding came to work together instead of competing vigorously.

"The real competition is abroad. Japan right now, but South Korea is coming up fast and then Brazil.

"We have to get British shipbuilding to slim down, abandon restrictive practices, get the trade unions on board, and buy steel and components much more efficiently and cheaply. And keep the politicians and media on board—that's where you come in," he added.

I was excited at the sound of this challenge, but I played a bit hard to get. I had now been in the Civil Service for eight years and had a top job at an established department, I told him. I was not sure I wanted to risk all that for a gamble in a dying industry.

I came to "What would the terms be?" I would join at managing director level, he told me—pay level fixed right then by Government at £16,500 a year, expenses, a PA of course, offices in London and at the British Shipbuilders' nominal headquarters in Newcastle. This had been a sop to the unions who had persuaded Callaghan's Labour Government to take not only shipbuilding, but also aviation and much of defence into public ownership.

"And there would of course be a car," added Mike as a kind of afterthought.

I pounced. "What sort of car?"

"Oh, up to a certain level—up to a Jaguar, I think," he replied.

My mind was revving fast—a rise of £4,500, the kind of new car I had wanted for a long time, and a new job with what sounded like an almost clean canvas. I was definitely on but I held back.

"I will think it over, talk to the department, and give you a call," in a day or two. "But I am very definitely interested."

Casey virtually took that as an acceptance, and started to tell me all the plans he had for changing a traditional industry in which Britain had for so long led the world, but now lagged badly behind its competitors.

I did indeed have a good job in the permanent civil service. I could retire at sixty and by then have accrued a good pension, especially as I was buying tax-free added years. Here I was with a wife and two children, risking it all to take a job in an industry that, if not doomed, was going to face a very bleak future.

Utter madness. On the other hand, instead of writing and talking about industry, I was going to be in the middle of one which made real giant-size pieces of machinery, competed in a world market, had thousands of workers and was vitally important to Britain.

I called Casey to say I was joining him.

A letter of appointment soon arrived. I would indeed join at managing director level in charge of all public affairs including media and political relations, and could bring in my own personal assistant, Kathy O'Brien, who happily agreed to join me.

I took a few days' break before starting at British Shipbuilders, but there was time to go to a Jaguar dealer at Hammersmith and collect my new, beautiful-smelling XJ6, finished in what was known as squadron blue with a cabriolet top.

When I started at BS, the Labour Government which had put the industry into public ownership was in power, but Margaret Thatcher, in Opposition, was starting to make the running. One of her key advisers, Sir Keith Joseph, was utterly opposed to us, as was one of his key lieutenants, Nicholas Ridley. The Tory chairman of the Trade and Industry committee, Sir Michael Grylls, seemed to hate our guts. Michael Heseltine, who had brought the Commons to a standstill when he picked up the Mace during his speech of opposition to nationalising ship repair, was equally against public ownership.

Improving our image was obviously the top priority. We needed better public support by demonstrating the positives about an industry which had huge yards, mostly loss-making, on the nation's major rivers like the Clyde, the Tyne, the Mersey, the Wear, and at Southampton, Portsmouth, and even down in sleepy Appledore in North Devon. And had a labour force of 87,000!

There were twenty-seven major shipbuilding companies, six marine engine works, and six general engineering companies taken over under the Act. Six repair yards were then included, which turned out to be an expensive mistake.

British Shipbuilders accounted for 97 percent of UK merchant build capability, 100 percent of warship building, all slow-speed diesel engine design and construction, and over half of the ship repair work.

It was quite an outfit with strong characters, built-in traditions and deeply embedded restrictive practices. After the miners, the workers in this industry were probably the most militant and craft-conscious in Britain. Each skill jealously guarded its differential in pay over the next lower grade to themselves, and would go to ludicrous lengths to protect it.

Talk of common purpose, even the threat from international competition, was tossed aside. They'd heard it all before. But we had to get across that this time it was different, the competition was more intense, and through their union leadership, some of them sitting as directors on the main BS board, it could all be so different.

First, I had to get to know and assess our team in the press and PR department, but I also needed to find out quickly who were the movers and shakers in the industry.

My deputy was John Pullen. He had been in the shipbuilders'

federation offices when the Government stepped in, as was Ken Pottinger. John was a decent man who showed no resentment at my arrival, though he came up with very few positive ideas. Ken was, however, quite enthusiastic, and also very helpful in saving me from putting my foot into a situation because of lack of background.

Then there was Michael Guy who edited *Shipbuilding News*. This was a lively eight-page tabloid on *Daily Mirror* lines, but I was astonished to find that as management we had very little say in what went into it each month. Because the unions had cooperated in setting up nationalisation and had three seats on the board, they had insisted on a completely independent editor. BS paid the bill for printing and publishing a nationwide distribution and staff costs, but had no say in content.

Upstairs on the management floor was the office of the chairman, Rear Admiral Sir Anthony Griffin, who had come to the job fresh from being responsible for the Royal Navy's own ship repair yards. He had captained the aircraft carrier *Ark Royal*, kept a meticulous daily log of his activities, and desperately wanted public ownership to succeed. But I found no drive there likely to make it happen.

He sent for me a few days later and told me to cease using the term 'through deck cruisers' for the three naval ships commissioned, the first of which, HMS *Illustrious*, was well ahead at the Swan Hunter yard at Wallsend on the Tyne.

"You can call them aircraft carriers now," the Admiral told me with a chuckle. The term had been invented to save face for Denis Healey, then Defence Minister, who did not want it to be seen he had given in to the naval brass and reluctantly agreed to order three new carriers.

I was at the launch on 1st December 1978 when Princess Margaret cut the ribbon accompanied by Earl Mountbatten who was on fine form.

Six months later he was assassinated—blown up by the IRA, sailing his small boat at Sligo in the Republic of Ireland. Very courageous.

Along the corridor was another Griffin—Ken—who was deputy chairman and came into public life from his electrical trade union background. I had known him over the years and knew he was a pretty sharp operator. A TU man, certainly, but not too wedded to hair shirts— he liked good restaurants, good wine, stayed at the five-star Atheneum Hotel in Piccadilly while in London, had selected a Jaguar coupe for official work—and had another at home! He was cunning, though, and had persuaded Whitehall that he was the man to sort shipbuilding's labour relations. He might have done, too, if he had put in a lot more personal effort.

He was a shrewd judge of people and it was Ken Griffin who was later to describe Mike Casey as a brilliant diamond which on first sight knocked one's eye out but then, on closer examination, possessed that tiny flaw. Spot on. He had a good one on me, too. He once gave me a high mark but commented, "Unlikely to be a candidate for the Diplomatic Corps ... "

Further along the corridor I found the open door of a man I might be looking for in the weeks ahead. The marketing director was a thirty-five-year-old Ulsterman named T. John Parker who had come to BS from being responsible for selling the best merchant ship ever produced in the UK—the SD14, built by Austin and Pickersgill at Sunderland to replace the ageing World War II Liberty ships. I liked the look of him immediately. He seemed to love his job; several balls in the air at the same time did not faze him. And he was clearly familiar with the sharp end of working in a shipyard, something about which few of the other directors had much of a clue.

I thought I had a good front man if Casey was not around. Amazingly, Casey had pulled off a coup when he set-up the industry and persuaded the then minister responsible, Gerald Kaufman, that as there was going to be so much travelling for board members BS needed an executive jet. In those days company planes were rather rare. That did not faze Casey, and although ours was on charter and there was no fancy British Shipbuilders logo on display, we had fairly regular use of a twin-engine HS-125. For me it was just like old times at the Northern Ireland Office when we used the RAF HS-125s to hurtle between Northolt and Belfast.

My first trip on the plane was to support a board meeting at Benton House, the headquarters building in Newcastle-on-Tyne. Rather than a four-hour train journey, we were up in the North East in little over an hour which was spectacular in time-saving. But I suspect it did not do a lot for the picture we were trying to paint of an industry with its back to the wall, facing a dearth of orders, a possible redundancy programme, and probably widespread yard closures.

We had to absorb the fact that shipbuilding was operating in a hostile environment. A private enterprise yard could be losing heavily, but it was not under the same spotlight as when it became owned by the taxpayer. Then it was fair game as far as the media was concerned. So getting a square deal was a matter of building relationships and taking into your confidence those you could trust—people like Ian Ross of the BBC, Ian Hargreaves of the *Financial Times*, and my old pal Geoffrey Goodman, by now industrial editor of the *Daily Mirror*. Another great supporter was Louis Heren, then assistant editor of *The Times*, who I persuaded to come to the Govan shipyard on a two-day visit.

Many rose to the exciting challenges as we shook up the industry, but not all. There were also major human problems, we knew, and many more ahead as we started a slimming-down process. To compete with the Japanese and Koreans our labour costs had to reduce drastically, and at the same time productivity had to rise. Yet we had to give the men in the yards hope that if we got concessions it would pay off for them.

I worked closely with John Parker, who had assembled a team from the merchant yards and identify possible orders BS yards might be able to win. The committee earmarked each ship order for a particular empty berth in a yard, and had conjured up quite a list.

"Could we publish this?" I asked Parker. Several around him shook their heads—not a chance. But Parker waved them down. "Let's think about this."

I explained that a kind of shopping list—so long as we knew we would definitely get some of the orders—would attract public and media attention and might swing support our way. Then when, or if, we did get an order we could announce it with a flourish. Also, with the likelihood that the Conservatives were going to win the impending General Election, a positive line might help to tone down the rhetoric against us.

A few days later, when I called a press conference, we had a good story to tell and plenty of facts and figures to back up the target list.

That evening the TV coverage was very good and next morning the papers were full of 'British shipbuilding's fightback'. Best of all my old paper, the *Daily Mail*, which had been very hostile to nationalisation, made us lead story. The honeymoon was unlikely to last long, but that morning the story of shipbuilding in the UK was looking good.

But it brought home to me the importance of *Shipbuilding News* and how crucial it was to integrate it into our operations. We needed to know the line it was going to take, and to synchronise its operations with the central PR message from British Shipbuilders.

I discovered the paper was being produced and published in Havering, Essex, at a printing press owned by Douglas Brown, once a distinguished journalist at the old *News Chronicle*. But there was a sleeping partner, it seemed … who turned out to be my old friend and colleague Geoffrey Goodman. That was a shaker. Geoffrey had never mentioned his involvement with *Shipbuilding News*, but it figured. He was a great believer in worker involvement, and the paper was supposed to be representing shipyard workers and the employers.

I invited Douglas and Geoffrey to my office for what looked like being an uncomfortable session. But then my luck turned. Michael Guy, the editor, asked to see me, looked me straight in the eye, and asked if I was going to go through with my planned changes.

I assured him I was quite determined. I thought Mike would quit right then. It would be a real blow, and hard for me to defend. Instead, to my astonishment, he announced, "If that's the case I would like to continue to edit the paper under your management."

I could have kissed him. I was being handed the trump card. Brown and Goodman could hardly argue when I told them their editor agreed with my changes and wanted to continue to edit *Shipbuilding News*. I never heard from Brown again but Geoffrey, as ever, bore no grudge, and over the years we continued to work together and remained good friends. But it might not have been the case.

As for Michael Guy, I brought him totally into our operations and he was able to get a much fuller picture. He had my input and active support.

Not long afterwards I sent him to Finland to visit the Turku shipyard to find out why its management, designers and workers had so decisively beaten our lead offshore engineering yard, Scott Lithgow at Greenock, for a North Sea drilling rig. Winning that order would have meant all the difference to the future of the yard. Though the wages of the Finnish workers were much higher and they had to cope with far more stringent weather, their productivity ran rings round us.

That week, *Shipbuilding News* contained a stinging shaft of realism under Michael Guy's byline, Filed in Finland. There was a lot more to come. Somehow BS needed to rouse its workers and get them to commit to major change.

The labour relations team under Ken Griffin were making big efforts to get a dialogue with the union leadership, but despite using *Shipbuilding News* I knew we needed to scale up the whole way in which we communicated.

I remembered the director of the *Tomorrow's World* TV programme we had made about the plastic bricks, and the bungalow we had built in the studio. It did not take too long to track him down and learn he was freelancing, so I invited him to my office in Knightsbridge and soon we worked out a plan. Using video to communicate was relatively new then in Britain, certainly in industry, and our plan was to make a special programme and to have it shown in every yard and facility in BS.

The beauty of the BS set-up was that I could push through an idea like that without having too many committees picking it apart.

We scripted a special presentation for Mike Casey, and then did slightly different versions for John Parker to address the men in merchant shipbuilding, and other variants for the head of warship and the head of ship repair. This was important because each section had different competition to face, varying order books, financial situations, and other problems.

I set off on a major tour of the yards with the videos and the equipment on which to show them. At each yard there was a short break for the men to watch the video and then hold an open discussion led by the local management. I would back them up, bringing a head office viewpoint, but the emphasis was on a chance for the yard's own workers to confront the problem of how to compete better.

There were huge discussions with several thousand men at Vickers in Barrow where we held several sessions—some for the submarine construction, and others for the section devoted to building artillery and naval guns.

As I toured the country I got to know much more about an industry I had always respected but of which I was now a part. It was a hard, but rewarding, journey and one which convinced me I had to continue using new methods of communication rather than relying on messages being passed down the line by shop stewards—or hoping men would pick up a copy of *Shipbuilding News*. I got approval to make quarterly videos to send out to the yards with up-to-date reports on how successful BS was on chasing overseas orders, introducing new ideas and building a better understanding.

The news that British Shipbuilders was to take a trade mission to China was very exciting. The team was led by Rear Admiral Griffin and Mike Casey. It included John Parker, George Snaith, head of research, Terry Harrison, who was very senior at Clarke Chapman, supplier of cranes, derricks and other equipment to fit out ships—and yours truly. My job was to set-up and present the audiovisual I had had made of British Shipbuilders, showing in fast-speed colour transparencies the industry at its best. With a slick soundtrack, it looked good.

We went from Hong Kong to Peking, or Beijing as it is now known. It really was very drab. Poor lighting, squalid so-called 'luxury' hotels complete with smouldering cloth burning in tiny tin cans to try to keep the mosquitos at bay.

We were driven around the capital in Russian cars kitted out with curtains; driven very slowly indeed because the whole city appeared to be on cycles, and cars had to hoot every few seconds to warn of their approach.

As for restaurants, we abandoned any idea of finding any. We were told there were one or two, but we never succeeded in finding any. And it was probably dangerous to wander around the streets in that era.

We found the Chinese shipbuilders very friendly indeed. Although none of us spoke the other's language we soon began to understand each other, and a good bond began to develop.

At one point we were split into two teams, and I was one of four with George and Terry and one other whose name escapes me, to travel by train to Nanking. It was a seventeen-hour journey on an inter-city express and as we clambered aboard we were closely watched by the other passengers. As soon as they found we were in berths in various compartments they swiftly reorganised so that the four of us were in the same compartment. And the Chinese did not have to share with a smelly foreigner from Britain.

Breakfast was an experience. Each coach appeared to have its own catering staff and they produced quite a good meal of bacon, eggs and tea—weak, but drinkable.

Looking out of the window, we could see the extent of the Chinese railways and the number of locomotives belching black smoke, as well as the bent backs of the coolies working knee-deep in the rice paddies. Even now it seems amazing to think that not only have most of the steam trains gone, but many of the workers too—away to the cities in search of work, just as ours did in the Industrial Revolution of the nineteenth century.

We found the Chinese shipyards appeared to be light years behind us in modern methods. Hulls were held up by wooden spars, just as we did it in Nelson's time; men scaled ladders, long since swept away in modern yards. Surely there was scope for us to sell new techniques in modern shipbuilding methods. And it looked encouraging when our

Chinese friends asked to come to the UK for a tour of our best facilities.

In fact nothing came of it, though the canny Chinese learned a lot which they took away for nothing. As I write, thirty-five years, later the Chinese have just launched their first aircraft carrier—and we have scrapped *Ark Royal* and *Invincible*. *Illustrious* is up for sale and we no longer have any Harrier jets—the US Marines have taken them over and developed the British technology. Now where have I heard that before?

And Beijing is teeming with excellent restaurants these days!

As part of the management team to try to turn around the shipbuilding industry I was becoming increasingly disappointed with Mike Casey. Whenever I could get to him, which was often becoming difficult, it seemed that whatever idea was put to him he wanted a paper on it. A typical civil servant's response. It was the same everywhere in the industry. It was a standard joke that if we could build ships with paper, there would not be a vacant berth in any of our yards.

The European Commission, alert to the slightest tendency on the part of BS to subsidise any construction, pored over any contract, determined, it would appear, to screw us somehow. Meanwhile, we watched the French, the Italians, and the Germans building luxury liners for the impending boom in ocean cruising quite oblivious to any restriction on subsidisation.

John Parker came up with a cruise liner concept where BS would build the hull in one of the bigger yards, but have the cabins, lounges, bars and kitchens all built ashore. Then, brought from the supply source, the assembled units would be slotted in, so cutting the man-hours considerably.

But we could not get the go-ahead, and since then the rival yards in Europe have cashed in while Britain just tossed thousands of skilled workers onto the scrapheap. We are watching a similar scenario in steel-making as I write.

We worked hard on lobbying and Labour MPs were naturally very supportive. The Tories, though, were strongly behind Mrs Thatcher.

I went to see Malcolm Rifkind and Norman Lamont, but I was wasting my time. I had a longer session with Michael Heseltine who

282

came to lunch with me, but he warned that the Tories would shut BS down if they won the impending election in 1979.

We even got Denis Thatcher, Margaret Thatcher's husband, to come in to Knightsbridge for lunch with the Admiral, Casey, Parker and Ken Griffin. He was not unsympathetic, but made no promises. We hoped Denis might mention over breakfast to his wife that those chaps down at British Shipbuilders were doing a good job ... it was, I understand, the Admiral who finally put the boot in for Mike Casey with the Government.

Mike's three-year contract was due for renewal but, while his charm and undoubted ability were recognised, his failure to follow through or to appear at meetings, began to tell against him. The word was that the Admiral suggested a new chief executive be sought and that Mike's contract should not be renewed.

He was angry, bitter, and felt he had been betrayed. He did not appear to realise that much of the problem was of his own making. That left us pondering who would come in to take the helm?

Ken Griffin, the deputy chairman and a former trade union official, had his ear to the ground in Whitehall, and picked up several names. But he never picked up the name of the new chairman, who turned out to be the nastiest man with whom I ever worked.

The word filtered through from Whitehall that the new chairman would be Robert Atkinson, of whom no one, it seemed, had ever heard. Eventually we discovered he had been chairman of Stag, makers of bedroom furniture, and also at one time managing director of Doxford, the famous marine engine maker, now part of BS. He had also had a distinguished wartime naval career, having served in corvettes, the lightly built naval vessels prominent in the campaign against German U-Boats.

How did he get the job, we wondered? Then we heard Atkinson had actually written in to the Department of Trade and offered his services—not at shipbuilding, but to take the chair at the National Coal Board. The permanent secretary, Sir Peter Carey, told him that had already been earmarked (Ian McGregor, Mrs Thatcher's nominee, who was soon to take on the miners in the epic year-long clash).

But Sir Peter, in effect, offered Atkinson the pick of vacancies in the nationalised industries. No assessment, no suitability check—just help yourself. It rather summed up Whitehall's view of the ailing shipbuilding industry, and of our chances of getting things put right.

Looking me straight in the eye, Atkinson told me, "I believe in public relations … GOOD public relations." What he meant, I knew instinctively, was anything praising the chairman was okay. But the slightest whiff of criticism would mean a witch-hunt to find the source.

He also indicated he was very hair shirt on expenses, so I was careful what I ate and drank but noticed this restriction did not seem to apply to him.

Lunch in the London executive dining room with the new chairman was a tense event. Ken Griffin summed it up well. He likened it to dining with Captain Queeg in the ship's mess aboard the *Caine* before the mutiny. "It's not as if he is counting the strawberries, but he watches what we all eat as if he is personally paying the bill."

Within a short period, several quite big names had been told abruptly to clear their desks and depart. Atkinson had started to do the Department of Trade's bidding and shed people, though the economies did not appear to involve *his* lifestyle.

And in myriad other ways it was clear times had changed at BS. Everyone knew they had to, but it would have been better if Mike Casey had addressed the issue sooner. Now it was going to get messy and there would be blood on the carpet. I was just determined it was not going to be mine.

Throughout my career I had followed a couple of maxims—never work for a person I did not respect or trust, and when a door opened to step straight through.

I knew that moment had arrived, but where to jump?

The phone came to my rescue. It was Jimmy James, deputy director general of the Confederation of British Industry, who told me they were seeking to replace the Director of Information, and he had been given my name. Would I have time to come to see Sir Terence Beckett, the director general?

I told my caller I could fit it in and was invited to the new headquarters of the CBI in Centre Point, the ugly new concrete tower at Tottenham Court Road, the following afternoon.

I told Kathy but otherwise kept my mouth shut, and slid away from the shiny shops of Knightsbridge, hardly an area to associate with the construction of magnificent ships, to the tatty environs of Soho, where the prestigious spokesmen of British industry were now located. It was the idea of CBI Director General, Sir John Methven, who fancied getting all the other employer bodies to move into Centre Point and to make the tower the power base for Britain's bosses. I think he even might have had the idea the tower would one day be named after him. Some hopes.

A few months later, though, Methven died suddenly in hospital when an operation on his leg went wrong and a blood clot killed him. His unexpected death threw the CBI into crisis, and a top name was urgently needed to replace him.

Enter Sir Terence Beckett, the chairman of Ford UK who had just announced record profits of over £300 million, enough to carry the loss that Ford of America had just clocked up. When I read of his appointment I remember saying the CBI had pulled off a coup. But then, at the autumn conference of the CBI at Brighton, which I attended to represent BS, Beckett hit out strongly at the Tory Government for interest rates at fifteen percent, not listening to the needs of British business, and generally falling down on the job.

It was a good speech, and well over a third of the delegates, myself among them, gave Beckett a standing ovation. But others present sat on their hands and felt it was not the done thing to criticise a Tory Government, certainly not one led by the blessed Margaret Thatcher.

There was a massive backlash the next day and several prominent members of the CBI resigned their membership—men like Frank Taylor of Taylor Woodrow, Barrie Heath of GKN, and Victor Matthews of Trafalgar. Ironically, five of these businessmen were made peers in the Conservative Party over the next year and all quietly rejoined the CBI.

So I knew all about the row when I was shown to the tenth floor at Centre Point and into the huge office of the Director General. He got quickly to the point. "I want you to join me," he said. "I've heard all about you and I reckon you are the man I need."

Interesting, but how did he know that? I found that when he had been hit so hard by the devastating backlash from the Brighton speech, he had rung the only top notch PR man he knew, Walter Hayes at Ford.

I had known Wally at the *Daily Mail,* and indeed had given his name to a headhunter when he rang and asked if I was interested in the Ford job. Wally had just been fired by Lord Rothermere from editing the *Sunday Dispatch*, so he was on the market.

"You don't need me," Wally told Beckett. "You need a political man. Try Keith McDowall."

"So why do you want me?" I asked Beckett.

"For your judgement," came the reply.

Well, that was interesting, but was he going to listen? No problem, it seemed. Every morning for a brief few minutes? Agreed.

How soon could I join him? I explained I would have to give notice at British Shipbuilders, but felt it would not take too long. In fact it was very quick. Atkinson was furious. He liked to do the firing, and did not like people jumping ship.

"Clear your desk at once, leave your car keys and get out of here," he snarled.

As *The Guardian* summed him up, "He was a mercurial and sometimes merciless manager with a choleric temper which unsettled senior colleagues."

I was not going to give him the chance.

I thought I was leaving without any pay and no car, but Philip Hares, in charge then of running the accounts and employment, called me to his room.

"You must be owed a lot of holiday pay," he told me, and arranged for a cheque. "And you can take your car."

You need a friend at times like that. I doubt if Atkinson was ever told. He would have demanded an immediate refund.

CHAPTER 16
CBI—the Voice of British Business

I had had an association on and off over the years with the Confederation of British Industry. On the *Daily Mail* I had long been keen that the employers should get their act together because the unions, and in particular its coordinating body, the Trades Union Congress, had been having it all their own way for far too long. Whereas it was like drawing blood to try to find an employer contact who would come up with a quote one could use in print.

I had picked up that the Federation of British Industry—mainly the large companies in the UK—the British Employers' Confederation, which concentrated on employment policy and pay, and the National Association of Manufacturers were in secret talks to create one body.

I had become friendly with Sir George Pollock, the director general of the BEC, and he kept me up to speed on how the tripartite talks were going on the strict understanding I would keep it quiet until the talks were successful, or at least concluded. I kept my word, and Sir George finally tipped me off to go with the story that the employers were to form one organisation.

I little thought then that more than twenty years later I would head up the press and communication function of what became the Confederation of British Industry.

Up on the ninth floor of Centre Point, at the junction of Tottenham Court Road and New Oxford Street, was the CBI's Information Directorate and I was its new director. I found the makings of a good team waiting. My deputy was John Dunkley, a journalist who had been on industrial work at *The Guardian* and then for several years at

287

British Steel. He and I had always shared an interest in sailing and had crewed together in the Round the Island Race on a catamaran. He was diligent and conscientious and had one of the best Pitman shorthand notes I had ever come across.

He summed up aptly what he thought my role was to be. "Your job," he told me, "is to get Beckett back on his horse."

That assessment was echoed shortly afterwards when I went upstairs to a pre-Christmas reception, and Sir Ray Pennock, President of the CBI, came over to introduce himself.

He did not use exactly the same words as Dunkley, but made it clear he wanted to see some steel inserted into the Director General who, Pennock told me, "is a bit shell-shocked."

Another old Fleet Street colleague in charge of the news room was Phil Ditton. He had been commercial reporter on the *Daily Express* when I was on the industrial beat so our paths had crossed fairly frequently. Phil took pride in producing fast copy, and believed in teaching youngsters the proper way to go about the job. I found him very dependable and enthusiastic about his work.

One of the best features of the CBI information set-up was that my predecessor had established the right for us to have our own people in each region, reporting direct to the Information department rather than through the regional centres. They were all professional journalists, mainly trained in the provinces, who knew their local media and could get the CBI case across on local TV, radio and in the newspapers. It worked like a dream.

The economic situation under Mrs Thatcher was deteriorating. Unemployment was rising sharply as were interest rates, and the morale in the country was poor. It was no great surprise that there was an outbreak of rioting in Brixton, in Bristol, Liverpool and other parts of the country.

As I drove into work it occurred to me that I was lucky to have a job, and at the morning meeting I told everyone to smile—we ALL had jobs. You could see the penny dropping. Instead of complaining and grumbling, people began to count their blessings. Not long afterwards

Phil Ditton came into my office and said, "I've been thinking, K—why can't *WE* find a job for a kid? What we need is what you and I did once in newspapers when we were the office boys. We really could use one here."

It was a great idea, but since I was being told to cut the staff I did not see how I could ask to recruit someone. Then we remembered that there was a Government scheme which meant if a youngster was employed the Government would find the wages.

We rang the local employment office and within a few hours we had set it all up. Next morning a pretty young black girl, whose home was indeed in Brixton, arrived at the office to start a three-month spell with us. It was not a great success because, although she was the daughter of a postman, we found she could only cope with one task at a time. If she was sent to Fleet Street to deliver a press release to, say, the *Daily Express*, she could not then continue next door and deliver one to the *Daily Telegraph*. She had to come back to the office for fresh instruction. But thereafter we had a succession of youngsters who were really great and we got one for the Library, too. He became so popular that when his turn came to depart, the Library staff came together to demand he be allowed to stay on. Which we managed, somehow.

By this time we had forged a relationship with a Youth Employment Officer in Grays, Essex, who sent us several youngsters. One day he rang to tell us he had a wonderful candidate who wanted to be a journalist. Though we told him we were not equipped to train journalists, he insisted we see this young lady. So an attractive blonde teenager promptly arrived and said her name was Denna Allen.

Quickly she found her feet as the dogsbody in the Press Office, but picked up knowledge equally quickly. When a full-time vacancy occurred she was first in line, and Phil and I nominated Denna to go on the national training scheme for journalists. Denna passed the interview with flying colours and went off for a year as a trainee at a local paper in Basildon. At the CBI annual conference in Eastbourne we fixed up for her to interview Sir Terence Beckett.

She sent us the cutting which made the point that scoffing at the

Government's youth employment scheme was unfair. "Look what it did for me," she wrote.

Sometime later she was appearing frequently in the feature pages of the *Daily Mirror* and her byline looked good. We were very proud of her.

We had on the team Squire Barraclough, who had been on the *Express* when I was on the *Mail* and who then joined the *Sketch*. Squire had talent and could write, but I discovered later he had a serious drink problem which was extremely difficult to handle. In several jobs I had had after leaving Fleet Street, I found I had a staff member who had an alcohol problem. One of the pitfalls of being in charge of a team.

Generally that was the exception to the rule. Over the years, though, I found that if given leadership and, when needed, a decision, it is possible to get people operating as a team with enthusiasm and actually enjoying their work. That was particularly the case with young people. There were numerous examples of seeing them succeed, and of me feeling quite proud of having had a hand in their career progress. I was fortunate in finding a top notch Secretary/PA in Susan Fellows on whom I could depend totally. She never seemed to forget a thing—and still even remember my birthday every year.

At my first Monday morning meeting at the CBI, however, it soon became clear that I had not joined a buoyant vessel. The organisation not only had a morale problem, it also had a financial one. It was sinking slowly. With the economy in a mess and interest rates now at sixteen percent, businesses up and down the country were feeling the pinch. A large number were going to the wall, and unemployment was rising sharply. So, quite apart from the fallout due to Beckett's 'bare knuckle' speech, a number of member companies were saying they could not afford to pay their subscriptions, and cancelling membership.

Beckett had the Ford gleam in his eye—cutting numbers was in his DNA. He used to argue that every January, like Ford, we should cut jobs at the CBI by five percent because through the previous twelve months employment would have built up quietly.

It was the way, no doubt, to run an hourly paid labour force, but not one likely to get the best out of a professional staff who would either be jaded or resentful. Certainly unlikely to come up with their best work.

Other section heads may have gone back to their desks with intentions to cut their staff as directed, but I determined to do no such thing. I called my team together and said it was quite clear to me we needed some new campaign themes; otherwise, why should member firms support us? And what was the point in claiming to be Britain's Business Voice if no one was listening? Or could hear us.

Over the next few days we kicked around ideas, and out of it came the thought that the best target was the Government's National Insurance Surcharge by which on top of taking a large slice of company profits to pay for pensions and employment services, the Government added on a further ten percent. And pocketed it.

The crafty tax was first introduced by Labour's Denis Healey when Chancellor in 1976. It slipped through virtually unnoticed amongst a raft of measures, and the impression given was that this was a temporary measure, soon to be abandoned.

Yet some years later it was still on the Statute Book and, as always, the Treasury had no intention of dropping it. The trouble was the language. Who the hell understood what the surcharge was, let alone why it existed? Business just paid up.

Suddenly there was one of those eureka moments—"Let's call it the Jobs Tax." When unemployment was soaring, how could an extra tax like the surcharge possibly be justified.

No, the Government would not like it, but they were supposed to be rooting for private enterprise and wealth creation—and for cutting unnecessary bureaucracy. That was surely the National Insurance Surcharge—the Jobs Tax.

I went up to the tenth floor and asked Beckett's new secretary to get me in to him as soon as possible.

I was in within seconds—and realised that in Linda Turner I had a potential supporter. She and I were to become good pals, allies, and to work together well.

Beckett quickly took the idea on board and liked the concept. We were not attacking the Government—we were attacking a measure by the previous government, which was ill-thought out, and an added burden commerce and industry should not have to carry. The Jobs Tax, we would argue, would have to go.

An immediate meeting was called of heads of economics, employment, small firms, and regions, to discuss it further. There was clear enthusiasm for a concept we could all get our heads around.

In the Information department, meanwhile, roughs were produced for car window stickers, special letter headings, briefing material for our information officers in the regions, and question-and-answer briefs for local businessmen willing to go on TV and radio and to meet local journalists.

For MPs we prepared special briefing, and targeted those within the Tory ranks better disposed to us like Chris Patten and Richard Needham, with whom I subsequently forged a long friendship.

A few days later we were ready, and the 'go' button was pressed. All over the country the sniping at the Jobs Tax began. Best of all, next morning *The Sun*, Rupert Murdoch's big selling tabloid and a great fan of Mrs Thatcher, led with 'Cut the Jobs Tax' as its Page One splash. We were off …

It was in the Budget some months later that, to roars of approval in the House of Commons, the Chancellor of the Exchequer announced the surcharge was to end. He managed to conceal the grudging irritation quite well, I thought.

For the CBI, and Sir Terence in particular, it was an important notch in the belt and meant that members' firms could see what he was doing with their money. Over the next few years we ran numerous campaigns, sometimes on our own and often in collaboration with others.

Quietly, I still had good contacts with the TUC, and though Beckett kept them at arm's length because of the strength of the right-wing supporters of Mrs Thatcher, he liked me to keep in touch.

As I have written, I knew George Woodcock well, but in later years would count John Monks and David Lee, on the TUC staff then, as friends and also, even in later years, TUC presidents like Alec Smith, secretary of the tailor and garment workers, and Fred Jarvis, leader of the main teachers' union.

The CBI were partners with the TUC on the National Economic Development Council which was originally set-up by George Brown in 1965. I was milling around with reporters outside including a young man named Nigel Lawson, then a City journalist. He would one day take the chair as Chancellor or the Exchequer. And wind up Neddy as it was known.

By then I was sitting, like Lawson, inside the conference room at Milbank Tower.

Before Lawson, Geoffrey Howe, as Chancellor, took the chair and one day came out with a wonderful quote 'Pray God send me a one arm economist!'

Neddey gave employers, trade union leaders, civil servants, nationalised industry chiefs, and politicians a chance to mingle informally and sound out ideas. It lasted 21 years and was killed off or pure political reasons—a pity, I thought.

So that was how the TUC came out to join us when the CBI launched a new campaign to end the annual ritual of putting the clocks back by one hour to Greenwich Mean Time and plunging most of the country into earlier darkened afternoons and gloomy nights. Apart from the view that Britons just did not work so well in winter darkness, there was also acceptance that, with Britain now in the European Union, it made more sense to be on the same time as our friends and rivals.

It looked as if, at last, we were going to get the so-called daylight-saving hour retained during winter. In World War II, when it was noted that people were working such long hours they were getting no sunlight or relaxation, the clocks were put forward by two hours.

Everyone loved it. But when peace came and the Government no longer demanded maximum output, the concept was abandoned. We knew if we could just get the one hour it would have been very welcome.

All was going swimmingly and there was widespread public support, except in Scotland. That was when David Waddington, then Home

Secretary, stood up in the Commons and threw out the hour change. It was done simply to appease the sparse number of Conservatives living north of the border. They had lobbied hard, and persuaded the Government that pushing the hours change through would lose even more support among the Scots Tories. Infuriating.

We were more successful in campaigning to get heavier lorries accepted on Britain's roads. The rest of the EU nations had accepted them and there was no doubt that payloads were much more economical if larger lorries were used. The trouble was that the term 'bigger' was being applied and no one wanted them on Britain's crowded roads.

But the freight hauliers were in a fix because in effect they had to operate two kinds of lorries—the larger European vehicles, and the smaller ones said to be more suited to British roads. David Howell, one of my old Northern Ireland ministers and now Transport Minister, was badly mauled in Parliament when he tried to get the changes through. He told me he was not willing to have another go unless the CBI drummed up better support.

So my team looked again at the issue, and found that the larger lorries actually had an extra axle and so spread the load more evenly on the road surface, meaning less damage. And in fact, side by side, the two lorries did not look all that much different.

We arranged to have them outside Parliament in Westminster, inviting MPs to come and have a look themselves, and also had them outside the Conservative party conference. We invited politicians to have a drink and look at the new not *BIGGER* lorries, but *HEAVIER* ones.

From then on we put the emphasis on the extra axle to lighten the impact on Britain's roads, and gradually our case won through. Next time, Parliament agreed to the vehicle changes without a vote!

Even after all these years, though, I sometimes get a nudge in the ribs when we are held up in traffic. "Is that one of your heavier lorries?" Brenda asks!

My boss Beckett was given the cold shoulder by the Prime Minister for the best part of eighteen months, and it made life difficult for him with CBI members. We were supposed to have influence with government, yet sometimes it did not look like it. At one meeting with ministers, when Mrs Thatcher was in the chair, she chided my boss, "Now, now, Sir Terence," she told him. "We've given you your Jobs Tax!"

I told him, "What she meant was she could no longer hold out against the CBI campaign."

We majored on two themes which nowadays have by-partisan acceptance-the need for infrastructure investment and for help in sustaining and restoring the role of manufacturing in Britain. To Beckett and to me these issues were vital to the nation's future. So whenever we got the chance they were worked into speeches, press quotes and publications.

One attraction of investment in new roads, bridges, airports and other major projects was that Beckett could argue they were non-inflationary and created jobs in Britain.

David Young, Thatcher's industry minister sneered, "Men don't make motorways—machines do."

It was a good line but it ignored all the employment involved in bringing a major project to the start line yet it summed up the Conservative Government attitude at the time.

Another comment I have never forgotten came from a Deputy Secretary at the Treasury when I pressed him to rethink policy on support for manufacturing. "You don't get it, Keith," he told me. "It's all about managing decline."

And that was the Treasury attitude. Besotted by the growth in the financial sector it saw that taking up the slack in job opportunities until the banking crisis of 2007–8.

These days the Chancellor can be heard extolling the virtues of creating jobs in the Northern Power House and in the Midlands. Just think of all the jobs we might have saved over the last fifty years if we had followed Germany's example.

One of the most effective weapons in our armoury was the fortnightly *CBI News*, which we developed from a routine newsletter to a readable full colour magazine. It went out to every member, as well as to the press, to MPs and peers and into Government departments.

When I arrived at Centre Point, the first issue set-up by my predecessor was about to be launched under the editorship of Peter Lawrence, formerly of the *News Chronicle*. But when I asked to see the front page splash on our Jobs Tax campaign I was told by Peter it was too late. As it was in colour, the front page went off three days early. It needed time to process. I told Peter to get the printer to come to see me. Very fast!

In came David Evans of Centurion Press, who took my critical outburst in his stride. He promised swift changes which were in hand by the time of the next edition. David was to become one of my best and oldest friends, and my very first customer when I set-up in public relations on my own. And I would help to write his inaugural speech when he was introduced as a Labour peer in the House of Lords.

Not long after I went to Centre Point, Bryan Rigby, another deputy director, came into my office to offer some advice. "Don't ignore FEIG," he said. "That's the only part of Europe that works."

It turned out he was referring to an outfit called the Free Enterprise Information Group, whose membership consisted of my opposite numbers in the various employer groups throughout Europe as well as Japan.

There was a weekend event looming in Madrid which I had been tempted to skip in view of the cost-cutting at Centre Point. But if I was being encouraged to go …

That turned out to be a life-changing experience. In that brief period in Madrid I forged friendships which lasted for the rest of my working career and, in some cases, long after I stopped.

FEIG was an inspired idea of a Swede, but embraced by all the people responsible in Europe for pressing the business case and promoting free enterprise. That meant one had a hotline throughout Europe—and indeed in Japan—which could really deliver.

My closest friends were Leif Fast and his wife Irma, from Finland, Jan Berg and Monica in Sweden, Per Bjorgan and his wife Inge Lisa, in Norway, Katsura Kuno and Aki in Japan, Viktor and Beatriz Bauer in Austria, and Claude-Oliver Rochet and his English wife Jill, in Switzerland. We also has contact in Spain, France, Denmark, and eventually in the United States.

We met twice a year and took turns to act as host nation. There was some competition as each of us tried to set-up some special events, drawing on our membership contacts, so we went to some splendid venues.

We had an understanding that if any of us had a good idea, FEIG members could freely take it and develop it for use in their own country. Beckett encouraged me to go to FEIG meetings, reasonably confident I would return with something fresh.

Our second event of the year was to attend, or sometimes run, the FEIG Industrial Film and Video Festival, which was a roaring success attended by 450–500 people. In those days, businesses spent considerable sums of money to produce films and videos of their products—particularly industries like motor manufacturers, pharmaceutical companies and steelmakers, but also official government drives on matters like training, health and recruitment. Quite often, there was great originality in the scripts and magnificent creative photography—particularly by companies like Bayer, the German chemical company, which ploughed in whatever it took to try to win the Best Industrial Film of the Year award.

The first year I went to Turin to see the Festival awards presented, I was delighted to find that a British company named Video Arts had won the training category with a highly amusing but very professional script. My colleagues told me how good it was, and when I saw the film myself I quickly realised the actor was John Cleese of *Fawlty Towers* fame. The production company, Video Arts, was the one later behind the great *Yes Minister* series which sent up British politicians and their civil servants. No wonder it made the Europeans laugh.

It was my turn to run the festival in London in 1984. My boss told me I could do it so long as it did not interfere with my work and did not cost the CBI a penny! Somehow I managed it, but at times it was a sweat.

We formed a special team on the festival project led ably by Bob Rangecroft (who fell in love with a Swedish girl he met in the judging process, and subsequently left his wife) and also Geoff Kelly, who was on secondment to me from Barclays Bank. Geoff had been sent to me for what his boss described as 'mind broadening' in preparation to taking over the bank's press and public relations.

Geoff took to our kind of work like a duck to water, as the cliché goes, and it was interesting seeing him loosen his grasp on the precision of banking, as it was then, to embrace our more flexible approach. After all these years he remains a good friend, but his attention to detail in running the festival was a boon just then to me.

I persuaded several client firms like Rank and Unilever to join the organisation team, and an appeal for funds brought in very welcome cheques from over twenty companies. So I was able to meet Sir Terence's stern condition that the London event should not cost the CBI a penny. Indeed, when it was all over I handed in a cheque, but managed to spend quite a bit of the £19,000 surplus beforehand. I made a substantial donation to the British Film Institute for saving old film, made of silver nitrate, rotting and in danger of catching fire, with the request it should be devoted to classic industrial films.

But it was not all hard work. We threw a magnificent ball for the festival delegates at Pinewood Film Studios, visited the dungeons of the Tower of London, and took a tour of Churchill's home at Chartwell. A highlight was a reception I persuaded the Government to fund at Lancaster House at which Princess Alexandra welcomed the delegates.

But the ball and presentation at one of my favourite hotels, the Park in Kensington, was the big awards night. I had seen several of my European colleagues' events in difficulty when it came to getting the final results listed in time.

Not only did we have them in a slip edition of the *Evening Standard* presented to every guest as they arrived, but with some slick footwork we had each award in silver, beautifully engraved in Clerkenwell. I was able to point out that this was the work of some of the longest-established craftsmen in London.

Throughout the week a team of Japanese followed everything that happened and all that we did, making copious notes. Katsura Kuno, then director of information at the Keidanren, the employers' organisation in Japan, had undertaken to stage the festival in Kobe, the first time it had ever been held outside Europe. He had a glorious success and made a bigger profit than me, but was smarter with it. Instead of getting rid of the surplus, he retained it in his information department and used it to subsidise the airfares for his delegates to attend future FEIG events. I never thought of that.

Interestingly, nearly all the key members of FEIG had a common interest in sailing. Over the years, Kuno and I, in particular, sailed together on Lake Geneva, out of Tokyo, and in the waters around Helsinki. Another close friend, Per Bjorgan, joined us a number of times—it seems most Norwegians are natural sailors. And Jan Berg of the Swedish employers owned a fine 34-foot yacht on which we cruised around the archipelago near Stockholm.

When the normal FEIG meeting was held in London, one weekend I took everyone to the Medway Yacht Club. With my boat and those of two friends we were all able to cruise down to the Thames Estuary and have a splendid barbecue. Well, it can't be all about work, can it?

Leif Fast, who ran the Finnish employers economic research centre in Helsinki, came up with the suggestion that we should make a tour to find how various nations promoted to children and schools the importance of jobs, skills and, above all, that profit was not a dirty word.

All our organisations gave us the go-ahead, so we flew first to Toronto to see coaches lining up outside the Schools Centre and children pouring into a building specially built to encourage children's involvement with, and interest in, wealth creation.

Inside, the kids were swarming around machines pulling levers, looking into viewing areas, trying on gear, and having a splendid time. The idea was to get them to see that work could actually be interesting and rewarding.

I told our guide I found the children's enthusiasm impressive—where did they get the idea?

"Oh, we saw it at work in the basement of the Science Museum at South Kensington in London," came the reply.

So there it was, slap in my own backyard. I had not been to the Science Museum in thirty years, but when I got back to London I went to the basement to find British kids having a great time and learning plenty.

We went on from Toronto to visit the headquarters of CNN, then newly launched by Ted Turner in Atlanta, and on to EPCOT at Disneyworld in Florida where America was also getting its young people interested in work and profit.

Inside, there were exhibits like the first electric car from General Motors, how rice was grown, and what the early space programme was revealing.

That night Leif returned us to EPCOT for a memorable and magical night. Apart from sailing, with our common interest in jazz we had been in some good clubs together around Europe. By the lake at Disneyworld that evening some of the best American big bands like Lionel Hampton, Count Basie, and a Benny Goodman copy orchestra were playing and we had a ball.

My strong friendship with my European and Japanese colleagues was extremely helpful to me when I set-up my own business. Years later, most of us remain in touch with the understanding that if one needs help in someone else's city, just pick up the phone.

It was a significant phase in my life and in my career, and I enjoyed trying to get across the employer point of view, which was by no means always negative. There was never any doubt in my mind that while the worker is fully entitled to be paid for the contribution he makes, there can be no future unless the enterprise in which he or she works is able to make a profit. Demanding a cut off the joint before the wealth is created is obviously self-defeating, but in the sixties and seventies there were many trade unions and their leaders who missed the point completely.

I was by then living with one of those trade union leaders, Brenda Dean, who was soon to become the general secretary of the largest print union, and confront the newspaper magnate, Rupert Murdoch, owner and publisher of *The Sun*, the *News of the World*, the *Sunday Times* and a number of other major publications, as well as Sky TV.

I had encouraged Brenda to put herself up for the top post in the union, and was delighted when she beat off a number of male candidates to reach the very top of a male-dominated union. But then clearly I had a problem.

The next morning when I had my regular meeting with Sir Terence, I told him that I had been watching a young woman fighting her way in the trade union world, but I had never been sure she would make it right to the top. But now she had, and I said I had to go. "I would never wish to embarrass you or the CBI, and I have to resign," I told my boss.

Beckett waved it aside. "Oh, that will be that young lass in the print union," he said. "Look, Keith, you have never had a high profile in the CBI and I want you to carry on here."

He was correct in that—I always took the view that it was not my job to engage in self-promotion. As I saw it, my task was to promote my boss and the CBI or keep it out of the news. Not to indulge in self-publicity, a delusion too many forget.

The penny dropped. MI5 had obviously tipped off my boss that his Director of Information was keeping 'dangerous company', but that did not faze Sir Terence one iota. I went back to my post, grateful to a very loyal boss who was taking quite a chance on his own career protecting mine.

Brenda was soon to become involved in leading the last major industrial dispute in Britain. Print workers staged a year-long demonstration outside the Wapping print works after Murdoch had sacked over 5,000 of them. I was able to keep my boss extremely well versed in what was happening in an industrial dispute that occupied the front pages of newspapers and swamped TV screens round the world for twelve hectic and violent months.

Over the years I was working for Britain's Business Voice, I enjoyed excellent relations with successive Presidents of the CBI like Sir Ray

Pennock, Sir James Cleminson and, finally, Sir David Nickson.

It was Sir David, though, who was to give me the chance to leave the CBI when the post really became untenable.

My boss, Sir Terence, had reached retirement and was quite keen to go, so the search to find his successor began. Headhunters were appointed and careful criteria worked out to find the best man—or maybe woman—for the top post speaking up for British business and manufacturing.

But at a conference they were dazzled by the performance of John Banham, then director for the Audit Commission. He came out quite irresponsibly critical of the public sector, designating most of those working in it as lazy and virtually a dead weight on business struggling to make its way. It sounded good, but anyone who knew what it was really like being involved in the public sector saw it was unfair and rabble-rousing. But as I feared—and Banham anticipated— the CBI delegates lapped it up. A month later I was called up to the tenth floor to be told that John Banham was indeed to be the next Director General. I was not at all surprised, I told Beckett. But then his secretary called through to say that Patrick Jenkin, until quite recently the Trade Secretary in the Thatcher Government, was ringing me.

"Keith," he appealed over the phone. "What on earth are you doing? This is the fellow who nearly sank my career. Does the CBI have any idea what kind of man this is?"

I told the MP, "Tell it to the Director General." Beckett's face went white as Jenkin tore into him about the appointment he warned was very unwise. For a man as cautious as Patrick Jenkin this was disturbing, Beckett told me. Then the phone went again.

It was Richard Needham, MP for Cirencester. "Are you mad?" he demanded in his usual forthright style. "There is no one in government who will touch Banham."

I passed the phone again to Sir Terence, whose demeanour became more agitated as he heard out Needham.

A few minutes later, a concerned Sir David Nickson listened as Beckett recounted the conversations he had just held over the phone.

They both looked at me. "What do we do?" asked Sir David. Though tempted, I replied, "Nothing."

I told them they had made a decision, maybe too hurriedly, but if it ever emerged that the Conservative Government had in effect blackballed Banham and forced the CBI to backtrack, its reputation would be rubbish. It would have meant the Government was having a veto on the CBI's most important staff appointment.

The two men agreed, and I went ahead to plan the arrangements for announcing Banham's appointment.

Shortly afterwards we met, and I questioned him to prepare a news release. Even then, I could feel that the incoming DG had strong views on what a press release should contain, and was not over-concerned about its accuracy—more what it should achieve than what it stated.

It was an early warning, and as he took over I found more and more that I could never be sure what Banham said, believed, or felt. He would say something to one person, perhaps a journalist, and within minutes would indicate the opposite to the next person he met.

I tried vainly to cope with the meteoric Mr Banham. I had more trouble getting past the personal assistant he brought with him. The new incumbent, who had come with her boss from his previous appointment, was very protective, refused to give out his diary, accepting engagements without bothering to tell anyone.

I had two options, it seemed to me. I had a good job, status, a fairly good salary, and could just keep my head down and let the inevitable smash into the buffers take place. But I knew my staff would have less respect to find themselves working for a doormat.

The alternative was to engineer a pay-off and get out. I had had a good run at the CBI and was very influential within the organisation, but this was no longer going to apply. My wife, Brenda, told me she thought I would have a heart attack if I stayed there.

My face must have told the story. As Sir David Nickson, the President, put it me, a few days later: "You don't seem all that happy, Keith?"

"Oh dear," I replied. "Does it show?" I came clean, and admitted I was finding it difficult to mesh with the new Director General.

Sir David asked if I would like him to see on what financial terms my departure could be arranged. Without too much thought I agreed it would be useful to know where I stood after seven years at the CBI.

He came back and told me the terms, which seemed quite attractive. The speed with which they were worked out made me think that down in the admin and human relations department, the chance to get me out and break the supremacy of the strongest department in Centre Point had been too good an opportunity to miss.

The money was quite generous, I could keep the car, there would be some holiday pay, but most importantly, my pension would be made up to age sixty-five though right then I was fifty-nine. That clinched it and I said I would go.

I had been thinking it was time I should set-up on my own and here was the opportunity. After journalism, a good spell in government and industry and then at the major employers' organisation in Britain meant I had wide experience and a fine contacts book. Having rubbed shoulders with some of the biggest names in business meant I ought to have an open door to some of the best.

Now was the time to find out if it was true.

CHAPTER 17
The Years When It All Came Together— Working for Myself

I was rather nervous on starting my first day employing myself ... after all, I had never done it before!

Brenda was great. Not only did she move out of her office at home and give it to me, but with her remarkable efficiency supplied stationery, notebooks, pens, paper clips and even postage stamps. Otherwise, I would probably have used up my first day wandering round a stationery store wasting not only money but time.

And that was going to cost me. I needed to face up to the fact that there would be no pay cheque at the end of the month, something that concentrates the mind wonderfully.

Quite quickly, remarkably, business started to roll in. Don Harker, a good friend and colleague who was in charge of public affairs at Granada TV, tipped me off that the *TV Times*, the weekly listings magazine, needed political help. David Mellor, then minister in charge at the Home Office of the arts, including television, was determined to end the grip the BBC and ITV had on their weekly listings.

This promoted the huge sales of the *Radio Times* and *TV Times*. Both had circulation figures in the millions. But there was intense pressure from newspapers that this monopoly—as they saw it—should now be broken, and Mellor was inclined to agree. Within a few days I had signed a deal for £3,000 a month to advise and work on resisting this Whitehall policy, or at least slow it down.

Next I was signed up by Prudential, the insurance and pensions group, to advise on public affairs and to help the in-house press and

PR team. My strong relationship with Sir Brian Corby, the CEO, who had been president of the CBI, certainly opened the door for me there.

Other clients were knocking, and I quickly realised that, far from starving, in fact I had a tiger by the tail and might not be able to cope. To complicate matters, Brenda had been invited to be a guest of the Australian print unions, and it was proposed I would accompany her. I wanted very much to go, but how did I explain to my new clients that when they wanted me I would be on the other side of the world?

I sat in our Gibson Square garden in Islington and offered up a little prayer—boy, did I need help. It was then that the phone rang and on the line was Brenda Laing, once my CBI regional officer in the North West, who had left to join the Thomson travel and airline business. I recalled that she had then quit to go on a year's trip around the world.

"I'm back from my travels," said Brenda. "Could you give me a reference?"

I told her I could do more than that—I could give her a job and she could start in the morning. She was cautious, but agreed to come round. I explained my dilemma and offered her a job to help me lay the foundations for Keith McDowall Associates, of which she would be the first.

The advantage for me was that Brenda Laing knew my working methods and philosophy. Above all, I could trust her judgement and be confident that she would be able to cope in my absence.

To her great credit she agreed to hold the fort for me while I went with my wife to Australia. She would not then agree to join me, but would think about it while I was away. In fact, it worked out remarkably well. We were able to keep in touch by fax, and when I returned home Brenda Laing had seen enough of the business to come on board.

Apart from having the problem of two Brendas under one roof, it worked out very well, and Miss Laing was involved in helping me get to a turnover of £100,000 within a few months. But it was cramped in the small office on the first floor of our house in Gibson Square. That was when Brenda L also had a hand in helping me find a new house. Going for lunch at the nearby Albion pub, we noticed a sign board offering a house for sale. It was No. 2 Malvern Terrace—a delightful, tree-lined tiny cul-de-sac containing only ten houses on one side and facing a park.

Double-fronted, two-storey and with a basement, we had found, as I put it, a country house in the middle of London.

It proved to be remarkably useful as KMA grew. With my wife Brenda a wonderful cook, we held dinner parties over the years attended by, among others, Neil and Glenys Kinnock, John Smith and his wife Elizabeth, Tony Blair and Cherie, and Sir Ronnie and Jane Hampel, chairman of ICI. We invited trade union leaders, MPs, and colleagues like John Robson, who had moved from government to head up the press and PR at Lloyds Bank, and David Severn, in charge of parliamentary affairs at NatWest Bank.

Over a decade that little house helped the KMA team to turn over several million pounds. All around Islington, people in the creative field were working from home and starting up new small businesses. We did not know it, but we were quite trendy, it would seem.

I also received what is known as 'recognition', which certainly helped in building my client list.

On 11th June 1988 it was announced that I had become a Commander of the Most Excellent Order of the British Empire, though I commanded nothing, and there was no longer an Empire to command. But henceforth I was to be a CBE.

I had been recommended for an honour by the CBI, and I know several prominent politicians contributed letters of support, so I was extremely pleased. Something might have come my way after the Northern Ireland work, but it collapsed so quickly and was overtaken by the snap general election that no one was recognised.

The best part of being gazetted is to receive letters from so many old friends and colleagues. People one has not heard from for years suddenly drop you a line of congratulation. Total strangers also write with their good wishes, which is gratifying.

Everything is extremely well organised at the actual investiture and the Palace staff have it stage-managed to perfection. On each occasion there are one or two knighthoods awarded, with the monarch's sword tapping the recipients on the shoulder. On my occasion, it was to see the overweight Rochdale Liberal MP Cyril Smith gasping as he sought to regain his feet. Subsequently, of course, the rumours of his penchant for small boys has become known publicly, and if he was still alive it is a fair bet Smith would have been stripped of the knighthood.

As we lined up alphabetically, the Queen singled me out for a few words and mentioned her visit to CBI headquarters at Centre Point a few months previously.

Brenda, my wife, came with me as did Clare and Alison. It was a long-standing family joke that I would warn them as children that unless their table manners improved, there was no way I could ever take them to Buckingham Palace. And here we were all together inside the Palace.

On reflection, the lunch afterwards in a hotel restaurant overlooking Kensington Palace Gardens was really the best moment of the day. My sister Jean was there, as was my cousin Ian McDowall, only son of my father's brother Jack.

"What did you get that for?" demanded Ian.

"For service to Queen and Country," I joshed, but I don't think Ian believed it.

A little girl made up the party. Edwina Reid, my first grandchild, was at the lunch in the top-floor restaurant overlooking Kensington Palace Gardens when the champagne flowed. Another first for Edwina. Several hours, and several bottles later, it was a good job Ken was around to drive me home …

When I was at the CBI I had a good relationship with an active member in the North West named Arthur Fairhurst, and I was taken to meet him when I spent a couple of days in Brenda Laing's region. Arthur was at Associated Octel, based on Merseyside, which produced the lead fluid that went into high performance engines and prevented 'knocking', as it was known.

Ironically, Arthur's company was fighting the allegation that the lead in petrol was harming children's health. Arthur was on the back foot when I turned up to offer assistance. He told me the company felt like a leper, and few had come forward to help in getting rational discussion and an impartial examination of the facts.

Oddly enough, Arthur and I found we had at least two things in common. His father-in-law turned out to be Mo Anglesey, who was assistant to the General Secretary of the National Union of Railway men when I reported the labour scene, and we were friends. Our other bond was a love of Cornwall, for Arthur had lived there in wartime, producing the crucial lead supplies at a second source in case the main plant in the North West was knocked out by a bombing attack.

Our relationship was strong, so when I started Keith McDowall Associates, I wanted to take on Arthur's account. That was not possible in the early stages, but as soon as Monty Meth came on board, that was to be his first account. Arthur and Monty clicked, and Monty knew Arthur's father-in-law too!

Another old friendship that bore fruit was with Denis Read, who had been one of those in the Royal Air Force Police involved in trying to start up its magazine. As the founder and first editor of *Provost Parade* I am proud to know the original editions are stored both at the Imperial War Museum and at the Royal Air Force Museum, not a bad achievement for a National Serviceman aged 18. The magazine is the longest surviving in the history of the RAF.

Denis and I kept in touch as he gravitated into the burgeoning security industry, and at one time I had dinner with his boss. What was he looking for, I asked him. It boiled down really to 'meeting people'.

Supposing I was to set-up a monthly lunch and bring along people from a wide spectrum. Would he be willing to pay towards that kind of operation? Most certainly, I was told.

It gave me the chance to work up an idea I had been mulling over, which would have fairly wide appeal. Each month I had seen the new issue of First Day postage stamps published by the Post Office, but they never seemed to me to be properly exploited in publicity terms.

How about a regular lunch to launch the stamps at an appropriate venue with a distinguished speaker and guest list? Alan Williams, the number two in the Post Office public relations department, had worked with me briefly when I was at the Trade department, and he was keen because he could see potentially good publicity for his outfit.

He obtained agreement that each month, as the new-issue stamps were published, many of them magnificent miniature works of art, he would get them printed on newly stamped envelopes addressed to the lunch guest of what became known as The First Day Cover Club.

The envelope became the guest's highly appreciated place name at the lunch. We chose appropriate venues according to the topic of the stamps. So we took our guests to the Armourers Hall, and to quite a few other Livery Halls in London like the Stationers, the Goldsmiths, and the Apothecaries. We went to St Paul's Cathedral, the Sherlock Holmes Museum, and quite often to the library at The Reform Club too.

My clients liked the occasion because we brought along MPs and peers, senior civil servants, diplomats, authors, cartoonists—you name it. If the stamps suggested a theme we located guests appropriate to that concept.

But there were always one or two 'bankers' on the guest list, people I could rely upon to mix and mingle, crack a joke and ask a question if nothing was immediately forthcoming. Among the regulars was the late Robin Corbett, Labour MP for Castle Vale in the Midlands, and later a life peer. I could also always rely on Sir Sydney Chapman, Conservative MP for Barnet and former Government whip, who loved the events. And my daughter Clare—always good for a laugh.

It was through the FDCC that Brenda and I met Alan Livingstone, the principal of Falmouth College of Art and Design, who sat on the advisory committee for the special stamps. He came regularly to our lunches and was a good mixer. A few years later, when we had bought a waterside home in Falmouth, we got to know Alan and his wife Isabella better, who were active locally. It was Alan's idea and his drive that enabled the concept of the Combined University of Cornwall, to be established at Penryn. We got involved in the struggle to get the matching funding for the new university. At times it was a close call, but we lobbied to get the funding. Today we are proud to have been associated with Alan in enabling Cornwall to have its own highly successful university with over 5,000 young students.

Back to the FDCC. In effect, I had created a wide band of support for the Post Office, which was itself entering difficult times and beginning the long period which led eventually to it being part sold off in 2013. The First Day Cover Club, in fact, was the Friends of the Post Office, and each month we ensured the guests got the Royal Mail's party line. When the issue came on the floor of the Commons or even the Lords, we could be sure of well-informed support.

The Post Office became one of KMA clients, an account we held for several years. We were closely involved in the lobbying trying to get across that it was a highly competent organisation, but needed greater commercial freedom. I worked in harmony with newly promoted Alan Williams who became a good friend as well as a client. I have always believed that the best clients are your friends or should become them. That's how you retain them.

A problem for the Post Office management was that as a fully owned arm of government it was not allowed to lobby, which was where I came in. But I had to tread carefully because too overt an operation would have brought a sharp rap on the knuckles from the Department of Trade and Industry or worse, the Treasury.

Another idea of bringing together the people we needed to influence was jazz— yes, jazz again. I put it to Alan, himself an enthusiast for my kind of music, that an impressive number of politicians liked it too, so why not arrange some concerts?

I contacted Dave Shepherd, the clarinetist, and sought his advice. He brought in trumpeter Digby Fairweather. Each month a number of well-established musicians like Dave and Digby played together at the Pizza Express in Dean Street, Soho, as the All Stars. Our idea was to rebrand them as the First Class Sounds, and get them to wear the light grey summer jackets issued to postmen, which looked quite good with their crimson flash. In the band, in addition to Dave and Digby, we had such well-established British jazz players as Len Skeat on bass,

Alan Ganley on drums, Tommy Whittle on tenor sax and above all, the incomparable Brian Lemon on piano. It really was a top-rate assembly, and they made two or three excellent CDs which the Post Office was able to send out at Christmas to 'friends' of influence. All the numbers recorded had a mail theme like 'Air Mail Special', or 'I'm Gonna Send Myself a Letter'.

Probably the best client we ever had was Kvaerner of Norway. They were big in shipbuilding and offshore oil technology. The lead came from my old friend Per Bjorgan, who had left the employers' federation in Oslo and gone to the company as its first real PR director. Per called me and said his company was interested in acquiring the Govan shipyard in the Clyde, and did I know anything about it?

Quite a lot, as it happened. During my spell at British Shipbuilders my duties had included serving on the board of Govan. So I was able to write a lengthy report on the potential for the yard, which Per put to his board of directors. The deal went through fairly quickly because the Thatcher Government wanted out of shipbuilding on political grounds—it was quite shameful. But Govan would be better with the Norwegians than the South Koreans, for example, Per and I agreed.

A few weeks later, when I was sailing in the Mediterranean off Majorca, I received a shore-to-ship phone call from Monty Meth in London. Kvaerner intended to list on the London Stock Exchange, and Per wanted to discuss retaining us as press advisers. With his City knowledge Monty was all for it, but Brenda Laing was opposed. We did not do City coverage and were out of our depth, she argued.

Both had a point, and, as the yacht pitched in the ocean off Palma, I had to make a quick decision.

I reckoned, with my relationship with Per and shipbuilding background, plus Monty's understanding of the financial world, we could do it. I told him to set-up the meeting as soon as I got back. That was one of my best-ever decisions.

Initially, our engagement was for six months as Kvaerner prepared to list using the Scandinavian merchant bank Enskilda, which, not surprisingly, had never heard of us. They recommended a well-known financial public relations company, and we knew in terms of firepower we were vastly outgunned.

But in Oslo Per Bjorgan had confidence in me because of our long relationship working together for the employer organisations. He argued that it was far better to retain a small, hungry company that wanted the business than just be a number to a financial PR company. That was an argument that tipped the scales our way because it appealed to a company in Norway, where industry is largely composed of small and medium-sized businesses.

We retained Kvaerner for nearly ten years. They were not only a most reliable client in a fascinating field, who paid regularly, but we became good friends with many of the key players. People like the Finance Director, Jan Magne Heggelund, and Kjell Ursin Smith who was to come to London and take charge of the group's activities in the UK, particularly in oil and gas.

Kvaerner was virtually unknown in London, but through my contacts, and Monty's in the world of finance, we succeeded in raising the profile. One of the best stories was in the 'Men and Matters' column of the *Financial Times*, which happened to have been written by my long-standing friend Roy Hodson. He did a good piece about the Vikings coming to London, and the story took off.

On the morning of the actual listing, the financial journalists and analysts were invited to the Stafford Hotel in St James's—not a tatty room on the well-trodden City circuit—and there we served chilled schnapps specially flown in from Norway, with tasty Scandinavian canapés. The journalists decided we were worth watching more carefully, and definitely undertook to come again.

We built a close relationship with the key people of Kvaerner, particularly the rather taciturn chief executive Erik Tonseth, and for several months our office was virtually their London base. Preferable to working out of a hotel, declared Jan Magne.

As our biggest client, Kvaerner would occupy a lot of our time. But the company was well received in Britain because it actually made things and employed many people. One of our first really big stories was when Kvaerner won a contract for six merchant ships. The plan was to build the first at one of the company's yards in Norway, and then the following five at Govan, the very yard which had been in the midst of labour relations battles with British Shipbuilders.

Just as well, because the shop stewards, led by Sammy Gilmore, had a formidable reputation. When the yard had been part of the Upper Clyde Shipbuilders group, they took on the Edward Heath government and forced a U-turn on government policy to stop all subsidies. It was a turnaround from which Heath never recovered, and also meant that Gilmore and his fellow stewards feared no management.

I found the changed attitude of Gilmore and his colleagues constructive. They were no fools, and realised that the Norwegians brought work and investment and knew what they were doing. For the time being Gilmore and Co. were on board.

One big campaign from which Gilmore and his pals saw the benefit was the first step in switching the yard to naval work.

A Whitehall decision had been made to build a new amphibious assault ship for the Royal Navy but to have the basic ship built in a merchant yard to cut cost and then taken to a naval yard for fitting it out with all the electronic gear and armaments which was specialist work.

There was only one order so who would get it. The battle was between a consortium led by Vickers of Barrow and Govan and the rival bid from Swan Hunter. The future would not be bright for the loser.

I worked on behalf of Kvaerner with the boss of Vickers and a young MP I thought had great potential, John Hutton who had taken the Barrow seat of Albert Booth. We campaigned and schemed hard and I told Hutton I could see him one day as the Chief Whip of the Labour Party. (I undershot a bit because he became a Pensions Minister and later Minister of Defence before going to the Lords).

When we won the order for what was to become HMS *Ocean* our glass-raising was somewhat subdued in the sad acceptance that we had probably signed the death warrant for the magnificent yard of Swan

Hunter on Tyneside. But long term I also thought it meant Govan—once again—would survive. As it has.

KMA had a coup as Govan completed their half of the ship when Monty and I tried out on Robert Janvrin, the Queen's Private Secretary at Buckingham Palace, the suggestion that the Queen might like to launch HMS *Ocean*. The timing tied in nicely with the Queen's annual visit to Scotland so it made a lot of sense and Robin liked the idea.

So it was that the Queen came back to the yard to name the ship on 11th October 1995, watched by most of the top brass of Kvaerner from Norway. Quite a day for the Yard that refused to die …

Monty and I took a succession of journalists up to the Clyde yard and got very good coverage for Kvaerner. In particular I remember taking our old friend Geoffrey Goodman, who was much impressed and wrote Kvaerner up well in his weekly column in the *Daily Mirror*. I was also pleased with a trip I organised to take Louis Heren, then deputy editor of *The Times*, who also gave Kvaerner a very good rating.

Monty led a group of industrial and financial journalists to Finland to visit the Turku yards, where a huge cruise ship was launched for Carnival Line, the cruise ship operator based in Miami, and the coverage was impressive.

Kvaerner was also big in energy, and I worked with Per Bjorgan to build up a relationship with National Grid in the UK to assess the feasibility of transmitting electricity under the North Sea from Norway.

Norway had cheap hydropower in abundance, yet Britain was desperately short of such power, having turned its back on coal-fired power stations. The general assumption was that sending electricity by cable over long distances was not viable because of the power loss. But I found out that great progress had been made in the cabling, and power loss was not now so much of a problem. Per and I managed to set-up talks between Statoil, the huge state-owned energy company, with National Grid and one of the major domestic suppliers.

We had frequent contact with Kjell Ursin Smith, who we christened the London manager, and he loved being located in the UK. With his wife Kirsten they toured the country, and even came down to our home in Falmouth for a New Year's Eve party.

When he had sorted out the suite of offices Kvaerner took over in King Street, off St James's Street, Kjell thought we should have an official opening and invite the clients to a launch party.

Over the years since CBI days, I had kept fairly good contact with John Wakeham, who had held a succession of Government jobs, but now just happened to be Energy Minister. It was not difficult to get an invitation accepted and to fix an opening time to suit the minister's diary. John arrived and stayed for lunch, glad-handing the guests. The minister unveiled a plaque bearing his name—and I bet that Kjell took that home with him when he departed some years later to become chief executive of the company which ran Norway's end of the North Sea oil and gas exhibition.

One afternoon I was telephoned by Jan Magne and asked to go to see a man named Brian Keelan at the merchant bank S G Warburg. Their offices just off Broad Street were an initiation into a completely new world of takeover, financial acquisition, meeting people who worked extremely hard—and played very hard, too.

Keelan explained that he had been asked to meet with me because Kvaerner rated my company, but he had never heard of us. He indicated he doubted if we were really in the right league. I disregarded that but said I reckoned Kvaerner was going to make a hostile bid and for one of three companies. I speculated on three, and when I mentioned AMEC it was pretty clear I had hit the target. I also said that I knew Kvaerner and its people well; they felt happier with us involved, and Keelan might come round to that way of thinking too.

There was a short silence as Keelan and I looked each other in the eye. Then he turned to a colleague and said, "I reckon he will do us nicely."

So KMA were on board for an attempted takeover of one of Britain's best known engineering and major contracting firms which involved not just City interaction, but also the politicians whose constituencies were affected, as well as the trade unions concerned. Not only did we have to strive to ensure the media accepted our takeover tactics for acquiring AMEC, but that our lobbying was on target, too.

Keelan was something of a buccaneer. He was in the office by 7 a.m. and stayed late, seldom bothering with lunch. And he would be on the phone constantly. He had a very loyal team at Warburg's, who obviously did well on bonuses when Keelan pulled off a big deal.

If Tonseth had a fault, it was that he could never seem to stop running. He always wanted to take over another company or industry. My old friend John Parker wisely queried, "He takes these companies over, but can he run them?"

Early on, I twigged that the press cutting service supplying Warburg's was not targeted to this takeover. So I started my own, which meant being up at 6 a.m. to read all the nationals plus the key provincial papers like the *Glasgow Herald*, the *Aberdeen Press and Journal* and *Lloyd's List*, the shipping paper. Sometimes they were closer to the action than maybe we were in London. Brenda, my wife, got up with me, and did the photocopying and then the faxing so that Keelan and the takeover team, plus Kvaerner, the lawyers and other key players, had the latest cuttings on their desks on arrival.

By then Brenda was in the House of Lords and it would probably have amused the recipients to know their press cuttings had the whiff of ermine about them.

That arduous but simple operation had a marked impact on the way KMA was perceived, and quickly we were absorbed into the takeover team. Keelan also grasped rapidly that KMA knew its way around.

It was a big chance for us, too—so long as we did not muck it up. That was fairly easy to do since there are complex rules, like those laid down by what is known as the Takeover Panel regarding what can be said and when. And by whom.

I took Eric Tonseth to meet a group of Labour MPs with the help of Richard Caborn MP, who was a good friend and useful contact. But not all the MPs present came on board; some had AMEC operations in their constituencies, and would not switch sides.

Most of the big investors were in support, however, and for a while it looked as if the bid would succeed. The convention was that the bidder would increase his offer at the last moment, but, on Keelan's advice, Tonseth said he was not going to increase his offer. What was on the table would stand.

It was a fatal error. Phillips and Drew, a finance house, held fourteen percent of AMEC, and were convinced that there was more to come. When they found out the truth they refused to sell, as did some other holders of AMEC stock. AMEC had survived.

Tonseth undoubtedly suffered a bloody nose, but I never found out why Keelan suggested the tactic, which was plainly wrong. To this day I wish I had spoken up, but to some extent I was out of my depth and kept my mouth shut.

I also had mixed feelings. Although I worked hard for Kvaerner, which had my total loyalty, I felt it rather a shame a good British company like AMEC should go under. As it was, it survived much longer than its Norwegian rival ... and some years later was to become a KMA client.

Here again, jazz played a useful role. Kvaerner's oil and gas people told us they were going to exhibit at the major industry exhibition held in Aberdeen in alternate years to Stavanger in Norway. They wanted to hold a grand reception to attract all the key industry players. Could we organise it?

Well, of course we could—but when we went into it we found that each of the four evenings of the industry show were already bespoke. Majors like BP and Halliburton were long established, and their events were those to be seen at.

We told Kvaerner that if they wanted to break into this cycle they had to offer something different—something which would entice the businessmen away from their regular drinking holes to visit the Norwegian newcomers.

Well, I suggested, "How about jazz?" Not a local band which would no doubt be able to make the right noise and play the right notes, but without much impact. I proposed a major international jazz figure with a worldwide reputation, who visitors to Aberdeen would want to see in person, and the name I came up with was Bob Wilber, an American who had studied the soprano saxophone under the great Sidney Bechet. I took Kjell Ursin-Smith and several Kvaerner colleagues to hear Bob playing at the Pizza on the Park. I had previously tipped Bob off, and both sides were so keen that we soon had agreement in principle.

Then I had a brainwave. What about commissioning a special piece of music and holding its first-ever public presentation at the Aberdeen Oil and Gas Show? Per Bjorgan agreed I could offer Bob Wilber a £1,000 fee for an original piece of work, and the deal was done.

It was only a week or two later that I realised how vulnerable I had made myself. Suppose the music flopped?

I arranged to drive up on a Sunday to Chipping Norton, in Oxfordshire, where Bob and his wife lived when in the UK, and asked if I could hear a snatch of the theme. He sat at the piano and with his left hand played a melancholy sounding roll of notes. "That's the North Sea," said Wilber. "Can you hear the majesty of those waves? And then this comes in over the waves …," and Wilber's right hand struck a neat, memorable musical phrase which was to be the theme. "I call it 'North Sea Sunrise'. Do you think it will do?" he said.

Did I? I was already thinking how that melody could be deployed at Aberdeen and indeed all over the world wherever Kvaerner sought to do oil and gas work. I rang Per Bjorgan next morning and told him to relax. His money, and all our reputations, were safe. We had commissioned a good piece of jazz music.

A few days later I met Bob at Heathrow with the musicians. He had engaged some of the best of British jazz players. Number one was trumpeter Kenny Baker, who had been a hero of mine since I first attended the Ted Heath Swing Sessions at the London Palladium in 1944. Also there were Dave Green with his bass (for which I found I needed to book a spare seat in the plane), Bobby Worth on drums, and Mick Pyne to play piano. Mick confided he had been practising the special piece at home, which augured well, I thought.

In Aberdeen I had help from Elizabeth Hall, who worked with me years ago at the Department of Employment, and was now the PR director of the University of Aberdeen. She already had three taxis laid on, and took us to the university where she had arranged a concert room for a rehearsal and the use of a good quality grand piano.

But no one knew who had the key to open the piano lid. As the college was closed for student vacation there were few people around, and none had the foggiest idea where the key might be. Eventually though, The Person Who Knows Everything (there is one in every organisation as a rule) turned up, produced the key from his pocket, and asked if music stands would be helpful? "Yes, please." As it was a totally new composition, the musicians needed to rehearse from scratch.

At last I sat in the hall with Liz and heard, for the first time, the full version of 'North Sea Sunrise'. It was quite a moment. Kenny Baker suggested a crescendo, and it was splendid, the kind of ending that makes an audience get to its feet.

Bob Wilber declared himself satisfied. So the musicians packed up their gear, and we took them to their accommodation—tiny, vacated student rooms which, in a city crammed with oil people, was all we could find.

A couple of hours later I drove them out to the art deco Beach Ballroom in Aberdeen, famous for possessing one of the finest dance floors in Scotland, and for its bounce because it floats on steel springs.

I had previously confirmed by phone that the ballroom had a piano, but the look on Bob Wilber's face told me something was wrong. "This is NOT a piano, Keith, this is a toy."

One look at the electronic keyboard told me he was right. I told Bob I would try to locate a proper piano, but asked the pianist Mick Pyne if he would give it a go. Mick, a true professional, was prepared to make the best of it.

I must have tracked down at least six grand pianos in the city, but in each case there was a problem in moving or getting permission at such short notice. So by 6 p.m. I had to tell Bob it was an electric keyboard or we dropped the project. By then he had cooled down and agreed to go ahead.

The first-ever performance of a piece of music dedicated to all who bring oil and gas ashore from the North Sea drew a big crowd, including the Mayors of Aberdeen and Stavanger. We promised that everyone who left their business card would be sent a tape recording of the concert, and this yielded many useful contacts for Kvaerner, which was, of course, the object of the exercise.

'North Sea Sunrise' sounded great, and Per Bjorgan and I glanced at each other during the performance, relieved that we had sailed extremely close to the wind and got away with it. Later that evening, the Mayor of Stavanger asked if we would bring the musicians to his city the following year and repeat the concert. Delighted, I told him.

And when I got into the taxi to my student studio, on the radio I heard a report of the musical event and a promise that as soon as a copy of it was available, it would be played on Radio Aberdeen.

Everyone, it seemed, knew that Kvaerner, the Norwegian oil and gas engineering group, had arrived in Aberdeen—which just goes to show that jazz has its moments and can make an impact.

But when we played the recording next morning the quality of the sound was horrible. The background buzz of talk, drinks and plates being scraped meant that 'North Sea Sunrise' was virtually obliterated.

A new jazz learning curve opened up for me. I had to find a studio back in London where a re-recording could be made, I had to re-engage the musicians and find a recording engineer, and a firm which would mass-produce a quantity of cassettes. Then I had to get the art work made for the boxes.

On those boxes I had printed 'Produced by Keith McDowall Associates', and felt my team had truly earned it.

A year later I was back at it again, only this time in Stavanger, the magnificent port which is the heart of the oil industry in Scandinavia.

"Got any more good gigs like this, Keith?" asked trumpeter Kenny Baker as he tucked into a splendid bacon, sausage, tomato and egg breakfast in the SAS Hotel.

There had been no difficulty getting the same musicians again because I was offering them an overseas trip, a first class hotel, and an enthusiastic audience. And good money.

They played in the main town square where the sound was difficult because of the traffic, but it made the point that the Oil and Gas Exhibition was starting, and that evening 'North Sea Sunrise' again opened the Kvaerner reception.

I don't think it has been played much since but it was a good piece of music and a number that occasionally I play in my car. When I do, the memories—and the heart-stopping moments in trying to organise its first public performance—flood back.

We developed many good friends within the Kvaerner Group—indeed, Monty and I were considered part of it. The head of Oil and Gas used to refer to us as The Terrible Twins, which I think was meant as a compliment. We went frequently to Oslo, to Stavanger, to Narvik, and also to Helsinki and Turku, in Finland, where Kvaerner had bought the big yards building the early generation of luxury cruisers. I was often in Scotland where the Govan yard was always at the forefront of the news. Kvaerner invested heavily in new facilities, which we at British Shipbuilders had never been able to achieve. Relations were good with the workers, too, and the shop stewards, with whom I had negotiated with the BS management, were well disposed to my reappearance.

But Erik Tonseth, the boss, kept seeking to acquire new businesses. The acquisitions flattered the balance sheet, of course, but not everyone was convinced. As my friend John Parker of British Shipbuilders, and later to run Harland and Wolff in Belfast, asked, "Had Kvaerner bitten off more than it could chew?" Then, in April 1996, I was asked by Jan Magne to go to see Brian Keelan again at Warburg's. My heart sank as I pondered what was likely to be on the cards. I had guessed correctly. Keelan had persuaded Tonseth that Kvaerner ought to acquire Trafalgar House, a sprawling conglomerate, built up since 1959 by a string of acquisitions. The company owned The Ritz Hotel and the *Daily Express* newspaper, and was also in construction, housebuilding, shipping, engineering and property. It owned John Brown's, the famous yard that built the *QE2* passenger liner, and it owned Cunard, the shipping line.

322

Yet with all its activities the company was in deep trouble financially. In its 1992 accounts the directors had to revise a £112.5 million profit downwards to a £30 million loss.

Keelan was thick with the Far East trading house Jardine Matheson, which held fifteen percent of Trafalgar House. In particular he hit it off with a JM man named Simon Keswick, who eventually took over the chairmanship, but even he could not turn it around. If the AMEC bid by Kvaerner had come off, Jardine Matheson would have done well—but if it could offload its Trafalgar House shares on to Kvaerner it would do even better.

All I knew about Trafalgar House was that it was a rag bag of companies, many of them losing money. "Where was the synergy in all that?" I argued with people like Jan Magne Heggelund, Kvaerner's finance director, but it was no use. Tonseth was like a little boy who had seen something sparkling in the toy shop window, and that was what he wanted. Now.

I was deeply concerned. I was only a public relations adviser, but I had moved in these waters for several years so pleaded with Jan Magne to talk Tonseth out of the deal. Jan Magne had proposed Kvaerner sold its shipyards to meet its cash crisis, but again his boss would not hear of it. Acquisition was the only way forward, Tonseth seemed to believe. So it was that, in April 1996, Kvaerner acquired Trafalgar House for £904 million and took 34,000 more people on the payroll.

As soon as the announcement was made I had several calls asking what my Norwegian friends were doing. A city journalist on *The Guardian*, David Gow, told me he had had an uneasy feeling about Trafalgar House ever since the press had been invited to a presentation of the company results in a special room at The Ritz and found themselves eating off gold-plated dishes!

Parkinson's Law predicts that in any merger the weaker will dominate the stronger. That was certainly about to happen in this takeover. I accompanied Tonseth to meet the senior Trafalgar House management in Eastbourne Terrace, alongside Paddington Station, and it was quite clear they had no intention of changing their ways.

One could almost see their noses turning up at this little fellow from Oslo coming along with his chequebook. They intended to carry on as before, losing orders and losing millions. No problem. Their jobs were safe, so were their expenses. The Norwegians were paying.

Despite the major concerns about the future, my short-term objective was to hold the contract of my best client. Per Bjorgan had retired, and it was extremely difficult to maintain contact with Tonseth himself. KMA's normal close relations with the management became harder and harder. And the financial performance continued to slide. The Norwegian financial press was in full pursuit, and there was little Monty or I could do from London.

It did not surprise us that, eventually, Kvaerner was taken over by another major offshore engineering group named Aker, while in the UK the yards were either closed down or sold off. One did survive. Govan was snapped up by BAe and developed into a warship-building yard, highly skilled and well-paid work, so the great survivor Govan had pulled it off again.

There was a tragic ending in Norway for Erik Tonseth. His wife and daughter set off in one car for the family's ski lodge, Erik following about ten minutes behind in his Land Rover. As he came round a bend he found there had been a major accident. A car had gone out of control and plunged through the crash barrier into the face of oncoming traffic. The occupants had been killed instantly. It was Erik's wife and daughter ...

In 1989, by which time KM Associates were running well, I received a call from our very first customer, David Evans.

"Keith," he enquired gently. "Do you know anything about pop music?"

I was my candid self. "Only that I can't stand the bloody stuff."

David laughed. "Pity about that, because I have got one of these pop radio pirates here, and I was wondering if you could come round and meet him." My clients' wishes were my command so I set aside my own prejudices and headed for Centurion Press to meet 'Gordon Mac', who was indeed a pirate radio man and quite well known, it turned out, even though I had never heard of him.

But I was up to speed on the Government's concern about widespread transmissions by illegal radio aimed at young people. The Home Office had a special unit tracking down the pirates and smashing their radio equipment. Pirates would broadcast their music from the most amazing locations—attics, airing cupboards, the back of a van, a canal boat.

It was costing money and effort, so the Home Office had reached the conclusion it was time to talk to the young people behind this phenomenon. "If you stop breaking the law and cease transmission, we will make some radio channels available and hold a competition to licence the winners," declared the Home Secretary.

Quite a lot of the stations continued breaking the law, but some were smart enough to see the opportunity. Gordon Mac was one, and he announced at a big rave night in Camden that his illegal station, Kiss, would apply. "Write and tell the government you support us," he told the cheering youngsters.

Then the hard work began as Gordon Mac realised he needed financial backing and some organisation to play in this league. David quickly grasped he was out of his depth, too. Hence the phone call to me.

Gradually I formed the view that there might be something in this commercial radio contest, which was how I became chairman of the organising team to try to win one of the radio licences which was to become Kiss 100 FM.

I insisted David had to second to me Malcolm Strivens, his accountant, with whom I had always got on well, and we started looking at what we were into.

Some quick digging told me that quite a few big business names were sniffing around. And while Gordon Mac and his fellow disc jockeys were none too keen on what they described as 'the suits', I told them they had not a chance of a look-in at the Home Office unless there were some suits around.

David was willing to speculate some money, but Centurion was not sufficiently known to be able to compete in the music market. We needed backers with known names.

After some thought I came up with that of EMAP, a publishing company which had been spun out of Eastern Daily Press. It had a wide variety of magazines and some good titles, particularly in motorcycling, teenage interests, and country living. It also had a pop music magazine.

So I rang Frank Rogers, the chairman of EMAP and formerly the general manager of the *Daily Telegraph*, who I had known over the years.

His genial voice came on the line. "What's up, Keith?"

Had his group any interest in commercial radio? I asked.

Frank told me he had no idea, but would get me an answer within twenty-four hours.

He came back next day and told me EMAP was definitely interested in taking a stake in a bid for a commercial licence, and was putting a lively young American, Tim Schoonmaker, on the project.

Very soon it was agreed that a third of the venture would be taken up by Centurion, a further third by EMAP, I would take two and a half percent, and Gordon would get a similar amount. We knew we would need to find more capital, but we had identified enough to make a credible start.

We met at least weekly in David's boardroom, and I was chairman. Gradually the project took shape, but there was a big gulf to bridge. Gordon and his young friends knew about their world—why, for example, a youngster would lust after a pair of trainers—whereas 'the suits' just did not get why a pair of gym shoes was worth more than a few pounds.

The hardest part was hammering out a 'Promise of Performance', in which the Home Office wanted to have set down in cold print just what it was intended to broadcast. There was a maximum of 120 words. And I think it was the hardest few sentences I have ever drafted.

We promised to play genres like hip hop, garage, blues—none of which meant a thing to me—but Gordon and his pals had very firm views here. Equally, I was determined not to use the word 'acid'. At the time there were so-called acid parties taking place at which a crowd of young people would descend on a property and hold a rave party, off the M25 motorway often totally unauthorized, then hurtle off again before the police arrived.

"Look," I told the youngsters, "no Home Secretary is going to put his name to a radio licence in these circumstances if the word 'acid' is used." For a while it was a deadlock, but gradually Gordon and his friends accepted that there was no signature on the bottom line—and no money—unless they gave ground. They caved in, and we were able to deliver the application just in time to the Home Office.

But there were nearly a hundred rival bids, and we were not complacent. We felt we were strong contenders, but all kind of groupings and alliances were being formed for this first bid for commercial radio.

Where I was convinced I had to take care was to avoid any lobbying since it might put up the backs of officials in the Home Office broadcasting section.

Mistake. A big one. To our shock, only one licence was announced, and it went to Jazz FM which, it turned out, had been lobbying like mad. It even had several MPs and peers on the board, and the people behind the idea of a jazz station (right up my street, personally) had been in and out of Westminster for weeks.

Their launch was spectacular. They brought the magnificent Ella Fitzgerald over from the US to sing at the Royal Albert Hall. And such was her eminence that the US Ambassador threw a party in her honour at his splendid residence in Regents Park. Because Brenda and I were on good terms with the Ambassador we were invited, much to the annoyance of the Jazz FM chairman who was distinctly irked to find Kiss people drinking his champagne.

"These are the people you have to worry about," he told his colleagues in my presence. "We have to run very fast before they get going." At that point I had no idea whether we would ever get going, but we had our hopes. We told all the disappointed Kiss fans to write in to the Home Office and say they felt let down. Hundreds of letters started piling up in the department's Whitehall letter box.

Meanwhile Brenda and I took the then leader of the Labour Party, Neil Kinnock, and his wife Glenys, to the Albert Hall for the Jazz FM launch. Neil had to go back to the House of Commons for a vote, but he hurried back and caught most of Ella's second act. When Ella reached the number Londoners particularly love—'Every Time We Say Goodbye'—tears were streaming down Neil's face and I felt very emotional. It turned out, in fact, to be the last time she came to London.

The Royal Albert Hall had quite a big audience that night, but it was by no means full, and I wondered how on earth Jazz FM could afford it. In fact they had overreached themselves, as we heard later, but I had learned a lesson. If ever we launched it would be a lot more modest, I decided. About a month later Richard Branson's organisation contacted us. They told us they thought there would be more radio frequencies made available by the Home Office, and that Kiss FM was very well placed to be offered one of them. Branson wanted to buy a third stake in the venture, and was willing to commit to a substantial investment. That made all the difference. I have never been a Branson fan, but I did not doubt his name carried some weight, and for us to have three serious companies as investors meant we stood out from the crowd.

A few weeks later we received a tip-off from the radio authorities that an announcement was imminent and we would be offered the FM frequency of 99.7, which Gordon Mac immediately latched on to and declared we could call ourselves Kiss 100 FM. "One hundred on the dial means the kids can easily find us," he said. We had six months to get ready to go on air—to gather in the financial backing, find some premises, set-up a transmitter, employ staff, and start to do deals to get backing for the new station. All that in the face of intense competition from the stations already well established, like Capital.

Gordon and his DJs all wanted to have studios in Camden. I checked the property prices, and found the going rate in the area was £20–£25 a square foot. Expensive.

What was so special about Camden? I demanded to know. It seemed that was where some of the original illegal transmissions had been made, the best clubs were located, and it was from Camden that the big rival, Capital, transmitted.

On my morning bike ride to Islington public swimming pool I thought about this problem, and as I waited by some traffic lights to cross Holloway Road in Highbury I noticed a building standing empty.

I made enquiries, and found I could get the new, three-storey building for £12.50 a square foot, half the price of a knocked-about place in Camden. Shortly afterwards a deal was done, and we took over the building as the headquarters of Kiss FM. It was hot, somewhat cramped, and had its problems, but we could place a big satellite dish on the roof to send out a good signal, and the building stood out as interesting in a student area and a busy London street.

Very soon we were contemplating our launch day. No way, I told Gordon and his colleagues, were we going to throw money at it like Jazz FM. We should have a launch which the kids behind us could attend, somewhere local.

And what better location than nearby Highbury Fields, a public park on a gentle slope which in a way provided a natural amphitheatre.

I contacted Terry Herbert, a Labour councillor I had come to know on Islington Council, and told him of my problem. I was bringing some multicultural teenage jobs to the area—could he help? A few days later Terry told me we could have Highbury Fields for the launch of London's new radio station—free! And several thousand young people could enjoy an open-air concert.

On the launch day Gordon Mac and his wife and I travelled up to Camden Lock on a small canal boat to declare the opening of Kiss 100 FM station to the strains of 'Our Time Will Come'. It meant something special to Gordon and his wife, but on the bankside crowds of youngsters cheered the arrival of their own station—never mind the song.

Back in Islington, Brenda asked me how I could put up with sounds of pop music which I loathed. "That's because I hear a different sound … a cash register."

In the months ahead it was often a struggle to keep the radio station alive. Everything depended on our ratings, which showed how many listeners, particularly younger people, were tuning in. That would affect how much advertising we could sell but, more importantly, how many sponsorship deals we could tie up.

We could see gradual progress but we were not making any money. I had two and a half percent of the stock, which meant I had already put in £49,000 to the Kiss venture when Martin, our financial man, warned it was time for what he described as reinvestment. Each of the main shareholders was expected to take a deep breath, dig deep and fork out some more funding for what was called a pre-rights issue.

I blinked, and waived my right to a share. I felt I had enough hard-earned money in a venture on radio.

That was a mistake because, a few weeks later, I had a call from David Evans to tell me Branson had sold his third to EMAP without even having the decency to mention it, let alone give David or me the chance to bid. Yet we had brought EMAP into the radio project in the first place. Now they owned sixty-six percent of the venture. Suddenly we grasped it did mean we now had a value price on the shares. Buy us out, too, at that price, we told EMAP. And they jumped at it.

David commissioned a lawyer to clinch the legal details, and about three weeks later we were out. David had a third of a million pounds, which turned out to be a godsend for his business in the sharp economic downturn ahead, and I had about £200,000 on which, of course, tax was due. But I emerged with about £150,000. So not a bad venture for me, after all.

As I told Brenda, I was right. I did hear a cash machine.

One account of which KMA were very proud, and which achieved much, was Carnegie UK, founded by Andrew Carnegie, a young Scot who went to the US, amassed a fortune making steel, and then set about giving his money away. He held the strong view that any man who had a huge bank account when he died was a fool. That money could be put to much better use by targeted charity, he argued.

Carnegie became one of the biggest and best known philanthropists in the world. However, he would not give a grant to any project of more than fifty percent, and only if effort was made locally to match it. When I first saw his name in 1951 over the entrance to the public library at Deptford in South East London, where I was a young reporter, I had never heard of Carnegie. His charity had donated half the cost of the impressive building. But then I realised I knew the name of Carnegie Hall in New York, where the famous 1937 first-ever Swing concert had been staged by Benny Goodman.

In Britain, Carnegie UK did similar good work but did it very quietly. It had never sought publicity nor had a public relations or even a press adviser. Which probably accounted for the fact that it had an exceedingly low profile and the charity's print work looked distinctly amateurish.

On the Carnegie UK board was Len Murray, the retiring general secretary of the TUC, who knew Monty and me and, I believe, thought well of us. He must have done, because he persuaded Geoffrey Lord, the director, that we could help with a project to improve the access of disabled people to arts premises all over the country. Len argued that such a drive would need publicity.

I admit I had never been aware of the problem, but it quickly became obvious that access to many public spaces like theatres, cinemas, libraries, museums and concert halls for those in wheelchairs or on crutches was quite appalling.

To lead the campaign and primed to become the driving force was a Conservative MP, Emma Nicholson. She had immense energy, but what amazed me was she was herself deaf yet could lip-read and was able to speak and debate in the House of Commons. Not only that, she played the organ and sang in a choir!

Over the years, KMA was involved with Emma in other issues, and we quickly learned she was not the kind of lady for whom a 'no' would suffice.

At the first meeting of the group I was introduced by Geoffrey Lord, who explained there would be a need to communicate to the disabled throughout the country so we had been brought in.

What we needed, I felt, was a good name for the campaign. There were several tossed around, but the best, which I seized on, was an acronym which spelt out as ADAPT, which was exactly what we would be seeking in all kinds of places. Not one West End theatre, for example, had decent wheelchair access, and a number said they could not admit them. So a lot of adaptation was likely to be needed.

It was true the old theatre buildings had never been planned to take wheelchairs, but ADAPT was not going to accept that in the 1990s. It was a time to name and shame.

Some theatre managers very quickly came into line, and found they could make an entrance suitable or put in a gentle slope where necessary. Others were adamant it was not possible to have wheelchairs, but eventually all West End theatre managers caved in.

This was an account that Monty quietly took over from me, and it was right up his street. He hit it off well with the Carnegie staff up in Dumfermline, and managed to persuade Geoffrey Lord's deputy that the annual report could do with a facelift—quite a breakthrough. When Geoffrey retired and was replaced by John Naylor, Monty quickly took him under his wing.

Monty was much involved in the Carnegie campaign to get the Third Age better understood and appreciated in the UK. Carnegie set-up a commission to assess the effects on health, pensions, activities, and other aspects of life for older people living longer in Britain. Quite forward thinking at that time. We even persuaded Brenda Dean to serve on the inquiry!

In later years Monty contributed to an excellent book called *Getting a Life: Older People Talking* in which he discussed his ten years' work with Carnegie UK and his lifetime campaign for the underdog, which in his later years took most of his time after retirement. He was involved in setting up a Seniors' Forum for older people in Enfield, which grew to 5,000 members. Not a bad achievement for someone supposed to be retired. But a campaign vehicle, right up Monty's street.

Another success by Carnegie UK was to give grants to help many villages in the country upgrade and improve their local halls. Many had been built after the First World War and were in a dilapidated state. Some villages did not have a hall at all. From Carnegie UK they could get a grant, but they had to make an effort, too, in raising the balance of the funding. KMA was proud that an enormous number of village halls were spruced up or replaced through the campaign.

That was true to the ideals and rules that Andrew Carnegie had laid down and which worked well all over the world. Carnegie UK was a client of which Keith McDowall Associates were extremely proud. And I was quite tickled personally one day at the Reform Club when looking at the pictures of some of the previous members to discover a portrait of Andrew Carnegie, and to find he had indeed been one himself.

The public interest in pensions was growing—a boring subject on paper, but in fact a very important consideration in the lives of millions, which led us to Scottish Equitable.

Liz Hall had left the University of Aberdeen and taken a post in Edinburgh with this long-established insurance firm. But it was a company set in its ways, and Liz found the going tough, so she gave me a call. I flew up to the splendid city where Liz introduced me to Stewart Ritchie, an actuary. Behind his steel-rimmed spectacles, the epitome of a pensions expert. Very precise in his thinking and his delivery. Was I going to do much with him, I wondered.

In fact I was just the man he was looking for, he told me later. He wanted to make contact with the political parties but was not sure where to start. I took him to meet John Denham, then drafting the Opposition policy on the subject for the impending general election, and Harriett Harman; and also to meet Steve Webb of the Liberals, Government ministers and civil servants. I found that once I had opened the door, so to speak, Stewart was away, and his knowledge, coupled with an ability to present the complexity of pensions in a digestible manner, was extremely successful and welcome at Westminster and in Whitehall.

At the time I had quite a lot of money with Equitable Life—no connection with Scottish Equitable—and the company seemed a very good place to invest. Must be, I told myself—after all, my accountant Peter Rodney revealed that he and most of his colleagues in their partnership were placing their pension money with Equitable Life. So were various lawyers, some judges, Members of Parliament and even some businessmen. It was the company where self-employed professionals were putting their cash.

Even so, Stewart Ritchie kept chuntering on about the dangers of Equitable Life, its autocratic boss, the dangers of an open-ended commitment to index annuities. "Great if you can do it," said Stewart, "but how could it be done?" Oh, how I wished I had listened to Stewart and confessed to him that I had a tidy sum with the rival firm. But it was the old story of not wishing to mix business with one's personal affairs, and I kept my mouth shut.

Suddenly, the company was into a lawsuit as some policyholders objected to the fact that Equitable Life was offering indexed annuities to some policyholders, but not to all, which would be quite impossible to finance. The company lost, appealed, and lost again. "No problem," they told us. "We are appealing to the House of Lords, and are strongly advised we shall win. Just sit tight and hold your nerve."

Wrong again. We all should have got out then, but held on, convinced that Equitable Life was a good, well-managed company, and our funds were safe.

They were not. I managed to get part of my savings out, but lost something like £200,000. We were all supposed to be protected by Government but the politicians squirmed, ducked and dived—as did the civil servants. It took a very determined action committee finally to wring some compensation out of the Government, but my cheque ten years later for £33,000 was derisory.

I never revealed my awful secret to Stewart Ritchie, but I do now wish I had listened and confessed.

My policy at KMA was always to keep lines open to both sides in politics, Labour and Conservative, but I did not bother much with the Liberals. I had never joined a political party, because I believed journalists should keep their powder dry.

Even so, I was on very good terms with John Smith, who had taken over the leadership of the Labour Party. He was determined to modernise and drive through his 'one member, one vote' concept, which would clip the wings of the trade unions and halt their domination of the Labour Party.

I got John invited to address the CBI conference for which he was grateful, even though some in the audience jeered him for warning them that change was coming. He came to dinner at our home with his lovely wife, Elizabeth, and I was also with John in Japan on the creation of the Anglo-Japanese 2000 Group. I found him a warm, straight-talker who, I felt, could even one day be loved if he became prime minister. But it was never to be.

In May 1994 we went to a Labour fund-raising dinner at the Hyde Park Hotel and met John, and I thought he looked tired, but when John spoke a thrill went through me because for the first time I felt he was really coming through as a future national leader. "He's got it," I said to Brenda.

At the pre-dinner drinks beforehand I met up with a young, happy Tony Blair, who discussed with me the impending date I had organised with him for dinner. "There's a future Labour leader," I told myself. I did not realise then how short the future would be.

The very next morning came news on the radio that John Smith had been rushed to hospital from his flat in the Barbican, where he had had a severe heart attack. It did not sound good.

I looked across the garden at the rear of the house Tony and Cherie Blair had bought in Richmond Crescent, and imagined what was happening there. Already speculation had begun in the party ranks, and Blair was probably warning his children that the day at school might be very different for them. It certainly was.

By then, poor John Smith was dead, and Tony Blair was in the opening day of his contest with Gordon Brown for the leadership of the Labour party and, ultimately the keys to Number 10 Downing Street.

Over the next three years we worked hard to build closer relations with Labour because the omens for a party victory looked good. Most of my clients, having totally ignored Labour for years, suddenly wanted to meet the top players. In recent times I had taken Mo Mowlem, Neil Kinnock, Jack Straw and others to lunch with the top people at Prudential, where the non-smoking rule in the boardroom did not fuss Mo at all. She just lit up and carried on!

Now there were many more demands. I took John Prescott to meet Sir Brian Moffatt, chairman of British Steel, and Margaret Beckett to exchange views with the top brass at the headquarters of British Standards Institute, among many others. It was heady stuff.

The election did not come for three years, but in July 1997 Tony Blair's new Government was swept into power on a landslide. For the six weeks of the campaign, Brenda and I were in Cornwall, where we sought to get Candy Atherton elected for Labour in Camborne. I drove our Ford Scorpio, bedecked in Labour posters, loudspeaker fixed to the roof rack, and I became quite adept on the mike.

I also canvassed possible voters door to door, which is exceedingly hard work. Meanwhile, Brenda worked in the office and persuaded the Millbank headquarters people in London to send down a party of MPs and peers to help our campaign. They flew in a chartered plane into Culdrose, the Royal Navy helicopter base, and we collected them in a cavalcade of cars. It was quite a day as we saturated places like the High Street in Redruth and took the politicians for tea in Tesco at Helston. On the day of the election Brenda and I drove to London for the results. We had been invited to the polling night rally at Royal Festival Hall, and though we were knackered and needed to share the driving to keep awake, nothing was going to stop us from getting there. We still did not know the result at Cornwall, as we saw Tony Blair arrive by helicopter at daybreak and tell us, "It's a wonderful morning." It certainly seemed it.

All the people we had known in nearly twenty years of Opposition seemed to be there, although, of course, others were at the election counts in their own constituencies. But for many, just like us, the South Bank was the magical place to be to see a remarkable piece of history enacted. It was an unforgettable occasion.

Gradually it dawned on me that the only place to be was bed. The lack of sleep had caught up with me. But as we drove to Islington and clean sheets, over the car radio came the final cherry on the cake— "Camborne and Redruth—Labour gain." Candy Atherton had been elected, and all that footslogging, poster hanging and door stepping had paid off.

A new Labour Government meant plenty of work for us trying to get meetings with the new ministers for clients, finding out what was planned for the first Queen's Speech, and briefing accordingly.

With our Labour connections, Keith McDowall Associates were extremely well-positioned. On the other hand, it was disappointing that many of the Labour MPs we had wined and dined for years in Opposition quickly forgot their friends. Two who did keep contact were Richard Caborn and John Prescott, both of whom KMA had helped in Opposition. John went on to become Deputy Prime Minister, so he was well positioned on the inner track.

His Parliamentary Private Secretary, Alan Meale MP, was quite a character, and dreamed up the idea of Labour backing the horse racing on Brighton Downs on the weekend eve of the first Labour conference in power. To this day I am amazed, but I managed to get sponsorship of three individual races—Kvaerner, Scottish Equitable, and even the Post Office took on a race.

John Prescott turned the pressure on the top Labour brass, who were made to come to the race track and rub shoulders with our clients. He even got the extremely difficult Gordon Brown, now Chancellor of the Exchequer, to attend with his entourage. That meant Scottish Equitable could ask about pensions, the Post Office could lobby about its plans for commercial freedom, and Kvaerner could lobby for help with offshore work.

One day in February 1997, I was picked up at Heathrow by Ken Tuppen, who had become our driver at KMA. He had previously driven Brenda Dean, my wife, who gave him a very high mark, and, as she was moving on from her job, it had meant Ken was looking around, too. So I took him on—an inspired decision.

He turned out to be an intensely loyal, conscientious companion. If a driver gets it wrong in his relationship with his boss, all is doomed. Ken knew when to speak, when to shut up, when to put his foot down, and when to drive gently.

Ken had been involved in my previous dealings with Brian Keelan at the merchant banker S G Warburg. "I have been told to take you straight to their offices," Ken told me at the airport.

On arrival at Warburg's offices off Finsbury Square in the City, I found my partner Monty Meth was already there, and we were quickly shown to the second floor where Keelan and his team operated.

This time, though, it was different. These slick City bankers were out of their depth, and so was Keelan.

The client was Co-operative Wholesale Society, the CWS, which was on the receiving end of a cheeky £1.2 billion bid from a cocky young entrepreneur named Andrew Regan. On the face of it, the audacious bid was doomed to fail. After all, the Co-op was Very Big Indeed. It was the largest farming landowner in Britain, the largest undertaker, second or third largest in the travel business, very big in insurance, a substantial contributor to the Labour Party—indeed, had its own political party affiliated to the Labour Party. There was even the Co-op Bank, used by many trade unions. Printing—yes, the Co-op had its own works in Manchester, and printed most of the trade unions' literature and magazines, as well as its own Sunday newspaper.

The list of its activities went on, page after page. Name any facet of British society and the Co-op was there, right in the middle. Maybe not the number one in the field, but a substantial player and one with ethics, a proud history, and a substantial labour force.

How was this kid Regan going to take over the Co-op with a hostile bid? Was he out of his mind? Had he no idea of the complex structure within the various Co-op Societies which made it almost impossible to get any decision, let alone tie up a major financial deal?

It soon became clear in the discussions with Keelan, and some of his team also, that they had little idea of the complexity of trying to buy a company or a project off the Co-op.

To Monty and me, this was of course meat and drink. As a young reporter in South London I became familiar with the Royal Arsenal Co-op, formed by workers at the Woolwich Arsenal at the turn of the century. I was used to reporting the quarterly meetings of members as they grumbled about food quality, dividend payments, and over-the-counter service. Monty had a similar story of reporting the activities of the LCS—the London Co-operative Society—and had a number of good contacts high up in the Co-op hierarchy.

There was no way anyone could come into the Co-op world, wave a cheque book, and buy out individual shareholders. Was there?

Regan seemed to think so. And Graham Melmoth, the chief executive of the CWS, was on his way from his Manchester headquarters at that very moment to hear how Warburg's, the merchant bankers he had retained, were going to stop him.

Keelan looked round the room. This one, he told us, was going to be different. We were not supporting a hostile bid, we were beating one off in a world which was quite different. Regan seemed to have the ear of the financial journalists, who regarded the Co-op as stuffy, old hat, poorly managed … you name it. As far as they were concerned, the Co-op had it in spades. They needed a shake-up.

The fact that the Co-op paid its many employees a fair wage, brought employment to areas where there was little else, built supermarkets in sleepy towns the big majors ignored, and carried out a variety of other public-spirited actions, meant little to the City journalists. They tended to read everything in terms of profit and loss and lauded the buccaneer over the sound, cautious banker.

Melmoth was shown into Keelan's office, and those who would become the key players in a slimmed-down team were introduced—in particular, John Turnbull, litigation partner at Linklaters, who would be a key player.

Melmoth, lean, tallish, grey, looked somewhat shaken. After all, it was a brave decision for the Co-operative movement to swallow its pride and go to some of the sharpest minds in the City and seek salvation.

Keelan emphasised that we would need quick responses from the Co-op. There was no time to call committee meetings if we needed to respond to, say, a press comment or a radio interview. Melmoth assured us that we would get them—any hour of the day or night. Which was very reassuring.

Afterwards, Monty and I decided we needed quickly to make contact with City and financial journalists likely to be covering the story. We knew some of them, but did not have the inside track that some of the bigger financial public relations companies clearly enjoyed. Our experience and nose for a good story should get us out of that hole, we told ourselves.

One journalist I had to get to know, however, was the city editor of the *Sunday Telegraph*, who had had an exclusive on the Andrew Regan bid. Apart from the sheer news value, there was also a supportive commentary arguing that each one of the 200 or so on the main Co-op executive could get a substantial one-off payment if they voted for Regan's proposal to dismember the organisation.

As we dug into the issue we discovered that this 'sell-off' idea was well down the road. Allied Irish Banks had expressed a serious interest in taking over the Co-op Bank, and Hambros Bank was equally interested; Sainsbury's had been sounded out about taking over the Co-op grocery chain. Also, the highly respected law firm Travers Smith found itself on the back foot, having confidential Co-op documents in its possession. It even hired the public relations company, Grandfield, which made matters worse by condemning the Co-op's actions as 'a sideshow and a distraction', to the main bid.

This was where the letter-writing skill of Linklater's John Turnbull came to the fore. In a handwritten note to Travers' senior partner, Melmoth (in Turnbull's prose) told him 'Please reflect on the following facts. One of your senior partners had sensitive and highly confidential CWS board minutes on his files. Anyone who can read will have known that they were confidential to the CWS. He knew that CWS would have nothing to do with Mr Regan, so why have any such documents? How then did he satisfy himself that the documents had come from a legitimate source or by legitimate means?'

With 'gold' like this to put out we were on a publicity winner, and as a succession of Melmoth letters were drafted by John Turnbull, knocking at some of the most prestigious names in the City, our growing friends in the press could not get enough. We were raining shot after shot onto the Regan camp, who had little with which to respond. They could hardly admit that they had stolen all the material!

One morning Keelan called me to his office and shut the door. This was clearly serious because he usually said everything at the top his voice with the door open so that his whole team could know what was going on. "I want you to engage a firm of top-notch private detectives to follow Regan to find what he is up to and who he sees," he ordered.

This was a bit hairy. My little company was extremely vulnerable if everything went pear-shaped. I had no insurance for this kind of activity. On the other hand, if I jibbed, Keelan would swiftly replace me with some other PR outfit. Outwardly confident, I assured him, I would do as bid.

Monty and I checked around, and agreed to contact two companies we had heard of, Kroll and Control Risks.

Next day I had an appointment with Kroll in offices in the Savile Row area off Piccadilly. So far as I was able, I outlined my requirements. In confidence, I explained who I was working for, but that I would be in charge of the brief. I listed all the names of the companies we knew had been involved with Andrew Regan, and I sought assurances that there would be no clash of interests.

We parted on the understanding that I would receive a call later in the day if there were any such clash, which would mean a case of strained loyalty. As it happened, there was a problem. Kroll had a client relationship with Allied Irish Banks and felt they had to withdraw. So out I went again and knocked on the door of Control Risks—a good name when you think of it, because that was exactly what Keelan and I were trying to do.

That was on a Friday, and on the Monday there was a call.

"Regan is having lunch in the St John restaurant at Smithfield. I am at the next table. Would you like to overhear the conversation?"

"No, thank you," I yelled down the phone. "Just record it and find out who Regan is entertaining."

Each day for the rest of the week I had similar calls, and it was obvious Regan enjoyed quite a comfortable lifestyle. On the other hand I was not certain that I was learning much except anticipating that Regan was going to have a weight problem.

Then on Sunday morning came a call at home. The CR boys thought they were on to something.

"We're in the car park at the Old Bell on the A40 at Gerrards Cross, and two blokes have just arrived to meet Regan. We are getting some very good photographs. We also have a car registration number. Could you check with your people if it means anything to them, please."

Easier said than done. The Co-op did not work Sundays!

Next morning, though, I collected a big wad of photographs from the Control Risks offices and took them to the Tower Hotel, where Graham Melmoth was staying.

"I think these will cheer you up," I said as I passed him the big envelope. Melmoth pulled out the pictures. The colour drained from his face. He said nothing, but put the prints back in the envelope.

"I'm going back to Manchester immediately," he told me.

Next morning, at the early meeting at Warburg's, there was no sign of Keelan. One of his lieutenants took the chair and we all reported on developments as we knew them, but there was a feeling in the air that there was something bigger around. Some hours later Keelan turned up and held an immediate meeting to 'put us in the picture'—an appropriate turn of phrase.

The saloon in the Bell carpark had in fact been that of Allan Green, a senior executive at the Co-op. He had been photographed handing documents to Andrew Regan, which turned out to show the full weekly takings in all the CWS grocery shops. Breathtaking treachery.

Green was fired, as was his henchman at the CWS, David Chambers. Both had been involved some months earlier in setting up a deal with Regan involving a company supplying the CWS, where Regan was chief executive.

On the Friday morning I went to the High Court in The Strand, where Andrew Regan's amazing gamble came to a grinding halt. His audacious bid to strip the staid but honest Co-operative Wholesale Society of some of its best assets was stopped in its tracks.

The judge heard a claim for an injunction brought against Regan's 'vehicle' company, named Galileo, and came down strongly on the side of the CWS. Hambros, the investment bank, until then with an impeccable reputation, was told to hand over stolen documents and fined £1 million. Three of its top advisers were forced to resign and apologise. It was the beginning of the end for Hambros. Also hit well below the waterline was the leading firm of City solicitors Travers Smith Braithwaite, its reputation totally shattered. One by one, the companies like Allied Irish Banks, which had rubbed their hands at the prospect at picking up CWS assets on the cheap, found themselves at the receiving end of the judge's withering verdict. The only company to emerge with its reputation unblemished was Sainsbury's, which had asked if the CWS approved of it being offered the trading figures of the grocery stores. When it was not satisfied, Sainsbury's returned unopened the letter containing the stolen figures.

When the judgement was concluded, Keelan's team gathered at the back of the court for mutual backslapping. It was quite a thrilling moment, and I knew KM Associates had acquitted itself well.

As costs had been awarded in our favour they had to be submitted quickly. John Turnbull asked me if I thought my figure would be around "The £200,000 mark?" And I confirmed it would be a good estimate, though in reality I had no idea.

What I did know was that I had worked on the story for many days non-stop, and I had been running on pure adrenaline because the issue was so exciting. But now I felt quite knackered. All my team—Monty, Mary Graham, Ken Tuppen, the driver, and Gordon Leak, ex-*Sunday Express*, who was working with us—had worked their socks off, too. As had my wife, Brenda, who had been up early each morning to help me to get the press cuttings over to Warburg's, Linklaters, the Co-op, and various others.

But now Brenda really came in to her own. She sat down and worked out a marvellous account for the days we had been engaged. It came in at a fraction over £198,000. "Not much water under the bridge, Keith," commented Brian Keelan drily as he glanced at my invoice. I said nothing, but thought of the huge fees Warburg's and Linklaters would be sending to Graham Melmoth at the CWS. My bill would look like petty cash among their invoices, but it was the largest cheque we ever paid in at our bank.

That was not the end of the saga. A few days later I received an invitation from Brian Keelan to dinner at a smart West End restaurant where my old friend, David Howell, Conservative MP, presided. He had been in our original team in Northern Ireland, and went on to be the Energy Minister in Margaret Thatcher's Government. On this occasion he was there as the London chairman of Warburg's.

Everyone who had been in the CWS defence team was at the dinner, and Brian Keelan thanked us all. Then he presented each of us with a beautiful miniature alarm clock made by Asprey, which my watchmaker in Cornwall described 'a gem of a clock'. I have it beside my bed at Falmouth, and often think of the days we routed the audacious bid to strip the good old Co-op of some of its best businesses.

I have mentioned my friendship over the years with Richard Needham, former Conservative MP for Cirencester, who did a great job as a junior minister in the Northern Ireland team and then went on to become, I believe, Britain's best-ever Trade Minister, for which, rightly, he was knighted.

But he stood down from John Major's Government and resolved, as he put it, "to make some money for Sissy"—his supportive

German-born wife, who had carried most of the constituency work while her husband was travelling the world.

I am sure Sissy would have preferred to see more of him at home, but with his customary zest Richard threw himself into building a consultancy, and soon had some extremely good clients. One was James Dyson, the British inventor, and for a while Richard was his deputy chairman, and I came in as public relations adviser.

There was a most exciting project when a wealthy Malaysian group asked Richard to become chairman of the Heart Hospital it had built off Harley Street, and which was equipped to state-of-the-art standards.

The trouble was, the private health sector was deliberately sending its patients elsewhere, where they owned the facilities. The worst were PPP, which not only owned the Harley Street Clinic, but also had a major stake in Wellington Hospital. So, although many specialists in Harley Street practice would have preferred to use the spanking new hospital on their doorstep, PPP told them, "Nothing doing."

It was tragic to see the gleaming new equipment standing idle. Richard tried negotiation and raising his voice, but PPP and others, like BUPA and some smaller private operators, had cloth ears. I told Richard we had to shout louder and asked, was he up to war?

He certainly was, and KMA set about making life distinctly uncomfortable for PPP. We placed stories in the newspapers and even got the PPP boss facing my old pal, consumer champion Anne Robinson, on the BBC. He was sweating when Anne had finished, but still would not concede PPP was in effect operating a restrictive practice.

Richard and I went to see the Office of Fair Trading and argued for an inquiry. They would not budge though, ironically, in later years the Competition Commission decided there was a case to answer. But that was not filling beds.

In the end the Malaysian investors told Richard to close the Heart Hospital. It would do better, they said, as a private apartment block with its ideal West End location.

I got Richard's agreement to approach Sir Ronald Mason, the chairman of University College London Hospital Trust, where Brenda had been his deputy.

Ron was enthusiastic and brought round his newly appointed chief executive, Robert Naylor, who I learned was one of the smartest operators in the National Health Service. The pair were keen, but where was the money?

Two months later Naylor had pulled off a coup. The Tony Blair Government announced it had put up £27 million to acquire the Heart Hospital. Better still, Naylor saw his chance to offer cardiovascular services to all the other London hospital groups struggling to cope with long waiting lists.

Within eighteen months the entire backlog of heart patients in Greater London had been cleared. What is more, NHS patients were spreading the word about the excellent treatment they had received for their bypass, stent or pacemaker needs at the Heart Hospital. It was good to know, and both Richard and I always have a warm glow when we recall the battle to save the Heart Hospital.

As for Keith McDowall Associates, we continued to flourish, and after a decade had built a sound reputation as reliable operators handling the inter-relationships between business, Government and the financial world. We had steady contracts in engineering, chemicals, insurance, the Post Office, Independent Television, a major charity, publishing and organisations like the Institute of Chartered Personnel Management. And the work did not all fall on my back. Increasingly clients were asking for Monty or Mary Graham, who had replaced Brenda Laing, and I was able to step back.

But Monty, who is older than me, was starting to feel the pace, and the two of us discussed the prospect of finding a buyer. I was becoming aware, though, that if ever we were to realise our full value and hopefully sell the business, we needed to get it out of our basement at home and into a suite of offices. I was loath, however, to go to the West End or the City and pay heavily for a prestige address. Surely it was possible to find a good address and offices in Islington, an area which over the decade had acquired a greatly enhanced reputation?

We found a suite of third-floor offices adjacent to The Angel underground station, and it was not so long afterwards the first serious feeler for a buyout emerged. There had been a couple of contacts, both of whom wanted to buy us for a song, but we told them where to go.

But a brief conversation with Peter Luff MP seemed more hopeful. I had known him for several years, and he did part-time work for a subsidiary of Bell Pottinger, by now a major player in advertising, City PR and polling, as well as being competitors in public affairs and lobbying. Peter undertook to have a word with the financial director, and a day or two later I received a call from Mike Smith. Shortly afterwards, we met for lunch, and I agreed I was seriously looking around with a view to sell.

Mike said he would make enquiries and get back to me.

It was time to talk to Peter Rodney of Bright Graham Murray, who had been our accountants since the very first day I had started to run my own business. Peter became a good friend and reliable source of advice. His company took care of our payroll and national insurance, and at the end of each year helped me to work out what bonuses I should pay the staff.

Monty and I went to meet Tim Bell, the affable head of the prospective buyer, and we seemed to get on well, but the deal went cold. We heard nothing for weeks. In the end I gave Peter Luff a call and asked him to find out if the deal was a dead duck. He called back shortly afterwards. "You should get a call from Mick Smith shortly," he told me. And we did. He made a firm offer to buy us out.

So began the process of unscrambling Keith McDowall Associates, which had taken ten years to assemble. In principle, they wanted to buy us and we wanted to settle, but how did we calculate our true worth? Peter Rodney came up with a formula for assessing goodwill, which, after all was the only value of KMA—the goodwill of our clients, and whether they would stick with us as we sold out.

Peter also found us a lawyer because in these kind of deals a major contract is worked out. All above our heads. Annoyingly, although we stressed there was no hurry, the two firms of lawyers decided to work through the night to tie up the deal—and charge us double-time to do it. What a racket. I was not surprised, though—I had seen it several times when working with Warburg's.

Throughout it Peter Rodney was our rock, and it was with great sadness that some years after I had retired Peter took his own life while living in New York. I imagine he was another victim of that deadly killer, depression. Very sad.

The deal with Bell Pottinger was in three parts—a third up front, a third in the middle, and a third at the end if all the clients had been retained and we had kept our side of the bargain. The agreed price was three quarters of a million pounds, of which I gave Monty a quarter. He had helped me to build the business, had restrained my enthusiasm, sometimes written joint introductions to news releases with me, and been my counsel over the years. For which I was truly indebted.

For a while we continued to work at our own offices at The Angel, but then were shifted down to spare rooms our new owners had in Russell Square, alongside Good Relations, another subsidiary. We worked a little with them, and at one time it was possible we would be merged, but nothing came of it.

Two newcomers did join us, however. With the election of Tony Blair's Government I became aware of the importance of the young people working in the various offices of ministers who clearly had a network. They had worked hard in Opposition, forged their own relationships, and were not at all bothered about the Civil Service system. I felt we needed to recruit one of these quickly. That was how we fell upon James O'Keefe, who had worked in Opposition, and during the General Election been at campaign headquarters. I had good vibes about James, and sometime after I departed he led a team out of Bell Pottinger and set-up his own company, which was

Top left: *Always a laugh with Norman Willis, General Secretary of the TUC. I met him as a reporter when he was personal assistant to Frank Cousins.* **Top right:** *Not many laughs though with Ian McGregor, National Coal Board chairman, appointed by Margaret Thatcher to see off the coal miners.* **Bottom:** *Sir Terence Beckett (right), Director General of the Confederation of British Industry received a standing ovation for his speech to the businessman's conference led by the president, Lord David Nickson (left). Speechwriting was a major part of my task at the CBI.*

Top: Barbados in 2010 with Brenda, my two daughters, Clare's husband, Andrew, and all the cousins – they are all the best of pals. *Bottom:* Former colleagues from some of the press and public relations teams I have enjoyed leading over the years helping me celebrate at The Reform Club.

Top: With my two daughters, Clare (left) and Alison (right). We all enjoy a good laugh. ***Bottom left:*** *My investiture at the Palace, June 1988.* ***Bottom right:*** *Reunion in Australia with Kathy, my PA at Employment & British Shipbuilders. She sadly died in 2015.*

Top: *Monty Meth sends me up to the amusement of my sister, Jean, and on my left, Betty Meth.* ***Bottom:*** *Switching off. Watching cricket at Capetown with jazz buff, Don Albert (left) and Jack Jeffery (right). England must have been winning ...*

highly successful. The sad thing about it was that Mary Graham was indignant when she found out the salary Bell Pottinger had agreed to pay James and she quit. That turned out for the best because she got a safe job with the Financial Authority, which meant she could start a family and not worry about taking maternity leave. Later, she and her husband set-up their own PR business in Suffolk.

The other recruit was David Hill, who had been in charge of the press operation of the Labour Party for several years, and really knew his way around in that area. He subsequently took my place as figurehead of KMA.

Monty and I were proud that we successfully retained all our clients over the two-year earn-out period, and handed them safely to our successors. Within six months most had gone. But we took our money, spread a little around and banked the rest. I will never forget the day I walked into HSBC at Islington and told Malcolm Wright, my friend there, I wanted to pay off the mortgage on 2 Malvern Terrace. He and two other staff members blinked. No one had ever asked them to arrange anything like that. Eventually I wrote out a cheque for £83,000 and the deeds were passed across the table. Not a penny was owed on 2 Malvern Terrace—fair enough, because the house had helped to earn most of the money in the first place.

We staged a big farewell party in the Library at the Reform Club, attended by many of our clients and contacts. Among them were John Prescott, Michael Foot, Sir Brian Pitman, boss of Lloyds Bank, Sir Brian Moffat, chairman of British Steel, several friends from the Kvaerner days, the chief executive of Carnegie Trust, the top brass of Royal Mail, and many others. The invitation did not spell out that we were retiring. It simply asked guests to join us '… to celebrate a few landmarks, remember friends, and raise a glass or two to the future …' which made it an intriguing come-on. It was a great night.

I made a speech which went down alright, but the highlight came when there were repeated calls for Monty to speak. He had determined beforehand that he was definitely not going to do so. But when the calls continued Monty made his way to the microphone, and we waited for his first words.

Instead came a song, well known in the trade union world: 'He's the man, the very fat man who waters the workers' beer … ' and then Monty paused and looked at me. 'He's got a yacht, a motorcar and an aeroplane … and he waters the workers' beer!'

It brought the house down—even though I insisted I did not water anyone's beer and tried to look after my staff. No one believed me after that rendition of Monty's.

After a few days without the need to go into an office I got around to thinking about what I was going to do with my life. I now had the freedom to travel, and with Alison, my younger daughter, married, and with her husband Graham settled in Texas with two children and a third on the way, I wanted to be able to go to the US as and when it suited me.

Then there was jazz. Since 1991, when I found in a jazz magazine an obscure reference to 'The Floating Jazz Festival' on board the SS *Norway*, Brenda and I have joined the cruise annually. We have just returned from our 25th! On our first trip it was Dizzy Gillespie's birthday, and I have a clear recollection of him cutting me a slice of his birthday cake. "Can't get better than this," I remember telling myself.

Over the years we have seen some magnificent talent like pianist Dorothy Donegan, clarinetist Kenny Davern, singer Joe Williams, Arturo Sandoval—who could hit terrific top notes on his trumpet— and many other excellent musicians from the East and the West Coast of America. I made friends with Bob Wilber, who played for me on Kvaerner gigs, with Derek Smith, an ex-Brit who plays riveting piano around New York, and most particularly with Jeff Hamilton, probably the finest jazz drummer in the world. For a number of years now, Brenda and I have had a regular dinner date on board the annual jazz cruise with Jeff.

Now I come to think about it, music has played a very large role in my life. I like all kinds of music, some classical, some opera, even some ballet, but I do like most of what today is called jazz, but which in earlier days was broken down into all kinds of categories, such as swing, boogie, big band, and of course, jazz.

I think it first got to me when I heard those early Glenn Miller 78rpm recordings in the Farm House Café at Addington, tunes like 'In the Mood', 'String of Pearls' and 'Juke Box Saturday Night', which had been on the hit parade as my Canadian friends boarded the troopship bringing them to the UK. They brought the music with them, which to me was a revelation.

I really got going buying my own recordings once I was at school and earning some pocket money. Whenever I had enough saved up, I would blow it on a wax 78rpm record. These were made of shellac, lasted just three and a half minutes each side, and if you happened to drop one that was the end. So we were very careful in handling them—but not so good at using expensive needles. We replaced ours with cheaper new steel needles, which over time scratched the recordings badly.

My first ever purchase was 'American Patrol' by Glenn Miller, which I played over and over again. And I built up quite a collection of his music. But at school, talking with school friends—particularly Brian Saker—we learned about trumpeter Harry James and the bands of Count Basie, Benny Goodman and Artie Shaw. And then another boy brought in a recent US recording of Duke Ellington so we added his name to our list of idols. And as money allowed, we slowly built up our collections, occasionally lending each other our treasured numbers. I still have my 78rpm collection and have had them all transcribed onto tape recordings.

In 1944, shortly after the D-Day landings, we learned that Major Glenn Miller was heading for London with the US Army Air Force Band—and what a band. In fact it was an orchestra comprising some fifty top American musicians handpicked by Miller, as they were drafted. He had them directed straight into his unit to entertain thousands of US troops who had arrived in the UK, and he did it brilliantly. He also lifted the people of Britain, especially kids like me and many of my schoolmates. He even broadcast special versions of his songs with German lyrics which Joe Voss, the West German labour attaché in London, years later assured me he and his friends were hearing.

"We were banned from listening to this Jewish music, as the Nazis called it. But to us it meant freedom, and we could not wait for it to reach us," Joe told me one night.

Then one morning in 1944 as I was on my newspaper round, one ear cocked for doodlebugs, I happened to glance at the front page of the *Daily Mail*: 'Glenn Miller missing.' He had boarded a small aircraft to fly over the English Channel to Paris one foggy morning and his plane had failed to arrive. I just could not believe it. How could Miller be so foolish? What would happen to the band?

Suddenly the door opened. "Do you mind if I have my *Daily Mail*?" asked the customer sarcastically.

In fact the US Army Air Force Band played on, and their magnificent music still stirs anyone of my generation who hears it. But soon Saker and I heard a new sound, and it came from a British band—could you believe it? No corny 'syncopation' as the BBC bands called their output. This was a sound to compete with the Americans by a fellow called Ted Heath. He had formed a new band in London and was making waves.

His first 78 was called 'My Guy's Come Back'. On the other side was 'Opus One', the original version of which, by Tommy Dorsey, we were eagerly awaiting arrival of from the US. But the sound and beat was good, and all my friends snapped it up and wanted to know more about this Ted Heath. The response was to announce monthly Swing Sessions on Sunday afternoon and evenings at the London Palladium, and Saker and I were there. We did not miss a concert and were enthralled. Jack Parnell was on drums—having his uncle, Val Parnell, running the Palladium had obviously been helpful, and a brilliant young trumpeter, Kenny Baker, led the brass section.

If the Ted Heath sound was how peacetime was going to be, bring it on, we felt. As the war drew to a close and the streets lights came on we heard more and more good music from names like Humphrey

Lyttelton, Harry Parry, Frank Weir, Billy Cotton, Geraldo, Jack Payne and Oscar Rabin. It was a wonderful era for hearing good music played and sung.

Over the Atlantic came Louis Armstrong, Duke Ellington, Count Basie, Harry James and Benny Goodman and even Frank Sinatra. It was amazing, The British never thought they would see Old Blue Eyes, but there he was appearing in 1963 at the Royal Festival Hall. Quite a moment.

By then of course we had all started to collect the so-called LP records—long-playing records, at a speed of 33⅓rpm, on unbreakable vinyl, and offering wonderful sound quality compared with our shellac ones.

I bought Frank Sinatra's *Songs for Swinging Lovers*, at the time the best-ever selling LP, and took it to a *Daily Mail* journalists' party. It was played non-stop as couples danced the night away.

I have a major collection of LPs, and though I have many more CDs and tapes there is no doubt the warmer sound quality of the long-playing classics is superior.

I have kept up an interest in my kind of music, and been to see many musicians playing. I feel strongly that there is nothing to equal seeing and hearing a musician or singer give a live performance. I have written earlier about the way I used live music to promote my clients to excellent effect, and as a result I came to be on friendly terms with a number of musicians, both in Britain in America.

In 2010 came the chance to do something positive and set-up some live events myself. The Reform Club, in Pall Mall, the centre of London's clubland where I have been a member since 1978, launched an appeal to buy a second-hand Steinway piano from the Wigmore Hall. At any one time it has at least two Steinways, one on the stage and the second in a pit below it. With the touch of a button the second instrument can be brought up for a duet or a quick replacement, should it be needed.

When it became known one of their pianos was for sale, some classical buffs in the club thought we should buy it and I made a contribution. Then I waited.

As I anticipated, a series of classical concerts were announced, a soirée here, a recital there—but nothing lighter. So I wrote a letter to the club magazine asking if a jazz pianist could touch the Steinway keyboard—or was the Reform 'too elitist?'

Rather like a Bateman cartoon, there was an almost audible clunk as shocked classicists contemplated such a dreadful thought. But then came a surprising response. Members wrote in asking why couldn't there be some jazz heard in the club? Jazz at The Reform, as the series has become known, has been running for five years as I write, and has enjoyed remarkable success.

One never stops learning, but the background I acquired over the years in this kind of music paid off as I found myself tracking down musicians, clinching them for events at the club, and then ensuring that the key sound equipment was in place, cheques were signed for payment, and seating was appropriate. It is amazing how much background work goes into presenting a musical event.

Before I leave the music theme I must pay tribute to my old school pal and fellow music fan, Saker—Brian as he was to me but Hugh as he preferred as his byline once he got to Fleet Street. As I have recorded, he did much to influence my decision to become a journalist. Our paths sometimes crossed in our early days in Fleet Street, but he specialized in crime and I went off towards industry so we lost touch. Whenever we did run into each other the wine flowed, there was much merriment, and it was just like old times.

One of the biggest laughs in Fleet Street was the one about Saker's journey home from his role as crimeman on the *Daily Mirror* when he was certainly 'tired' but unlikely to be 'emotional'. The *Mirror* put him on a very late train to East Croydon. The news desk rang his home at Addington, near Croydon, and persuaded his wife, then in bed, to take the car to the station and collect Hugh.

Vivienne Batchelor was no stranger to booze in Fleet Street because she herself was a distinguished writer on the *Evening Standard*, and prior to meeting Saker, also then on that paper, had been married to

Tom (Duncan) Webb of the *The People*.

Not best pleased, Viv put a housecoat over her nightie and shot off quickly to East Croydon because the trains are fast from Victoria and there was not much time. With a grunt, Hugh Saker got in the passenger seat and promptly went into a deep sleep while his wife drove.

But Viv had not had time to spend a penny—and realized that she did not have one with her. So as her car reached the more rural Shirley Hills, she parked and crossed the road in search of appropriate tree cover.

Just at that moment her husband awoke, and found himself sitting in the passenger seat. He was surprised at his sagacity, but getting behind the wheel saw that he had forgotten to remove the ignition key. Still, he felt up to driving home so switched on and set off.

It was before the breathalyser, but cars did have rear-view mirrors. Even so, Saker missed seeing Viv frantically running after him, waving and shouting.

It says much about a Fleet Street man's ability to recover rapidly from a skinful because he drove home to Featherbed Lane in Addington, put the car safely in the garage, went indoors and locked up. Within seconds he was in bed and fast asleep again.

Ever resourceful, Viv found a lit phone box, which did little to alleviate her shivering, but she had no money to call home. Only thing—dial the emergency 999 number.

"Oh yes, dear," replied the ever-helpful New Scotland Yard. "Lost your purse, have you? Business not so good tonight ..."

It took all her resourcefulness—of which Viv had a lot—eventually to convince the two patrol car cops who eventually arrived, hardly able to keep a straight face. Nor to forget they had heard it all from distraught women, many times over.

But eventually they agreed to drive her home to Addington, where she could prove that her husband really had left her standing by the roadside.

Only trouble was that by the time the police car arrived, Hugh was well away and nothing was going to wake him. No amount of hammering on the front or back door resulted in a sound from the house. Vivienne's credibility once again was on the line.

Only with the reluctant agreement of her roused neighbour that he certainly did recognise her, and would give her a bed for what was left of the night, brought the curtain down on the drama for Vivienne. But wait till she got her hands on Hugh Saker in the morning.

He was quite unfazed—wondered where the silly cow had got to … hadn't even left him anything to eat … he was thinking as there was a hammering on the front door and his wife stood there.

It was some time before normal relationships were restored …

As I have mentioned, Saker and I were actually at school together in Croydon during the war, and good personal friends. In those days he did not have the huge belly he presented at the *Daily Mirror*. In 1944 I think of a slim, lithe Brian Saker (as he was then) who became a school hero in being selected for trials in the same year for Crystal Palace Juniors and the cricketing Surrey CC Colts.

He lost an eye when we were playing soccer in the school playground with an inch-diameter marble, and a kid named Harrington gave it an almighty kick. Naturally, Saker tried to head it, and I remember a huge lump appearing quickly on his forehead. But it soon went down and the game resumed. In any case, as we were not supposed to be kicking a ball in the playground, there was no case of Saker seeking first aid from a teacher.

A fellow named Peter Kinsley has written that Hugh Saker lost his eye as a rear gunner in the RAF when attacked by a German fighter plane, but I think that sounds distinctly like Saker's very keen sense of humour. We both left school aged 16 in 1945, intending to become reporters, and we both started on papers in South London—but we kept in touch with a joint love of newspapers and, indeed, big band jazz. Hugh tragically died at 37 from a huge tumour in his stomach. But he was always a hell of a laugh, and he and Viv dined out for several years on the tale of their crossed paths in Shirley Hills …

One ambition I was determined to achieve was to make a major voyage in my yacht *Selangor*. She now lay on a good mooring in Falmouth harbour. *Selangor* was my fifth boat and I kept her for the longest—over twenty years. She was thirty-eight feet in length overall, which is a good size for British waters, could sleep seven, had a good oven, fridge, heating, running hot water, a shower, and very comfortable accommodation. Best of all, she had a dependable Volvo 44 hp diesel engine.

Brenda and I sailed her happily for many years, sometimes on cruises to the Brittany coast, inviting friends and family to cruise with us and dine and wine on board. At other times Brenda and I would cruise together up the magnificent River Fal or spend the weekend anchored in the Helford, less than ten miles from our house in Cornwall. Entering the Helford, it is said, is to behold one of the most magnificent river scenes in Britain.

Selangor was a far cry from my little 21-foot LOA (Length Overall) Time & Tide, a wooden Martini class, which I bought with the proceeds from my libel action as I mentioned earlier.

I bought *Selangor* in Mallorca, where the original owner had sailed her from Poole, but he did not want to bring her back. That was my initial intention, but then Brenda and I decided we ought to have a look around the Mediterranean water before getting back to the UK. In the end, we had three seasons there. We kept the boat at Calle d'Or, and who should we find had a house there but David and Eileen Cassidy, old Medway Yacht Club friends. We had lots of other friends out to stay aboard like Roy and Fay Hodson, Ian and Diana Wright, Ron Weedon—friends from the Medway Yacht Club—from where came regular crew like John Baynes and John Greenwood. Another regular member of the crew over many years was Paul Wood, Brenda's second cousin, who first came to us as a student and ended up a distinguished member of the staff at St John's Cambridge, teaching chemistry.

But *Selangor* eventually came back to the UK, and after some east coast adventures we moved her to Falmouth. I could sit on the bathroom loo and see my boat ... a yachtsman's paradise. When I sold out KMA my plan was to take *Selangor* to Scotland, so I formed a crew of experienced friends—Roy Hodson, Ian Morton-Wright and John Robson, who had been in my Government team at times and held the top public relations post at Lloyds Bank, and Noel Lewis, ex-BBC political correspondent and then on the staff of the *Daily Mirror* at Westminster. All of them had sailed with me and knew *Selangor* well. I bought plenty of charts showing the route up the Irish Sea, and more for the second leg across to the Western Isles of Scotland, surely one of the most beautiful cruising grounds in the world. In the right weather ...

We set off on a good morning from Falmouth, and once round the Lizard made a rapid journey into St Mary's on the Scilly Isles. Just as well we had a good mooring because the wind came up to gale force, and I was grateful I had not chosen that night for the big passage. But by next morning it had passed through, and we were on our way. *Selangor* sailed and motored 200 miles dead north, clearing a major headland well, leaving the Isle of Man away to our starboard, and the Republic of Ireland to our port. As a nasty black cloud came towards us, we headed into the neat harbour of Arklow. A quick tidy-up of the boat and ourselves, and within 200 yards we found a splendid pub and good food. We all slept exceedingly well that night.

After that came a comfortable sail along the east coast, skipping Dublin but putting into Hoath, a magnificent yacht club where, we were told, a prominent member was Charles Haughey, the departed prime minister. His name brought back memories for me as he had been associated with the early gunrunning to supply the IRA. He had not lost his touch—there must have been a load of EU money ploughed into Haughey's little harbour. Still, we enjoyed the enhanced facilities. As we did when we got around the next headland, and sailed into Belfast Lough. I laughed as I recognised the various flashpoints of my Belfast days when I was there with Whitelaw. In my wildest moments I could never have imagined going back there for a sailing holiday!

A few phone calls brought my old Northern Ireland Office pals with some local journalists on board for drinks, and we had a hell of a good party. There is nowhere in the world like Northern Ireland, I maintain, where they throw themselves so enthusiastically into a party and then tell everyone next morning, "Wasn't that good crack?"—or craic, as they spell it.

Within ten minutes they had worked out a crew of friends to accompany *Selangor* and me across the North Channel to Scotland in a week's time, safely avoiding the strong tides off the Mull of Kintyre and entering the Sound of Jura to Gigha. *Selangor* had made it to Scottish waters and seemed very content.

Next morning we set off for Oban, where our crew departed to get the ferry back to Belfast, and I waited for Brenda to arrive. She flew up to Glasgow and hired a car.

Brenda and I had the best part of three months cruising the Clyde—to Tobermory, up Loch Linnhe towards Fort William, in and out of Oban and generally enjoying those magnificent waters. Family and friends came up to join us—Clare brought Henry and Alex, who loved crabbing using our best bacon as bait.

We began our homeward journey by making the tricky journey through the Crinan Canal accompanied by two good friends, Andy Wood and his wife, who came over from Belfast. Andy had my old job as director of information in the Northern Ireland Office but had fallen foul of Mo Mowlem, the incoming Labour Northern Ireland Secretary, so the chance to come with us through the canal took his mind off his problems for a while.

The Crinan Canal was at record low levels due to an absence of sufficient rainfall that year so for a while it was touch and go whether *Selangor*, with a draught of 5 feet 9 inches, could get through, but eventually the canal authorities gave us the go-ahead. We hired one of the ex-employees of the canal, who cycled ahead and was ready to open the gates at each lock as *Selangor* arrived, take our lines and help us through. Then as we waited for the level to rise, he would cycle off to the next lock ready for our arrival.

There were no snags as my crew were all quite sharp on the

fenders and adjusting lines. So we were through in a few hours, and made fast to enjoy a good meal and open a bottle or two … another sailing ambition achieved.

We subsequently made our way through the Kyles of Bute, and spent a night in Rothesay where we woke to find *Selangor* hopelessly aground on one of the lowest tides of the year. We got off the mud later and reached the Clyde at last. Most people knew it then as a working river with shipyards and busy quays, but towards the mouth of the river it has quite magnificent scenery.

We made for Kip Marina and that was the end of my retirement cruise, a great adventure. I paid a professional crew to sail *Selangor* back to her home port.

CHAPTER **18**

Spin, Slipping Standards—and the So-Called 24-Hour News Cycle

There is no doubt in my mind that journalism and its way of thinking has provided me with my career, taken me around the world, opened the doors to some apparently impenetrable places, found me some great jobs and, most of all, given me some wonderful friendships.

When strangers ask me about my former job I say 'journalist', but sometimes these days I hesitate. I hate to confess it, but I am no longer as proud as I was to say what I did for a living.

To many it conjures up phone-hacking, corner-cutting, sharp practice and that phrase the late Nicholas Tomalin conjured up— 'a rat-like cunning'. Occasionally I might plead guilty to that charge.

But does the journalism I loved, and which gave me my whole career and life, still exist? Sadly, I think not.

I cut a few corners in my days as a working journalist—we all did— but in those highly competitive days of Fleet Street, before television came along, we had some standards. Most of us had come through local papers where we were taken by our seniors to the local branch of the National Union of Journalists and signed up. I can still remember my very first meeting in 1946 of the South East London branch over a pub near Lewisham station. I was proud to have been admitted. And I am proud to be a Life Member of the NUJ.

That was where we became aware of the NUJ's Code of Conduct, which laid out clearly for youngsters like me that there were lines not to cross. And a code to try to respect.

On the *South London Press* we were also fortunate to have some seniors who knew the ropes, but had also just come back from fighting World War II so they had some personal standards of dignity, and had seen tragedy at close quarters. So they would not accept sloppy work, getting a reader's name wrong or failing to call back on a phone request.

Defining 'intrusion' was often a delicate matter. But we knew if we overdid it there would be awkward questions to face from the editor—or even the owner. Possibly even from the National Union of Journalists to which we all belonged because the *South London Press* was what was known as 'a closed shop'. Losing one's union card might make it difficult trying to enter Fleet Street.

Later, working in the newsroom of the *Daily Mail*, one would be unwise to plead the NUJ Code of Conduct too strongly, but since most of us were in the union we all were aware of where the line was drawn. I recall arguing strongly with Paul Sargent, then the late night news editor, about being asked to go back a fourth time to a home where there had been a tragedy. Nobody fired me.

Watching some of the evidence in the Leveson Inquiry, I found the conduct of many of today's journalists appalling; I felt ashamed. How any journalist could subject the McCann family to such inhumane hounding based on pure fabrication took my breath away. Like anyone else, today's reporters have mortgages to pay and mouths to feed, but have they no pride left? Would they rather take Richard Desmond's shilling on the *Daily Express* than tell him where to put his job if it meant inflicting further torture on the McCanns, falsely accused of murdering their own child?

The phone tapping cases at News International and the *Daily Mirror* and the crocodile tears when journalists were made to face charges I found hard to swallow, particularly the claims that no one in authority knew what was happening. It is inconceivable, at the *Mail,* that my former editors like William Hardcastle, Mike Randall or Arthur Brittenden would not have been seeking assurances about the source of a story even if they were not told the actual names of informants.

As for executives at the *News of the World* and the *Daily Mirror* signing off large sums of money to informants without assuring themselves of their veracity, that strains credibility past breaking point.

On ethical standards—these could long ago have been sorted in a hotel room by four people accepting their responsibilities. Lord Rothermere, Rupert Murdoch, and their counterparts at the *Telegraph* and *Mirror* Group could have agreed lines in the sand which were not to be passed by their employees.

Instead they hid in the background in the public spats, and let their employed editors take the flak in so-called pursuit of freedom of the press, which actually was freedom to make money without hindrance. Yes, we must fight hard for genuine freedom of the press, but surely with that comes responsibility too?

The press has set-up what it calls the Independent Press Standards Organisation and I have been to hear its chairman, a retired eminent judge, discuss his approach. A little laid back I thought but these are early days. Will today's journalism raise its game or simply use the new body as a fig leaf while it gets back to 'business as usual', which, let's face it, has been indefensible at times.

That does not imply that all current journalism is poor. There are some excellent men and women striving around the world to get at the truth and bring it to us, but the outlets are fewer and fewer. Thank goodness the foreign pages still remain open to them at the *Financial Times*, *The Times*, *The Guardian* and in television and radio, particularly the BBC World Service. In Britain we are fortunate still to be able to buy some good daily papers and to have such a wide range of TV and radio at our disposal, though much of the output of the former is pap.

There have been some notable achievements, Nick Davies of *The Guardian*, who pegged away at the phone-hacking scandal for years, deserves recognition. So do the *Sunday Times* reporters who exposed a deep and dangerous criminal network buying up land before the Olympic site at Stratford was bought by the Government. These crooks were so dangerous that Scotland Yard admitted in court that it had abandoned any hope of bringing them to justice. The *Sunday Times* did not chicken out, though.

The whole question of standards also arises in my 'second career' in Government Information Service (GIS). As a journalist of some experience I was able to work closely with a top Conservative, Whitelaw, later to become Deputy Prime Minister; and with James Callaghan, then Labour Home Secretary. Neither doubted my integrity, and both accepted that as a civil servant there were party political lines I could not cross. It was the same with Tories like Peter Walker on the Tory left wing and Nick Ridley on the right, and with Michael Foot, as left-wing as they come, from Labour's ranks.

I stuck to the mantra 'Never lie to a reporter', a theme I hammered into the young people who worked for me in Whitehall. Maybe avoid the question or change the subject, but never, ever, mislead. I knew myself what I would do to a press officer who deliberately misled me.

Today, I believe Government credibility is on the line because the public seldom believes what the Government tells it. Using so-called 'spin', an American term, recent Governments have cried wolf too often. And that is serious because when it is vital that the public responds, the man and woman in the street just shrugs it off. Often we are told a politician today 'will say' something, but we seldom see the speech reported, or whether Mr Bloggs MP actually got a word out of his mouth.

Mind you, if today's media will take this kind of manipulation, they are the mugs—just chasing each other's tails. In my time we would insist a speech was made before we reported it. Supposing the politician was hit by a car or missed his train and never made the speech anyway?

The truth is that, nowadays, neither the politicians nor the journalists—TV, radio, and print—care. So why should the public?

I know of several GIS senior people who were itching for the arrival of a new Labour Government, as were a number of senior civil servants who wanted change, though that did not mean they were willing to abandon their own code of conduct.

But those around Alastair Campbell, Tony Blair's spokesman at Number 10 Downing Street, did not appear to care a fig, were supremely ignorant of the potential of a professional Government Information Service, and quite happily watched it cut to pieces.

Why worry? They had the kids they'd brought in, now well paid as Special Advisers, chatting away to the media, just as they had done in Opposition, oblivious to the public duty to tell the truth, the need to uphold Parliamentary standards, and the integrity of their ministers.

The cynicism of the young woman at the Transport department, who sent out a note on the day of the 9/11 New York Twin Towers disaster suggesting 'It is now a very good day to get out anything we want to bury' rather summed it all up.

The recently elected Conservative Government has no claim to integrity in this field either, since it has simply adopted or worsened the Labour practice. They have brought in even more SPADs, got rid of the last few civil servants remaining in Government information work, or put them on short-term contracts. They have treated the public to a daily bombardment of so-called 'news'. Again and again there is a Government announcement of a development which quite often is a rehash of previous news.

This is a practice to which the public have wised up. They wait now to see the fine print, and the Government cheque, before going out to wave in the street.

Similarly, Prime Minister David Cameron's policy of making a speech virtually every day is quite counter-productive. He gives the impression of never being in the office. Does he ever have time to read his in tray, the man in the street must wonder.

There was a time when the prime minister was at the hub of the Whitehall–Westminster machine, and when he made a speech, it mattered. What the PM stated was closely studied. Today the public frequently dismisses what its prime minister says as yet another photo opportunity.

I recognise this may appear the rantings of an old man, and that the speed with which information girdles the world has created problems for today's politicians, and for newsmen something which maybe I do not fully comprehend.

But I believe that, more than ever, the public crave sound thinking and leadership from the people they elect, and are at the moment profoundly disappointed with cavortings to please the 24-hour news cycle.

It has only become this non-stop treadmill because politicians and their so-called 'spin doctors' have not the nerve to get off, occasionally, to have time to think—and give the voter a chance to do the same.

Maybe it is time for some determined journalists to give a lead. They could refuse to accept a story just broadcast as genuine, but insist they check it first for accuracy. And for a true source, more than just a behind-the-hand whisper of a 'special adviser'. And if they think they are being told a pack of lies, then to say so. Yes, it might endanger a future 'source', but maybe it might yield some respect, too.

For all I know it may be the same with so-called Social Media which nowadays seems to be a dominant prime source for so-called 'news'. A one-line rumour can go halfway round the world in seconds yet no one has checked a fact of it. It would seem that any nutter can witter on Twitter and their banal thoughts are then avidly looked at by millions on their mobile phones when it would be a good idea to be looking where they are going. Or read a newspaper. Cameras in phones are changing news systems too. All too frequently someone snoops with their phone on some incident and within seconds has despatched it widely on Facebook, Twitter or what-have-you. But no attempt is made to check the facts or assess the situation before they press the Send button—and may be about to destroy someone's life.

That is what happened to a young woman filmed on a tram in Croydon in an apparent racial outburst. Yes, she said things she regretted but it was not until she was in court that it emerged she had severe mental problems and at the time was on medication which had strong side effects. There was no mention of an apology from Piers Morgan who had tweeted 'I want this woman arrested and deported. It makes me ashamed to be British'.

So that's my view, and that's my story. Thanks for coming along. As Frank Sinatra sang, 'Yes, I Did it My Way, and now I Face the Final Curtain.'

I have heard this song played many times at memorial services, most notably in Westminster Cathedral when I remember George Brown, number two in the 1964 Labour Government, who certainly did things his way. Some say the song is corny, and Sinatra certainly loathed it. But for many it sums up rather well one's feelings in the sunset of life.

Paul Anka's lyric, when scanned carefully, does indeed capture what a lot of us feel. 'Regrets, I've had a few, but then again, too few to mention.'

But for me, Shirley Horn, the American jazz pianist and singer, tells it much more the way I feel.

Her song 'Here's To Life' topped the US charts for several weeks, and I keep playing it in my car. I would like to have it played at my funeral.

'No complaints and no regrets, it begins. I still believe in chasing dreams and placing bets.'

'I've had my share, I drank my fill

So here's to life … and every joy it brings.'

'To dreamers and their dreams.'

Then it has some beautiful lines like:

'But there's no yes in yesterday.'

And then the lyric peaks:

'So here's to life, and every joy it brings'

May all your storms be weathered,

And all that's good, gets better.

Here's to life, here's to love, and here's to you.'

That will do it for me.

I have had a good life, wasted little time, enjoyed a good standard of living—which I achieved by my own efforts—cherished strong family ties, been a close observer, even participant, at a few historic moments. I have rubbed shoulders with some remarkable politicians, industrialists, journalists, trade union leaders, and many others in various walks of life. It has been a privilege, and I would certainly argue that journalism has been a splendid way to see the world at close quarters.

Above all, I have been able to cherish long friendships across a very broad spectrum. The trouble with growing older, though, is that one loses so many of one's friends. When I first met Roy Hodson all those years ago, I little thought that he would be my best man when Brenda and I married in 1989, nor that one day I would organise his funeral, write the service, give the eulogy, and provide the final photograph of him enjoying lunch with us at St Mawes. And to think Roy always maintained he was a better photographer than me ...

My long-time jazz pal Brian Perren and I used to talk two or three times a week and would go together with our wives to musical events in Britain and, of course, on our annual jazz cruise. Brian was cruelly struck down by a stroke, and I still miss him.

As I miss sailing companions like John Baynes, John Greenwood and Nick Nichols, who over many years helped me fit out my boats and sail them on the Medway, in Mallorca, in Scotland, or round the wonderful coastline of the South West of England.

Cricket has provided me with new companions in my disengaged years, and I have come to love the game and enjoyed watching it, not just at Lord's or Edgbaston, but in Australia, South Africa and the West Indies with new friends like Keith Bradshaw, David Gare, Terry Bailey, Jack Jeffery and their wives.

Watching tennis—now that I no longer play it—at Wimbledon, Queens and other venues has also been extremely satisfying. Brenda and I have enjoyed in recent years a good friendship with Tim and Elizabeth Phillips—Tim was the quietly influential chairman of the All England Tennis Club and kindly invited us to the Royal Box on several occasions. A lifetime's ambition achieved. There is no better vantage point on Centre Court than watching from that box.

Messing about with classic cars has been fun. Just looking at my E-Type Jaguar I find quite moving—rather like studying a painting. From whatever angle one regards the vehicle, it is a work of art in itself and cannot, surely, be surpassed. And I still keep in touch with my friends of the Singer Owners' Club, which has lasted over sixty years and is still in remarkably good health.

Then there are—or were—the swimming companions at Highbury Pool, out of which I formed a monthly lunch club we call the Craftsmen, mainly because most of us can't remember very much. But we have a good time eating, drinking and conversing on politics, theatre, film, or issues of the day. And we regularly discover good pubs in Islington serving some fine food.

I have never embraced the term 'retirement'. I always tell people I am 'disengaged' when I am asked what I do. I explain I am so busy I sometimes find it hard to see how I had time to work.

In 1978 I joined the historic Reform Club and have enjoyed its atmosphere over the years. Brenda and I held our wedding 'breakfast' in the magnificent Library in 1989, with music played by my old friend Dave Shepherd.

In the Club we have held many events like my eldest granddaughter's twenty-first birthday party. I am proud that in 2014 Edwina came to me and said she wanted to become a member herself.

In 2013 I decided it was time to give a hand in running the club, and put myself up for election to the General Committee. It has meant more involvement, but I have enjoyed putting something back into an institution to which I have belonged for thirty-seven years.

The most important aspect of being disengaged is to keep one's brain fully involved, to be aware of what is going on around one. Above all, to enjoy one's family and the present. That has been my philosophy for many years, and to date it has served me well.

I'll tell you if it continues to operate in the sequel to this book. Thanks for coming along for the ride …

'Here's to Life.'

ABOUT THE AUTHOR

Self-reliance forged in an exciting wartime childhood during the years of the Battle of Britain, the Blitz and dodging V1 and V2 attacks led Keith McDowall to become a young newspaper reporter in South London.

It was the start of more than twenty years in highly competitive journalism that later took him to work closely with major British politicians covering top level policy. His most demanding challenge was in Northern Ireland working closely with William Whitelaw when direct rule was introduced to try to halt the bomb and bullet campaign by the IRA wrecking the province.

He later spearheaded the public affairs effort of British industry to influence government policy before running his own successful agency.

The endorsement of the first woman speaker of the House of Commons, a deputy prime minister, a highly successful trade minister, leading industrialists and a top flight journalist/author vouches for the range and scope of McDowall's memoirs and underlines his disdain at today's emphasis on 'spin' in politics.

Keith McDowall is married to Brenda Dean, who as a young woman led the print workers in their one-year campaign against Rupert Murdoch's move of his newspapers to Wapping – the last major industrial dispute in Britain. He has sailed his own boats for over fifty years, is a classic car buff and sadly recently sold his E-type Jaguar. He has six grandchildren and one-year-old Margot is his first great-grandchild.

INDEX

Pullen, John 274–5
Pyne, Mick 319, 320

QE2 (*Q4*) 89–90

radio 324–30
Ramelson, Bert 103
Randall, Leslie 82, 83, 84, 101–2, 104
Randall, Mike 102–3
Rawlinson, Sir Peter 227
Read, Denis 309
Redcaps 223–4
Redcliffe-Maude, Lord 171
Reform Club 251–2, 333, 353, 357–8, 373
Regan, Andrew 338–43
Richards, Morley 81
Ridley, Nicholas 155–6, 274
Rigby, Bryan 296
Ritchie, Stewart 333, 334
Roberts, Tom 136–7, 175, 176, 192, 197, 206–7, 222, 236–7
Robson, John 362
Rodney, Peter 334, 347–8
Rogers, Frank 326
Rolls-Royce 150–1
Ross, Jack 10, 12, 14–15, 100–1, 269
Rowley, Alan 197, 225–6
Royal Canadian Artillery 9–12, 14, 15–17, 27
RTE 217–18
RUC (Royal Ulster Constabulary): and B-Specials 122, 127, 129, 130–1, 224–5; confidential phone line 207–8; in Derry 196; and intelligence 207–8; 226; joint Task Force 223–4; leadership of 131, 132, 195; press officer 207; and riots 129,

130–1; shootings 133, 245; uniform 132

sailing 299, 361–4
Saker, Brian (aka Hugh) 355–60
Sargent, Paul 63, 68–70
Scanlon, Hugh 181, 251–2
Scarman, Lord 224–5
scouts 23–5, 26–8, 29–32
Seaman, Dick 115, 117, 193–4, 202–3, 214
security vetting 180–1
Selangor (yacht) 361–4
Serpell, Sir David 172
Sewell, Eric 97
SG Warburg 316–18, 322, 338–9, 342, 344
Shepherd, Dave 311
Shepherd, Neville 147–8
shipbuilding 89–90, 272–86, 324; Kvaerner 312–16, 322
Shipbuilding News 275, 278–9
shop workers' union 88–9
Shore, Peter 113–14, 116, 118–19, 121, 123, 124, 261
Singer cars 47–8, 55
Singer Owners' Club 48, 372–3
'Slippery Emperor' 43–7
Smith, Cyril (industrialist) 108–9, 110
Smith, Cyril (MP) 308
Smith, Douglas 240
Smith, John 335
Smith, Mike 347
Smith, Ron 105
smog 39–40, 41, 42
social media 370
South London Press: and Baldwin, Freddy 55–6; and Carr-Gomm, Richard 38–9; closed shop 366; and competition 49–50; editor of